Botanical Poetics

BOTANICAL POETICS

Early Modern Plant Books and the
Husbandry of Print

Jessica Rosenberg

PENN

UNIVERSITY OF PENNSYLVANIA PRESS

PHILADELPHIA

Published by
University of Pennsylvania Press
Philadelphia, Pennsylvania 19104-4112
www.upenn.edu/pennpress

Printed in the United States of America on acid-free paper
10 9 8 7 6 5 4 3 2 1

Hardcover ISBN: 9781512823332
eBook ISBN: 9781512823349
Cataloging-in-Publication Data is available
from the Library of Congress.

CONTENTS

Contents

NOTE

In quoting from early modern texts, I have followed original spelling, while silently modernizing *u/v, i/j,* and *vv/w* and expanding contractions. I have followed the same principle for the titles of early modern books in the endnotes, though I have made the fonts uniformly italic and give words printed entirely in capitals in lowercase. Titles have been capitalized when they appear in the text.

The endnotes refer to several frequently cited sources in abbreviated forms. *OED* and *ODNB* refer, respectively, to citations from the *Oxford English Dictionary* (OED Online), Oxford University Press, https://www.oed.com, and the *Oxford Dictionary of National Biography*, Oxford University Press, https://www.oxforddnb.com. Unless otherwise noted, biblical quotations refer to *The Bible: Translated According to the Ebrew and Greeke* (London: Christopher Barker, 1599). I have drawn quotations from Shakespeare's plays from Stephen Greenblatt et al., eds., *The Norton Shakespeare*, 3rd ed. (New York: W. W. Norton, 2016), though where appropriate I refer to early quartos, folios, and other modern editions.

A full bibliography of sources cited in the endnotes, as well as the complete data set of early modern plant books, is available online at http://jmrosenberg.net/botanicalpoetics.

INTRODUCTION

And all in war with Time for love of you
As he takes from you, I ingraft you new.

The final image of Shakespeare's Sonnet 15 leans on a tree to make a promise of posterity.[1] Though preparing for the survival of the young man, the poet may also be making a claim of posterity of his own: the etymology of "ingraft"—from the Greek *graphein*, to carve or to write—underscores a deep connection between poetic composition and horticultural procedure, between the power of inscription and the excision, transport, and reinsertion of a fruit-bearing branch (or scion) into a new trunk (or stock). The poet, it seems, is in the business of severing and reattaching, wielding penknife and waxcloth. Shakespeare's metaphor relies on its faith that, at the other end of this procedure, the fruit has a future. Though it heralds the power of the poet, Shakespeare's couplet depends on the power of the plant: vegetables, cut into pieces, turn out to be capable of quite a lot.

The way that early modern writers understood the shared capacities of plants and texts is the subject of this book. Rather than the tree or the root, I follow the rangier paths of segments like grafts and slips as they join writers, planters, readers, and poets in the labors of circulation and cultivation. Not all of these labors, however, are performed as confidently as Shakespeare's at the culmination of Sonnet 15. More often than not, for example, metaphors of grafting announce the illegitimacy of the scion and its fruit and riff uneasily on the strangeness of a hybrid tree.[2] A grafted plant threatens to forget the stock from which it came: would a scion even respond, some agricultural writers wondered, if its original stock withered or died?[3] For this very reason, though, vegetal capacities of fragmentation and reassembly offered a useful model for the materiality of writing and the procedures of composition, printing, and circulation. A generation earlier than Shakespeare's couplet, the verse collection *The Arbor of Amitie* (1568) described its author, the young poet Thomas Howell, as the "tender graffe that growes in grove, / that tooke the stock but late."[4] Other young Elizabethan poets depict themselves as grafts in their own work, especially ones newly set, and accordingly both agents and objects of cultivation.

Grafting took on a more specifically iconic role in the business of print— taking seriously perhaps the injunction of Sonnet 11 to "print more." A grafted olive tree features in the printer's device of the Estiennes, the renowned printing house based in Paris and Geneva; there, invoking Paul's image in Romans 11:17 of gentiles grafted onto the body of the church, the large tree shows several branches cut off and six more newly grafted on. On the Estienne olive tree, the joints remain visibly bundled in a dressing of (perhaps) clay and waxcloth. The device's iconic status extended to England, where multiple stationers had their own copies cut. A single bundled joint appears at the center point of the English stationer Richard Grafton's device, a rebus of his surname that shows a grafted tree growing out of a tun, or barrel. These outsized bandages betray the work of the craftsman: both trees are incised, cut, bound, and joined. Their conspicuously marked artifice, however, is not the whole story. Grafton's joint, like Estienne's, is the visible index to an invisible process.[5] Having performed this assembly, gardener and printer wait as the tree completes the work of incorporation, a process already invisibly underway within these bindings.

As temporary orchardists, poets and printers are craftsmen in touch with the capacities of plant life for severance, reassembly, relocation, and regrowth. With its emphasis on the bundled joint before the growing branch, this repertoire of practices suggests a strange version of what a plant is. We tend to define vegetables by the qualities that they lack but that beasts and humans possess, like sensitivity, reason, and free locomotion.[6] The early modern plants that figure in the following pages challenge this prejudice: as possessors of enviable capacities of longevity, fragmentation, and relocation, they exceed the fate decreed in Genesis, that "every greene herbe shall be for meate."[7] Instead, *Botanical Poetics* uncovers a countervalent tradition, one that in sixteenth-century England came to offer a powerful account of what plants and texts were made of—and, moreover, of what they could do.

What, then, was a plant for early modern readers, writers, and planters? John Maplet introduces the treatment of the vegetable kingdom in *A Greene Forest, or Naturall Historie* (1567) by describing how his subject got its name.

Plants are called "plants," he writes, because they are "planted & graft in the earth." The earth, nurse-like, feeds the plant rooted in it, which is "fostered up by his roote and by that nourishment that the roote taketh and feedeth on ministred and put to it by his Nourse the earth." Many of us would likely say something similar if asked to define vegetable life: plants are rooted things, growing from the earth, fed by light and sun and rain. But Maplet's discussion does not end here. The sentence following his "Etimologie" turns decisively from the root: the pieces of a plant, if engrafted or replanted at the right time, are able "by secret force of Nature to take and resume againe like life and power."[8] This is because plants are "in everie their chiefe part," such that, once cropped, slips might take up life in new soil and eventually grow back to their full shape. This is the genius of the vegetable: its potential, in only fragments, for relocation and resumption of life anew.

A *Greene Forest*'s depiction of vegetable life was not unique in early modern England. But, as I have suggested, it troubles long-standing assumptions about what plants are and what they can do. Maplet's interest in this vegetable capacity takes its cue from Aristotle, who was also fascinated by plants' potential for propagation from partial cuttings. Maplet observes, echoing Aristotle, that plants' capacity for partitioning makes them like "those small and siely Wormes" who are called "Insecta that is, in part and member distinct and severed, having for all this life proportionably and equally besprent throughout the whole bodie." Despite their famous rootedness, plants share with wasps and worms a body that comes *in sections*. For these insects and plants, life is "besprent" through the entire body: like dew, blood, or tears, sprinkled across all of a creature's parts. But the power of plants to "resume againe like life and power" exceeds the more limited capacities of insects.[9] As Aristotle writes, plants "when cut into sections continue to live, and a number of trees can be derived from one single source." Aristotle attributes this power to the nutritive soul, the force that distinguishes vegetable life, which "while actually single must be potentially plural."[10] It is not only their present forms that distinguish plants, but the potential plurality of their future patterns of growth.

Early modern writers joined plant-thinking and book-thinking according to these shared capacities: the vital sufficiency of the fragment, the possibility of relocation, the many potential paths of growth and propagation. In collaboration with gardeners, herbalists, and printers, those writers developed what I call a *botanical poetics*, a theory and practice of inscription that understands books' material form and possible futures on the model of vegetable life. Printed texts seemed loaded with distinctly vegetable capacities for reuse and propagation. Aristotle's definition of the vegetable soul—as a faculty of growth without ratiocination or will—includes this proliferative and expansive trajectory within it. In this view, the energy of books, like that of Maplet's vegetable, seemed attached not to the rooted organism but to the segmented plant: plucked, besprent, and, as Aristotle writes of the nutritive soul, single in actuality but "potentially plural." This style of plant-thinking understands the vegetable world as a kind of matter resistant to personal possession. A slip, branch, or bud can be taken from a plant without diminishing the original stock, and those cuttings can generate copies that take new root far from their place of origin. Plants and texts helped make sense of each other's distinct materiality; as bearers of latent capacities, both have the potential to act at a distance and at a delay.

In early modern England, writers and printers registered the sympathy between plants and books in titles like *The Garlande of Godly Flowers* (1574), *The Garden of Eloquence* (1577), and *A Posie of Gilloflowers* (1580); in epistles and dedications that describe an author's labor of harvesting and gathering; and in an exuberant vocabulary of forms and procedures—grafting, slipping, cutting, weeding, transplanting. This phyto-bibliographic lexicon reflects the conventional use of "flowers" to refer to rhetorical ornament and draws on legacies of medieval florilegia and ancient anthologies, both terms that (from Latin and Greek) meant gatherings of flowers. A "posy," in the sixteenth century, could name either a bouquet or a small piece of *poesy*.[11] At times, such analogies between texts and plants grew conventional to the point of seeming inert; a reference to the "flowers of rhetoric" may not often have evoked the particular curve of petal or stamen. Nonetheless, these dead metaphors came vigorously to life during Elizabeth's reign. Curious about where their printed texts might be scattered, writers and stationers reimagined the textual force of vegetable life: as slips redistributed, seeds dispersed on new ground, grafts taking hold in new wood.

The botanical poetics those thinkers generated imagined the meaning and materiality of texts, like those of plants, in terms of their capacity to circulate. The formal and social capacities of books and plants were shaped in turn by their piecemeal composition and their lively embeddedness in networks of readers and users. We have already seen one consequence of this framework in Maplet's account of the vegetable: culled or "discerped," meaning broken down into pieces, the plant is severed from its original "nurse," the earth, and no longer bound to any particular ground.[12] "Discerped," like "excerpt," derives from the Latin verb *carpere*, to pluck; and, like it, suggests the possible futures available to borrowed fragments. The pieces of a plant may be held in many hands and many soils, quietly linking reader-planters across time and territories. At an historical moment that saw a rapidly growing traffic in both plants and texts, this capacity for travel helped fuel a global fantasy of boundless transmissibility shared by naturalists, merchants, consumers, and colonists.[13]

While this picture of vegetable life is familiar to any who have gathered slips for a bouquet or planted them in a garden bed, it is not the model that has most influenced literary study. The botanical poetics I describe here offers a sharp contrast to the most common links between plant life and poetic form in English literature. Building on Romantic conceptions of organic unity, vegetable aesthetics have generally followed Coleridge's vision of plant and poem as living wholes, each part radiating together into a common purpose.[14] In Cleanth Brooks's mid-twentieth-century formulation, the parts of a poem should relate "not as blossoms juxtaposed in a bouquet, but as the blossoms are related to the other parts of a growing plant"; the beauty of a poem thus reflects the "flowering of the whole plant, and needs the stalk, the leaf, and the hidden roots."[15] *Botanical Poetics* suggests an alternative model. The gardens, nosegays, and forests in the pages that follow reflect instead the ideals of textual abundance and disunity that inspired the terms "florilegia" and "anthology" and their piecemeal gatherings of flowers—what Brooks dismisses as the "mere assemblage" of the bouquet. Examples from sixteenth-century England make visible an account of reading that follows the etymology of *lego, legere*: to read, they remind us, is to gather or pluck—or, as Maplet writes, to *discerp* and re-collect vegetable or textual matter.

The attention of early modern planters and poets to the fragmentary and piecemeal reflects the period's interest in small, useful forms, an interest cultivated in classrooms and practiced in habits of reading, copying, and reusing texts. Promising their readers profit and delight, a wide swathe of early modern books took a pedagogical posture that relied on expectations of fragmentation and portability, especially of verse or short sayings.[16] Thomas Tusser's rhyming *Five Hundreth Points of Good Husbandry* (1573) offers readers poetic lessons that are "points of them selves, to be taken in hand."[17] He is echoed by Philip Sidney, in his *Defence of Poesie*, who praised imitation that, in both teaching and delighting, can "move men to take that goodnesse in hand."[18] These formal investments animated a literary culture attentive to piecemeal forms, the joined crafts of writing and reading, and the openness of textual fragments to future reuse.[19]

As old analogies came newly into contact with techniques and styles of practical horticulture, the identities of reader and text took shape according to the protocols of craft and the conceptions of materiality it entailed. To early modern plant-thinking, a text in pieces is also a text in process, susceptible to human labor and manipulation. And, in turn, it is with habitual use that an intimacy with vegetable capacities is won. Maplet explains the potential plurality of vegetables, for example, by reference to the practice of grafting—he knows that "men in time of yere use to cut them off, such as are thought to prosper better in another place, and graffe them into a new stock."[20] Printers and poets likewise wrestled with, and depended on, the capacities and tendencies of the matter with which they worked; in this way, they understood their labors as continuous with the craft of gardeners, husbandmen, and practitioners of herbal medicine.

Husbandry and gardening, like printing books or writing poetry, are sites of quotidian creativity, shot through with imaginative and speculative outlooks, whether the material practice of provisioning, experiments in manuring or compost, or edging out the beds of a kitchen garden.[21]

Practical engagements with books and plants were shaped by an understanding of the innate "vertues" they shared. This key term choreographed the collaboration of poetry and practical knowledge in the period, framing both plants and books according to a logic of latent capacity, those forces that Friar Laurence in *Romeo and Juliet* calls "the powerful grace that lies / In herbs, plants, stones, and their true qualities."[22] Across the abundance of nature, each creature was seen to hold an innate force and distinct operation, divinely endowed and held *in potentia*.[23] Taking up the rhetoric of practical books, textual gardens and nosegays demanded readers' "right handling" of the virtues in front of them. This collaborative and ecological understanding of virtue fueled a model for textual and herbal interaction that built on habits of practical, embodied knowledge. Such virtues, moreover, could travel, scattering their potential energy across a wide field of cultivation and reception. Their paths, in this sense, track the contours of what Laurie Shannon describes as a sixteenth-century cosmos of "scattered microsovereignties and dispersed capacities."[24] This dispersed picture of cosmic sovereignty in turn supports a scattershot version of the book of nature—and of the nature of the book.

These configurations of horticultural and textual practice reflect a literary culture in which poetic production was not sequestered from the labors of everyday life. During the sixteenth and seventeenth centuries, discourses of poetic virtue, botanical form, and horticultural labor belonged to overlapping spheres of cultural practice. The concord between poetry and practical knowledge shaped the careers of poets like Barnabe Googe, whose translation of Conrad Heresbach's husbandry manual outsold his original verse several times over; and like George Gascoigne and Isabella Whitney, whose texts ask readers to join practices of herbal medicine to the reading of poetry. (Gascoigne was also responsible for parts of an elaborate entertainment presented to Queen Elizabeth in 1575 at the Earl of Leicester's gardens at Kenilworth—including the delivery of an ostensibly extempore speech in the person of Sylvanus, God of the Woods.)[25] Many of the printers responsible for poetic collections matched their literary business with a lively trade in practical books of instruction, often advertising their value in the same language of pleasure and profit.[26]

The engagement with husbandry by aspiring poets like Googe and Gascoigne reflects a revaluation of agricultural labor that took place over the course of the sixteenth century, a period that saw the wider dispersal of land among a growing class of landowners as well as a return to classical works on farming.[27] As theory and practice, husbandry supplied a powerful model for household order, for textual storage and composition, and for good governance. It was, as Googe wrote in his translation of Heresbach, "the Mother and Nurs of al other artes" and an appropriate occupation not just for yeoman but for gentlemen.[28] Husbandry also structured emergent accounts of the materiality and social lives of printed books. While the long furrows of the plow offered a ready analogy for the lines of the printed page, the affiliation between printing and husbandry came to turn less on the labor of tilling than on the uncertainty of waiting. Like the farmer who plows in hope, writers and printers of early modern books sowed their seeds and ceded to fate and the seasons. Against the anonymity of an expanding market, the horticultural processes evoked by these texts helped put a name to books' uncertain futures and situate the new adventure of print within that most ancient discipline of risk management: agriculture.[29]

Habits of thought about vegetables have long been future-oriented, woven closely into a lexicon of growth, yield, and harvest. Recent theoretical and philosophical work on plants has emphasized their capacity to imagine the future—what Natania Meeker and Antónia Szabari call "the speculative energies unleashed by the plant."[30] The philosopher Michael Marder, whose work has spurred the nascent field of critical plant studies, writes that the exuberance of vegetable growth helps plants enact "a constant projection of themselves into the future."[31] Early modern plant-thinking boasts its own version of this orientation to the future: one embedded in the familiar rhythms and unpredictable outcomes of the harvest calendar, in the household accumulation of provision, in vegetable paths of growth, proliferation, and decay, in the latent energies of herb or seed. In their imagination of future time, the "speculative energies" unleashed by early modern plants suggest versions of survival that do not sit easily with either classic ideals of poetic posterity or modern values of preservation. These longer temporalities inform Joshua Calhoun's recent proposal for an ecology of texts—an environmentally attuned practice of book history that attends to the human and nonhuman agencies that shape textual form and meaning.[32] As materials that might persist or decay, books—like plants—proceed on a historical timeline indifferent to human designs and desires.

Botanical Poetics uncovers a distinct style of early modern plant-thinking as it developed in early modern England, one that called upon the contingent open-endedness of vegetable life to reimagine the material text and its reading, use, and reception. In calling this style of plant-thinking a botanical poetics, I do not intend to limit its influence to the period's vernacular verse, or even to the production of the written word in general. Rather, a botanical poetics governs the relation of form and meaning across a range of settings, on the printed page, planted field, and in the kitchen garden. Botanical poetics figures each of these sites as arenas of practical collaboration among sundry active participants, including human, text, plant, and—from time to time—spider or pig. I take as my starting point a set of figures and concepts elaborated in the middle years of Queen Elizabeth's reign, at a moment when the language of plants proliferated across the landscape of English print. Linking the crafts of printing, planting, and poetic production, these examples elaborate a complex theory of literary practice—one that, animated by the slipperiness of cuttings, shaped debates about the moral and cultural status of poetry and resisted emergent ideas of textual property and authorial power. This strain recurs in early modern literature, retooled, reordered, and sometimes parodied. But, wherever it appears, botanical poetics carries with it the suggestion of contingency and redistribution, calling into view the potential plurality that plants and books share and the possible futures they help us imagine.

Plant Lives in Print

Maplet's *Greene Forest* was published in June 1567 by the stationer Henry Denham, folded in a tidy octavo with its title bordered in broad, laced ornament (Figure 1). Between 1566 and 1568, the compositors in Denham's shop would reassemble the small cast-metal pieces that formed this border at least a half dozen times on other titles that included octavo editions of Edmund Tilney's *Flower of Friendship* and Thomas Howell's collection of verse, *The Arbor of Amitie* (Figure 2). Denham, or someone in his shop, was likely responsible for the titles of both the *Arbor* and the *Forest*: both had been entered in the Stationers' Register under different titles but were renamed prior to publication under the aegis of the vegetable kingdom. Though all three texts fall into different literary genres—natural history, prose dialogue, poetic gathering—Denham saw a link between them, one that he registered visually and verbally on their title pages.[33] With these titles, Denham makes a literary and a commercial choice: he carves out a place for them in the market under the wide canopy of plant life.

Denham's publication of these volumes in the late 1560s marks the beginning of a decade-long vogue in books whose titles link them to the world of plants. I refer to this class of printed texts as *plant books,* to name the kind of hybrid objects their titles announced to readers. Printed books had been called "flowers" and "nosegays" since the earliest days of print in England, and, throughout the sixteenth and seventeenth centuries, the language of plants dotted the landscape of English print. Whether objects you could carry (like bouquets or nosegays) or spaces you could enter (like an intimate bower or disorderly forest), botanical titles promised a book composed of many smaller pieces—what Randall Anderson calls a "recombinant text."[34] From the late 1560s through the following decade, the market share of these recombinant plant books more than doubled. An analysis of data from the English Short-Title Catalog (ESTC) shows that this trend extended from 1567 to about 1583, significantly outpacing an overall increase in the number of books printed by London stationers.[35] Though plant books rarely made up more than one-twentieth of the titles printed in any year, stationers often applied these botanical frames to experimental forms and new genres. At this

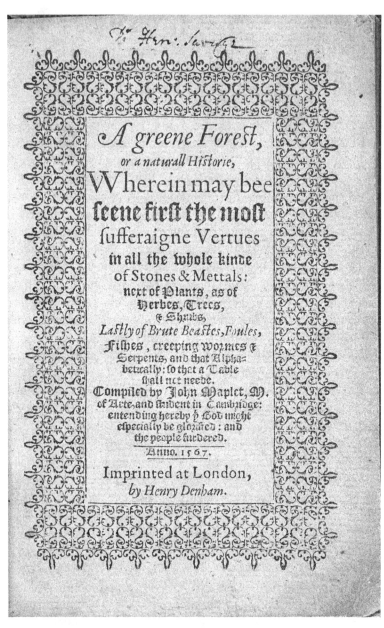

Figure 1. John Maplet, *A Greene Forest* (London: Henry Denham, 1567), title page. RB 59181, The Huntington Library, San Marino, California.

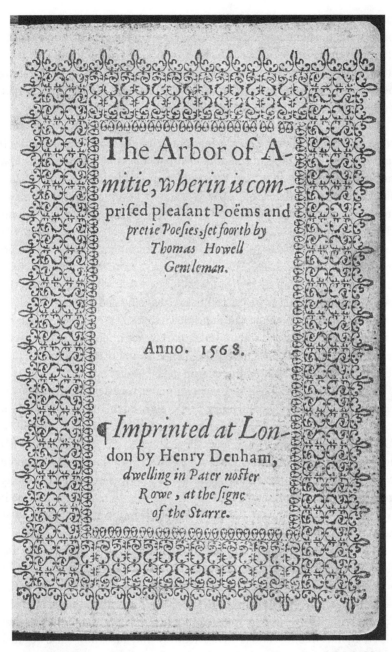

The Arbor of A-
mitie, wherin is com-
prifed pleafant Poëms and
pretie Poefies, fet foorth by
Thomas Howell
Gentleman.

Anno. 1568.

❧ Imprinted at Lon-
don by Henry Denham,
dwelling in Pater noster
Rowe, at the figne
of the Starre.

Figure 2. Thomas Howell, *The Arbor of Amitie* (London: Henry Denham, 1568), title page. By permission of the Bodleian Libraries, University of Oxford. Shelfmark 8° H 44 Art.Seld. (2).

transitional moment in England's consumer culture and in the business of bookselling, the language of plants helped fashion the printed book as a legible and even desirable commodity, making sense of its composite form and plural material existence. A book, like a plant, was many things in one thing, and one thing in many places. To the makers of plant books, these properties looked like distinctly vegetable capacities.

Titles that alluded to horticultural spaces and vegetable matter reached across genres and formats: duodecimo prayer books, poetic miscellanies in quarto, octavo collections of epigrams. Most are the kinds of collections, epitomes, or translations that have been only marginal to literary and intellectual history. As the data from the ESTC shows, several features of this set remain consistent across more than a century of printed books with botanical or horticultural titles. Nearly all are miscellaneously composed of smaller pieces: poems, brief histories, prayers, recipes, commonplaces, or some combination of those forms. As Leah Knight argues in the most comprehensive treatment of these titles to date, botanical titles reflect a culture of collecting that encompassed texts as well as plants, one that emerged in tandem with the sixteenth century's growing trade in printed herbals.[36] While their popularity as measured by both new and reprinted titles waxed and waned, this class of plant books never fully disappeared, even after the use of such figurative titles seemed (to some) antiquated and quaint.

The sixteenth century in fact saw two major waves of plant books: one beginning in the later part of Henry VIII's reign, lasting from 1539 to about 1550, and one in the middle of Elizabeth's reign, approximately from 1567 to 1583. In the years leading up to 1550, the first wave reflects translations like Richard Taverner's *Garden of Wisdom* (1539) and Nicholas Udall's *Floures of Terence* (1534), which were issued in multiple editions, as were the well-selling, figuratively titled devotional books by Thomas Becon. The second surge in plant books, which begins in the late 1560s, at the moment of Maplet's *Forest* and Howell's *Arbor*, reflects a much greater number of *new* titles, especially miscellaneous gatherings of various kinds, including poetry, prose, and useful proverbs. Included among them are a subset of poetic collections influenced by *Songes and Sonettes*, the multiauthored collection of short verse that had been published by Richard Tottel in 1557.[37] The bibliographic language of plants will play an outsized role in announcing the forms of poetic anthologies that, like practical books on horticulture and husbandry, also began to be published in greater numbers in these same years. Those anthologies' motifs of floral collection will recur at the turn of the century in the group of commonplaced anthologies that included *Englands Helicon* and *Bel-vedére or the Garden of the Muses* (both published in 1600.)[38]

Titles from the Henrician and the Elizabethan waves of plant books draw on similar metaphors and build on many of the same textual practices of copying and compiling. However, there are important differences when it comes to the contexts of their publication and reception, which we can better understand through a measure that Alan Farmer and Zachary Lesser define as "first-edition weighting." In their anatomy of structures of popularity in early modern English print, Farmer and Lesser suggest we draw a division between classes of the Elizabethan book market according to the portion of titles in a given genre that represent new first editions. These distinctions reflect the kind of decision a stationer is making in publishing a certain kind of book: how likely is a title to recoup a publisher's investment, to sell most of its first printing, or require to additional reprintings? Most of the books composing the surge in the middle of Elizabeth's reign fall into the class that Farmer and Lesser call "innovative": occasionally reprinted, but not as sure a bet as those genres of books they class as "mature."[39] In the earlier wave, 37 percent of total editions are new titles, while in the second wave 59 percent are first editions.[40] In the 1560s and 1570s, then, plant books fall into a portion of the market that represents a significantly greater financial risk. Many of the horticultural titles published in this later period are also generic or formal experiments, like the miscellaneous poetic collections published by Denham or Richard Jones. More than some other titles, then, plant books faced an unknown audience, even as they drew on a familiar lexicon. In this same decade, plant books begin to give newly speculative accounts of themselves and of their possible courses of reception. As their techniques of self-figuration reflect a greater interest in both novelty and in contingency, the book itself comes to seem a new kind of adventure.

The many plant books published in the 1530s and 1540s coincide with a wave of Protestant humanist printing during the reign of Henry VIII, much of it giving English voice to habits of textual gathering advocated by Erasmus and exemplified by dozens of continental florilegia and anthologies.[41] Collections of flowers reflect practices of textual commonplacing that, building on the teachings of Erasmus and Agricola, shaped humanist classrooms and fueled composition in and beyond it.[42] Schoolboys were trained, in Erasmus's words, to "flit like a busy bee through the entire garden of literature," gathering choice sentences into their own hive of notes, a topically organized treasury of pieces of wisdom.[43] Breaking down their content into small textual pieces, the format and framing of books like Taverner's "garden" and Udall's "flowers" advertised their readiness for copying and for practical application as storehouses of ready matter.

Across early modern Europe, the sixteenth century saw countless books published as *florilegia, anthologia, flores*, and *manipuli florum*, energized by these models of textual gathering.[44] These printed volumes embraced humanist models while building on practices of textual compilation and organization developed by medieval scribes and scholars.[45] As Ann Blair has shown, many were extensive compendiums in which scholars grappled with the vast amounts of knowledge available in written form, as they gathered examples from literature, history, and natural philosophy into sizable catalogs. Nani Mirabelli's *Polyanthea*, for example—a title that, in a twist on the etymology of "anthology," suggests "many flowers"—included many flowers indeed: Blair estimates the first edition, of 1503, at 430,000 words, and editions a century later topping out at over two million words.[46]

In England, most plant books published before 1550 were significantly more compact than Nani's. Nearly all were epitomes and translations of continental examples, including a number of schoolbooks provisioned with Latin exemplars worthy of students' emulation. One of the earliest plant books printed in England, Wynkyn de Worde's 1513 edition of *The Flores of Ovide de Arte Amandi*, gathers sentences in English and Latin.[47] A more elaborate version of the same basic structure, Nicholas Udall's *Floures for Latine Spekynge Selected and Gathered oute of Terence* (printed in octavo by Thomas Berthelet in 1534) gathers examples from Terence's plays, assembling a treasury of Latin sentences from which schoolboys might learn and practice.[48] It would be issued in at least ten editions by the end of the sixteenth century.[49] A translation of Erasmus aimed at schoolboys, Richard Taverner's *The Flowers of Sencies Gathered out of Sundry Wryters*—or, in its parallel Latin title, *Flores aliquot sententiarum ex variis collecti scriptoribus*—went through at least five editions in the decade after its 1540 publication. During the same period, Taverner published at least another four editions of his two-part commonplace book, *The Garden of Wysedome*. Many of these titles remained in print through the end of the century, and all remained in circulation. The authors and compilers of plant books from the later sixteenth century had largely been trained in humanist classrooms and studied exemplary collections like the *Flores poetarum* and schoolbooks like Udall's and Taverner's. Those later publications, issued a generation or more after Henry VIII's reign, would experiment with well-established practices of gathering and compilation, combining useful *sententiae* with assortments of prose and verse, and with the lexicon of forests and flowers that framed those earlier texts.

By the middle of the 1570s, horticultural titles indicated to readers not just that the books they named were part of a tradition; they also identified them as part of a trend—a distinct strain in what William Webbe in 1586 would call the "innumerable sortes of Englyshe Bookes, and infinite fardles of printed pamphlets, wherewith thys Countrey is pestered."[50] Among those infinite fardles, plant books were linked by both printers and readers, and they were characterized by a cluster of material features: extensive use of printer's ornament, small literary forms, long prefatory materials, and intent alliteration both in titles and prefaces. All qualify the book as an artifact, a fashioned commodity. John Bishop seems almost apologetic for the title of his 1577 *Beautiful Blossomes* in confessing that he has been "infected with the common contagion of oure time, whiche maketh us small smatterers in good letters." More specifically, he apologizes for the conventionality of his title, which he, "following the manner of these daintie dayes, who do delight to dalley with the letter, named *Byshops Blossomes*."[51] Despite his apology for letter-dallying, Bishop does it enthusiastically here and throughout the prefatory material. And he had company: booksellers' stalls in mid-Elizabethan England would have been littered with alliterative titles, many of which converged with the horticultural conceits that were so popular in the same years: *The Arbor of Amitie* (1568), *A Petite Pallace of Pettie His Pleasure* (1576), *A Gorgious Gallery of Gallant Inventions* (1578), *The Forrest of Fancy* (1579). Like a figurative title, or an ornamental border, the preponderance of alliteration draws attention to the surface of language and its status as a fashioned thing. Titles like "bower" and "nosegay," like those that frame books as a galleries or cabinets, reflect "the fashionability of a certain kind of commoditized book," as Jason Scott-Warren argues; they situate it as part of the print market and as part of domestic material culture, promising a treasury or warehouse of materials on which reader or consumer might draw.[52] The titles of plant books add an additional twist to this trend, endowing the material cultures of bookselling and book use with the specific capacities of vegetable life. In turn, they frame the book according to a version of craft and commodity that understands it as something more than *mere* matter, endowing it instead with a prodigious potential for dispersal and regeneration.

Readers in the period linked these titles as well, even when the content of particular collections may have seemed incompatible. The single surviving work of the Elizabethan poet John Grange offers one example of how a reader ranged across different kinds of plant books and of how a model of reading as discerping or excerpting fueled the composition of poetry and fiction. The prose narrative in Grange's *Golden Aphroditis* (1577) tracks the story of two lovers across a landscape that echoes *The Adventures of Master F.J.*, published a few years earlier in Gascoigne's *Hundreth Sundrie Flowres* (1573).[53] It is a terrain littered with bibliographic landmarks. In his attempts to communicate to his beloved the rare virtue of his affection, Grange's protagonist compares his devotion to a long series of minerals—including asbestos and chalcedony—in terms drawn directly from Maplet's *Forest*. Grange's narrative at this point even closely paraphrases Maplet's dedication, which suggests he may have had the book in front of him while composing, or, more likely, had copied into a notebook long passages from both parts of the earlier volume.[54] Later, seeking aid from the muses, Grange's protagonist finds them at home in a flowery dale "commonly called the *Arbor of amitie*."[55] With these allusions, Grange follows the cues of Denham's marketing strategy, linking his reading of these decade-old octavos, and rifling through both, along with other miscellanies, for material. Grange is one example of figures whom Scott-Warren calls "the readers that print built": those whose habits of consumption and interpretation hungrily absorbed the fashions in newly printed books.[56] He pays a culminating homage to these trends by naming the collection of poems that concludes the volume "Granges Garden," a gathering to which I will turn in Chapter 3.

Of the readers that print built, none were more influential than stationers, and it is in the decisions made by stationers that we find the strongest links between plant books. At the junction of literary figure and commercial advertisement, bibliographic use of horticultural idiom calls on the joint agency of author and stationer. Some titles clearly originate in the printing house, devised as part of an effort to frame a text for consumers, or to illustrate the stationer's editorial role in gathering a volume. (Several printers whose business joined an interest in plant life to the work of bookmaking will recur throughout this study, including Henry Denham, Henry Bynneman, and Richard Jones.) Other titles are explicitly claimed by the writer responsible for part or most of a text's content, with the vegetable conceit woven through the form and structure of the volume. For the most part, though, when it comes to botanical conceit, the roles of author and stationer cannot be distinguished, for a good reason. These conceits emerge where the labors of literary production and invention meet the making of the book as an object; where the energy of printers is most speculative, as those responsible for the making and publication of texts imagine new and enthusiastically vegetable futures for their pages.[57]

Botanical poetics emerge at this intersection, marked by the joint energies of poetic and bookish invention. It should be no surprise, then, that we find most of plant books' figurative botanical material in the segments of the book that scholars often call paratexts: in the content of prefaces and epistles, on title pages, in running titles, and in divisional subheadings. Though often in prose, such entryways represent a kind of *poiesis* of the book itself; these elements are relational, future-oriented, and performative.[58] In collaboration with page design and book format, titles and other paratexts make a codex an intelligible object—both a thing unto itself, akin to a bower or a bouquet, and a meaningful participant in a field of other books. Marked by this coherent repertoire of formal and rhetorical conventions, plant books represent a distinct print genre. However, as a principle of classification, botanical titles operate not according to what a book says but according to what it does, how it calls itself into being as an artifact. Plant books take shape, in other words, according to their presentation of their own bookishness.[59] It is a bookishness, though, in a distinctly plant-like guise. Specifically, the patterns of plant life illuminate two dimensions of the printed codex's multiplicity: first, the internal complexity of the codex, its composition in multiple folds, leaves, and parts; and, second, the multiplicity of the printed book as a reproduced object. Alongside the "thereness" that Andrew Piper ascribes to books as objects, plant books also project an "elsewhereness."[60] Any given text—posy, letter, recipe, or anthology—can always be in multiple hands at multiple sites.[61] These two kinds of plurality capture what sometimes seems strange about the materiality of both plants and printed books; the next two sections of this Introduction treat each dimension in turn.

"A Very Curiouse and Artificiall Compacted Nosegay": Composite Forms

The cultural imagination of the codex has long reflected a tension between scattering and gathering. Building on images from Virgil, Dante, and Petrarch, a conventional fantasy takes the codex as a closed volume, one that promises to repair and regather the leaves lost by the Sibyl, just as Dante, gazing into paradise, seems to see restored and bound in a single volume "that which is scattered in leaves throughout the universe."[62] But early modern books were also unavoidably composite things—unbound, or merely cracked open, a book was once again a multiple object, imminently subject to scattering if not already scattered. The codex in this view suffers from a version of wave-particle duality, as it oscillates between the book as a single bound object and as a promiscuous assemblage of loose pages.

Horticultural titles give form to this central tension between scattering and binding. Early modern writers frequently linked the bindable capacities of pages, flowers, or slips—a word that referred equally to paper and to vegetable fragments. A fascicle, for example, could name a gathering of either pages or flowers, as long as it was compactly bound together. Thomas Elyot's dictionary links the gathered quality of the Latin *fasciculus* with its status as a "handful," noting that it may be a pamphlet or a bundle of letters, or "a grype, or thyng bounden togither. It is also a nosegay, or any thynge knytte togyther, whiche maye be borne in a mannes hande."[63] Here, Elyot disregards the contents of the bundle, keying his definition instead to the gathered form of a "thynge knytte togyther." John Palsgrave, introducing his 1540 translation of the comedy of *Acolastus*, uses "nosegay" as a term of praise for how his source is gathered: "I esteme that lyttell volume to be a very curiouse and artificiall compacted nosegay, gathered out of the moche excellent and odoriferouse swete smellynge gardeynes of the moste pure latyne auctours."[64] Under the sign of titles like "nosegay" and "bouquet," these dynamics of scattering and gathering generate a robust account of composite forms, a poetic vocabulary for what Cleanth Brooks called a "mere assemblage": horizontally organized, mixed forms will be described as "knotted," "compact," "loosely bound," or composed of "slips."[65]

Plant books thus participate in what Jeffrey Todd Knight describes as a "culture of compilation," an approach to texts that values their potential to be reordered and reorganized into new gatherings.[66] Recent scholarship in book history, like Knight's work, has emphasized the piecemeal and provisional quality of early modern books—the literal and figurative ways in which material texts were cut up, pieced together, copied, and torn apart. At times, the work of redistributing textual pieces reflects the material practices of readers, like the physical labors of cutting out and compiling paper slips, or binding multiple pamphlets together into a *Sammelband*—a kind of megabook in which multiple shorter imprints were bound together.[67] Other times, the redistribution of parts gives shape to the stories that books tell about themselves—in the texts that are my subject here, a story told in the language of plants.

As gatherings of small forms, plant books register their diverse composition rhetorically and typographically. These volumes are crowded with visual differentiation, marks of distinction that break up both sections of the book and the text blocks of individual pages. At the beginnings and ends of sections and chapters, and at shifts between poetry and prose, a reader finds transitions marked by type ornament or even a fully bordered divisional title page. In books of sayings and in collections of poems, a lively repertoire of single-spot type ornaments marks out the work's composite pieces. Taverner's carefully crafted volumes offer an early example of how stationers used the toolbox of print to form their texts according to the piecemeal reading strategies associated with commonplacing. Building on traditions of manuscript annotation, marks like manicules and hedera (visible in Figure 3) give visual form to the metaphorical labors of plucking choice flowers from the text. Readers like Ben Jonson penciled marginal flowers or trefoils in the margins of texts, marking parcels of text worth noting, copying, or remembering (illustrated in Figure 4, from Jonson's copy of Thomas Tusser's *Five Hundred Pointes of Good Husbandrie* [1580]).[68]

In the *Garden of Wisdom*, printed by Richard Bankes under Taverner's supervision, each hedera or manicule is a mark of significance, fragmentation, and diminution. As we will see at greater length in Chapter 5, other volumes join these symbols to a varied assortment of typefaces (roman, italic, black letter, at different scales) to mark different kinds of writing—prose or verse, Latin sentence or English translation, abstract or editorial gloss. Such pointing helps constitute the page as a visual field, while indexing a fragment's capacity for reuse and repetition.[69]

The popularity of books of sentences persisted across the period, as did the graphic architecture that marked out these rhetorical slips on the printed page. Published more than forty years later, Thomas Crewe's *Nosegay of Morall Philosophie* (1580) (a translation of Gabriel Meurier's *Bouquet de philosophie morale* [1568]) organizes its brief pieces of proverbial wisdom in a witty question and answer format. Some of those brief answers explode into more copious forms.[70] For example, the *Nosegay*'s thirty-two answers to the question "What is the life of man properly?" supply a treasury of paradoxical wisdom: it is a true "Cave of fantasies" and "Shoppe of deceites," the list begins, and eventually concludes, a true "Kinde of base haughtines"(Figure 5).[71] Here, the

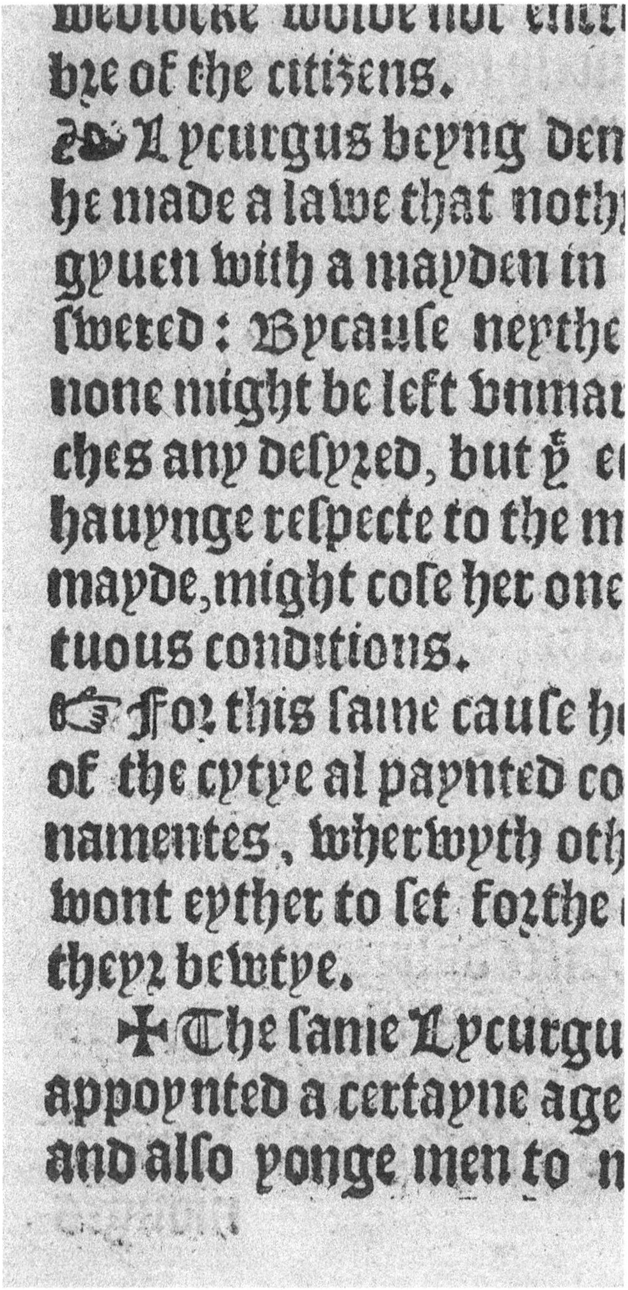

wedlocke wolde not entr[...]
bre of the citizens.

⁊ Lycurgus beyng den[...]
he made a lawe that noth[...]
gyuen with a mayden in [...]
swered: Bycause neythe[...]
none might be left vnmar[...]
ches any desyred, but ⱳ e[...]
hauynge respecte to the m[...]
mayde, might cose her one [...]
tuous conditions.

☞ For this same cause h[...]
of the cytye al paynted co[...]
namentes, wherwyth oth[...]
wont eyther to set forthe [...]
theyr bewtye.

✠ The same Lycurgu[...]
appoynted a certayne age [...]
and also yonge men to n[...]

Figure 3. Richard Taverner, *The Garden of Wysdome* (London: William Copland for Richard Kele, [1550?]), sig. A8ᵛ (detail). RB 51809, The Huntington Library, San Marino, California.

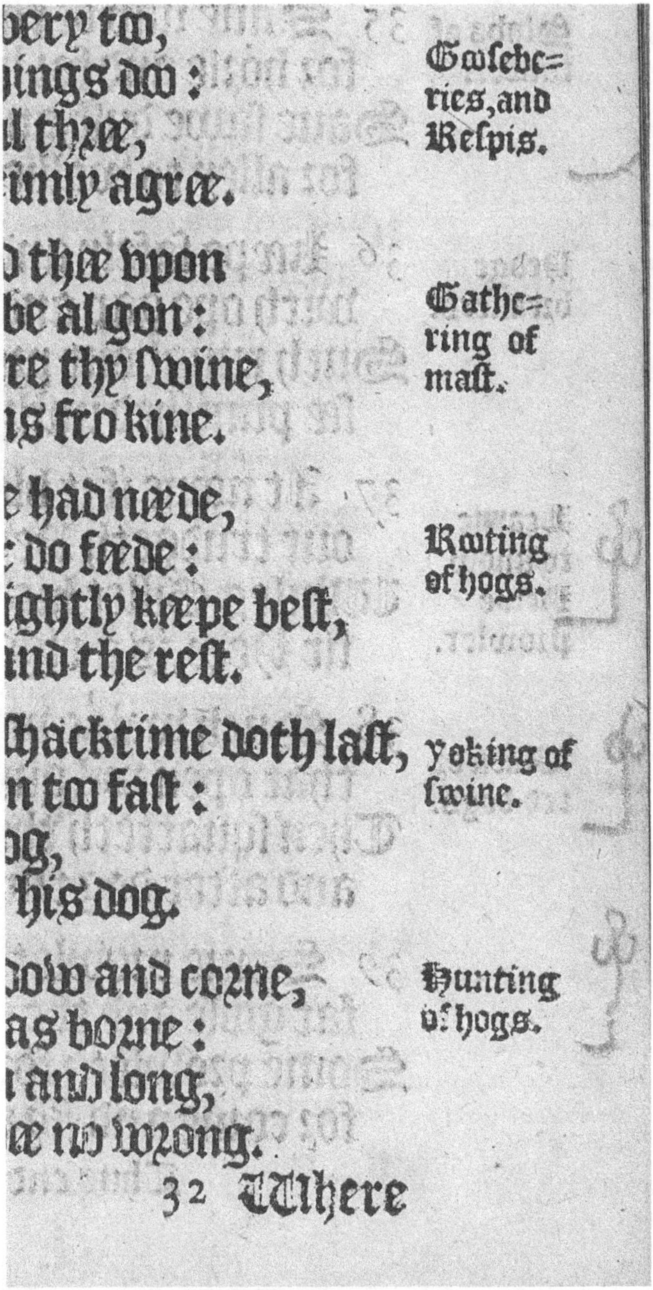

Figure 4. Ben Jonson's marginal notes in Thomas Tusser, *Five Hundred Pointes of Good Husbandrie* (London: Henry Denham, 1580), sig. E4ʳ (detail). By permission of the British Library. Shelfmark C.122.bb.19.

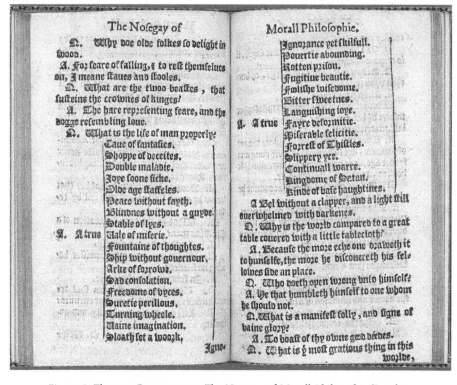

Figure 5. Thomas Crewe, trans., *The Nosegay of Morall Philosophie* (London: Thomas Dawson, 1580), sigs. E5ᵛ–E6ʳ. RB 51755, The Huntington Library, San Marino, California.

mise-en-page of the *Nosegay*'s printer, Thomas Dawson, gathers its examples into a kind of shape poem: long brackets running alongside the short lines of text give visual form to the parceled bundle of the nosegay. Reading through the *Nosegay*'s gathered answers offers a pleasure in itself, as the page invites the reader to experience a profusion of similarity and difference. A nosegay like Crewe's recalls Elyot's definition of a fascicle, or Palsgrave's curious, compact nosegay: it binds together a great variety in a small bundle, as the rhetorical intensity of answers suggests the infinity of invention possible within a closed space.

The density of printer's marks and numeration in plant books gives a concrete visual rendering to their distinct blend of copiousness and brevity. In this, they play out the practice of rhetorical abundance that Erasmus gave the name of *copia*—a display of richness in words and matter foundational to rhetorical education in the humanist classroom.[72] Like the husbandman and housewife, compilers, printers, and poets were in the business of ordering and sorting large quantities of *stuff*. Every florilegium or commonplace book supplies a lively tank of rhetorical fuel, a resource to be tapped in moments of need, or as occasion demands.[73] Making reference to the *Odyssey*'s locus classicus of vegetable productivity, Arthur Golding advertises his translation of Ovid's *Metamorphoses* as "This Ortyard of Alcimous"—so full of useful examples that "there wants not any / Herb, tree, or frute that may mans use for health or pleasure serve."[74] On this model, botanical gatherings promise not just to meet every need but to *continue* to meet those needs, undiminished by use or consumption.

At times, the fecundity of vegetable life posed a challenge to protocols of order. Printed herbals, which grew in popularity over the course of the sixteenth century and into the seventeenth, grappled intensely with the tension between the capacious world of things and the finite capacity of the codex.[75] But practices of gathering and cultivation also offered models for handling that immensity. And, as Leah Knight has shown, that same energy to anthologize drove the engagements of early modern readers with both plants and the books in which they were gathered.[76] In herbals as in rhetorical gardens, competing forces of copiousness and compactness register in the visual form of the collected page. The first herbal printed in England (now known conventionally as *Banckes' Herball*) was published by Richard Bankes in 1525, fourteen years before his professional relationship with Richard Taverner would produce the Erasmian *Garden of Wisdom* and *Flowers of Sencies*. Like the garden gathered by Taverner, *Banckes' Herball* brings a world of practical knowledge into the portable codex, transplanting the flowering field to the printed page.

As products of gathering, translation, and compilation, plant books take a characteristically minimalist view of the role of the author, editor, or translator in a text's generation or transformion. The epistle to Crewe's translation of Meurier's *Bouquet* humbly frames his own role as the transporter and gatherer of foreign slips: "The slips hereof were set in sundry Italian gardens, & with branches therof I met at Paris, which smelled so sweetely, that I tooke the paines to transport them hither into England, and to binde them up in this small nosegay, the which I pray your Ladiship so to accept." Crewe's combination of geographical ambition and personal humility specifically echoes the blend of gathering, translation, and transportation suggested by the long title of George Gascoigne's 1573 *A Hundreth Sundrie Flowres,* which are described as "bounde up in one small Poesie. Gathered partely (by translation) in the fyne outlandish Gardins of Euripides, Ovid, Petrarke, Ariosto, and others: and partly by invention, out of our owne fruitefull Orchardes in Englande." Evoking a geographic texture that is both specific and imaginative, Crewe and Gascoigne counterpoise the rangy variety of their sources with the compactness of the bound gathering: transported to England, Crewe took pains to "binde them up in this small nosegay," while Gascoigne's flowers are "bounde up in one small Poesie."[77] Both "vegetable authors," in this account, paint themselves as binders and transporters—conduits but not creators.

In the final third of the sixteenth century, their shared capacities of condensation and fragmentation figured plants and texts as supremely portable things: whether seeds, flown abroad or broadcast; scions of fruit trees imported to graft on English stocks; or slips or samples carried on ships from the East or West Indies. In a description that might apply either to Gascoigne's gathered posy or to national dynamics of crop importation, William Harrison's *Description of England* (1587) introduces gardens and orchards as amalgams of specimens "brought hither from far countries," fueled by the "natural desire that mankind hath to esteem things far-sought, because they be rare and costly, and the irksome contempt of things near-hand."[78] The value of plant materials had long driven projects of settlement and of commerce, including the long-standing and long-reaching international traffic in spices. But the transportation of plant materials accelerated many times over during the sixteenth century, driven by European colonization, consumer demands of a growing population, and a global economy increasingly shaped by the transatlantic slave trade. In the following two centuries, the science of botany would continue to develop alongside European colonial expansion, as growing collections and emergent taxonomies depended on access to widening territories. Colonial projects were in turn fed by profits from botanical imports, including seeds, spices, roots, resins, and other parts of edible and medicinal plants.[79] The copiousness of herbals printed in Europe reflected these networks of transport, as they grew to incorporate examples from ever further afield. The Spanish physician Nicolás Monardes became the foremost written authority on New World *materia medica*, maintained a medical practice, and carried on a profitable traffic in imported medicines and dyes, all without traveling outside of Seville. His treatise on new medicines was published in English translation as *Joyfull Newes out of the Newe Founde Worlde* (1577), in an edition that promised to share the "rare and singuler vertues of diverse and sundrie Hearbes, Trees, Oyles, Plantes, and Stones," along with guidance for their medicinal use.[80] The compiled form of his book reflected the fantasy of New-World copiousness it endorsed; in turn, the virtuous capacities of plants enriched Monardes's book, just as they enriched him.

Loose Bindings: Use, Dispersal, and Reception

The capacity of plant life to proliferate, travel, and begin anew suggested powerful models for reimagining poetic reception and textual circulation. As objects defined by their capacities for use and transaction, plant books consistently defer to the power of readers and conjure the possibilities of circulation. In the late sixteenth century, the printed book's internal diversity—so often as a composite of sentences, commonplaces, poems, or other small pieces—was paired with a growing sense of the potential diversity of its readership.[81] However, the stationers, translators, and poets I consider here face the uncertainties of reception without trying to contain or control them; instead, with the help of plants, they generate fictions. As the market for print was expanding, and books as a commodity form could be indifferently and untraceably exchanged, the language of horticulture naturalized that field of risk and speculation, giving imaginative form to an otherwise invisible social field of reading and consumption.[82]

Like Maplet's *discerped* cuttings, sent to dispersed places, botanical poetics reorganizes the energy of creation, sending it away from the position of gatherer, editor, or author, and casting it instead toward readers and users. Sometimes, the titles of plant books conjure particular relations with readers, defining and delimiting the proper kinds of objective and manual engagement with the book. A plant book's direct address fragments the body of a fantasized reader: into hands (to grasp or extract), nose (to smell or savor), and, more rarely, bosom (a corporeal vessel in which to hold and carry the book). Spatial metaphors like gardens and bowers promise to absorb the whole body of the reader but still evoke specific sensory attunements, especially smell, touch, or sight. The sensory claims made by these texts upon their readers rely on a Renaissance discourse of taste and textual consumption that was filtered through the terms established in Horace's *Ars Poetica*: to profit or delight, "aut prodesse . . . aut delectare."[83] In Ben Jonson's translation, "Poëts would either profit, or delight, / Or mixing sweet, and fit, teach life the right."[84] Jonson's phrasing filters its dualistic view of reception through a materialist discourse of taste: sweet mixed with bitter, or salty, as realized at the moment of textual consumption. In publisher Richard Tottel's preface to the *Songes and Sonettes* (1557), a gustatory logic weeds out less discriminating readers, but offers to retrain their taste.[85] He asks the unlearned to read more skillfully, and to "purge that swinelike grossenesse, that maketh the swete majerome not to smel to their delight."[86] Influenced by Tottel's inaugural salvo on aesthetic distinction, printed poetic collections participate in a discourse of aesthetic legitimacy repeatedly grounded in a scene of herbal consumption. They encounter potential readers through the portals of their noses and tongues.

Plant books were especially interested, however, in readers' hands: they asked to be used. In this way, early modern plant books make a distinct contribution to the suggestion, made by a number of scholars of the history of reading in recent years, that we reframe the field's central questions around a conception of book *use*.[87] This attention to how books were used (or, at least, how they asked to be used) reflects the central humanist principle that reading should be oriented toward future action and common profit.[88] Plant books understand "use" even more concretely. In dialogue with practical handbooks and craft knowledge, these texts reflect a practical lexicon of use that draws a continuous arc from the skilled propagation and distillation of plants to the skilled handling of books. The articulations of reception and readerly engagement we find there amount to a situated theory of reading, one that understands the reception of books in the hands of users on a continuum with other manual practices.

This is not to say that botanical titles always came out on the side of utility and profit; poets in particular often played at the limits of profit and delight, coyly suggesting the possibility (and pleasures) of uselessness. Even in those cases, though, vegetable textuality offered a powerful tool in the period's debates about the cultural status of poetry. This was especially true when those debates turned on the potentially dangerous effects of verse on poets, on readers, and on the commonwealth. Faced with detractors who attacked poetry and drama as sources of temptation and idleness, and its producers as vain, indulgent, and dangerous, an herbal account of textual substance promised a ready-made authorial defense: readers, like skilled herbalists, were responsible for knowing how to handle the material in front of them so that its effect was curative and not poisonous.[89] Stephen Gosson, in permitting only the "right use of auncient Poetrie," aimed to limit the range of poetic activities that qualified as profitable; that same logic, though, could exculpate the poet, as George Gascoigne understood when he defended the "Weedes" included in his *Posies* (1575) by deferring to the skill of the reader. There was no weed "so vile or stinking," Gascoigne suggested, "but that it hath in it some vertue if it be rightly handled."[90] The very substance of the verse awaits the reader's handling. This logic defended verse against the threat that it might be actively wasteful: it held, like earth's other creatures, some potential to serve humankind.

Faced with accusations of wastefulness, poets assumed for themselves the promising latency of plant life. In comparing himself to a new graft, Thomas Howell solicits the reader's cultivation, suggesting that, if properly watered and cared for, he too might grow into something more profitable. This is a version of the poet subject to what Patricia Akhimie calls the "ideology of cultivation," a figure capable—like untilled soil—of improvement.[91] Howell shares this quality with the group of writers that Richard Helgerson influentially called the Elizabethan prodigals, young poets whose literary production was framed within a narrative of wasteful errancy—one that those poets often patterned on horticultural processes of growth and decay. At once environmental and economic, the paired logics of profit and prodigality embed verse and even poets themselves in a natural economy.

As they defer to a reader's right handling, plant books are loose bindings: I intend this phrase to name both the hold of the whole volume on its mixed contents and the hold of the book on the reader. Plant books repeatedly promise to free up readers to find their own paths through the text, a readerly liberty they key to the composite forms of both garden and codex. Nicholas Breton, for example, suggests that readers who dislike a given poem should "turne ouer the leafe, and you shall finde somwhat els to your contentment," while John Lyly compares the readers of *Euphues* to lovers who, "when they come into a Gardeine, some gather Nettles, some Roses, one Tyme, an other Sage." Whether offering a page to turn or a nettle to gather, plant books ensure this freedom with their copious and composite forms. As Lyly writes, "Lette everye one followe his fancie, and say that is best, which he lyketh best."[92] The ill-fated butterly of Spenser's *Muiopotmos* practices this same readerly freedom as he "enjoy[s] delight with libertie" in that poem's garden of riotous variety.[93] (In practice, as his fate in that poem implies, that exercise of looseness does not always end well.)

By imagining divergent and multiple futures for their texts, the gatherers of plant books fit uneasily into Michel Foucault's definition of the author function as "the principle of thrift in the proliferation of meaning."

Ostentatiously prodigal versions of that principle, these poets, printers, and compilers fashion themselves instead as sites and inciters of textual proliferation. Attuned to the proliferative potential of plant life, some of those poets sketch out a distinctive theory of poetic authorship—one that preserved the loose hold of the codex over its parts and its readers. They suggest in turn a horticultural fantasy of free circulation and common property—a fantasy that we will see put to the test in Part II of this study.[94]

While the composite forms of botanical collections free up readers to approach the book as they please, they also qualify a book to address multiple readers. As these unregulated readers suggest, the law of genre uniting plant books is necessarily a loose one: the nature of such miscellaneous works is their refusal to prescribe an order of approach or to closely govern the reader's response. Instead, they speculate, sketching out anticipatory histories of their own reading. In this sense, they encounter—from the opposite side of the coin—the same epistemological problems that have nagged historians of reading in recent decades. As Roger Chartier has argued, the history of reading has always been "vagabond," chasing errantly after traces and ghosts.[95] Whether in the form of prodigal poets, far-fetched herbs, or regifted nosegays, plant books tell their own vagabond histories of reading. It is this fictive work of anticipation that animates the approach of botanical poetics to circulation.

Conjuring a social world of readers and their habits is an imaginary exercise that is also prescriptive—hailing readers and managing their approach to the book, a technique that surely as often produces failed interpellations and disobedient readers. The language of virtues offers one strategy for managing such a divide. On the one hand, it endows plant books with it the generic and prescriptive force of practical genres like herbals, manuals of physic, and gardening books: all texts that empower readers to repeat methods and regenerate forms at new sites and in new settings. But virtues could also travel, and the capacity of virtuous slips and excerpts to circulate afforded printers and authors a powerful imagination of the future itineraries of their books. Drawing a resilient connection between the present text and its future satisfaction in the hands of a reader, the logic of virtue conscripts single copies as deputies on assignment in the hermeneutic hinterlands of country or city, closet or lane.

ɣə   ɣə   ɣə

The chapters of *Botanical Poetics* immerse themselves in the class of texts I have defined as plant books, following the tendrils of particular scenes, images, and formal patterns as they unfurl across early modern England's printed books. These titles form a motley archive: pamphlets, practical handbooks, gatherings of useful sayings, anthologies of tales, books of private devotion, and the jumbled gatherings of short verse now usually described as "miscellanies." Each chapter combines readings of literary and practical genres, a reflection of the overriding premise that the worlds of poetic production and everyday practice were not as distinct in the period as we might today imagine. Guided by this archive, I take a special interest in what we might call the long 1570s, a period from about 1567 to 1583 in which the number of plant books brought out by London stationers increased dramatically. The literature of this period has received less attention than that produced either before or after, cursed perhaps by C. S. Lewis's indelible assessment of it as the "Drab Age."[96] But, closely considered, the poetry and plant books of this period offer unfamiliar and provocative accounts of familiar literary categories: the author, the single poem, literary property, textual reception and circulation. *Botanical Poetics* explores what early modern literature looks like from the vantage of this archive.

Botanical Poetics proceeds in three parts, each of which tracks the entanglement of book-thinking and plant-thinking through the lens of two central themes: the loose and miscellaneous associations of plants, poems, and people; and virtue, the latent material force carried by both texts and herbs. Each of Parts I and II comprises two chapters and a shorter case study, or "branch," which revisits a familiar or canonical work of Renaissance literature in light of the preceding chapters.

The first part, entitled "Bound Flowers, Loose Leaves: The Form and Force of Plants in Print," considers the surge of plant books published during the middle part of Elizabeth's reign in order to introduce what is distinctive about their understandings of the matter of the book and its circulation and use. Horticultural metaphors, these chapters argue, plant seeds of textual miscellaneity and active readerly engagement, while carving out for both author and reader an ambivalent freedom. Chapter 1, "'What Kind of Thing I Am': Plant Books in Space and Time," addresses two trends that distinguish titles from this period: first, the use of knots, ornaments, and graphic division in the built environments of books and gardens; and, second, the role of husbandry in the efforts of printed books to anticipate their reception in the hands of readers. The instructional writer Thomas Hill, whose gardening books reflect these phenomena, and his publishers Henry Denham and Henry Bynneman serve as guides through both trends. Part of the period's aesthetic vocabulary for complex forms, design elements like knots and printers' ornaments seem to fix both book and garden as closed objects, determinate gatherings of matter. These closed forms, however, are only ever provisional—as readers are reminded by the divisional title pages that join gatherings of verse onto longer books and recur within these titles. Knots, ornaments, and other enclosures multiply throughout the spaces of book and garden, where they invite non-linear reading and suggest an experience of division and indeterminacy. In poetic anthologies, this material and formal variety appears alongside structuring metaphors of husbandry, which compete to define what kind of object or event the printed book (or individual poem) should be. The chapter concludes by showing how the deferred temporalities of agricultural labor shape poetic collections of the long 1570s, reframing both planting and publication according to a patient practice of risk management.

Chapter 2, "On *Vertue*: Textual Force and Vegetable Capacity," turns from the forms assumed by plant books to their force. To do so, it introduces another defining feature: the lexicon of "vertues" that endows vegetal-textual forms with a latent capacity for getting things done. A cousin of Aristotle's *dunamis*, or potentiality, virtue named the potential to break into worldly action. By tracking the lexicon of virtue across plant books and practical handbooks, the chapter charts this vegetable latency as it pulls humans into an ecological collaboration with nonhuman matter. These capacities emerge within a cosmology that understands worldly virtues as divine provisions, packets of divine potential distributed across the earth, often copiously packed into small forms like poems, herbs, or printed pamphlets. A central character in the period's literature of craft knowledge, vegetable virtues reframe the role of the reader according to this artisanal model. Texts, like medicinal herbs, demand skilled handling: reader-practitioners capable of managing their transformative potential, especially the potentially dangerous virtues of poetry. The chapter concludes with an analysis of George Puttenham's reliance on a logic of virtue in *The Arte of English Poesie*; though Puttenham's handbook takes a collaborative and practical engagement with material virtues, he ultimately frees the poet from the dependence of the craftsman.

Part I concludes with an analysis of Shakespeare's *Romeo and Juliet*, showing how the botanical tradition uncovered in the previous chapters illuminates the play's tragic entanglement in the circulation of plants, texts, and people. The world of Shakespeare's Verona is overrun with small, powerful things—including flowers, poems, poisons, and the young lovers themselves.

Infused with what Friar Laurence calls the "mickle" and "powerful grace that lies / In plants, herbs, stones and their true qualities"(2.3.11–12), the play's virtuous materials consistently misfire. Botanical poetics lends the play this dynamics of diminution, where the closed logic of small forms breaks into a world of accident and contingency.

This model of dissemination, collection, and readerly engagement laid generative soil for poets writing in the middle years of Elizabeth's reign, especially as they considered the peril and promise of appearing in print. Part II, on poetic gardens of the 1570s, examines botanical poetics at the peak of plant books' Elizabethan popularity, showing how a conjunction of plant-thinking and book-thinking helped poets and publishers negotiate access, judgment, and the problem of poetic value. In Part II, the formal tension between gathering and dispersal introduced in Part I plays out as a social problem. The assemblers of Elizabethan poetic gardens, both poets and stationers, turn their imaginative energies toward the scene of reception and the capacities of vegetal materiality, as they ask who can and who should have access to printed gardens.

The first of these two chapters ("Sundry Flowers by Sundry Gentlemen") takes as its central focus a set of books of poems called "gardens" or "flowers" published by young members of the Inns of Court in the 1570s. While each of these poets organizes his poetic garden around a fiction of hospitality and friendship, each also imagines the harm that might be done to the text through uprooting, shredding, or castration. These imagined vulnerabilities, I argue, figure the poet himself according to a vegetable logic of ongoing growth, as a figure whose poetic properties are valuable precisely because of the harm that might be done to them in the present. The second chapter in this section, "Isabella Whitney's Dispersals," revisits this same scene from the perspective of a reader. Whitney's *Sweet Nosgay* (1573), among the first works of secular verse printed by a woman in English, forcefully rewrites the gardens of the male poets examined in the previous chapter. By relying on gathered "slips," I argue, Whitney assembles an account of "slippery reading" that taps into the logic of botanical virtues to rethink the social potential of vegetable and textual circulation.

Like Part I, Part II concludes with a case study, entitled "How to Read Like a Pig." This second "branch" gathers images of pigs as bad readers of poetry, arguing that such metaphors help writers give form to what is strange about the matter of printed poetry. Proverbially incapable of enjoying sweet smells, swine supply ready figures for bad readers. However, as trespassers in poetic gardens, they are also destructive, nuzzling, groining, and uprooting its poems. I conclude by showing how this tradition is inverted in the destruction of the Bower of Bliss in Edmund Spenser's *Faerie Queene*, which offers a rejoinder to these earlier collections. Spenser's Bower stands as a culminating—and transformative—example in a series of gardens invaded by swine.

Part III "An Increase of Small Things," includes a single chapter, "Richard Tottel, Thomas Tusser, and the Minutiae of Shakespeare's *Sonnets*." Here, taking the poetic couplet as a case study, I look at the preservation, circulation, and accumulation of small vegetable and verse forms, generated at the intersecting rhythms of poetry and practice. Connecting Thomas Tusser's rhyming horticultural advice (first published in 1557) with the poetics and rhetoric of Shakespeare's sonnets, I show how a pedagogical investment in rhyming couplets shapes the sonnets, tying their rhetorical work of memory to a tradition that emerges from the literature of husbandry. The sonnets' "minutiae" signal this indebtedness, shaping the poems' famous engagement with the work of memory according to a piecemeal logic of practical cultivation. In Tusser's *Pointes*, the botanical poetics of small forms (including the first indented couplet printed in an English book) emerges in concert with Tusser's imagination of the field, the household, and the passage of time.

An epilogue concludes with an examination of plant books by two figures significant in the development of the so-called "New Science" in the seventeenth century: Hugh Plat's *Floraes Paradise* (1608) and Francis Bacon's *Sylva Sylvarum* (1627). Despite the protestations of both figures that their collections are rhetorically plain and formed without methodical order, the botanical poetics explored through these chapters haunts the small forms that Plat and Bacon both call "experiments." In calling their collections a paradise and a forest Plat and Bacon signal that their numbered experiments are available for reuse, reordering, and extraction. The looseness of these collections, like those in Chapter 3, promises to free up the reader, loosening the hold of the order of the book on their encounter with its contents. They also force us to confront, however, the environmental legacy of the versions of textual and horticultural use described in the previous chapters—and to question the fantasy of an infinitely generative nature they sometimes entail.

The exuberance, multiplicity, and fugitivity of vegetable life underscores the divergence, which I noted earlier in this introduction, of botanical poetics from other frameworks for understanding printed books, both the kind of things they are and the kind of work they do. In the account they offer of bibliographic reproduction, early modern associations between books and plants break from the more familiar model of textual paternity. Frequent metaphors of printing as parenthood bring with them norms of legitimacy and lineage that link printed offspring to the influence of its human parent; they also conscribe textual futures within the horizon of heterosexual (and often dynastic) legacy and inheritance.[97] However, the model of paternity can only ever weakly imagine a printed text's many possible paths of circulation and dispersal. The lexicon of vegetable propagation and transport charts a model of textual reproduction that, instead of lineage, emphasizes proliferation and distribution. Traveling as slips, grafts, and seeds, these fertile textual fragments could start anew and forget the stock or root that bred them. With its more exuberantly horizontal forms of replication, vegetable life suggests a more itinerant and dispersed model for reception.[98]

In his famous description in *Areopagitica* of books as "not entirely dead things," John Milton reveals the tension between these two models of reproduction or proliferation. Books are vessels, he writes, that "doe contain a potencie of life in them to be as active as that soule was whose progeny they are; nay they do preserve as in a violl the purest efficacie and extraction of that living intellect that bred them."[99] Milton suggests an image of publication as human parenthood and material inheritance, in which he casts the author as father to the book. But his language is shot through with suggestions of non-human capacities, like the preservative "violl," which seems to echo the distilled floral perfume figured by Shakespeare in Sonnets 5 and 6. Milton's next image, though, which draws on the myth of Cadmus, is ambivalently agricultural: "I know they are as lively, and as vigorously productive, as those fabulous Dragons teeth; and being sown up and down, may chance to spring up armed men." Cadmus had traditionally been associated with the origin of writing, credited with importing the alphabet from Phoenicia to Greece. According to Erasmus, the letterforms in this alphabet and the dragon's teeth were the same in number; planted and recombined, those teeth would sprout forth into fully armed, fully grown men who fought and destroyed each other—an allegory of language and discord. But Milton's image joltingly mixes metaphors. Though organized verbally and conceptually around a masculine conception of authorial parentage, it depends on plant propagation for its understanding of circulation and conservation. The dragon's teeth are scattered and sown in soil furrowed and prepared by Cadmus—an agricultural labor vividly rendered in Ovid's *Metamorphoses* and in Renaissance emblem books' illustrations of the myth (Figure 6). Giving a sense of orderly ubiquity, Milton's sowing "up and down" locates this repetitive labor along the lined furrows of the field—*versus* in Latin, like the lines of verse also sown with letters. In emblems, these plowlines unspool horizontally like lines of text, in distinct ridges and furrows across a landscape of open fields.

Though writing is produced and reproduced by the linear recombination of letterforms, human life could not, to Milton's knowledge, either be extracted in a vial or planted in the soil. Milton's mixture of metaphors in this moment joins two competing impulses: a desire, clinging to the model of parenthood, that the life preserved and propagated in the book be that of the author/father; and, on the other hand, a recognition of dispersive and proliferative patterns of textual survival that exceed human reproductive patterns and outlast human lifespans. For these powers of books, Milton needs plants.

Figure 6. Cadmus sows the dragon's teeth. Andrea Alciati et al., *Omnia Andreae Alciati v.c. emblemata: Cum commentariis* (Antwerp: Ex officina Christophori Plantini, 1577), 600 (detail). Courtesy of The Rare Book & Manuscript Library, University of Illinois at Urbana-Champaign. Emblems 853 AL17Oe 1577.

PART I

Bound Flowers, Loose Leaves

The Form and Force of *Plants in Print*

CHAPTER 1

_____

"What Kind of Thing I Am"

Plant Books in Space and Time

Like many Elizabethan books, *The Forrest of Fancy* begins by repeatedly offering itself to its readers. The quarto, published by Thomas Purfoote in 1579 and attributed only to "H.C.," promises "very prety Apothegmes, and pleasaunt histories, both in meeter and prose, Songes, Sonets, Epigrams and Epistles, of diverse matter and in diverse manner."[1] Even before a page of commendatory verse and a prose epistle, the collection directly hails its potential reader with two poems. The first, "The Booke speaketh to the Buyers," presents the *Forrest* to customers in the voice of the book, affirming:

> What kind of thing I am,
>   my shape doth shew the same:
> No Forrest, though my father pleasde,
>   to tearme me by that name.

These lines are a coy beginning and present an ambiguous offering: the title page's "Forrest" is an arbitrary label, serving the pleasure of the volume's "father" but missing the mark when it comes to the "shape" of the book. With this opening division between name and kind, the *Forrest* performs the magic of "fancy" to translate between two worlds: between the pleasure of imaginative naming and the thing truly described.

The poem that immediately follows continues to complicate the status of the book on offer. This second poem, "The Authour to the Reader," casts the poet in the role of husbandman, who "when meetest time shall serve, / doth plow his ground, and sow good seedes therein."[2] The extended analogy recalls a conventional association between poetry and plowing, inspired by the double sense of the Latin *versus*, which can refer to both a line of poetry and the turn of the plow.[3] In this case, the "Authour" builds not from the patterned form of the furrow but from the shared sense of timing that frames both labors. Poet and plowman carve their lines when "meetest time" serves, and then wait for harvest. The stanzas that follow describe the gathering and storage of grain with precision, as the harvest is scattered, divided in sheaves, threshed, heaped, and fanned. These latter steps, especially the work of storage and sorting, occur at a delay, "at the last," after "a while he suffers it to bide." Some of these labors, we eventually realize, await the participation of the reader. As the poet shifts from metaphorical forest to agricultural field and barn, the first poem's promise—of "what kind of thing I am"—is revealed as a work in progress.

The *Forrest* was published at the tail end of the period considered in this chapter, a span of just over a decade, from 1568 to 1583, in which printed collections called "forests," "gardens," "arbors," and "flowers" increased severalfold. Its title especially emphasizes the miscellaneity that characterizes all of these volumes: drawing on ancient meanings of *silva*, a "forest" signified to early modern readers the unformed promise of its diverse raw materials. The double movement suggested by H.C.'s opening poems plays out a dynamic that we encounter across multiple titles from this era: an attention to the material "shape" of the book—in the *Forrest*'s words, "what kind of thing I am"—and to the shared labors of author, stationer, and reader, a temporally extended literary process rendered in the language of husbandry.

This chapter surveys the archive of plant books from the long 1570s through a discussion of these two trends, which especially distinguish this period's horticultural titles: the spatial forms they give their contents, through metaphors of enclosure and through the graphic arrangement of the page; and the techniques by which authors and printers anticipate their works' reception and circulation, which increasingly figure as future events according to the patterns and protocols of horticulture and husbandry. These two trends shape gatherings across a range of genres of prose and poetry, including the poetic collections and practical handbooks that both saw a growing audience during these same years. Reading practical and poetic books in dialogue, the chapter asks how this paired dynamic shapes those printed anthologies that included sections of short poems, many of them issued under the titles of flowers or gardens. Crafted and compact, the architecture of their bookishness visible on the surface of the page, such volumes recall Palsgrave's 1540 description of "a very curiouse and artificiall compacted nosegay." They are further in dialogue, as we will see, with the compartmented styles of landscape architecture that characterized both gardens of the nobility and gardening guides for the middling sort in the same period—captured in the style of the "curious-knotted garden" (1.1.237) of *Love's Labour's Lost*. These collections call up long-standing links between poems and flowers, drawing on ancient and medieval traditions that link the pleasures of poetry to the sensual offerings of enclosed gardens. A more surprising turn appears in their prefatory materials: books with titles that emphasize comfort and recreation—the more floral, odoriferous, or pleasurable aspects of a garden or arbor—turn not to flowers in their preliminaries but to images of husbandry. In place of the ornamental pleasures of gardens, we find accounts of labor. In place of perfume, the plow.

Together, the two trends define a strain of early modern bookishness that emphasizes the material circumstances of both composition and reception. On title pages and in printed preliminaries, plant metaphors draw attention to the conditions of gathering and *mise-en-page* that give the book its determinate form. However, this variety of bookishness is not an aesthetic quality that resides autonomously in the object itself. Rather, the Elizabethan surge in plant books advances a conception of book form that incorporates the future events of reading and handling. These editions represent an inflection point in the longer history of plant books, a change that takes shape around the time of Henry Denham's publication of *The Arbor of Amitie* (1568), as these volumes articulate a new relationship with their readership and a new relationship to time. In this way, plant books of the long 1570s reinvent the floral rhetoric of copiousness so important to Erasmus, Taverner, and the humanist classrooms in which Elizabethan poets were educated. The mid-Elizabethan redeployment of this vegetable lexicon balances the event of publication on the edge of the question: Will people like it? What will become of the text in the hands of new readers? Indexed in an idiom of vegetable growth and dispersal, these common concerns yoke a volume's form and format to the imaginative field of its reception.

This double vision is exemplified by the conceit of Thomas Hill's *Gardeners Labyrinth* (1577), an instructional handbook published after Hill's death by the stationer Henry Bynneman. A labyrinth encompasses both a fixed, complex form—in Renaissance gardens, of paths or alleys wrought from herbs or hedges—and a narrative series of winding turns that is unfixed and unsettling. In Hill and Bynneman's title, it names both the form of the book and the path a reader takes through its pages and through the labors of gardening. A popular medieval and early modern understanding of the spelling *laborintus* saw its etymology composed of two words meaning "the labor within." That labor within might be a completed work, or opus; but it might also stand for the extended toil the labyrinth demands of its captive visitors. The word captures a combination of formal fixity and incompletion; both open and closed, a labyrinth is a determinate artifact and an ongoing labor.

The first part of this chapter explores what I suggest we think of as the built environment of the Elizabethan book: by placing gardening books alongside printed anthologies, it shows how the graphic architecture of these volumes supports an aesthetic of discrimination and division. The second half of the chapter tracks the language and practice of planting through some of these same examples, following mid-Elizabethan plant books as their syntax of bookishness moves into the future tense. By orienting the material forms of plant books toward a conjectural future, comparisons with husbandry reach beyond the evident materiality of the book to imagine the role of readers. While title and title page may seem to take a snapshot, fixing a portrait in two-dimensional form, metaphors of horticulture and husbandry tell a story: these frameworks unfold both the book and its author as processes, protagonists of a story either consummated or disappointed in the event of reception. This chapter therefore suggests we view these two tendencies dialectically—between, on the one hand, the book as an artifact and offering, as a formed and fabricated thing; and, on the other hand, the book as an unfolding process, the fruit of labor and contingency, one (its authors and publishers help us imagine) on a narrative arc that extends beyond its creation. It was, after all, from these two perspectives that Elizabethan readers encountered plant books: as formally fixed and ornamented objects, which might be owned, shared or admired; and as ongoing events that link the labors and experiences of writer, printer, reader, and others. These perspectives shape the composite gardens and books that occupy the first part of the chapter and the experimental verse anthologies that inhabit the second. It is the double view of this botanical poetics, as we will see, that empowers the makers of those collections to figure the printed poem as both object and event.

Border, Labyrinth, Knot: The Built Environment of the Elizabethan Book

The title page of *The Gardeners Labyrinth* (1577) employs a doubled visual logic: on its upper half, an ornamental border announces its status as a printed artifact; below, a woodcut displays the horticultural labors on which the book will offer instruction (Figure 7).[4] Printed after Hill's death by the stationer Henry Bynneman, the *Labyrinth* was arguably the most important general gardening book printed during Elizabeth's reign and, by the beginning of the seventeenth century, had gone through more than ten editions. Though attributed to "Dydymus Mountaine," the pseudonym was likely decipherable to Bynneman's customers: Hill had already been responsible for the first English printed book devoted to gardening, issued almost twenty years earlier and, at the time of his death in the mid-1570s, was a well-known writer and translator on topics related to natural knowledge, including physiognomy, meteorology, and dream interpretation.[5] When Bynneman printed the *Labyrinth* in 1577, he had already taken over the printing of Hill's earlier *Profitable Arte of Gardening*, so that, by the end of the decade, he was simultaneously selling two gardening books by Thomas Hill.

In the decade before the *Gardeners Labyrinth* was printed, English printers had begun widely using typeset, modular ornament like that which forms the upper half of the *Labyrinth*'s title page. Unlike the architectural woodcuts that also enclosed printed frontispieces, these so-called "printers' flowers" could be cast and copied, their pieces reordered and reused in new arrangements on title pages and on inner leaves. There, they composed a volume's visual infrastructure, marking the spacing and division of the book and its parts. In the late 1560s and through the 1570s, some of the printers responsible for botanical titles were also the most enthusiastic users of modular ornament. Following French and Italian models, Henry Denham may have been the first English printer to begin using typecast ornament in the mid-1560s, and he deployed it in different combinations in about one-third of his publications between 1566 and 1571.[6] Bynneman followed soon after. As we saw in the introduction, Denham in 1567 and 1568 published John Maplet's natural history *A Greene Forest*, Thomas Howell's poetic collection *The Arbor of Amitie*, and Edmund Tilney's marital dialogue *The Flower of Friendship*. All appeared in octavo with the same distinctive interlaced border. A customer who saw these titles for sale, or Henry Bynneman's editions of Plat's *Floures of Philosophie* (1572 and 1581) and Lodovico Guicciardini's *Garden of Pleasure* (1573), would recognize the volumes' visual and rhetorical affinity. In each case, the border recapitulates the rhetorical work that the title performs, gathering the page's cluster of letters and words into a coherent frame and offering the book as a legible and valuable object.

Bynneman's title page for *The Gardeners Labyrinth* echoes these distinctive ornamental borders but goes only half the way there: in the lower half of

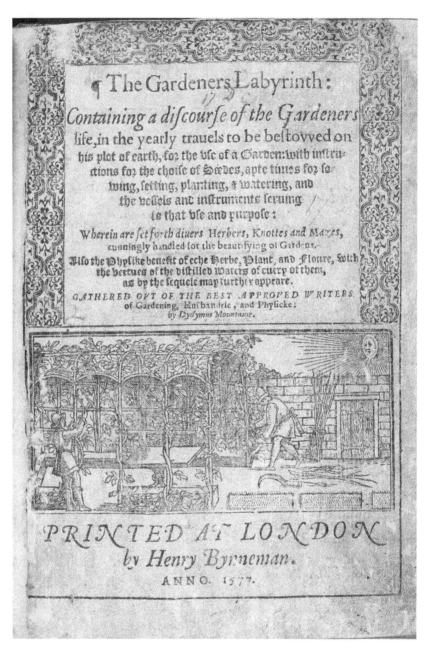

¶ The Gardeners Labyrinth:

Containing a discourse of the Gardeners
life, in the yearly trauels to be bestowed on
his plot of earth, for the vse of a Garden: with instructions for the choise of Seedes, apte times for sowing, setting, planting, & watering, and
the vessels and instruments seruing
to that vse and purpose:

Wherein are set forth diuers Herbers, Knottes and Mazes,
cunningly handled for the beautifying of Gardens.

Also the Physike benefit of eche Herbe, Plant, and Floure, with
the vertues of the distilled waters of euery of them,
as by the sequele may further appeare.

GATHERED OVT OF THE BEST APPROVED WRITERS
of Gardening, Husbandrie, and Physicke:
by Dydymus Mountaine.

PRINTED AT LONDON
by Henry Bynneman.
ANNO. 1577.

Figure 7. Thomas Hill, *The Gardeners Labyrinth* (London: Henry Bynneman, 1577), title page. By permission of the British Library. Shelfmark 453.a.3.

the page, the ornamental border opens to a woodcut into the garden, like a gate through which the reader enters its multidimensional world. This distinctive visual structure survived decades of new editions. It balances the formal self-consciousness of the full border—an ornament that by distinction and division marks off the book as a discrete and admirable object—against the ostensibly worldly reference invoked by the woodcut. The title performs this same doubleness: the book itself is a labyrinth, a piece of garden design that gardener-readers are meant to enter and whose turns they will be expected to follow. The two roles of this hyphenate figure—gardener and reader—are joined in the book's rhetoric of its own bookishness, bridging the garden inscribed on the landscape and the garden imprinted in the book.

The printers' flowers that frame titles and that mark off division within volumes are not, of course, *actually* flowers. The winding patterns that fill these inked ornaments, sometimes known as "vinets," fall under the category of ornament that historians of art and design call "arabesques"—elaborate winding designs that originated in Islamic art and design and first appeared in printed books in sixteenth-century Venice, before being developed and copied by French and then English printers. Though some were based on botanical forms, their intricate patterns are abstracted from worldly referents. In an important series of articles, Juliet Fleming argues against reading printers' flowers mimetically, suggesting instead that we resist the temptation to find allusions to a real world of flowers or foliage outside the text. These type ornaments, she argues, refuse the attempts of readers to make symbolic or referential sense of them. Instead, they draw the eye to the patterned surface of the page, where they seem to work *like* letters—filling up space and taking form—without being legible *as* letters.[7]

We should, I agree, resist taking the composed environments of either book or garden as natural forms. To extend Fleming's observation about type ornament, gardens impressed on paper and those imposed on the landscape serve analogous functions: to break off space, to engage the eye, to demonstrate the aesthetics of division and symmetry. Frances Dolan suggests that we view printed borders in light of the hedges used in the period to enclose and divide fields—boundary markers that become spaces of visual interest and human sustenance in themselves.[8] The following pages extend this observation back to the built environment of Elizabethan plant books. Literary and terrestrial gardens in this period work in a parallel fashion: fascinated with their own thresholds, they rely on and reinstantiate the prescriptive and regulative functions of inclusion, exclusion, and discrimination.[9] A closer look into the "window" of the *Labyrinth*'s woodcut reveals a world as formed as the title page itself: a garden composed of compartments and a built arbor, with suggestions of knots or perhaps even labyrinths beyond. The represented garden, like the *Labyrinth*'s printed border, shapes the reader in the experience of pattern, repetition, and division. This garden may, in fact, look something like a book.

The split design of the *Labyrinth*'s title page offers an insight into how Bynneman understood the volume's genre and its market of potential readers and buyers. Among his contemporaries and in the opinion of modern bibliographers, Bynneman holds a reputation as a judicious and elegant printer, qualities that supported his early career, and his publications generally bear carefully constructed title pages.[10] While the doubled arrangement of the *Labyrinth*'s title page is distinct, its core visual features of woodcut and border characterize other titles produced at his shop in the same period. Though Bynneman printed title pages with woodcuts on fewer than a dozen occasions, each surviving example outfits a book of practical advice and makes visible some aspect of its content—such as the diagrams on his editions of Leonard Digges's *A Geometrical Practise, Named Pantometria* (1571) and *An Arithmeticall Militare Treatise, Named Stratioticos* (1579), or the woodcuts of hunting scenes or navigation that correspond to the content of other texts' instruction.[11]

A much greater number of Bynneman's titles, however, feature the kind of ornamental borders that he and Denham began to use in the 1560s. Between 1568 and 1580, 46 percent of titles printed by Bynneman featured bordered title pages; of the publications for which Bynneman likely took financial responsibility in that period, more than 60 percent were printed with borders. Those borders appeared more commonly on titles that were, like Hill's, described as gatherings, translations, or both. Of translations published by Bynneman between 1568 and 1580, twenty-six of thirty-three were printed with bordered title pages. As a vernacular work of practical instruction that reflected learned practices of textual gathering and translation, Hill's *Labyrinth* linked these two threads of Bynneman's business—both of them represented in the *Labyrinth*'s pairing of woodcut and border.

By using title and title page to join the form of the book to the landscape form of the labyrinth, Bynneman merges book design with what he seems to have taken as one of the volume's selling points. He builds the architecture of the book from the same formal masonry as the architecture of the garden. Other enclosures, in text and image, appear throughout the pages of

Hill and Bynneman's *Labyrinth*. The first chapter opens by describing ancient gardens as "a smal & simple inclosure of ground," and the text turns soon after to methods of fencing by which the Romans enclosed their gardens, including brick, stones, willows, and, for the poor, mud, dung, and chaff. Hill observes in the following chapter that he prefers the quickset hedge of brambles and white thorn, which is the "most commendable inclosure for every Garden plot."[12] (The best kind of enclosure, Hill and others agree, is a living one that repairs itself.) Further on in the volume, knots and borders function as both instructional guides and as elements of bibliographic form. The *Labyrinth* includes more than a dozen images of knots and mazes, in addition to woodcuts illustrating the layout of beds in compartment gardens alongside walls, watering machines, and arbors.

Like the *Labyrinth*'s design, its woodcuts align the reader's way of seeing the book with ways of seeing the garden, positioning the gardener-reader both above and within its plots. Alongside designs for mazes and knots, a number of woodcuts bend geometry to show both the practical labors of gardening and the garden's diagrammatic form. For example, one image (Figure 8) shows geometrically plotted garden beds from a neutral vertical position, while the labors of two gardeners appear three-dimensionally, from a slightly elevated angle; above them, the depth of a planted arbor is perspectively rendered, beneath which four fallen grapes cast a shadow leftward, a reminder of the uses of the vine and the space of the arbor—and, with their long shadows, even the time of day.[13] Woodcuts like this join geometric plotting with naturalistic depth, going as far as to imply the kinds of narratives that might play out across the rectilinear plots of garden beds.

The *Labyrinth*'s images reflect what Katherine Acheson calls "mixed-coding orientation," a visual strategy that these garden diagrams share with other settings in which space was understood mathematically, especially works of military strategy. Such diagrams, Acheson observes, merge the neutrality of an aerial point of view with "icons figured according to a naturalistic or iconographic tradition."[14] This same double perspective governs the representational conventions of Bynneman's 1579 edition of Digges's *Stratiocos*, for example, which also relies on mixed coding to render the arrangement of human bodies and the built environment in space. The geometry of such plots invites the reader's eye into a position outside the space of the garden, set above a terrestrial plane of labor and uncertainty.[15]

This double vision structured English garden design in the sixteenth century outside the pages of the *Gardeners Labyrinth*. While an interest in the benefites of walkes and Alleyes in any Garden ground: whiche the Gardiner of his owne experience may aptly tread out by a line, and sift ouer with sand, if the owner will, for the causes afore vttered.

The forme of the disposing the quarters into beddes, and apt borders about, with the sowing, choise and defence of the seedes, and weeding of the beds. Chap. 13.

He quarters well turned in, and fatned with good dung a time before, and the earth raysed through the dunging, shall in handsome maner by a line set downe in the earth, be troden out into beddes and seemely borders, which beddes (as *Columella* witnesseth) raysed newly afore with dung, and finely raked ouer, with the cloddes dissolued, and

D. stones

Figure 8. Thomas Hill, *The Gardeners Labyrinth* (London: Henry Bynneman, 1577), sig. D1ʳ. By permission of the British Library. Shelfmark 453.a.3.

sightlines and theatrical spaces traveled northward from Italian Renaissance gardens, as John Dixon Hunt has shown, these same points-of-view shaped the era's intricately formed landscape designs, especially the knot. Garden historians have generally considered knots the distinctive innovation of Tudor garden design, as a form that reached from luxurious gardens like those at Nonsuch and Theobalds to the worlds of the middling sort, as Hill's collection suggests.[16] While mazes and labyrinths more specifically suggested formally winding paths, a "knot" could name any orderly partition and usually suggested an artificial and interlaced design—one standardly described as being "made" or "cut." As built and planted forms, mazes and knots encourage particular spatial relationships and reward certain sensory experiences of the garden: they are best viewed from above, from a prospect, mount, gallery, or walk, a perspective encouraged by the popularity of galleries and mounts during the heady years of Tudor knot-making.[17] Each of these related forms, however, pairs a view from above with only a partial view from the ground, just as a labyrinth reveals a completed form to those in a position to see it, while refusing that view to those trapped in its paths and turns.[18] Its infuriating power to defer and digress has made the labyrinth an emblem of narrative form itself; for Petrarch, and for those writing poetry under his influence, it stood for the vexations of poet and lover.[19]

As a way in and a view from above, the *Labyrinth*'s title page bridges these two positions: a bordered title page presents the book as a closed, rectilinear space, the unity of which is broken by the fractured pages of a multiply folded, composite object. As I mentioned at the outset of this chapter, a popular etymology of "labyrinth" understood it to derive from *labor intus*, and, echoing this association, early modern orthography often renders the word with an *o* following the *b*.[20] This spelling brings to the lexical surface two kinds of work: the "labor within" of the gardeners depicted on the woodcut, whose manual toil represents the *Labyrinth*'s instructional content; and the "labors within" of garden and book *as works*, made and crafted things, like the woodcut's compartmented beds or the printed border. As a deponent verb meaning "to slip" or "to err," *labor* could also suggest the potential peril of what happens within the maze—a hint of risk and contingency to which we will return. The title's metaphorical "labyrinth" reaffirms this doubleness: the formed enclosure of both book and garden, their status as wrought objects; and their status as narrative forms, sequences of turns shaped of time and contingency.

While knots and mazes hold an important place in the division and em-plotment of Tudor books and gardens, their place in the greater scheme of Hill's instructional project is more ambiguous. Garden historian Jill Francis notes that chapters on knots in gardening books detail less labor than other sections do, as they emphasize instead the pleasure they provide visitors and the liberty they afford the gardener.[21] Authors and publishers in turn under-stood illustrated knots as special features of the book as a commodity.[22] In the first issue of the *Labyrinth* in 1577, Bynneman devotes a full, unsigned quire to woodcuts of knots and mazes, some of them apparently newly cut and others reused from earlier titles.

As part of an instruction in horticulture, mazes represent a culmination of the reader's discretion—glossed by Hill in 1563 as "no necessarye commod-ity in a garden, but as an ornament upon pleasure."[23] As the saying went, "The knot garden for pleasure, the pot garden for profit." When woodcuts of mazes first appear in Hill's gardening books of the 1560s, they are introduced almost as an aside: "Here by the waye (gentle Reader) I doe place two proper Mazes."[24] In the same way that a knot or maze supplements the garden, these printed mazes are "by the waye" as a visual supplement to the progress of the text, a gentle digression from the preceding instruction. Descriptions of knots coincided with authors' most extreme deferrals to readers' whims in other gardening books as well—for example, in the *Country House-wives Garden*, where Gervase Markham writes that there are as many knots as "as there are devices in Gardners braines."[25] The knot's position as ornament and supple-ment admits a space for the variety of human preferences—a fact of psychol-ogy provisioned for by its "extra space" in the garden and the book.[26] This extra space, in other words, makes space for the reader.

One exceptionally elaborate knot first appears in the 1568 and 1572 editions of *The Profitable Arte of Gardeninge*. Larger than the *Arte*'s octavo pages, the image is folded into the volume according to instructions printed alongside it (Figure 9). In fact, two sets of instructions accompany the cut: one, an imperative to the assembler or user of the book as to where to put the knot ("Place this knot Folio.188"); and a gentler suggestion to the gar-dener that the knot be planted "where as is spare roume enough, the which may bee set eyther with Tyme, or Isope, at the discretion of the Gardener." One side of the knot tells its place in the book; the other, more open-endedly, imagines its place in the "spare roume" of the garden.

There is no obvious thematic reason that the knot should be placed at fo-lio 188, where it follows Hill's secrets of sowing and planting and precedes a

Figure 9. Thomas Hill, *The Profitable Arte of Gardeninge, Nowe the Thirde Time Sette Forth* (London: Thomas Marsh, 1572). RB 30052, The Huntington Library, San Marino, California.

collection of precepts on gathering and preserving herbs, flowers, seeds, and roots. Instead, the interstice itself provides the occasion to *place this knot*: the inserted image divides the two books, serving the printed book's structure rather than the content of its instruction.[27] The same image again functions as a supplemental mark of division in Bynneman's quarto editions of the *Gardeners Labyrinth*, where it joins the larger collection of knots and mazes that divides the *Labyrinth*'s first and second parts. There, by holding space within the book, the knot provides ornament and infrastructure.

Scholars of garden history have observed that this knot may not be instructional at all: it is not clear how these elaborately interlaced threads would be rendered with thyme or hyssop. More likely, the image has been imported from an embroidery book.[28] What is it doing, then, as part of a series of instructions on how to form garden knots? Francis suggests that the elaborate knot—to which the main body of the text never refers—was "simply added by the printer to separate the two parts and therefore had little relevance to the text."[29] That is, the knot is not a piece of practical gardening instruction, but a mark of bibliographic differentiation, mediating between one division and the next.[30] Bynneman's knot in this sense echoes John Harington's instruction to his printer, Richard Field, that an "Allegorie" in his translation of *Orlando Furioso* be introduced "with some pretty knotte."[31] The *Labyrinth's* advice to its reader also applies to Bynneman's reuse of the woodcut: it should be cast "as there is sufficient roome."

As this invitation suggests, the ornamental status of knots within the book and within the garden aligns them with the reader-gardener's discretion and desire: they supplement the garden, as they do the codex, by filling out and beautifying space. They can thus come to seem emblems of artifice for artifice's sake, form unhooked from function. When George Cavendish praised the famous garden at Hampton Court under Cardinal Wolsey, he found its knots both admirable and difficult to describe: "The Knotts so enknotted, it cannot be exprest."[32] The circularity of Cavendish's phrasing echoes the artifactual force that Fleming identifies in printers' ornament: refusing the desire of a reader or viewer to see through to a worldly reference, it leads the eye instead across an intricately differentiated surface. In this articulation, enknottedness is per se a positive aesthetic value, just not a describable one. It does, however, offer a useful vocabulary of formal organization: "knit," "knotted," and their cognates mark the craft and density by which forms are gathered. As these examples suggest, knots were transmedia forms in early modern material culture: as a fashionable piece of Tudor garden design, as a building block of sewing and embroidery work, as a term of art for any well-formed thing.[33] Gardens, books, and embroidery all knit together matter in a compact space, bundling and binding into a closed form.[34]

Sometimes, well-knittedness describes a distinctly poetic quality: *Palladis Tamia* (1598), citing Seneca, offers praise for "the well knitte and succinct combination of a Poem."[35] C. Thimelthorpe, introducing his *Short Inventory of Certayne Idle Inventions* (1581), ascribes well-knittedness to the printed gatherings of poetry available to Elizabethan consumers, which are "cunningly devysed, and severallye knyt up togeather," enabling readers to "for a penny have in your pocket choyse of many prety toyes at al times to delight you." Thimelthorpe merges the force of poetic and bibliographic "knitting," by which copious but still pocket-sized collections owe their delightfulness to artful composition, their curious quality of mixture.[36] As we have seen, the act of knitting could also specifically refer to book forms—a nosegay or fascicle, in Thomas Elyot's definition, is something *knit together*. While gardens and books were certainly associated with bound enclosures, they were enjoyed as much for their modular and iterative forms: their knots, subsections, tales, poems, parterres, groves.[37] Both kinds of garden promise a simultaneous experience of extension and of intense abundance.

We can now see one mechanism by which "curious knotting" translates into the form of a codex. In printed books, floral ornament does more than block off a book's title page: its pieces, often impressed from the same metal type, reappear throughout the volume, dividing its contents. Like the borders and compartments of a formal garden, they give visual substance to the composite structure of a book, supporting patterns of modular and iterative composition as much as an aesthetic of enclosure. In doing so, they intensify the invitation to non-linear reading always present in the codex form, and in turn serve the labors of discrimination in which early modern readers were regularly asked to engage.[38] For example, the same pieces of cast type that border the title page of Humphrey Gifford's *A Posie of Gilloflowers* (Figure 10) return to mark divisions between sections: at the end of a new dedicatory epistle introducing the volume's verse, and again after prefaces to longer poems later in the volume, once again mediating between verse and prose, and between text and paratext. As a mark of continuity and differentiation, the repetition of ornament gives concrete form to the *Posie*'s subtitle: "eche differing from other in colour and odour, yet all sweete." The same material substrate that blocks off the space of the book also breaks down the book's contents, carrying readers from prose to verse and back again.

Sometimes ornaments repeat to form entirely new enclosures. In the case of Gifford's *Gilloflowers*, the title page's enclosing ornament reappears fully assembled at signature H4ʳ, where it introduces a new section of poems, and so more decisively marks a shift from one part of the volume to another. The *Gilloflowers* is not alone in marking this formal division. Mid-Elizabethan plant books include divisional title pages with unusual frequency, many sporting a full ornamental border that they follow with a new dedication or preface. These marks of interior architecture are signs that many books are gathered in one and (even if continuously printed, as they usually are) that

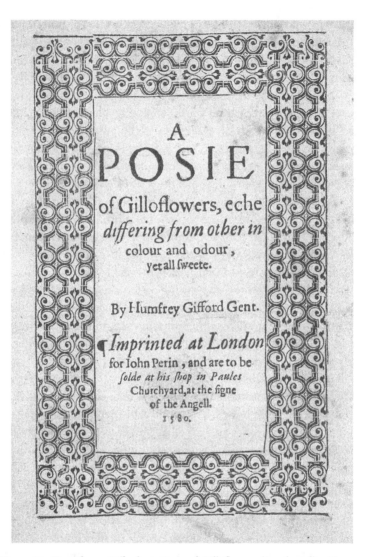

Figure 10. Humphrey Gifford, *A Posie of Gilloflowers* (London: [by Thomas Dawson] for John Perrin, 1580), title page. By permission of the British Library. Shelfmark 239.g.33.

they might be broken apart. As such, these volumes form a kind of virtual *Sammelband*, a bound composite that makes visible readerly habits of editing and compilation.[39] Like that preceding the collection of verse attached to Gifford's *Gilloflowers*, many of these divisional title pages announce a gathering of the author's short verse. There, they present those miniature gatherings as supplements to the volume's other elements, like longer narratives or prose epistles, often translations by the author of the original verse that follows. A partial list of these mini-anthologies includes the "Pleasures of Poetry" appended to Hugh Plat's *The Floures of Philosophie* (1572); "the Garden of Unthriftinesse" included in George Whetstone's *Rocke of Regard* (1576); John Grange's "Garden" (1577); and Timothy Kendall's "Trifles," attached to his *Flowers of Epigrammes* (1577). George Gascoigne's *Posies* (1575), in revising his *Hundreth Sundrie Flowres* (1573), introduces bordered divisional pages between three sections of flowers, herbs, and weeds.[40]

We might think of these miniature gatherings as supplemental, or prosthetic, anthologies. In each case, a vegetable lexicon energizes the aesthetics of division and supplementation that joins a poetic gathering to the body of the book: a handful or bouquet is a portable (and replaceable) prosthesis, the garden a necessary ornament to the house. The vocabulary of supplementation—by which additional parts are "joined," "added," or "annexed"—encompasses the material craft of both the printing house and the scholar's study.[41] In the codex as in the home and garden, craftspeople join a range of functions across divided spaces.

Like walls and borders, bibliographic divisions generate visible frames for distinct kinds and stages of literary activity. In pairing gardens or bouquets of poems with more useful examples, printers and authors use the structure of the book to join pleasure and profit, offering that Horatian pairing to a reader and displaying the author's mastery of both modes of composition. George Whetstone's *Rocke of Regard*, for example, elaborates the logic of spatial division by ordering its sections according to a progressive narrative. Each region of the book renders a stage in an allegorical progress. By sequestering most of the collection's short verse into a single section ("the Garden of Unthriftinesse"), Whetstone frames it not just as a space within the book but as a period in the life of a young gentleman—a period, the structure of the printed volume makes clear, with boundaries.[42] In a dedicatory sonnet to Christopher Hatton, Edmund Spenser describes *The Faerie Queene* as "ydle rymes" to which he should "lend litle space," an image of poetic sequestration and superfluity that suggests these same practices of aesthetic division and readerly discrimination.[43] Richard Helgerson argues that titles referring to gardens or bowers block off the activity of poetic production from the more profitable dimensions of an aspiring young man's career, corralling verse in a walled—and thus finite—sphere.[44] These miniature anthologies, each one a "litle space," deploy the elements of landscape architecture to metaphorically fortify their defense of poetry.

By simultaneously joining and separating pleasure and profit, these divisions rely on the psychological benefits of variety to strengthen their defense of poetry's utility. By 1580, plant books and other gatherings advertise their composite form on the basis of salubrious variety as much as on the pleasures of intricate artistry. While fewer anthologies of secular verse were published as the decade progressed, models of formal division and aesthetic variety continued to shape a subset printed books, especially those that drew on the language of plants. As Louise Wilson has shown, the category of "recreation" had begun by the 1580s to shape readers' experience of literature according to an idea of "leisure time" sequestered from other parts of the day.[45] The virtual *Sammelbände* that I have discussed on the previous pages, their divisions marked out by recurring title pages, preserve an affiliation between recreative time and horticultural space. For a reader, the composite volume offers myriad paths for comfort and for recreating the mind. The same compositional rhetoric plays out in the decade's devotional books, especially the small-format prayer books that began to take up a greater part of Henry Denham's business in the 1580s—such as Abraham Fleming's *The Diamond of Devotion* (1581); William Hunnis's *Seven Sobs of a Sorrowfull Soule for Sinne* (1583), including *A Handfull of Honisuckles*; and Anne Wheathill's *A Handfull of Holesome (Though Homelie) Hearbs* (1584).[46] Printed in duodecimo, with borders throughout that echo the ornamentation of manuscript devotionals, these books render in even more compact form the copiousness of floral collections.[47]

Denham printed William Hunnis's *Seven Sobs of a Sorrowfull Soule for Sinne* in 1583 with a series of internal title pages: following the titular *Seven Sobs*, a translation of the Psalms of David, there is *A Handfull of Honisuckles*, promising "Certaine short and pithy Praiers," some printed with music; *The Poore Widowes Mite*; and *Comfortable Dialogues Between Christ and a Sinner.*[48] Though continuously printed, each section of *Seven Sobs* has its own title page, with an ornamental border and the full publication information and date. The volume's briefer forms (those classed as "honisuckles" and the "poore widowes mite") are gathered into their own sub-books, an organization that allies the collection with the verse anthologies popular in the previous decade. This link to printed lyric is not a great departure for Hunnis, a musician who was master of the Children of the Chapel, and who had poems included in (and may have been involved in an edition of) *The Paradise of Dainty Devices* (1576).[49]

Small forms are even more intricately gathered in Fleming's collection of prayers and precepts, *The Diamond of Devotion* (1581).[50] Fleming was a prolific compiler, indexer, and translator whose literary career was wrought at the conjunction of the printing house and poetic composition.[51] Like Fleming's editorial work, which incorporated complex systems of numbering and reference, the *Diamond* makes canny use of the resources of the printshop to structure the book's contents, including a series of running headers, enumerated lists, and bordered divisional title pages, some of which mimic the organizational systems of learned treatises.[52]

Denham and Fleming clearly saw this minutely articulated variety as a selling point. Those six divisional titles are listed on the title page alongside page numbers, an extension of the *Diamond*'s conceit, as "Cut and squared into six severall points." The *Diamond* joins the practical architectures of the book to a series of figurative conceits, rendering its visual strategies of enumeration and division according to the fractal-like metaphorics of plant life. One section breaks its contents into a series of "branches," each composed of a set of numbered "blossoms," each containing a series of numbered points. In the style of learned treatises, *A Plant of Pleasure, Bearing Fourteen Severall Flowres* and *The Swarme of Bees* count their progress in the running title, so that readers, looking to the top of the page, see both which flower or honeycomb they have reached and what page number. A plant, like the guide, like a swarm, like a honeycomb, is made up of pieces—a structure that Fleming and Denham reiterate throughout the book's architecture. All of this piecemeal variety, however, is captured within an aesthetic whole, gathered in the repeating bordered patterns that enclose every page.

These microdivisions of the book are governed by the rhythmic reappearance of new title pages, which regularly return the reader to a new beginning and a new gathering of small forms in prose or verse. Fleming and Hunnis both gather short forms of verse or song into their own divisions—like Hunnis's *Handfull of Honisuckles* or Fleming's *Plant of Pleasure*, which advertises its "fourteene severall flowres" as comfort and recreation, to satisfy the "naturall inclination of man, for the delighting and solacing of himself." In framing this section by a logic of recreative variety, Fleming imports topoi from the previous decade's gatherings of secular verse and prose; the variety of this small section, he writes, defers to the various tastes of readers. It is, he writes, "put partlie in rythme, and partlie in prose, for the satisfaction of sundrie Readers desires, some beeing addicted to this, and some delighted in that kind of writing."[53] Though he expresses passing moral ambivalence about the practice of recreation, Fleming closely echoes the arguments for variety in the *Forrest of Fancy* (discussed below) or Gascoigne's *Hundreth Sundrie Flowres* (discussed in chapter 3). In each of these cases, the book's figurative and graphic architecture seems to fix it as a determinate object, all while freeing up readers to pursue their own ends and their own pleasures.

The sense of order that these title pages provide is not binding—and sections like these might be literally disbound, like a copy of *Granges Garden* that survives at the Folger Shakespeare Library without the prose narrative alongside which it was printed.[54] In fact, like *Sammelbände*, divisional title pages do as much to undermine the order of the book as to enforce it. They suggest that ordered divisions were once unbound and might be rebound, that the book itself is one contingent compilation among many possible. A peculiarity in the structure of Gifford's *Gillofowers* reminds us of this contingency: Gifford almost certainly intended its two title pages to appear in the opposite order. The general epistle to the whole volume describes the examples immediately following as "christened . . . by the name of *A Comfortable Recreation*," while the dedication following the division introduces the poems that follow as "a posie of *Gillowflowers*, collected out of the gardens of mine owne inventions." Only the pages of verse that follow include the running head "Giffordes Gilloflowers." While this switch may represent either an error or an editorial decision, it is a reminder that repeating forms are also slippery ones, readily susceptible to substitution and recombination.[55]

Husbandry, Printing, and the Future Estate of All Things

While the titles of many Elizabethan plant books advertise a space of comfort and recreation, a reader might encounter (with just a turn of the page) the grittier, sweatier realm of husbandry. The remainder of this chapter considers plant books' representations of agricultural practice, especially as they shape the temporal outlook of several important poetic anthologies. I will delve, first, into the work outlook of Thomas Hill and then turn my attention to Thomas Howell's *Arbor of Amitie* (1568) and H.C.'s *Forrest of Fancy* (1579).

The allusions to husbandry that accompany these printed volumes make some sense: conventionally, preliminary epistles and poems enrich the book by reference to the labor of the author or compiler. They also conscript the reader into an extended process of cultivating meaning, asking them to water or tend the text, or to sort or process its harvest. This rhetorical turn toward the labors of cultivation alters the temporality of the book. As we saw in the previous section, the lexicon of gardens, bowers, and paradises can serve to prop up the book as an achieved and closed artifact—a space edged out by walls, hedges, gates, knots, and other closed or enclosing forms. The rhetorical turn to husbandry, on the other hand, frames both book and author as works in progress, products of labors still ongoing. With this turn away from static vegetable ornament, time takes on a more powerful role, subjecting book, reader, and author to the variables of harvest, seasonality, and deferral.

When they appear in the prefaces to printed books, metaphors of husbandry embed printed collections in environments of alteration and change. These projective roles converge in preliminary materials, as printed books look forward to their reception and consumption in the idioms of plant life. The language of husbandry offers an especially richly imagined example of the microstructures (like promising) that J. K. Barret has shown scaffolded early modern literature's encounters with future time.[56] Agriculture brings with it additional temporal infrastructures: the seasonal and yearly rhythms of harvest, the repetitions of household practice, the longer lifetimes of orchard, pasture, and estate. Whether oriented optimistically toward harvest or unhappily toward dearth, an agricultural lexicon places the printed book in a position of anticipation: balanced between sowing and reaping, between the event of publication and the adventure of reception.

Like publishers, farmers and gardeners were experts in anticipation, well practiced in deferring to a fertile medium to power dispersal and growth. English humanists took a special interest in husbandry, valuing its training in habits of order and the practical arts of good government.[57] Inspired by classical models of Xenophon's *Oeconomicus*, Virgil's *Georgics*, and the agricultural writing of Columella and Varro, scholars in sixteenth-century England brought out new translations of these texts as well as continental works on husbandry and household by Heresbach and Tasso. The language of husbandry in turn infused humanist pedagogical theory and classroom practice. When he prescribes the reading of Virgil's *Georgics* to schoolboys, Thomas Elyot praises the poem's literary variety and gives particular attention to husbandry's knowledge when it comes to "the future astate of all thynges": "What ploughe manne knoweth so moch of housebandry, as there is expressed? . . . Is there any astronomer, that more exactly setteth out the ordre and course of the celestiall bodyes: or that more truly doth devine in his prognostications of the tymes of the yere, in their qualities, with the future astate of all thynges provided by husebandry, than Virgile doth recite in that warke?"[58]

For humanist teachers and scholars, this uncertainty provided valuable occasions for exercising prudential judgment.[59] For gardeners and husbandmen, however learned or unlearned, action in face of uncertainty was a daily vocation. An attention to the "future astate" of things frames Thomas Hill's gardening advice: the *Labyrinth* guides aspiring gardeners through the turns of their yearly labors, offering tips and tests meant to lay a foundation for future success, beginning with how to choose a plot and test (and even taste) the soil to best choose a ground. According to Hill, gardening is an art that must confront "the uncertaintie of the time to come."[60] Offering methods for managing risk but never fully containing it, the point of the *Labyrinth* is twofold: to learn the technique of risk management in the garden, along with the rhythms and habits of living with uncertainty. Like the other writers and poets considered in this section, Hill saw publication and circulation as energetic encounters with risk—consequences of an orientation to the future, not necessarily for the sake of posterity but in hope of making it from one season to the next, from sowing to reaping, from writing to reception.

"The uncertaintie of the time to come" was a theme throughout the wide range of topics on which Hill published.[61] Like gardening, physiognomy, palmistry, dream interpretation, medicine, and meteorology are expressions of practical wisdom that turn on arts of interpretation. Predictive and conjectural, they require judgment and prudence, and Hill accordingly teaches his readers to interpret signs of character, health, constitution, and clues to future events. This orientation is especially evident in Hill's interest in the weather, reflected in his almanacs and handbooks on gardening, like the "husbandly conjectures" first appended to the third edition of his earlier handbook (*The Proffitable Arte of Gardening* [1568]), and in works like his *A Contemplation of Mysteries* (1574). The *Contemplation* classes events like earthquakes and comets as "the fore note of hunger, and dearth," while the "husbandly conjectures" reflect critical worries about harvest failure and offer tools for interpreting signs of coming dearth or plenty. Like Hill's side hustle in almanacs, these prognostications prepare readers to engage with the natural environment's limited predictability.[62] God, Hill wrote, sends messages, tokens, and wonders "to forewarne us, if we were not dulheades, we might perceyve the same."[63]

Contemporaries recognized futurology as a special dimension of Hill's expertise, but not all saw it as an asset. A prefatory poem praising his treatise on physiognomy singles out his ability to teach readers to

> learne to shunne those ylles to come,
> which may turne thee to paine.
> And also thou thy luchie fate
> mayst learne so too foresee:
> That by preferring of the same,
> good haps may rise to thee.[64]

By imitating Hill's skill to "foresee," readers might make their own luck, shunning ills and welcoming "good haps." However, unlike the general practice of prudence, the more specific arts of prognostication threatened to exceed the lawful purview of mortal knowledge. They also failed to have the sure basis of a true science, as William Fulke argued in his pamphlet *Antiprognosticon* (1560), which specifically targeted Hill and others for their "vayne and unprofitable predictions."[65] In his treatise on dream interpretation, Hill defended his teaching against charges of unlawful divination by allying it with other permissible and useful arts of foresight. The foresight of dream interpreters is no different, he argues, from the judgment exercised by physicians, husbandmen, and soldiers, all of whom frame their actions according to judgment of future events: "If it be superstitious (gentle Reader) and therefore denied of some men, to have a foresyghte and judgmente in things to come, whye is not then denyed to learned Phisitions, skilfull warriours, weary husbandemen, and polytycke Captains, to have knowledge in the Artes of divination? . . . Al Artes of forknowledge hath beene of longtime had in great price and estimation. In tymes past the noble warriours, the grave Senatours, the myghty Princes, & almost every privat man, did direct al their doings, and wayghty affaires, by conjectures and divinations."[66] The addition of husbandmen's conjectures recalls Hill's own publications on gardening instruction. Echoing Xenophon, it also links the specialized crafts of dream interpretation and husbandry to the honorable offices held by captains, warriors, and princes; all are united in the exercise of foresight and served by practiced judgment of "thinges to come."[67]

Hill exercises another dimension of this judgment in his management of his career in print. Several of Hill's publications feature lists of future titles, including those composed and awaiting a printer and those he has not yet finished writing. He suggests, for example, that readers eager to see certain unpublished manuscripts may seek out the author directly at the shop of stationer Christopher Barker. As such notes suggest, Hill was actively involved in the craft and business of print, maintaining relationships with multiple stationers and speculatively laying the groundwork for future endeavors. Hill understood making a living as a professional writer and translator as a project: one built of the kind of speculative energies that fueled growing portions of the labors of stationers in this period.[68]

When he addresses readers about their reception of his books, however, Hill's attention shifts to his own impotence. In a conclusion printed nearly verbatim both in his *Proffitable Arte of Gardening* (1568) and *Contemplation of Mankinde* (1571), Hill expresses far less confidence in this role than in his activities as gardener or physiognomist.[69] Instead, Hill depicts publication as a risk undertaken on untested ground, an event not only vulnerable to accident but forged by it: "for wel I wote, that no treatise can alwayes be so workemanly handled, but that somewhat sometymes may fall out amisse, contrarie to the minde of the wryter, and contrary to the expectation of the reader."[70] As workmanly as his contribution may be, it might still "fall out amisse"—a circumstance Hill hesitates to figure with any specificity, admitting only that it may "somewhat sometymes" fall out.

At the limit of his "workemanly" handling, Hill sees no method to assure a courteous reception, throwing himself optimistically on the courtesy of the reader. This strain in Hill's depiction of publication runs counter to the policy of prudential virtue that otherwise governs his advice. In his conclusion, Hill elaborates an analogy between print publication and military combat—another of the canonical sciences of the future he had named in defense of dream interpretation. His first example tells the story of Falarus Thebanus, a captain about to go into battle with his army despite being "marveylously (at that instaunt) vexed with a sore disease of the Lunges." In battle, he is cured after launching a courageous attack, "and beeing then stroken on the breast with a speare, his griefe ceassed, and was for ever after healed of the same." Next, Hill relates the case of a Tuscan king with a stubborn piece of iron in his neck, also marvelously cured while undertaking a prototypically masculine, noble activity: out hunting, he is thrown from his horse, and "the fall was so boystrous, that the little piece of yron flewe out of his mouth, and so was healed." In a synthesis of military and medical action, each figure cures himself in the act of endangering himself.

When it appears in the *Labyrinth*, "boisterous" is an unambiguously negative word. However, in Hill's concluding epistles, the quality that is a force of destruction in the garden is a panacea in the hunt or on the field. Both examples depart from the care and skill prescribed in the chapters of Hill's books. Unlike those future-oriented methods, these happy outcomes could have been neither predicted nor planned for. Instead, Hill conveys the surprise with which both men were "contrary to their expectation healed of their griefes." Despite Hill's humble self-accounting, print publication emerges as a bold masculine activity like hunting, soldiering, and adventuring. But it does so in the *absence* of expectation, without any "husbandly conjecture."[71] Here, humanist protocols of management and prudent conjecture run aground on the courtly demands of grace, surprise, and authorial submission.[72]

Instead, Hill bases the interaction of author and reader on trust. The reader's acceptance, he writes, will encourage him "to truste more unto thy curtesie." We might hear echoed in these lines a sentiment that Hill paraphrases from the Roman agricultural writer Columella, in a discussion of planting: "Have no mistrust in the committing of seedes to the earth."[73] Or, we might analogize, in the committing of books to the public. Formulations like this join the practices of printing and planting at the limits of mastery. In the seventeenth century, as Peter Harrison has shown, God's grant of dominion to Adam in Genesis would authorize large-scale agricultural projects of land reclamation and colonization, worldly enactments of the imperative to "subdue the earth."[74] Against this reclaimed dominion, Hill sounds a different note. The farmer who scatters seeds, like the writer who scatters copies, releases them, and waits: they both commit their seeds to the earth.

By linking agricultural practice to textual circulation, Hill represents a kind of prequel to the agricultural-textual strategies that Wendy Wall describes as "Renaissance national husbandry." As Wall shows in the case of Gervase Markham, who published prolifically on husbandry from the 1590s through the first decades of the seventeenth century, Markham's many books on farming and housekeeping imagined a national community of readers bound by the soil and its cultivation. In cultivating a national identity, Markham's project linked the work of husbandry to the printed book and its field of reception.[75] A generation earlier, in the texts under consideration here, both the text itself and its imagined community are more provisional: a hybrid of foreign and native slips, dispersed into the hands of a readership that remains fictive and uncertain. It is in this hesitant turn toward that future that mid-Elizabethan poets and printers call upon husbandry and the latent capacities of vegetables for dispersal and growth.

Hill's examples reflect a trend evident in other mid-Elizabethan printed books: a depiction of the event of publication as a kind of adventure, a risk of reputation and well-being undertaken with bravery and perhaps foolishness. We can see these dynamics play out in a trio of books by the poet George Turberville, published respectively by Denham and Bynneman in 1567.[76] Comprising two translations and one gathering of original verse, these titles represent the young poet's first ventures in print, and they express acute concern about how those poetic experiments will be received. Here, the language of husbandry figures a practice of patience and deferral. In a prefatory poem to his *Epitaphes, Epigrams, Songs and Sonets* aimed at "the rayling Route of Sycophants," Turberville draws a military model for the boldness of poetic publication, aligning the poet with the fearlessness of those who charge with "dreadlesse hart and unappalled brest."[77] Turberville's combative poet is a cousin to Hill's captain, but the poet makes more contentiously explicit that the enemy—the occasion for the author's courage—is a putative bad reader. In a similar spirit, Turberville's translation of Ovid's *Heroides* (1567) concludes with a poem addressed from the translator to "the captious sort of Sycophants." Taking a less combative approach, it begins with an analogy to the plowman:

> The Ploughman hopes in recompence of toyle,
> And winters travaile past, to reape the graine
> That he (goodman) hath sowen on his soyle,
> Wyth great encrease of crop and goodly gaine:
> And reason good why so he should in deede,
> For he thereon long earst bestowde his seede.[78]

The next lines suggest an analogy with the fisherman, whose labor is also a practice of patience; in laying his hooks, he "doth trust at length by happie hap" to catch a store of fish "and bring him in the mucke / That ventred life in hope of happie lucke." Rather than the labors themselves, it is each figure's patience in face of uncertainty that forges his continuity with the poet. In both examples, Turberville brings out the delay between investment and recompense; the plowman "long earst" bestowed his seed, the fisherman trusts "at length" that a fish will find his hook. Here, Turberville builds on proverbial and biblical associations of the labor of plowing with the virtue of hope, as in the famous phrase from 1 Corinthians 9:10, that "he which ploweth may plowe in hope."[79] The plowman is also a figure of hope in George Wither's emblem book, introduced with the couplet, "The *Husbandman*, doth sow the Seeds; / And, then, on *Hope*, till *Harvest*, feeds."[80]

However, in the unhappy complaints of the *Heroycall Epistles*, as in Turberville's original verse in *Epitaphes, Epigrams, Songs and Sonets*, the plowman has little reason for hope: as Helen says to Paris, "Why should I fondely seeke / to plough the barraine sand?"[81] Images like these of lost labor run through poetic anthologies published during Elizabeth's reign, as poets who plow in hope in their poems' prefatory materials worry acutely—though in the same agricultural idiom—that their erotic efforts will prove unprofitable. In this, Turberville and other poets of the 1560s and 1570s echo *Songes and Sonettes* (1557), the anthology published by Richard Tottel a decade earlier and a model for poetic collections of the following decades. As Catherine Bates argues, love poems in *Songes and Sonettes* frequently render the traditional position of erotic complaint in economic terms, as an investment that leaves a lover "nothing but diminishing returns."[82] The poems' recurrent language of husbandry frames the fruitless labors of the lover, as well as his stubborn hope in face of rejection or indifference.[83] The poems' accounting, Bates argues, extends the economic framework introduced by Tottel's preface, which advertises the liberation of its poetic contents from "the ungentle horders up" of that treasure.

Economic and agricultural frameworks likewise extend from the preliminaries to the poetic contents of collections published in the wake of *Songes and Sonettes*, like Turberville's similarly titled collection, and like the *Arbor of Amitie* (1568) and *Forrest of Fancy* (1579), both discussed further below. In these Elizabethan examples, the language of husbandry shapes both the verse itself and the volumes' paratextual depiction of their economic and literary enterprise. However, the epistles and prefaces of these Elizabethan collections are full of the energy of anticipation: instead of unlocking treasure in the present, the books' reflexive economy turns toward the uncertain possibility of future harvest. The erotic logic of expectation in turn is tangled in the social and material anticipations of publication, as both poet and lover wait to see if their spent labor will pay off.

Turberville's third poetic publication of 1567, a translation of Mantuan's eclogues issued by Denham in an octavo with a now-familiar interlaced border, gives us some insight into the kind of loss against which plowman, fisherman, and poet press their optimism.[84] In the eighth eclogue, a shepherd rehearses a prayer for the safety of farm and harvest against the many mishaps that plague rural life. "O Virgin," he appeals,

> save from thunders rore
> the Drinke we lately brewde.
> Kepe wel the blossomd Ewes from cold,
> the Calves from stinging Flie.

The full prayer catalogs dozens of quotidian enemies to survival before asking, in more general terms, "That Ploughmens labour be not lost / O Goddesse do thy best."[85] Though appealing on the part of the plowman's labor, the shepherd resists at this moment performing labor himself. Instead of proactively interpreting the weather, as Hill's handbooks explain, Mantuan and Turberville's shepherds take a distinctly lyrical approach, in apostrophe to a goddess who may or may not be indifferent to their supplication.

Catherine Nicholson has shown how poetic eclogues, particularly those written in vernacular in the middle decades of Elizabeth's reign, gave poets a ground on which to work through the strange nature of poetic labor, with its close resemblance to idleness.[86] Though pastoral poetry is not my focus here, the examples I consider in these paragraphs reflect the work of some of the same poets, publishers, and poetic forms. It is especially suggestive, then, that these references to husbandry in printed poetry emphasize not the exertions of plowing but the excruciations of waiting. In the case of Turberville, for example, the poet's investment in print is wrought not of the sweat of his brow but by the passive virtue of his patience. In these mid-Elizabethan examples, the deferred temporality of print publication reframes poetic labor. Time, in other words, does its own kind of work—the *ergon* of printed poetry unfolds beyond the reach of its author, on a timescale unconcerned with human effort.

The remainder of this chapter tracks the anticipatory mood of husbandry across two other printed poetic collections, Thomas Howell's *Arbor of Amitie* (1568) and H.C.'s *Forrest of Fancy* (1579). In these examples, the rhetoric of husbandry extends beyond preliminary materials to shape the poems within, where it informs both love poetry and versified advice.[87] Agricultural anticipation fuels the way in which both collections fashion themselves as composite printed volumes and structures the erotic and didactic energies of the poems they contain. In preliminaries as in poems, a discourse of thrift posits that you put work in now to get profit out later. This process, however, is marked by different degrees of contingency across different spheres of investment—erotic, friendly, mercantile, and poetic.

In Howell's *Arbor of Amitie*, expectations of profit fall (or fail) under the rhyming assurance of the axiom "No pain, no gain." Neither pain nor gain, however, turns out to be evenly distributed across all labors or laborers. Published by Henry Denham in 1568, the *Arbor* was one of the first assays in what would prove to be a vogue for similar titles in the next dozen years.[88] It survives in an octavo volume comprising one part of a *Sammelband* from the collection of John Selden now at the Bodleian Library, bound with other titles that share some similar qualities: many of them gatherings of verse or short fictions, including two printed by the prolific miscellaneous compiler Richard Jones, as well as *The Flower of Friendshippe*, in an edition published by Denham in 1571.[89] At the time of the *Arbor*'s publication, Howell was in the household of George Talbot, 6th Earl of Shrewsbury, and dedicated the collection to the earl's daughter-in-law, Lady Anne Talbot.[90] The Talbots' name appears scattered throughout the collection and some dimensions of Howell's anticipated reception fit the model of a patronage relationship. Nonetheless, a current of anticipation and loss runs through the *Arbor*, reaching from its preliminaries to the poems themselves. This topos, like the future orientation that sustains it, tangles the themes of the verse in the material circumstances of the book's publication and reception.

Like the double vision of Hill's woodcut, the *Arbor*'s interest in the cultivation of plants joins the space of the titular *Arbor* to the horticultural processes undertaken there; it represents both a locus of retreat and an environment of vegetal growth.[91] Its preliminary materials include verse and prose epistles by Howell in praise of Lady Talbot, and another poem, by Howell's friend John Keper, addressed "To the curteous and gentle Reader."[92] Keper's poem shifts the volume's speculative energies away from the scene of patronage and toward a more anonymous scene of reception. There, he anticipates the work of reading along two parallel paths: one, which emphasizes reception as a process, projects responsibility for the text's cultivation onto the reader; the other takes the poet as the subject in process, a locus of youthful potentiality and deserving repository of the reader's patience and care. Keper's poem introduces the poet and his poems through a humble comparison to a grafted branch:

The tender graffe that growes in grove,
   that tooke the stocke but late:
From slender spraies his leaves he shootes
   but small and young of rate.
Which length of time will strengthen strong,
   his yerely fruites to beare:
Whose braunch then buddes in stronger stem,
   least frowarde wight it teare.

Thus it is with Howell, whose fruits are still in their infancy:

So Howelles hart and hardie hande,
   hath plight his pen to set
And graft this braunch, the fruites whereof,
   are young and tender yet.
             (sig. A.v^r)

The analogy is slightly uneven (Howell seems at first the newly set graft, but is ultimately the orchardist, the pen his grafting knife, *this* branch the *Arbor*, and the fruits the poems it bears), but the technicalities are less significant to Keper than the chronology they imply: that which shoots leaves but small and young of rate may yet bud. Whether fruit, poems, or young men, it all gets better. Keper's developmental interest in Howell offers an example of what will be an important theme in the following pages: while analogies to gardening and husbandry regularly figure circulation as a deferred process, this deferral can also extend to the author. We will see again in Chapter 3 how, in poetic collections, the extended temporalities of agricultural practice slip between these two strains—the delayed development of the author and the deferred satisfactions of reception.

It is according to this structure of deferral that the *Arbor* packages its potential appeal. Following the image of the graft, Keper's poem reorients its energies toward the present volume, initiating a cluster of temporal deictics: Howell's branch *now* begins to spring and *now* begins to bring profit. Keper infuses the *now* of the text with the novelty of first fruits: the present text, these *now*s reinforce, is just that—an artifact of the present that begins to spring but that will be superseded by mature future production. The *Arbor* advances a developmental narrative. Like the youthful poetry of Horace and Virgil (respectively, their "trifling toyes" and "sielie gnat," Keper writes), the triviality of Howell's juvenile *toys* suits the poet's station in life.[93] It also promises greater things:

> But length of lyfe, shall Howell holde,
>   on stronger stem to stay:
> By cunning skill of setled braunch,
>   to beare the bell away.
>   (sig. A.v^{r-v})

Keper's poem initially undercuts Howell's collection, advertising its inadequacy while promising something better down the road. Offering a botanical variation on the *humilitas* convention, by which a poet presents his work in a scene of self-abnegation, the poem culminates in a coded request for patronage and investment on the part of the reader.

Despite its deference to convention, we should take seriously Keper's marketing of the *Arbor*'s incompletion, juvenility, and smallness: these are selling points. In framing the collection according to the latent capacity of the tender graft, Keper primes the reader to experience the work according to an assurance of future yield. Keper promises long lines—"length of time will strengthen strong"; "length of lyfe, shall Howell holde, / on stronger stem to stay"—in an image of longevity and posterity that anticipates Shakespeare's fantasy of poetic survival in Sonnet 15, as we will see in Chapter 5. If poet and book thrive in a narrative of investment, risk, and eventual profit, the "slender sprays" represented by the *Arbor* place reader and text on this arc at a moment of maximum contingency. More solid things are yet to come, but the uncertain present offers its own satisfactions.

By the second half of Keper's commendatory poem, something else has changed. To this point, the burdens of transformation and growth have fallen on Howell the poet. At the twenty-ninth line, just past the poem's midpoint, Keper transfers the burden of future fruit to the reader: "Then cease ye not, to helpe the grounde, / where this good graffe doth growe." This moment acts as a volta, as Keper pivots to a prescriptive conclusion from the previous lines' descriptive scene of tender growth. What waters this ground? Praise. Shifting to the imperative, Keper abandons the metaphor of stock and scion, and instead focuses straight in on the earth. Good readers do more than decline to tear branches from his tree. They actively contribute to its growth: "learned wits will further forth, / and laude his lore that's rare."[94] A narrative of authorial growth has become a labor of readerly love.

With a tremendous pun on Howell's name, Keper then places the hope of the plowman in the hands of the reader: "Then hope I *well* my *Ho* to plie, / some greater woorke to see." As he signs off, Keper asks the readers to "*maintaine* this braunch now shute" (my italics) such that "Then will he spring in time full trim, / to yeelde you larger fruite" (sig. A.vᵛ). Unlike the strengthening lines from earlier in the poem, this branch will not fruit on its own. Instead, Keper resolves the essential agricultural uncertainty of yield by redistributing the burden of risk onto the reader: *if* you help the ground, *if* you maintain this branch, it will spring and yield larger fruit. Reading becomes a practice of reputational maintenance, performed on an author's behalf. Introduced as a "tender graffe," Howell (with Keper's help) does more than apologize for immaturity and promise greater things; he also qualifies himself socially as someone capable and worthy of cultivation.[95]

Keper's poem introduces two themes that recur across Elizabethan plant books: an author figure who emerges as developmentally incomplete, paired with a deference to the responsibility of the reader. Keper's poem imports the model of plant life first to make a promise—that the poet is a creature in process, still maturing—and then to make a demand—that maturation depends on the reader's response. Both gestures rely on the duration of horticultural process. The framework of husbandry renders the plant book a work in progress, whose appeal as a pleasing object in the present depends on the fiction of its future development—and the reader's assistance in that developmental course. Consider, for example, C. Thimelthorpe's *Short Inventory of Certayne Idle Inventions: The Fruites of a Close and Secret Garden of Great Ease, and Litle Pleasure* (1581), which links the contingent form of the published book directly to the scene of the printshop. At the end of the volume, nine stanzas are attributed to the voice of the compositor, addressed in turn to author and reader. By imbuing the matter of the book with the aura of its material composition, the compositor's verse asks the reader to engage the *Inventory* as a fabrication rather than as an abstract text. Lines addressed to the author figure the poet as sower of seeds and readers as reapers ("Thou sowed hast the seede for us to reape, / We of thy toyle the sugred sweete do taste"). Here, the compositor identifies as another reader, while the agricultural image renders Thimelthorpe's labors the seeds and the sweetness of them, once germinated, the readers' profit. As the compositor's voice turns toward the reader, however, it becomes clear that even with those seeds sprouted, the author's youth demands special cultivation, or "mending," from the reader.[96] Like the two parts of Keper's poem, the compositor's framing interest in the making of the book ultimately occupies itself with the making and remaking of the author. The craft of verse remains an open process, its performance a valuable dimension of published poetry.

In the *Arbor*, the future fruit that Keper promises does not hold up across the collection's other investment schemes. Like other Elizabethan anthologies influenced by *Songes and Sonettes*, the *Arbor* is largely composed of two kinds of verse: love poetry, usually from the position of a dejected lover, and monitory poems offering advice to friends, many of them phrased in direct imperatives. The language of husbandry, harvest, and profit shapes the operation of foresight across both kinds of poem.[97] The results, however, are split. Poems in the collection that are addressed to friends promise happier husbandmen than those addressed to potential lovers. While Howell's poems frequently frame erotic investment as an unsuccessful agricultural effort, poetic advice to friends makes more confident promises about future yield.

Howell's advice poems generate the temporal structure of investment by the proverbial coupling of "pain" and "gain." In "To one that faine would speede, yet doubtfull to proceede," the rhyme of "pain" with "gain" is repeated three times. The poem's advice is assembled from proverbial analogies that turn on investment: the cat (who wants a fish, but hates getting his feet wet), the hardworking ant (who works through the summer to survive the winter), and the bee (whose sweet profit "comes not by lying still"). The merchant and the plowman provide examples of figures who labor in search of gain:

> The Marchant eke men know,
> Great goods by travaile gaines:
> The Plowman seede doth sow,
> To reape rewarde for paines.
> (fol. 19ᵛ)

Howell imports both the scene and vocabulary of practical husbandry. Future store relies on hard-won beginnings—a proverbial truth assured by the consonance of pain and gain.

> For travaile is the way,
> Eche noble gift to gaine:
> Use therein no delay,
> And spare thou not for paine.
> (fol. 19ᵛ)

Through its proverbial structure, the poem operates by generating and reapplying an axiom of practical knowledge.

The pairing at the center of the profit logic also shaped the promissory structure of the period's how-to books: an investment of labor or substance now assures profit down the road, an economic analogue to the expectancy and eventual sonic satisfaction of the rhyme. The title page of William Lawson's *A New Orchard and Garden* (first edition, 1618) carries the motto "Skill and paines brings fruitfull gaines," vertically arranged, alongside a woodcut showing orchardists plying the tools of their trade. I have argued elsewhere that, in printed instructional books, the proverbial coupling of pain and gain follows the deferral of textual reception: from the author's pain in writing and experience to the reader's gain in fruitful harvests.[98] Thomas Tusser's first point for January, following the winter holiday, advises his readers to return to their labors with the reassuring echo of this same rhyme: "Be myndefull of rearing, in hope of a gaine, / dame profit shal geve thee rewarde for thy payne." In Tusser's verse, Dame Profit gives allegorical form to husbandry's central law of painful investment and gainful return, while the echo of the rhyme rewards the ear of a reader willing to wait "in hope."[99] The 1573 edition of Tusser's *Five Hundreth Points of Good Husbandry* includes the rhyme more than a dozen times.

Pain and gain are unyoked, however, in Howell's love poetry. (And it may be, by the measure of his verse, that Dame Profit is the only woman worth counting on.) Across the various registers of anticipation that appear in the *Arbor*, love represents the cruelest economy. Howell's poems consistently describe erotic desire as lost labor, figuring women as unreliable soil for investment. In the voice of a spurned lover, Howell returns to the language of cultivation that characterizes the preliminaries, comparing himself to the "crooked clowne" who plows diligently in hope that "paines and restlesse woes" will be rewarded.

> The crooked clowne that drawth the plowe
>   with all his yerely toyle:
> Receives at last rewarde of worke,
>   bestowed on fertile soyle.
>   (fol. 9^r)

As we saw for Turberville, the skill of waiting sometimes seems as significant as the labor of sowing. The plowman, with his "yerely toyle," belongs to the cyclical timescale of husbandry; when he receives "at last" his reward, it is at the conclusion of the agricultural calendar, part of a seasonal cycle of repetition. In the lines that follow, Howell draws a comparison with the poet-lover who, though he also toils cyclically, never reaches a rewarding "at last." Reduced to a social station below that of the humble plowman, who at least *receives* some reward for his labor, the poet worries that he will instead be "prest in simpler sort," a verb that, as Wendy Wall has shown, suggests both the experience of being imprinted and a passive sexual position.[100] Here, Howell enfolds the roles of plowman, poet-in-print, and lover, unified in their subjection to fortune and unhappy reception.

In another poem, the unrequited lover is like the breeding bird who builds a nest only for others to "take the gaines and fruites of them," and like the humble plowman: "The crooked clowne so earth the toyling fielde, / But oft the crop, remaines to other men" (fol. 3ʳ). The poet is not optimistic about his chance of profiting from this attachment:

> Well time may come, wherein my fruitlesse part,
> So ill bestowde: some others may bewaile
> And wish they had, receivde my yeelding hart,
> Whose loving roote, tooke grounde to small availe.
>   (fol. 3ᵛ)

The poet's hoped-for end is—quite literally—reception: that his heart should be "receivde" by the fruitful soil of a loving recipient. But, in contrast with the tender graft that described the poet in the preliminaries, Howell's "fruit-lesse part" and "loving roote" promise little joy. Breaking from the promissory structure of Keper's preliminary poem, these poems unhook the investment of labor from the enjoyment of profit: the crop, the poet complains, falls "to other men."

The imaginary erotic triangle on which the poem is premised reiterates a topos from *Songes and Sonettes* ("The lover lamenteth other to have the frutes of his service") and from Turberville's *Epitaphes* ("He sorrowes other to have the fruites of his service"), which also ascribe the general danger of lost labor to the more specific threat of an interloping third party. They further echo a more distinctly agricultural worry from Virgil's first eclogue: the shepherd Meliboeus, having been driven from his lands, asks, "Shall wicked soldiers have and hold these fallow fields so trimd? / And strangers reape this crop of mine."[101] In these variations on Meliboeus's complaint, the political dispossession of land is rewritten as erotic rejection, with competing lovers in the role of undeserving strangers (in Latin, *barbarus*) who reap the crop they did not sow. Like any love triangle, this configuration draws a homosocial link between the poet and his competition; as agricultural analogy, the triangles imagined by Howell, Turberville, and others further reframe the female beloved as territory of which the poet has been dispossessed. But here the poet's sense of native entitlement issues not from the circumstances of his birth but from the sense that someone might take it away. We should not forget, though, that the lost labors of sowing and trimming (the lover's fruitless service) include the writing of poetry. From this angle, the agricultural model of poetic publication casts the reader of the printed copy as the third point in this triangle: the overhearer of lyric, the latecomer to a field already cultivated by the labor of another. With the poet dispossessed of his labor, it is the reader who—belatedly—harvests fields of his verse in his absence.

Howell suggests a glimmer of optimism in another poem about erotic economy, "Desirous to requite for manie giftes, one to his deare beloved." Here, in the context of romantic gift exchange, the poet once again frames the experience of the lover in a vegetable lexicon of gain and reward. He is less doleful, though, as he takes on an extended metaphor about briars and grapes. For the moment, however, he confesses he has little to offer:

> For I to writhing thornes am lyke,
>   in course of present trade.
> Therefore receyve this simple signe,
>   my springs yet dried are:
> But yet of thorns account this one,
>   which nowe my briars are.
> My budding tree cannot as now,
>   some other fruits disclose
>   (fol. 9ᵛ)

Howell's vegetable analogy extends the volume's economic framework ("in course of present trade," "account this one") and more robustly interweaves writing and vegetable growth: in the echo of "writing" in "writhing thornes"; in the invitation to "receyve this simple signe"; in the budding tree, which reminds us we are meeting just one citizen of Howell's bound *Arbor*.

The analogy between writing and vegetable growth, however, turns on fruitlessness. The poem further elaborates the interweaving of horticulture and publication in its image of what it is *not yet* able to offer: "My budding tree cannot *as now*, / some other fruits *disclose*." Twisting Keper's promise of future fruit into an image of present withholding, the thorny poet offers a single rose, since "I a Briar now perceyve, / that I a Briar am": "So I with charges presse thee still, / but no rewarde I sende." The poem's transactional lexicon of pressing and receiving echoes the experience of the "crooked clowne" in the poem discussed above, though it suggests the possibility of a more active role for the poet. The conclusion assumes a provisional image of future growth:

> But if in time from thornes I may,
> of Vine tree take the shapes,
> Thou shalt in steede of Briars sharpe,
> receyve my springing Grapes.
> (fols. 9ᵛ–10ʳ)

Howell's "springing Grapes" convey the erotics of reception in an innuendo that is not terribly subtle. Nonetheless, he makes this prediction within an intricate set of conditions. The phrase is a conditional (*if* he takes this shape), with an ambiguous temporal modifier: *in time*. With reference to this indefinite length of time, Howell's erotic deferral renegotiates Keper's confident promise about Howell's future production: there, in time, the slender spray promised greater fruit. Here, Howell opposes present briars to future grapes. The contrast has changed from a distinction among life stages to a difference in kind. However, the relationship between present disappointment and future satisfaction (*in time*) draws on a transformation more radical than the gradual development of the tender graft: *can* a briar spring a grape? Howell folds a range of biblical references into these lines, each of which embeds the image in a different horizon of expectations: the curse of Genesis 3:18 ("Thorns also and thistles shall it bring foorth to thee"); the patient prophecy of Isaiah 55:13 ("For thornes, there shall grow firre trees: for nettles shal grow the myrrhe tree"); and, less optimistically, the paradox of Matthew 7:16 ("Ye shall knowe them by their fruites. Doe men gather grapes of thornes? or figs of thistles?"). More pragmatically, Howell also calls up a range of contemporary debates about the power of cultivation: just how much can human art alter the course of nature?[102] How much is Howell's identity—as poet, lover, or young man attached to the Talbot household—limited by the logic of kind, or by the circumstances of his birth?

This uncertainty extends to the volume's promises to its readers. If we trust the poem's second-person assurance that *we*, as readers, will in time receive the springing grape, then this poem recapitulates the promissory structure of the prefatory verse. But this last allusion may give the poem's addressee less cause for optimism than Keper's opening poem suggests as to the poet's potential for transformation. If we doubt whether this briar of a poet might ever bear fruit, or whether we can know poet or lover by his present fruit, the scenarios of the poems might warn us against trusting its earlier promises. Though the collection as a whole asserts Howell's capacity for social and poetic cultivation, his identity as a lover follows a path of improvement that is far less linear.

This chapter's final example returns to H.C.'s *Forrest of Fancy*, the collection of poems introduced at the outset to ask "what kind of thing I am." While *The Arbor of Amitie* addresses its reader by soliciting maintenance and cultivation, the *Forrest* takes a more epistemologically dramatic approach to its potential diversity of readership. As we saw at the beginning of this chapter, H.C.'s *Forrest* begins with a prosopopoeic poem that disavows and then reclaims the title of "Forrest." The poem confesses the title was an imprecise inheritance from the volume's father, but then reclaims that moniker in a final pitch to a potential customer:

> To thee my friend, before thou passe,
>   this present plot of grounde.
> Put hand in purse for pence,
>   to purchase me withall:
> What foole a Forrest would forsake,
>   that sees the price so small.
>   (sig. A.ii^v)

At the site of commercial transaction, the book takes full ownership of its name: the fancy that renders it a forest affirms its value, and so still holds sway on "this present plot of grounde" where books are bought and sold. The voice of the book, in crediting the value of this fantasy, subscribes to a certain economic realism.

From this "present plot," the subsequent agricultural metaphor walks away. In an extended metaphor that links husbandry to the writing and circulation of poetry, the subsequent prefatory poem, from the author to the reader, expounds on the theme of seasonal patience, as each stanza describes a stage in the harvesting of grain. The analogy remains very much tangled in the temporal anticipation of consumption and reception that has been a theme throughout the latter part of this chapter. Once again, this labor of anticipation is projected in the idiom of agriculture: the husbandman "doth plow his ground, and sow good seedes . . . reapes it up . . . to his Barnes he beares it ready bound" (sig. A.ii^v).

Through the first two stanzas of the poem, H.C. weaves an account of his book through a shared lexicon of printing and planting, invoking words also associated with the writing and making of books: plowing, sowing/sewing, scattering, dividing in sheaves, binding. With an earnestness that echoes the previous poem's conclusion, he then takes ownership of the conceit:

My selfe I count to be the Husbandman,
For in this booke, as in a ground most fit,
To sow the seedes of my unwildy wit,
I scattered have my fancies in such wise.
And senst them so, as I can best devise.
        (sigs. A.ii^v–A.iii^r)

H.C.'s presentation of his own labor emphasizes scattering before binding: he has "scattered" his fancies, and "senst" them as best he can, but he implies a limit to his power of devising. Instead, scattering fancies and seeds across the space of the book, he presents the poetic collection as a broad field for dispersed reading. Repeated twice, "scattering" provides the key link between husbandman and the author. However, H.C. leaves a crucial labor of poetic making incomplete: "Desiring thee that thou wilt take the payne, / All thinges amisse to put in perfect frame" (sig. A.iii^r). Like Thomas Hill, he recognizes the possibility the text should "fall out amisse." Here, however, the final piece of pain is not the author's but the reader's. And he leaves "framing," a core activity in early modern poetic making, to the reader, as the *Forrest* rises from the threshing floor as a thing unmade.[103]

Even with this deferral of responsibility, the venture into print remains a presumptuous leap of faith. The final stanza of the poem from the author to the reader turns from its dominant agricultural framework to newly imagine the perils of publication. It isn't vanity or a desire for praise, but "sloth to shon" that is "the cause why I presumed have, / To thrust my selfe amidst the surging wave." This surging wave embodies the mass of printed material it joins upon publication, one that invites the masculine "thrust" of venturing into print.[104] The maritime image aligns print publication with military and mercantile hazard, giving some dramatic heft to the daunting crowd of printed books and aspiring poets.[105] With the turn of a page, a reader sees this phrase echoed in a commendatory poem by R.W., who relocates H.C.'s surge to the Hellespont, in the story of Hero and Leander:

> What led *Leander* to presume,
>   so oft to swim through surging seas:
> But hope to fynd his *Hero* there,
>   where he ariv'd his hart to ease.
>   (sig. A.iii^v)

Repurposing words from the end of the preceding poem, these lines recast the author-husbandman as romantic hero, braving the seas of public scrutiny and poetic competition to land his book in the right hands. The surging wave gives elemental form to something essential about publication—the possibility of absorption, disappearance, and submission to the smothering immensity of the sea.[106] The adventure of publication, the allusion suggests, is a kind of crossing. And its danger is existential: however hopefully they thrust, Leander and the poet risk being absorbed and subsumed into this formless mass. Despite their diverse styles and genres, husbandry, authorship, and romantic adventuring all share this hopeful venture into the unknown, risking loss of self and substance to a greater and uncertain force.

As in Howell's collection, motifs of hazard and adventure shape the poems throughout the volume, as both moral advice and erotic aspiration turn on logics of investment. The *Forrest*, however, places itself in a landscape defined by variety and alteration. It is on these terms that, in the face of an uncertain field for the book's reception, H.C. assembles a kind of insurance policy. Like much traditional agricultural risk management, the *Forrest* relies on a practice of diversification.[107] Facing what Hill calls "the uncertaintie of thinges to come," H.C. acknowledges readerly diversity: the volume, he promises, assembles a variety of matter to suit a variety of readers. Instead of making conjectures or predictions, he offers broadly demographic knowledge about people in general: "So variable are the minds of men (gentle Reader) and so diverse their opinions, that amongste twenty, it is hard to fynd twaine that agree all in one thing. For commonly that which one man lyketh, another loatheth, that which one man praiseth, another reproveth" (sig. A.iv^r). With this consideration of the diversity of taste, H.C. offers a natural, cognitive, and even appetitive argument for the disorder of the *Forrest*'s organization.[108] Even his consideration of human diversity is organized around hazard: the epistle draws distinctions between the young man and the ancient sire, the courageous captain and the scholar, according to how they engage with "perrill." By his own logic, the poet joins the ranks of the risk-taking young man rather than the more sober "aunciente Syre."

H.C.'s belief in the human appetite for variety dictates the form of the book, in which are "gathered togither in one small volume diverse devises, as well in prose as meeter, of sundry sortes, and severall matter, which at idle times (as wel to sharpen my wits, and shake of sloth, as to satisfye my friendes, that had occasion to crave my helpe in that behalfe) I have heretofore as occasion served, diversly framed, supposing the same to be fitte for this present time, and agreable with the mindes of moste men" (sig. A.iv^r). Alongside his repetition of "diverse," in several forms, H.C. layers a series of "occasions": his friends' occasions to seek his help, his own occasions to diversely frame, and—as we will see as the volume progresses—the reader's occasional encounters with poems in the disorder of the forest. Michael Hetherington has shown how, in the case of George Gascoigne, the contingent force of accident helped shaped the diverse form of the printed collection.[109] Both "accident" and "occasion," as Hetherington notes, derive from the Latin verb meaning "to fall"—it is into this world of uncertainty and accident that Thomas Hill worries his books might "fall out amisse." The "things amisse" that H.C. asks his readers to frame are likewise those accidents still strewn—"dispersedly"—in the *Forrest*. Framed as a hermeneutic encounter with contingent particulars, the *Forrest* recapitulates habits that humanist educators hoped the literature of husbandry might inculcate in students, and which we saw witnessed across various facets of Thomas Hill's career. I suggested in the introduction that sixteenth-century plant books are defined by two competing forces: that of binding and enclosure, on the one hand, and scattering and dispersal, on the other. The *Forrest* rewrites this tension in narrative form. In describing his collection according to "the disordered placing of every perticuler parcel thereof, being rudely and dispersedly devided," H.C. maps botanical and bibliographical dispersal onto a landscape of accident and contingency. The job of the *Forrest*, in this sense, is to bundle and redistribute occasion, so that the reader too might have an occasion to be surprised.

The Forrest of Fancy models this happenstance encounter with pleasure in several places throughout the volume, two of which I will describe here before concluding. The first is a poem that narrates a surprising experience of discovering and eating a hazelnut in the forest. Aligning the poem's setting with the conceit of the collection, "Certaine Verses written in commendation of the Nut cornell" presents a model of reading that turns on chance and occasion.[110] With its description of the poet's indirect path through the woods, the poem's narrative mimics a reader's happenstance itinerary through the admittedly disordered collection. Walking abroad, the poet "by chaunce" enters a great wood, where he encounters a thicket of disordered variety, including oaks, asps, elm, birch, and box trees:

> By chaunce I lighted then,
>   Upon a huge great wood,
> whereas in rankes right goodly trees,
>   of sundry sortes there stoode.
>   (sig. D.iii^r)

There, the poet echoes a commonplace language of variety as he praises flowers in "sundry sent and hue," and, echoing the epistle to the reader, notes that "every thing that hart could wish, / a man might find it there." From this store, the poet makes a choice and happily plucks from a filbert tree:

> Then from this Philbert tree I pluct,
>   A cluster that were clong,
> Togither fast in seemely sort,
>   as on the tree they hung,
> And when I had them in my hand,
>   not knowing how to use them,
> I was at last by reason taught,
>   betwixt my teeth to bruse them,
> which having done I found therein,
>   A Cornell fayre enclosde,
> which for to be of pleasaunt tast,
>   I also then supposde.
>   (sig. D.iii^v)

The remaining lines praise the nut's taste and medicinal virtues before concluding that "of all fruict the best, / the Philbert *cornel is*." H.C.'s image of the kernel—along with the poet's brusque technique of bruising the husk to reach its interior—recalls a conventional image for allegorical reading—and, indeed, invites an allegorical reading of the poem's account of discovery and pleasure. The poem's message, however, is far more particular, as the poet's bruising of the nut results not in a revelation of concealed truth but of personal taste: "the philbert in my minde, / Doth seeme most pleasaunt in the tast." A reader, of course, has had an experience much like the poet's: we have encountered this "nut cornell" of a poem in the middle of a forest (or, *Forrest*), the disorder of which is literalized by H.C.'s and Purfoote's printed codex. The concrete form of the book—as a miscellaneous gathering—structures a contingent reading experience, freeing up readers to discover the pleasures of the forest, according to the particularity of their own taste.

Later in the collection, another poem—"Certain verses in written commendation of the Rose"—reiterates the poet's account of his own taste. Like H.C.'s praise of the "nut cornell," his praise of the rose amplifies the epistle's arguments about human variety. Here, the language of sundriness serves an argument for even greater aesthetic contingency:

> As sundry sortes of men in world there be,
> So sundry mindes in them also remayne,
> And in one point they sieldome do agree,
> That one thinkes good, another thinketh vayne,
> That one desyres, another doth disdayne,
> And I that doe in Flowers great pleasure take,
> Desyre the Rose, my nosegay sweete to make.
> (sig. H.i^v)

The final couplet returns in each of the following stanzas, as H.C. proceeds through a sort of estates satire, naming the various aspirations of cowards, astronomers, prisoners, husbandmen, and others. (The answers, respectively: to live in peace, to see the stars, their freedom, and full barns.) Despite the strength of his praise of both the rose and the "nut cornell," H.C. does not try to universalize these claims for their value or beauty; instead, his "I" and its desire and pleasure remain firmly planted in both articulations of praise. Both build instead on some combination of chance and choice, and thus hold out space for what is arbitrary and contingent in the generation of pleasure.

In setting the woods as a scene of alteration and contingency, then, H.C. preserves a space for a certain amount of freedom—or, room for will or fancy to operate. As the epistle had argued, the mind works like the stomach and becomes cloyed without the pleasure of variation. There, this fact of psychology underwrites a powerful argument for variety: "no man be he never so well stayed, that will adict himselfe to one thing onely, and refuse all other" (sig. A.iv^v). The language of addiction in this formulation suggests that variety frees up mind and stomach from a kind of indenture to sameness, giving them freedom to wander or reorient.[111]

The necessity of variety recalls the interstitial knots of Thomas Hill's gardening books, which likewise break their addiction to the order of the book in making room for the diversity of readers' taste—since there are, as Gervase Markham wrote, as many knots "as there are divices in Gardners braines." In both cases, the deferral to readers' desire is realized in the order of the book: in those moments of punctuation where the progress of the codex pauses, where a text block opens or closes to ornament, or offers a reader free passage between the parcels of the forest or the page. Printers and poets collaborated on this visual architecture for the contingency of reading and reception—a labor that, in giving determinate form to the printed book, left the potential paths of readers undetermined and unfinished.

ᙢ   ᙢ   ᙢ

Before turning to Chapter 2, I would like to make a final observation about the two poems from *The Forrest of Fancy* discussed in the previous paragraphs. Alongside the contingency of taste that I have pointed out here, both also sound a second and distinct note in their respective praise of "nut cornell" and rose. "Such vertue in this *cornel* is," H.C. writes, that "Phisitions use it many times, / their patientes paines to stay" (sig. D.iii^v). Of the rose, he writes,

> Distild it makes a water wondrous sweete,
> Of vertue great, and good for many thinges.
> The oyle thereof, full many thinke more meete,
> Because much ease in them it often bringes.
> (sig. H.ii^r)

Virtues, in both cases, offer a powerful stay against contingency and illness. Accordingly, the poet's syntax turns away from the first-person voice of taste and desire.

The language of "vertue" suggests an alternate practice of praise, one that builds not on the experience of the poet but on the forceful internal capacities of each kind of matter. Those capacities will be the subject of the following chapter, and, as we will see, their material resilience will offer a certain stay against the contingencies of circulation and reorganization. As it does in the examples considered in this chapter, however, the lexicon of plant virtues tells a story about reuse and circulation that builds on the latency of textual and vegetable matter—as the kind of stuff that can travel between here and there, self and other, past and future.

CHAPTER 2

On "Vertue"

Textual Force and Vegetable Capacity

"Vertue" with an *e*

The climax of George Puttenham's *Arte of English Poesie* comes at the end of its last substantive chapter, as the handbook's author arrives at a new articulation of the poet's singular capacities. To this point, Puttenham has committed much of the chapter's discussion of the relation of art and nature to the ways in which artisans engage their materials. In the final paragraphs, however, the "maker or Poet" breaks from this comparison and does not work *on* nature, but "even as nature her selfe working by her owne peculiar vertue and proper instinct and not by example or meditation or exercise as all other artificers do." It is in these respects, Puttenham writes, that "it is not altogether with him as with the crafts man."[1]

Even as Puttenham frees the poet from the exercise of craft, he paints his distinct capacities in the lexicon of the artisan: "even as nature her selfe," he writes, "working by her owne peculiar vertue and proper instinct." To this point in Puttenham's chapter, "vertue" has accompanied the work of skilled laborers: like the physician, who might nourish the virtues of a weak and unhealthy body; or the gardener, who might enhance the color or virtue of a choice flower. Beyond the sphere of Puttenham's *Arte*, "vertue" was similarly entangled in the transmission and exercise of practical knowledge. It haunted the pages of practical manuals and fueled the artisan's labors and the huswife's ingenuity. For sixteenth-century readers and printers, it also gave a name to the work that printed books promised to perform in the world. It is to this dimension of "vertue" that this chapter will attend, turning from the horticultural forms that books assumed to the botanical lexicon of bibliographic and poetic force. The following pages ask what it means for a book, or a piece of language, or a piece of vegetable, to carry this sovereign agency: What does that agency look like, and what are the consequences for humans and nonhumans entangled with it?

A resonant and agile term in the period, "vertue" named the latent force and potential utility of different kinds of matter: the capacity of one herb to heal and another to purge, the potential of one metal to draw or repel another, the power of stars to guide the course of terrestrial lives. Though in less common use today than the moral meaning of "virtue," this material sense was widespread in early modern England, providing a primary frame through which the rhythms and capacities of the natural world were understood. It is nearly always in this material sense that Puttenham uses "vertue" throughout the monumental treatment of ornamental language undertaken in the *Arte*'s third book: in chapter 20, to model the interaction of art and nature; and in earlier chapters, to capture the potential force of poetic language. Book 3 opens with Puttenham's classification of ornamental language according to its two distinctive virtues, and, in the chapters that follow, particular tropes and figures are said to have their peculiar "vertues." Before Puttenham's elevation of the poet to a second nature, "working by her owne peculiar vertue and proper instinct," material virtue has been a property not of people but of language—matter molded or transformed by the art of the poet.

Though marked by an *i* in our contemporary spelling, "virtue" standardly appeared in sixteenth-century printed books with an *e*: *vertue*. More than 99 percent of the uses of "virtue" and its English cognates in print prior to 1600 were spelled with an *e*. In books printed before 1650, "vertu-" appears more than 97 percent of the time.[2] It is not until the second half of the seventeenth century that "virtue" comes to compete with, and eventually outpace, "vertue." Remarkably standard in an era of unstandardized spelling, this persistent *e* brings the notion further from *vis*, *vir*, and *virtù*, and closer to *veritas* and *verité* (the "vertue" of a thing being, to some degree, the very thing). It joins forces there with Lady Ver and the propulsive energy of springtime. And, crucially, it marks a silent orthographical alliance with the turns of rhetoric. Physical and poetic "vertues" convert, invert, divert, and subvert— that is their "mickle" and "powerful grace," to recall the words of *Romeo and Juliet*'s Friar Laurence. A "vertue" in this sense acts not just *like* a rhetorical trope, but *as* one—linked by close orthographic contingency if not actual etymology. As we will see below, Renaissance writings on poetics and rhetoric consider ornamental language itself to be virtuous, a repository of latent force that empowers poetic language as well as the form and matter of books. In handbooks like Puttenham's *Arte of English Poesie*, the "vertue" of a figure is that which does the turning, converting, and inverting—the germ of its operation and efficacity.

The etymological connection between *vir* and *virtus* has been a commonplace of scholarship on the European Renaissance, planting the codependence of virtue and virility deep in understandings of Renaissance culture.[3] What changes if we see, through the eyes of early modern readers, the turn of the *e* instead of the masculine uprightness of the *i*? To be sure, the *i* that links the Latin *vir* and *virtus* was visible to any Elizabethan trained in a humanist classroom; for educated readers, the manly fortitude described in Cicero's *Tusculan Disputations* and exemplified by the *vir virtutis* of Stoicism was a common point of reference and emulation. In his *Boke Named the Governour*, Thomas Elyot echoes Cicero in writing that "A Man is called in latine *VIR*, whereof saythe Tulli, *VERTUE* is named."[4] And yet, boldly rendered in printed majuscule, the page's spellings of "VIR" and "VERTUE" pose a silent resistance to this family resemblance. The long-lived *e* of "vertue," a relic of the word's descent into English via Anglo-Norman, remained in regular use more than a century past the ostensible triumph of humanist teaching, withstanding the influence of Latin orthography and of Italian *virtù* in learned and courtly circles. It resonates in counterpoint to Roman *virtus*, calling instead upon an inclusive chorus of plants, beasts, and stones, each in its particularity endowed with capacity for virtuous action. We might (however anachronistically) call this a more ecological view of the cosmos, one that places human artisans in positions of interactive dependence, subject to the rhythms and patterns of nonhuman capacities. "Vertue" decenters natural sovereignty, by imagining these capacities distributed among creatures and across territories.[5]

When used reflexively in early modern printed books, "vertue" summons the encounter of textual with human agencies—an encounter in which it preserves the primacy of nonhuman capacity. As a consequence, the bounded forms of book and poem are both subject to Friar Laurence's warning that "Within the infant rind of this weak flower / Poison hath residence and medicine power"—like Thomas Becon's *Flour of Godly Praiers* (1550), "of synguler vertue and myghtye in operacyon"; or the "weeds" of George Gascoigne's *Posies* (1575), which despite their name have "some vertue if it be rightly handled."[6] Calling on analogies with artisanal practices, these examples reiterate that virtues are put into use when found and properly handled. Until that moment of actuation, they rest in latent suspense. Like the moral virtues, ecological virtues are forces *in potentia*, harboring the capacity for action but not constituting actions themselves. An expert poet or orator, like a husbandman or gardener, taps into what Julia Reinhard Lupton calls "those capacities that subsist in things," inciting them to fill the office that their nature entails.[7] The word's use in early modern texts belongs to a longer history of virtue and potential energy, one that leads from the distinction between *dunamis* and *energeia* in Aristotle's metaphysics to Renaissance debates about the reality of occult virtues and the morality of their manipulation. Like Machiavelli's distinctive and influential conception of *virtù*, these material virtues speak ambiguously to moral virtue. Though patterned like the moral virtues on repeated habit and potential action, material virtues might be forces for good or for evil.[8]

The use of "vertue" in Elizabethan printed books and poetic and rhetorical theory reflects an important shift in the analogy between plants and texts, which was conventionally emblematized by the "flowers of speech": with its emphasis on the *force* of both plants and language, the connection between the two reaches beyond the structure of the metaphor to engage the reader in an active process of repetition and reproduction. The figure opens to the possibilities of practice and technology. As a language of force, virtuosity is not strictly borrowed from a domestic lexicon of flowers and herbs; it can also name the invisible persuasive force of rhetoric and poetic language. In *The Boke Named the Governour*, Elyot describes the eloquence of sentences that, "by a vertue inexplicable, do drawe unto them the myndes and consent of the herers."[9] A language of virtuous force enters printed collections under the colors of botanical conceit but educes by the same stroke the occult physics of rhetorical force. The lexicon of "vertue" thus participates in "the world-changing power of verbal eloquence" that Jenny Mann describes as an Orphic poetics, a physics of the natural world (and word) "unfolded in figures and fables and attuned to occult traditions."[10]

In what follows, I argue that an understanding of the innate "vertues" of plants and books shaped the identities of reader and text according to a logic of innate capacity—that is, the idea that matter holds a potential force within itself awaiting release by a skilled hand. Its distinctive latency and replicability make "vertue" a concept especially well suited to the material and social conditions of the printed book. Inscribed and implanted in matter prior to its manipulation or handing, virtue's agency inhabits textual or vegetable copies and is distributed with them. It is realized only at the site of reception, as poison or medicine, on the ripeness of occasion or with the right or abusive handling of reader or apothecary. Material virtues model a portable and proliferative kind of power, one that enlists both plants and texts in a cosmos of distributed sovereignties. In the context of Elizabethan plant books and botanical collections, as "vertue" becomes a key term for the vegetable materiality of the book, it is not the poet who is presumed to wield this artisanal mastery but the reader.

As this chapter will show, the practical and collaborative sense of virtue is countered by a second strain—one that especially values the autonomous springing of virtues, their capacity to copiously burst forth in the absence of human intervention and without regard to human utility. Nonetheless, I will argue, it is the practical sense of virtue that prevails across Elizabethan print culture, as it places uses of the word in intimate contact with the rhythms of practical labor and the demands of everyday ethics. With their emphasis on either spontaneity or collaboration, however, these two views on virtue suggest divergent accounts of textual reception and poetic authorship. The final section of this chapter will see these two strains come to a head in the play of "vertues" in Puttenham's *Arte*.

A World of Virtues

In the beginning, countless early modern histories and books of secrets tell us, God endowed creation with virtues. Since then, earth's creatures, even the thorny ones, have held their uses and capacities. Sir Walter Raleigh, in his *History of the World* (1614), argues for the peculiar virtues of stars by drawing an analogy to terrestrial creation. "We may not thinke, that in the treasury of his wisedome who is infinite," he writes, "there can be wanting (even for every Starre) a peculiar vertue and operation; as every herbe, plant, fruit, and flower, adorning the face of the Earth hath the like."[11] Raleigh here plucks "vertue" as the thread from which to draw the fabric of creation, as he asks his readers to extend their faith from the familiar terrestrial capacities of plants to the more far-flung powers of the heavens. Raleigh's reference to stars' and creatures' "peculiar vertue and operation" registers the infusion of virtue into each trivial-seeming piece of creation, a distribution of capacity with reach both intensive, down to the very smallest thing, and extensive, to the cosmos's furthest reach. As marks of the universe's abundant particularity, virtues "dispearsed upon the whole face of the earth" (in Robert Mason's 1609 framing) offer a reminder of this primal endowment.[12] A virtuous vision of creation imagines the cosmos as a field of distributed sovereignty, peopled with tiny deputies each infused with divine force.

But these dispersed virtues rarely rest as objects of praise unto themselves, and their encomiums travel in fellowship with attention to a second endowment. While God infused the earth with abundant virtues, he also granted mankind the capacity to make use of them.[13] These twin endowments are commonplace in books that promise techniques for accessing the hidden powers of natural things—the so-called "books of secrets" that taught readers across sixteenth-century Europe methods for manipulating nature to their own ends. In his introduction to the first English translation of Alexis of Piedmont's widely read book of secrets, William Warde invokes this doubled endowment to defend the techniques propagated in the following pages—the divine gift of what he calls "perfitte usage." "In all these thinges are certaine secrete vertues," Warde writes, arguing that both virtues themselves and the God-given power to use them are signs of divine love.[14] A similar argument recurs in the prefaces of printed handbooks on healing, where it authorizes the practice of medicine: it is not only acceptable to use the virtues of natural things to heal, they argue, but incumbent upon readers not to neglect the double manifestation of God's love.[15]

As this commonplace suggests, practical knowledge, in its transmission and exercise, grappled with material virtues. Engagements with the virtues of plants and other natural materials were everyday and embodied, effected (for example) through the sensory organs of the nose or the manipulations of the hand. When they advertise access to the powers concealed in natural things, books of secrets promise the ability to manipulate what are occult forces in the most basic sense: those qualities known through their consequences but never perceived in themselves.[16] Pamela Smith argues that, for early modern artisans, a practical relationship to matter turned on experiential engagements with the innate virtues of substances: in the words of the Italian metalworker Vannocchio Biringuccio, "those things that have such inner powers, like herbs, fruits, roots, animals, precious stones, metals, or other stones, can be understood only through repeated experience."[17] In this embodied and iterative theory of the physical world, Smith writes, "matter is something to work through, something in which to explore resistances."[18] Though virtues are natural endowments, powers that rest hidden in material things, written accounts consistently link them to the artisanal practices that make them known and useful—in Warde's words, to "perfitte usage."

Plants were an especially ubiquitous vehicle for virtues, an affiliation that found its origins in ancient pharmacology and had been cataloged in herbals for centuries. The capacities that herbals and medical texts describe as virtues were rendered in Greek as *dunameis* by ancient physicians, including in the herbal writing of Dioscorides, who was still honored as the father of herbal medicine in sixteenth- and seventeenth-century herbals.[19] *Dunamis* is a central concept in Aristotle's *Metaphysics*, where, in opposition to *energeia*, or actuality, it names the potentiality of a substance.[20] Scholars of ancient medicine now believe that Diocles, a fourth-century BC medical writer, was likely responsible for this transfer of *dunamis* from philosophy to pharmacology.[21] This new context reoriented the term's primary emphasis away from a substance's own process of becoming and toward its potential to transform substances around it.[22] An Aristotelian conception of potentiality in turn left its mark on the conceptual form taken by herbal virtue. But, like the "vertues" of herbs, the *dunameis* of pharmacological substances are defined by their capacity to transform the creatures and environments they encounter.[23]

The abundance of virtues in creation lends itself to particular literary and bibliographic forms—especially those based on inventory and enumeration. It was commonplace, as we have seen, for early modern writers to draw on the vegetable kingdom as a thesaurus, or forest, of symbolic language. It was even more common, however, that texts should leverage the world of plants to project an image of storehousing itself, drawing on a fantasy of gardens and fields as treasuries of value readily detached and redispersed, of natural properties freely appropriated. Practical enumerations of virtues were best represented in herbals, where the "vertues" of a plant were inventoried along with its names and the places it might be found.[24] Like creation itself, printed herbals were repositories of vegetable capacity. William Turner's *A New Herball* of 1551 emphasizes this set of properties by dividing each entry under two headings, the first including a description of a plant's name, location, and form; and the second, its "vertues."[25] We will see below how virtue plays much the same role in the inventory of rhetorical tropes and figures offered by Puttenham's *Arte of English Poesie* as it does in herbals. Thus collected, virtues become the preliminary but latent stuff of a storehouse—awaiting their consummation into one kind of action or other.

While herbals explicitly present themselves as published catalogs of the virtues of plants, treatments of virtues tracked into other genres of books, carrying with them the logic and style of the inventory. Thomas Hill's gardening books introduce virtues as "annexed" to particular specimens, an adjunct property of the plant itself, cataloged and stored in kitchen garden or field, on call to be realized by a skilled herbalist or huswife. In his *Profitable Arte*, the virtues and uses of kitchen herbs are gathered under a separate heading, annexed and appendixed to the main body of the book. In many surviving copies, readers have treated this prose section as a collection of recipes, translating descriptions of plants' virtues into the language of curative method: "for the head," for example, or "to kill the worme."[26] Dense marginal comments like these turn Hill's book into a battery of potential action, in collaboration with and in imitation of the virtues of creation. Formally, as virtues invite listing and enumeration, their bounty comes to seem both essential and supplementary, to earthly creation as to particular substances: they are both annexed to the plant and at the very heart of it.

What might it mean, then, to think of books themselves as virtuous? For plant books, those Elizabethan titles printed as flowers, gardens, or other vegetable collections, a language of virtue suggests both the energetic copiousness of their contents and their readiness for use. The cosmology of virtue shapes an understanding of the book as a composite of many small forms; as a container of latent forces, awaiting their actuation; and, lastly, as a useful object, its purposes available to those with "perfitte usage." For example, Thomas Knell Jr.'s prefatory epistle to John Northbrooke's *Poore Mans Garden* (1571) explains the virtue of the book by describing God's implantation of healing force into nature itself: "GOD in the beginning when he created the earth, gave vertue to the same, to bring foorth every hearbe of the fielde, that might beare seede in him selfe, after his owne kinde, without gardening, digging, sowing, plantyng, weedyng, or any other travayle of man."[27] As it invites readers into Northbrooke's garden, Knell's epistle signals the kind of book it is: like manuscript *flores patrum* or *flores doctorum*, a collection of sentences on doctrine, virtuous fragments laid out in sequence and ready for plucking. Like herbal simples, each virtuous slip offers an antidote to poisonous counterarguments. They are curative, healing, and multiple—dispersed across the book (in orderly fashion) like virtues across the face of the earth. Both kinds of virtue place human practitioners in the position of *making use*—a process that consists of gathering, extracting, and applying.

Through the course of the sixteenth century, European colonists and traders came to see the Americas as an especially rich garden or treasury of virtues, a capacity advertised and performed by books focused specifically on New World *materia medica*. In this context, virtue promised a kind of movable property, one that might be extracted from its place of origin to provide a source of value and healing in new locales. But the transformation of plant, animal, and mineral virtues into abstract, portable value was not always straightforward: it was not clear, for example, whether a medicine from one location could successfully treat patients or ailments from other climates. Nor, moreover, was it always evident how newly discovered specimens could be transported such that their virtues remained fresh and ready for use months or years later. In the case of an especially influential example, English editions of the Spanish physician Nicolás Monardes's *Joyfull Newes Out of the Newe Founde Worlde* (1577) promised to declare "the rare and singuler vertues of diverse and sundrie Hearbes, Trees, Oyles, Plantes, and Stones." Its translator, John Frampton, saw the virtues of those materials as an assurance of the value of the book, which he introduces by comparing its contents to other materials extracted and brought back across the Atlantic. After extolling gold, silver, griffons, lions, melons, dyes, and pearls that have "stored the whole world," he claims that the medicines of the West Indies "doe exceede much in value and price all the aforesayde thinges."[28] Organized in print as an inventory of commodities and their virtues, the material form of the *Joyfull Newes* emblematizes the storehouse of riches as which Monardes (like Thomas Hariot, below) wishes his readers to see the Americas. Here, the value and virtue of book and plant emerge in tandem; while the virtues of plants affirm the value of the book, the imagined fixity of the book stands in for the portable resource of novel medicinal virtues.[29]

An appreciation of their value, however, does not necessarily entail an understanding of their use. Europeans in the Americas struggled to find and to exploit virtuous specimens. Monardes repeatedly complains about the reluctance of natives to share the secrets of local plants—both their use and where to find them. It would, he says, "be a thing of great profite, and utilitie to see and to knowe their properties, and to experiment the variable and greate effectes, which the Indians doe publishe, and manifest with great proofe amongest themselves, which they have of them."[30] At the same time, other travelers insist, while those Indians may understand the practical virtues of plants (and, crucially, know where to harvest them), they have no understanding of their spiritual value. Written accounts of these capacities sometimes felt the need to explain how non-Christians could make use of virtues without understanding their true origins. Both books of secrets and travel accounts accuse heathens of misinterpreting God's gifts, reading each creation, in its particular virtue and operation, as a God unto itself. Infidels, Alexis of Piedmont tells us, "beynge ignoraunt from whence that gyfte came: who, notwithstanding their ignoraunce, did so reverence the wonderful vertues of thinges created in the worlde, that they thought that eche of those thinges had had in it selfe a certaine divine power, or els that there was of every thinge a several god or creatour."[31]

These calculations also extended to the ostensible virtues of books. Thomas Hariot famously describes the encounter of native Virginians with his Bible in a myth of misrecognition. Like their encounters with clocks, loadstones, or "reading and writing," which he also describes, this scene turns on the reading and misreading of virtues. Hariot writes that they tried to embrace, stroke, and otherwise materially worship his Bible, "although I told them the booke materially & of itself was not of anie such vertue, as I thought they did conceive, but onely the doctrine therein contained."[32] As James Kearney shows, this belief in the Bible's material virtue marked Hariot's indigenous interlocutors as both barbarous and idolatrous, drawing on Reformation discourses of fetishism and on the fixation in travel literature upon the excessive value that native people placed on trifles and trinkets.[33] Hariot disavows, in other words, their belief in the material agency of earthly things. Though both Hariot and Alexis of Piedmont intend to correct these superstitious misreaders, each nonetheless presents a version of nature in which it is possible to imagine oneself surrounded by tiny but powerful deities. The very necessity of correction reflects the particularity with which virtues are distributed across creation, and the ease of misunderstanding the origin of their efficacy.

Nonetheless, as these accounts of heathens' mastery of virtues admit, a user need not understand the cause or origin of virtues to be expert in their application and manipulation. Here, the inability to properly *value* dispersed natural virtues in no way impedes one's ability to *use* those virtues. This disconnect will serve as a goad and frustration to the period's settlers, traders, and soldiers eager to tap the medicinal riches of the East and West Indies. One need not buy into a theological account of virtues' origin in order to access their capacities. This lesson extends to the virtues of books and fundamentally shapes the account of authorship that discourses of textual virtues imply. The distributed sovereignty that virtues model can do as much to obscure the origin of technological power as to display or amplify it. An understanding of creation as filled with dormant virtue underwrites a particular conception of the book, one that consistently locates the operation of textual force outside the will of the author. Instead, paratextual references to the "vertue" of a printed book grant decisive power to its material virtues and their handling by a reader. The event of the virtuous book occurs at the site of reception, not creation. Like physic gardens or fruitful fields, books offer a repository of latent virtues for skilled readers. However, in redistributing sovereign force, they erect an effective screen between a user-practitioner and the origin of a text's meaning or power.

Springing: Virtues Published and Compact

As latent capacities within a book or in the earth, virtues are pockets of potential action. They await consummation and even perception. Both poets and natural historians, for this reason, describe them as laying hidden, or concealed. Friar Laurence in *Romeo and Juliet* says, "O, mickle is the powerful grace that lies / In herbs, plants, stones, and their true qualities." John Parkinson writes in his *Paradisi in Sole* (1629) that God has given herbs and flowers "such vertues and properties, that although wee know many, yet many more lye hidden and unknowne."[34] We will see this echoed again below in George Herbert's "Vertue," in the description of spring as "A box where sweets compacted lie."[35] The capacity of virtues to make visible, to bring into lively being, links them to the power of poetry to make images, and to printing as a model for bringing out and making public.

Virtues do not, however, always need an invitation to emerge. And here, we can begin to see an alternate account of material and poetic virtuosity take form—one less reliant on skilled handling but fueled instead by copious nature's innate proliferative force. As latent wells of active principles—founts of healing, and even of rebirth—virtues fueled the season and action named by "spring." The early modern spelling of "vertue" legitimated this association, linking it materially to "Ver"—the familiar if antiquated name for the season. Spring's generative force reaffirmed this alliance, with its proliferative power to clothe the earth in virtuous and verdant life. Variety, abundance, and power all copiously and virtuously *spring*.[36] In his handbook of astronomic measurement, Thomas Hill writes that the coming of spring "stirs up" the earth's virtues: "the hidden vertues againe of the earth," he writes, "hee then beginneth to loose, open, chearish, and stirre up by his lively heate, and both looseth and sheadeth forth the dew moysture inclosed."[37] Loosening, cherishing, opening, and stirring up: Hill's litany of verbs grasps at the season's distinctive action of making present—of emergent energy at the instant of its arrival, the visible introduction of action where stillness had been.

When, in *King Lear*, Cordelia asks for the help of the earth in healing her father, she summons (in spelling of the 1608 quarto) "all you unpublisht vertues of the earth," asking them to spring:

> All blest secrets,
> All you unpublished virtues of the earth,
> Spring with my tears; be aidant and remediate
> In the good man's distress. Seek, seek for him,
> Lest his ungoverned rage dissolve the life
> That wants the means to lead it.[38]

Cordelia responds here to the doctor's promise that nature offers "many simples operative" to grant Lear rest, but she turns from that practical reassurance to a more lyrical mode of address. Her apostrophe to its "unpublisht vertues" suggests an enchanted and capacious vision of the earth, one in which the secrets of creation harbor capacities for springing and for hearing her plea. In the lines that follow, Cordelia instead directly commands her attendants to "seek for him," a midline turn that reveals the two modes of sovereignty at stake: in one, a hopeful apostrophe summoning a sovereign salve; and the other, a sovereign speech act to loyal inferiors. We may not be so confident, though, that this command for virtues to display themselves will work out, or that virtues, once displayed, will last—a caution that Cordelia and her sisters taught us in the play's first act. In this way, her words play out the poetic and political paradox of deputization that virtue carries with it; the virtuous capacity to spontaneously spring may also be a capacity to autonomously resist.[39]

The loosening energy of springtime, with its power to deck nature in visible virtues, had long provided a setting for poetry—we might think for example of April's generative force at the beginning of *The Canterbury Tales*, when the month has "bathed every veyne in swich licour / Of which vertu engendred is the flour."[40] In the later sixteenth century, poets more often evoke virtues' springing and budding from a distance, in moments of reflective grief, as they come and go with the seasons. The November eclogue of

Spenser's *Shepheardes Calender*, for example, calls upon the springing of virtues from an elegiac position, as "the flouret of the field doth fade, / And lyeth buryed long in Winters bale," a contrast with spring when "vertues braunch and beauties budde."[41] The vibrant branching of "vertues" indexes the movement of the year, as they flower and fade with the passing seasons. Extending the harshness of winter to the whole year, Thomas Middleton's early poem, *The Wisdome of Solomon Paraphrased*, describes a "barren earth, where vertues never bud." In the glum scene painted by Middleton, the burial of virtues in the earth takes on a funereal and almost apocalyptic guise—a barren landscape which he likens in turn to a "fruitles wombe, where never fruits abide."[42]

In these cases, "to bud with virtues" gives vernacular form to the Latin verb *viresco, virescere* (to grow green, or become verdant). The same convergence fuels the proverb "Virescit vulnere virtus" (Virtue flourishes in the wound)—a sentiment that marks the cyclical and seasonal alternations of cutting down and springing out. Raleigh, in his *History of the World*, joins *vertue, virescit*, and the greening of the world in his account of God's operative power in natural things. "It is Gods infinite power, and every-where-presence (compassing, embracing, and piercing all things)," he writes, that drives the nourishing movement of the weather—empowering the sun, vapors, clouds, and eventually rain. "So all second and instrumentall causes," he concludes, "together with Nature it selfe, without that operative facultie which God gave them, would become altogether silent, vertuelesse, and dead: of which excellently ORPHEUS; *Per te virescunt omnia, All things by thee spring forth in youthfull greene*."[43] The movement of springing, fueled by divine omnipotence, is also a movement of disclosure.

George Herbert's "Vertue" plants the season of spring in the "Ver" of the poem's title, which was spelled with an *e* in its first appearance in *The Temple* (1633) and throughout the seventeenth century. Across its four stanzas, the poem balances the word's moral and material senses, before turning in the final stanza from the seasonal flux of material "vertue" to the "season'd timber" of the virtuous soul.[44] The ecological sense of "vertue" specifically shapes the third stanza, where the preceding stanzas' addresses to "Sweet day" and "Sweet rose" give way to "Sweet spring, full of sweet dayes and roses, / A box where sweets compacted lie."[45] "Sweet spring," naming the act and the season, seems to gather the sweet days and roses within it, sheltering them—compacted—in the striking image of the stanza's second line.[46] "A box where sweets compacted lie," as I mentioned above, recalls the evocations by naturalists and herbalists of the virtues that "lay hidden" in the earth, awaiting discovery or reinvigoration.

The sweets *compacted* of the third stanza of "Vertue" tell us something further about the composition of books and plants. Like "spring," "compact" often accompanies "vertue" in early modern English prose and poetry, where it calls up a tradition of thinking about virtue itself as a kind of composite body. Rather than our more common contemporary sense of compression, compaction here denotes mixed composition—in the sense that nature is *compact* of the four elements, or, as Thomas Elyot writes, that moral gravity "is compacte of two vertues, Constance & Prudence."[47] "Spring" and "compact" convey what is multiple and assembled about the virtues, both moral and creaturely. The aesthetic effect of compaction reaches its greatest intensity in the third stanza of Herbert's poem. Following its opening address to spring, this is the most multiple of the four stanzas in its imagery—in the abundance of spring itself, the repetition of "sweet," the box's heterogeneous collection of days and roses. Miriam Jacobson places this stanza in the context of both floral and poetic posies, as gathered things themselves.[48] It is easy enough to imagine that this "box where sweets compacted lie" extends to the stanza or to the poem—itself a gathering of sweets, days, and roses. It might also, in an echo of Palgrave's 1540 description of "a very curiouse and artificiall compacted nosegay," name the printed and gathered *Temple* itself.

A compact plurality orders the operation of virtue both as physical force and as the moral components of character. Persons and things in sixteenth- and seventeenth-century England were standardly described in terms of the collection, compaction, and abundance of virtues. Tilney's *Flower of Friendship*, for example, praises Queen Elizabeth "for that in the person of your Majestie, are assembled the rare vertues."[49] Another moralizing example compares one's assembled virtues to an engrafted tree, crediting Cicero, "that gay Gardener, and cunning Arborer," with "graft[ing] upon this Tree of Vertue: foure brave branches: out of which, bud many springing sproutes, very necessary and spectant to perfection, and heale the miserable maymes of mans life."[50] No mere appendages, the virtues of Prudence, Temperance, Justice, and Fortitude make life whole. And it was as assemblies that virtues traveled. This diversity is an asset when it comes to praise: a poet or orator gets to list things, a strategy for which both early modern poetics and early modern books offered a plethora of rhetorical and typographical tools.

Nonetheless, the rhetorical force of enumerations of virtues carried a certain ambivalence: a style of praise reliant on rhetorical inventory can make its object seem to disintegrate. Troilus is "a minced man," Cressida says in Shakespeare's play after hearing a list of his virtues from Pandarus.[51] In their plurality, his assets break him down to mincemeat. Some writers resolve this danger by addressing the grace of virtues' assembly—a project for which flowers, gardens, and posies offer helpful templates. Barnabe Rich writes that a wise man loves a woman of virtues who "so tempereth her selfe in all her demeanors, that vertue hath seemed to settle her selfe in her lookes and countenances, and that the graces are there heaped together like a pleasant posie, compact and made of many flowers, and that of the most faire and excellent in the garden."[52] A wise man loves the heaping and compaction of graces and virtues in his beloved as much her honesty and sobriety—the gathering of the posy as much as the flowers themselves. He knows to subject both kinds of heap to the ordering logic of temperance.

We have seen how the balance between part and whole shaped the imagination of the book and of the garden in early modern England. In the context of virtue, a tension between the one and the many—the distance between the minced man and the pleasant posy—also revisits an ancient philosophical problem: just how many virtues are there? Are particular virtues, like temperance or piety, part of a whole, or different names for the same capacity? What kind of thing is *virtue* when what we see in practice reflects particular *virtues*?[53] The question of the "unity of the virtues" figured in in Plato's *Protagoras*, in which Protagoras advocates teaching the *one thing* every citizen needs before going on to name virtues seriatim. The principle of unity later becomes an ethical touchstone for the Stoics.[54] At times, the multiplicity of virtues seems to alienate the very idea from the rhythms and protocols of human life. Plutarch criticizes the Stoic philosopher Chrysippus for the monstrous plurality that results from his insistence that each virtue has its own quality. In Philemon Holland's translation (1603) of this passage in the *Moralia*, Chrysippus "raised a swarme of vertues never knowne before" and "so pestered Philosophie with new, strange and absurd words, more iwis than was needfull."[55] Here, the supplemental virtues with which Tilney describes Queen Elizabeth as being "adorned" have become chafingly superfluous—going so far as to *swarm*, like a pestilent army.

In Thomas Hoby's translation of Castiglione's *Courtier* (1561), the variety of virtues both troubles and adorns civil life, where it behooves the courtier "not onely to set his delite to have in himself partes and excellent qualities" but moreover to order his life so that "the whole may be answerable unto these partes." He should "make one body of all these good qualities, so that everye deede of his may be compact and framed of al the vertues, as the *Stoikes* say the duetie of a wiseman is." The courtier emerges like a well-gathered posy, in which "all are so knit and linked one to an other, that they tend to one ende."[56] Extending a formal logic that he also gives the names of framing and compaction, Hoby's use of knitting imagines a force that joins diverse things, bringing grace and harmony to Chrysippus's "swarm."[57] A knot, as we saw in the case of compartmented gardens, is a well-formed complexity. "Knit" and "compact" both name without explaining the subtle force by which mixed forms gather, performing an invisible and latent coherence between complete works and the particular virtues that fuel them. Such accounts of compacted virtues offer an aesthetic solution to a philosophical problem of proliferation, by which virtues are both essential and supplemental, super-fluous and the primary source of grace and substance. As a work of instruc-tion, Castiglione's book names but does not quite teach this magic of coherence. In the *Arte of English Poesie*, where this compaction goes by the name of "decorum," Puttenham also never demonstrates exactly how the many virtuous tropes and figures that compose his catalog should be made to *fit*, despite his instruction that they *should* fit.

Moral handbooks of the virtues mobilize the compacted form of the codex to impose order on Chryssipus's swarm.[58] In N.B.'s *Smale Handfull of Fragrant Flowers* (published by Richard Jones in 1575), the main body of the text is structured as a didactic inventory of feminine virtues, the fragrant flowers a virtuous lady should gather into a small handful she can carry with her. In this way, the *Handfull*'s moral and spiritual advice echoes the formal strategy of the printed collection: a virtuous woman gathers qualities within her as a nosegay or handful of fragrant flowers gathers virtuous slips. *The Boke of Wisdome Otherwise Called the Flower of Vertue* (1565), translated by John Larke, organizes a parade of virtues—part of a dream vision that takes flight from a springtime scene of flourishing birds and flowers. The ensuing collection of sayings follows the sequence of this parade. There, virtues are bound together in the book, just as they ought to be bound together in the reader, modeling virtuousness by modeling a restrained multiplicity. None-theless, the composite form of both codex and individual poem makes demands on readers. The following section considers how early modern discussions of the virtues of poetry endorse a skilled and piecemeal handling of poetic matter.

Right Handling: Poetry's *Materia Medica*

Poetry and plants are matter that demands handling: to be treated, differentiated, pieced out with skill. The active logic of virtue traced throughout this chapter amplifies the role of the reader, an emphasis that characterizes a wide range of sixteenth-century books of poetry and practical knowledge. The following section of this chapter examines the way that sixteenth-century writers on poetics frame poetic reception in pharmacological terms, figuring the force of poems according to the medicinal virtues of plants. By explicitly plugging into genres and vocabularies associated with the dissemination of practical knowledge, these analogies cast plants and humans as collaborators in virtuous action. From the perspective of the reader of poetry, these same virtues are elements in a text's composition, latent properties awaiting discovery and extraction.[59] In the debates about the dangers or virtues of poetry that occurred in the final decades of the sixteenth century, both enemies and defenders of secular verse deployed the pharmaceutical logic of material virtues. One authority for framing poetry's power in pharmacological terms was Plutarch's essay on how a young man should hear poetry, which relies on an herbal logic of force and effect to describe the active participation of the poem in the world of the reader.[60] In doing so, the essay relies on some of the artisanal analogies—with the gardener or physician, for example— which Puttenham will assert but ultimately disavow. Philemon Holland's 1603 translation explicitly links the essay's argument to defenses of poetry, entitling it, "How a yoong man ought to heare poets, and how he may take profit by reading poemes"—the latter phrase a gloss that explicitly links Plutarch's essay to Tudor defenses of poetry according to pleasure and profit. Plutarch's essay responds implicitly to attacks on the dangers of poetry much like those articulated in the late sixteenth century, in which its enemies impugned it as a mere vanity and waste of time or as a dangerous temptation. Scaffolding his argument that poetry is profitable for those who know how to use it properly, Plutarch's analogies align poetry with the double sense of the Greek *pharmakos*: it has the power to be both noxious and curative. The translation by Holland (who was also a physician) renders these potentialities "vertues."[61] This ambivalent vision of the poem's capacity leaves the reader with a heavy burden: to extract poison or cure, to act (as the analogy will run) as a spider or as a bee. As Plutarch's framing makes clear, and as Holland's repetition of "how" in the title reiterates, poetic reception is another kind of know-how: any profit that poetry may generate depends on the reader's handling.

Throughout the essay, Plutarch's prescription turns on knowing how to manage the internal variety of the text at hand. That is, the reader's share of virtue corresponds to the poetic work's quality of mixture. In some of Plutarch's medical examples, the antidotes to textual poison may be found in other segments of the text. The solution to poetic danger, it follows, is not to uproot the textual vine but to ensure textual variety. As such, readers are able to rely on portions of a work to inoculate themselves against others, just as the expert apothecary knows that the wings and feet of the Spanish fly counter the poisonous effect of its body.[62] Readers or listeners of poetry may likewise inoculate themselves by partitioning language: "even so in the Poemes and writings of Poets, if there be one Nowne or Verbe hanging to a sentence that we feare will do harme, which Nowne or Verbe may in some sort weaken the said hurtfull force, we are to take hold thereof, and to stand upon the signification of such words more at large." A poem, too, should be dissected: anatomized but not wasted or destroyed.[63] Like the double endowment of natural virtues, the proper use of poetic language depends on the human exercise of discretion and skill.

Holland uses "mingling" to capture the piecemeal approach to poetry that Plutarch's essay prescribes. In the story of Lycurgus, Plutarch's pharmaceutical reasoning returns to reject the king's decision to fight widespread drunkenness by having the kingdom's vines exhaustively "cut downe and destroied." This was a grave error: Lycurgus should have known that mingling, not uprooting, was the solution, and should instead have brought spring water nearer the vines, to "keepe in order that foolish, furious and outragious god *Bacchus* as *Plato* saith, with another goddesse that was wise and sober." As he goes on, "the mingling of water with wine, delaieth and taketh away the hurtfull force thereof: but killeth not withall the holsome vertue that it hath" (19). The same is true of poetry, which "we ought not to cut off, nor abolish," because we may in the process amputate some piece of wisdom. It is not poetry's suppression of but its increase in variety that resolves its potential menace: the collection of more, not less.

Plutarch draws his conclusive illustration from the apothecary's cabinet: "For as the herbe Mandragoras growing neere unto a vine, doth by infusion transmit her medicinable vertue into the wine that commeth of it, and procureth in them that drinke afterwards thereof, a more milde desire and inclination to sleepe soundly: Even so, a Poëme receiving reasons and arguments out of Philosophie, and intermingling the same with fables and fictions, maketh the learning and knowledge therein conteined to be right amiable unto yoong men, and soone to be conceived" (19). Here, the mandrake infuses the vine with "vertue" as philosophy infuses poetry with "vertue," a mingling of kind effected by proximity.[64] It is curious that Plutarch turns to the mandrake—a mythical icon of the danger of taking up a root—in an argument against the uprooting of poetry. All of these botanical allusions suggest strong moral consequences. Both of Plutarch's medicinal examples—mandrake and the beetle cantharis, or Spanish fly—are aphrodisiacs and, for early modern readers, erotic bywords, an intimation that the essay may in fact be couching in these medicinal analogies a disquisition on the dangers of sexuality in poetry.

Each of Plutarch's examples presumes a heterogeneous composition of textual matter, as he prescribes that the text be taken as a miscellaneous store to be used and handled, not as a univocal message, moral, or command. In Holland's introductory summary, the presence of "intermingling" guides the profit a young man should take from poetry—"That the sentences intermingled here and there in Poëts, do reply sufficiently against the evill doctrine that they may seeme to teach elsewhere" (18). Holland uses versions of "mingle" or "intermingle" seven more times in his translation, to indicate both the mixture of genres and forms and the mixture of substances, like water and wine (18).[65] In each case, the intermingling of forms and substances inclines the young man toward taking profit from poetry, putting him in the position of a skilled collector.[66]

A commonplace of this projection of responsibility onto the reader is the proverbial coupling of the spider and the bee, an analogy found throughout late sixteenth-century prefatory materials and addresses to readers. Paired with the spider, the bee represents not just the organized gathering and storage of sources into common placed cells, but the moral management of that textual matter—even, in some cases, its active purification. The analogy also finds a source text in Plutarch, who writes: "like as Bees have this propertie by nature to finde and sucke the mildest and best honie, out of the sharpest and most eager flowers; yea and from among the roughest and most prickly thornes: even so children and yoong men if they be well nourtured and orderly inured in the reading of Poemes, will learne after a sort to draw alwaies some holesome and profitable doctrine or other, even out of those places which moove suspition of lewd and absurd sense" (43). The spider and bee bequeath to the reader the burden of extracting virtue from even the most malicious literary example. A good reader—in both moral and aesthetic senses—operates not just by pruning (or uprooting, like ill-judged Lycurgus) but by approaching miscellaneous matter with an eye to analyzing, selecting, and purifying. Here, the closeness between the multiple meanings of "virtue" is rhetorically enabling: a text may be "virtuous" in the sense of "efficacious" while its moral virtues remain ambiguous at best.

For Elizabethan poets and publishers, casting readers as spiders or bees belongs to a general articulation of readerly ethics. At the same time, the analogy conveniently offers a ready tactic for authorial defense, empowering poets and editors to dismiss potential detractors as morally venomous or aesthetically perverse. The spider and bee frequently figure in prefaces and epistles to introduce approaches to managing classical texts. There, the commonplace reminds readers to inoculate themselves against veins of paganism or obscenity, while giving them license to proceed with their personal virtue unthreatened. Arthur Golding, as he warns readers of potential dangers lurking within his translation of the *Metamorphoses*, casts the metaphor as a prescription:

> Then take theis woorkes as fragrant flowers most full of pleasant juce.
> The which the Bee conveying home may put too wholsome use:
> And which the spyder sucking on too poyson may convert,
> Through venym spred in all her limbes and native in her hart.
> For too the pure and Godly mynd, are all things pure and cleane.[67]

The first couplet of these lines tells the reader how to take, or receive (*recipe*) the text, a rhetorical strategy that will be echoed by Isabella Whitney's own recipe at the conclusion of her translation of Hugh Plat's "flowers," where she helpfully instructs her reader to read just like the figure described as a profitable bee by Golding. Curiously, here, conversion, the *Metamorphoses*' central trope, is assigned to the venomous spider, while the bee merely conveys and "puts to wholesome use"—something that it does once it has conveyed the juice "home," a touchingly pedestrian word in this context, evocative of a domestic scene better suited to the distillation and concoction of an herbalist than the wild classical geographies of Golding's translation. Through this troping on conveyance and conversion, transformation and transport come to represent two different kinds of reading, while translation itself is revealed as a not entirely benign method of "conveying home."[68]

The reader's power to draw either medicine or poison from the same kind of matter informs George Gascoigne's revised *Posies* (1575), which asserts an elaborate argument for readerly "right handling." A revision of his 1573 *Hundreth Sundrie Flowres* (explored in greater depth in Chapter 3), *The Posies* draws on practical discourses of plants to sketch out the virtuous properties of the text and the responsibilities of the reader. Ostensibly revised in response to an unspecified scandal, the corrected *Posies* promises to redeem both the prodigal poet and his questionable verse.[69] In a departure from the previous edition, the volume is organized according to what seems a firm vegetable taxonomy, which classifies the different values and "vertues" of its content according to three classes of botanical use. Those poems classed as flowers, Gascoigne explains, are more pleasant than profitable, and the herbs, more profitable than pleasant. The compilation's "weeds," on their face both unprofitable and unpleasant, in fact hold an occult power available to discerning gatherers capable of discovering and unleashing their virtues through skillful handling. "But as many weedes are right medicinable," Gascoigne writes, "so you may find in this none so vile or stinking, but that it hath in it some vertue if it be rightly handled."[70] This serves as a powerful apology for the book: even the worst bits, it suggests, aren't as bad as they look, if you know what you're doing.[71] Gascoigne's use of "vertue" preserves a provocative ambiguity: he does not clarify whether weeds promise moral or material efficacy or both. Indeed, his metaphor seems to elevate a reference to pharmacological "vertue" to the status of moral excellence. As was the case in Holland's Plutarch, the contiguity of these two senses of "vertue" underwrites his textual analogy; and, again, the realization of poetic capacity depends upon the reader or listener's proper handling of poetic matter.

In writing that a weed "hath notsome vertue if it be rightly handled," Gascoigne echoes Thomas Becon's warning that the virtues of his spiritual flowers are only realized when "ryghtelye used." In both of these cases, the operation of virtue implies know-how on the part of the reader, while the specific vocabulary of "use" and "handling" locates the moment of the book's actuation in the material scene of reading. There, a skillful reader wrings virtue from what might otherwise fall to vanity or waste. Reading thus becomes a kind of craft knowledge akin to the right artisanal handling of medicinal herbs, an analogy that implies a correct and skillful way of "handling" the book as an object.[72] Nonetheless, Gascoigne prescribes no actual method for eliciting the virtues of weeds, beyond his more general references to the reader's "right" and "skilfull" handing. This vagueness is a central tactic in *The Posies'* broad defensive strategy, one that displaces responsibility without offering concrete prescriptions, thus preserving the kind of readerly liberty that seemed so troubling to putative critics of *Hundreth Sundrie Flowres*.

Though Plutarch's sense of mingling turned explicitly on the segmentability of grammatical parts, Gascoigne's virtues reside in the formal variety of the printed anthology. The mingled body, in other words, is the book itself. Like Plutarch, Gascoigne links both venom and cure to variation and mixture. Updating Plutarch's physic according to a more contemporary idiom, Gascoigne introduces *The Posies* by comparing the written word to a Paracelsian view of matter: "*Paracelsus*, and sundrie other Phisitions and Philosophers, declare, that in everie thing naturall there is to be founde Salt, Oyle, and Brimstone. And I am of opinion, that in every thing which is written (the holy scriptures excepted) there are to be founde wisedome, follie, emulation, and detraction."[73] At this moment in *The Posies*, the invocation of Paracelsus alights upon the figure of venom that runs through the work, as it does through Holland's translation of Plutarch, and as it does in Friar Laurence's reflections on herbal medicine. Though Paracelsus's understanding of the composition of matter may have been known to Gascoigne's readers, the German physician was best known for his related theory of *arcana*—namely, that any substance (however powerfully poisonous) could be curative in the right dosage.[74] Matter is not, in itself, harmful or curative; it simply demands, like a poem, "right handling."

In an epistle addressed to "the youth of England," Gascoigne tells the "lustie youthes, and gallant Gentlemen" that attacks on his earlier volume arose from the perceived danger that "your mindes might heereby become envenomed with vanities."[75] The figure of venom, as we have seen in Plutarch's essay and in Gascoigne's elaboration of his "Weeds," is repeatedly tethered both to vanity and to a certain style of reading. As Gascoigne writes later in the epistle, his detractors worry that his book is "more likely to stirre in all yong Readers a venemous desire of vanitie, than to serve as a common myrrour of greene and youthfull imperfections." This "venemous desire of vanitie" is a danger for those young readers who have neglected Plutarchan literary cultivation—those who, we might say, neglected to break off the wings and feet of the Spanish fly. Gascoigne's riposte, appropriately, is drawn directly from Plutarch: "Whereunto I must confesse, that as the industrious Bee may gather honie out of the most stinking weede, so the malicious Spider may also gather poyson out of the fayrest floure that growes."[76] The ambidextrousness of the text is the flip side of its heterogeneous composition (and, as Gascoigne asserts in his Paracelsian analogy, of textual matter in general): readers take of it what they will, and so whatever they take is their own responsibility. Variety serves not just as a source of pleasure but as an argument for authorial exculpation.

Puttenham's "Double Vertue"

My final example considers the sense of virtue from the perspective of the creation of poetry. Puttenham's use of "vertue" in his *Arte of English Poesie* further removes its sense from the context of morality and reframes it according to policy and technique. Though "vertue" plays an ultimately ambivalent role in Puttenham's account of poesy, it serves a crucial role in the success of the *Arte* as a handbook—a how-to guide in the production of courtly verse. In the *Arte*'s concluding depiction of cultural and artisanal production, the poet or maker is at first a craftsman akin to gardener or physician, who manipulates the virtues of language as those other artisans manipulate the virtues of natural bodies, whether plant or human. The proximity of these poetic discourses to practical genres helps shape the place and sense of "vertue" within them. But Puttenham ultimately expresses a deep ambivalence about this practical outlook—and the management of material virtues it entails—and turns away both from an artisanal view of poetic production and from the possibility that his practical guide might actually teach its method.

Puttenham's treatment of poetic ornament, which composes the third, longest, and most significant of the *Arte*'s three books, is bookended by "vertue."[77] "Of Ornament" begins by classifying all "ornament Poeticall" into "two sortes according to the double vertue and efficacie of figures" (119); later, as we have seen, in a concluding chapter on the nature of poetic creation, "vertue" acts as a flashpoint between art and nature, a common thread between the labors of poet, gardener, and physician. In the intervening pages, many of them comprised of a long catalog of figures, the term appears regularly, peppered across descriptions of individual examples. There, it names what is distinctive and useful in those rhetorical building blocks: the qualities and capacities of linguistic matter. This important book on poetic ornament is thus framed and perfused with "vertues." While some are explicitly botanical or physiological, and others linguistic or poetic, such a division does not easily survive Puttenham's own distinctions and elaborations.

Throughout much of book 3, then, "vertue" functions as a term of art in its own right, at the heart of how Puttenham understands the strange matter of poetic language, with its capacious activity and openness to human artifice. Especially in the catalog of book 3, figures *have* virtues and readers are taught to use them. In this sense, the *Arte* operates much like an herbal in form and function—the most important compendiums of virtues available to early modern readers. Like an herbal, Puttenham's catalog of figures offers a didactic storehouse of these potential energies, examples to be both admired and learned from, referred to and reused.

Analogies between rhetorical handbooks and herbals extend to other works on poetry and rhetoric. These connections between gatherings of figures and plants are made more generically explicit by Henry Peacham, who frames his 1577 rhetorical handbook as *The Garden of Eloquence*, from which a reader might gather "all manner of Flowers, Colours, Ornaments, Exornations, Formes and Fashions of speech." With this invitation, Peacham welcomes the orator or poet to pluck these instrumental flowers, while Puttenham, perhaps more subtly, simply structures the third book of the *Arte* as a catalog of ornamental "flowers," with guides to their properties, virtues, and right handling. Both titles inventory the properties of different kinds of things and give an accounting of the storehouse of nature and language. Readers, in turn, are meant to breed and gather more, to take extractions, and to make forceful use of those material capacities.

Though the place and frequency of the word is not nearly as regular as in herbals, "vertue" nonetheless acts as a specific term of art, prescribing the use of a figure and its characteristic property. Allegory, which Puttenham calls "the chief ringleader and captaine of all other figures," possesses "vertue of so great efficacie as it is supposed no man can pleasantly utter and perswade without it." When he defines it in the next paragraph, it is introduced "properly & in his principall vertue" (155)—a formula that recurs at moments of definition and distinction throughout book 3's catalog of ornament. As the example of allegory, "the ringleader," makes clear, virtue musters a language of power: it describes what figures can effect, and allegory, with its "vertue of so great efficacie," takes a hierarchically superior position.

Throughout, serving as shorthand for the operation of poetic power, virtue resides at the heart of Puttenham's understanding of "ornament Poeticall."

At the outset of his chapter introducing the nature of poetic language, Puttenham classifies ornament into what he calls the "double vertue" and efficacy of figures. As he elaborates this distinction, however, the meaning of "vertuousness" seems increasingly ambiguous. "This ornament then is of two sortes," he begins, "one to satisfie & delight th'eare onely by a goodly outward shew set upon the matter with wordes, and speaches smothly and tunably running: another by certaine intendments or sence of such wordes & speaches inwardly working a stirre to the mynde" (119). The first, he explains, was termed *enargia* by the Greeks (after *argos*, light); the second was "called *Energia* of *ergon*," or work, "because it wrought with a strong and vertuous operation."[78] As Katherine Craik and Rebecca Wiseman both show, Puttenham's understanding of poetic operation turns on an understanding of the sensitivity and receptivity of the body.[79] Accordingly, he classifies each kind of ornament according to how it works on its audience. The first, *enargia*, through analogy with visual effect, results in aural stimulation—it "satisfies and delights the ear only by a goodly outward shew set upon the matter with words." Its workings and its effects are external, on the level of the surface. The second works with more depth, "by certain intendments or sense of such wordes & speaches inwardly working a stirre to the mynde." By the end of this paragraph, however, the virtuousness of the double virtue with which we began has become a problem. *Enargia* is defined restrictively; it satisfies and delights the ear *only*, it gives gloss *only*. The language of force and virtue meanwhile—which the title of the chapter promised as a "double vertue and efficacie"—leaves luster behind and attaches itself to *energeia*. As a term of classification and discrimination, virtue names the duplicity of language, or of linguistic and poetic performance. But as property and power, it gives its force only to *energeia*—not to the surface of language but to its forceful substance. This tension is at the heart of Puttenham's conception of poetic language and of the work of the poet: is it an ornamental performance—a kind of show or luster? Or is it an operation of work and energy—that is, virtuous? What was introduced as a "double vertue" turns out to be a split between ornament's more and less virtuous functions.[80]

"Vertue" takes another central turn in the chapter that serves as the *Arte's* effective conclusion, a discursus on the respective roles of art and nature in the making of poetry. Here, our key term wears several potentially contradictory guises.[81] In a discussion of how and when the courtly poet ought to dissemble, Puttenham asks where art should appear and where "the naturall is more commendable than the artificiall" (249). As he turns to the classic debate between art and nature, Puttenham calls upon not just Renaissance discourses of poetry but discussions of teaching and gardening, among other topics.[82] Puttenham divides the relations between art and nature into four categories, of which the first two turn centrally on the role of virtues. First, art may be an "ayde and coadjutor" to nature, a "furtherer of her actions to good effect." He calls upon the physician and gardener as examples of these "good and cunning artificers." The art of physic supplies the wants of nature "by helping the naturall concoction, retention, distribution, expulsion, and other vertues, in a weake and unhealthie bodie" (253). The gardener, meanwhile, waters, weeds, and "cherisheth" his plants, and "so makes that never, or very seldome any of them miscarry, but bring foorth their flours and fruites in season" (254). This model of engagement follows the virtues and inclinations of the materials at hand: it "further[s]" those "actions" that nature already has underway. This is also the traditional position of craft, the embodied and iterative engagement with material virtues that characterizes the expertise of the artisan. The position that Puttenham describes here—of being an adjutant to nature—also appears as a Latin motto on the title page of Thomas Hill's 1568 *Proffitable Arte of Gardening*: *Ars naturam adjuvans*. As this echo reminds us, becoming an aide and a coadjutor to nature is the role that practical books offer to hopeful readers.

But art might also do more with respect to nature's actions, and, in a more aggressive role, act as "an alterer of them, and in some sort a surmounter of her skill, so as by meanes of it her owne effects shall appeare more beautifull or straunge and miraculous." The physician, for example, might be able to give his patient long life "many yeares over and above the stint of his first and naturall constitution." The gardener, by his own art, might alter the course of nature, and "make an herbe, or flowr, or fruite, come forth in his season without impediment, but also will embellish the same in vertue, shape, odour and taste, that nature of her selfe woulde never have done." The "embellishment" of "vertue" brings it beyond its natural state, to a position that would have remained unrealized without human intervention. Such operations, Puttenham writes, are "most singular, when they be most artificiall" (254). Despite their differences, both kinds of specialized labor are defined by their relations to innate capacities. The identity of the artisan turns on this ability to tap into, solicit, cultivate, and manipulate those same aspects of vegetable and human matter to which the gardener and physician direct their interventions and collaborations. As Puttenham has suggested to this point in the chapter, a poet or orator, working with language's "double vertue," likewise engages those capacities, furthering, altering, or fitting them to new settings.

However, these analogies are not the final word on the poet's engagement with his virtuous materials. At the end of the chapter, Puttenham's logic takes an abrupt turn, as his argument breaks from the comparisons with gardeners, joiners, and physicians that have guided him to this point. Despite what the poet shares with these figures, Puttenham writes, "it is not altogether with him as with the crafts man" (256). Each previous example shows art acting on and through nature. Yet, he claims that the poet or maker (the figure cultivated throughout the handbook to this point) is neither alterer nor coadjutor, but more like nature herself: "in our maker or Poet, which restes onely in devise and issues from an excellent sharpe and quick invention, holpen by a cleare and bright phantasie and imagination, he is not as the painter to counterfaite the naturall by the like effects and not the same, nor as the gardiner aiding nature to worke both the same and the like, nor as the Carpenter to worke effectes utterly unlike, but even as nature her selfe *working by her owne peculiar vertue and proper instinct* and not by example or meditation or exercise as all other artificers do" (257; my italics). The poet works not *with* nature but *like* nature herself, who works spontaneously" by her owne peculiar vertue and proper instinct." The novel likeness with nature herself is of a different order from the analogies that precede it. Eloquence becomes a virtue in itself—not an arranger or gatherer of found virtues, operating not on or through nature but as a nature, with the poet relying solely on his proper organs and faculties (including "invention," "phantasie," and "imagination"). Language and utterance now stand as "the vertues of a well constitute body and minde"—a human possession (255).

The "example or meditation or exercise" that Puttenham rejects here are the techniques of pedagogy—that is, the ostensible instructional project of the *Arte* and the promise it offers its reader. The poetic maker likewise casts off the prosthetic yoke of the craftsman's tools, and, indeed, of analogy itself, as Puttenham dramatically disavows the previous pages of artisanal comparisons and asserts for the poet a radical autonomy—more akin to courtly standards of grace and *sprezzatura* than to the collaborative exertions of gardening or medicine. Puttenham rejects the pedagogy of practical knowledge but replaces it—perhaps discordantly—with "vertue," though in an unfamiliar guise.

Puttenham's poet seems to resolve the debate between art and nature by *becoming* nature. He is only slightly less bold here than Philip Sidney is in a famous passage from the *Defence of Poesie*, where he writes that "Onely the Poet disdeining to be tied to any such subjection, lifted up with the vigor of his own invention, doth grow in effect into an other nature: in making things either better then nature bringeth foorth, or quite a new, formes such as never were in nature." This may be the moment of the *Defence* most difficult to emulate or apply, least readily assimilated into a progressive and teachable account of poetic craft.[83] The poet here is more *vates* then craftsman. As it breaks from the familiar technologies of gardening and carpentry, Puttenham's abrupt literary naturalism is not easily reproduced or imitated; there is no method to follow or repeat. Rather, the passage throws off method, abandoning its project of instruction—rejecting, in effect, the relational and collaborative approach to literary virtues that the *Arte* has endorsed to this point.[84] It is here that the terms of Puttenham's analogy with craft shift into the negative: though he may sometimes look like a craftsman, the poet is also *not* like the craftsman. This represents not just an ideological shift (in terms of what a poet is and the embeddedness of poetry in the world) but a generic one: the book becomes useless—it has nothing more to teach—at the moment it casts off this prior sense of worldly "vertue."

An attention to "vertue" brings this discussion of the *Arte* into conversation with a question that has long nagged scholars of Puttenham's handbook in particular and of instructional books in general. Practical books and manuals of instruction represented a significant portion of material printed in the sixteenth century, and a rhetoric of utility was central to their self-presentation. But, as literary scholars and historians of science and art have asked: Just how useful were they?[85] How and what do they instruct, and how do readers engage with them? The utility of Puttenham's *Arte* represents a specific point of disagreement in modern scholarship. With its complex structure and rambling style, its frequent undercutting of its own lessons, and its long discourses on courtly manners, the *Arte* has driven modern readers to wonder whether such a book can actually *teach* someone to write vernacular poetry.[86] From this angle, its lessons on decorum—an expertise Puttenham eventually leaves undefinable—are more important than its lessons on prosody. Whether in an herbal or in Puttenham's *Arte*, "vertues" empower a work's pedagogical project: these capacities are ostensibly transferable, available for redeployment in the hands of a skilled and self-improving reader. And yet the rendering of virtue at the conclusion of book 3 sets it as a limit case for this kind of technology transfer. In this way, "vertue" operates in concert with Puttenham's treatment of decorum, a concept that, as Derek Attridge argues, undermines the *Arte*'s instruction at every turn. Discourses of both decorum and virtue in the *Arte* challenge the possibility of teaching either poetry or courtliness.[87]

Tellingly, though, it is still to a language of "vertue" that Puttenham turns in this crucial moment. But it is a "vertue" of the poet's own possession, not one that resides in the capacities and rhythms of his materials. If, throughout the *Arte* and in herbal practice and textual culture, "vertue" represented an alternate sovereignty, a capacity proper to things, vegetable slips, or poetic figures, Puttenham has here reclaimed it as the poet's private property and personal power: in a feat of authorial self-possession, the poet now works "by his own vertue," according to his own sovereign nature. By the same stroke, Puttenham transforms the relationship of the book and the world. He cuts loose the gardener and physician, leaving them still entangled with the natural "vertues" of their plants and patients; and he sets loose the imaginative, self-naturalizing poet. As such, he absolves him of the relationships of dependency and supplementation that are the stuff and energy of craft. But even this last turn is only possible because of the collaborative ecologies he had described only lines earlier and the practical genres alongside of which the *Arte*'s project becomes legible. In the very word by which Puttenham asserts the poet's autonomous power—"by his own *vertue*"—he also asserts his indebtedness, the tense survival of this ecological thread in the moment of its disavowal.

The Traffic of Small Things in *Romeo and Juliet*

Minutiae

The world of Shakespeare's *Romeo and Juliet* is traversed by small, powerful things, minutiae whose traffic across the stage and across Verona drives the play's fateful movement. Ranging from Queen Mab and her fairy attendants to flowers, potions, and letters, this inventory extends to the small verse forms that Shakespeare implants throughout the play, like the sonnets of the opening prologue and the lovers' first encounter, and to Romeo and Juliet themselves, especially Juliet, whose very name, like Capulet and sonnet, is marked by miniaturization in its suffix. Seeing these minutiae in a list reveals something absurd about its set of juxtapositions: it is the rare metaphysics that groups together herbal potions, young Veronese women, short poems, and fantastically tiny fairy monarchs. These are, after all, different orders of matter. But they are, in the play as they are in the genre of narratives from which Shakespeare drew his plot, orders of matter that participate in the same economy, subject to exchange and to the same physics of potential energy.[1] *Romeo and Juliet* is deeply informed by what the previous chapters described as a botanical poetics—by the print culture of sonneteering, as others have argued, but also by the traffic in plants, poems, and other minutiae so vigorously pursued by books printed decades earlier in the sixteenth century.[2] Rather than the full book of nature, the play reads from the virtuous force of nature's letters, flowers, and slips.

The following pages, the first of two branches off of *Botanical Poetics*'s longer chapters, show the power of plant-thinking in the play's distinctive assemblies of form and force. *Romeo and Juliet* repeatedly directs us to the great violence of the very small, offering a treasury (if we look closely) of miniature forms and minute enclosures whose force seems to exceed their scale.

The "infant rinde of this small flower" (in Friar Laurence's words in the First Quarto), the flood of tears overpowering the bark of Juliet's "little body," vials and drams of poisons and potions, the Friar's undelivered letter to Romeo, which "was not nice but full of charge."[3] In this phalanx of small things, Queen Mab and her atomic fairy attendants lead the charge. Articulated in the first act of the play, Mercutio's fantasy trains an audience in the method and madness of seeing small. Advancing from the charm of the "joiner squirrel" (1.4.60) to the prick of "breaches, ambuscados, Spanish blades," the monologue's progress from imaginative delight to irresistible violence offers a sober reminder that the especially small is also especially capable of travel and trespass. Several scenes later, Friar Laurence's reflections on the virtues of plants—the great force in the flower's infant rind, the virtue that turns vice if misapplied—take this same shape, growing from comedy to tragedy in an arc that mimics the play's generic mixture.

The small verse forms woven through the play form another part of this collection. Georg Gervinus, writing in the nineteenth century, identified these "external forms" in the lovers' sonnet (1.5), Juliet's anticipatory epithalamium (3.2), and the lovers' aubade (3.5); as lyric Easter eggs tucked throughout the play, these embedded forms were corollaries (he argued) to its rendering of the "innermost nature of love."[4] Building on Gervinus's observation, Walter Pater describes *Romeo and Juliet*'s appropriation of lyric forms as part of a "perfect symphony"—one that, rather than partitioning the play, imparts to the drama the superior unity of lyric.[5] Rather than resolving these "external forms" into a deeper unity, we might instead see this conglomeration of small forms as the labor of upfilling the tragedy's own "osier cage," to repurpose Friar Laurence's ritual of gathering—a mixed bundle in which the infant rind of the sonnet will prove an especially powerful small form.[6] By this view the play's miniature poetics participate in a lyric culture that valued mixture and contingency—its composite pieces inhabitants of a small-time world that seems to sit uneasily with the grander scale of tragedy.

The play invites us to understand these dynamics according to the logic of material virtue. Friar Laurence's musings on the virtues of plants in 2.3—spoken while gathering slips—offer a position paper on the play's dynamics of diminution. As we saw in Chapter 2, "virtue" named what was marvelous and inexplicable in the potential energy of compact matter and language across a range of settings and genres in the sixteenth century. It could convey the greatness of moment in the very smallest form: Thomas Elyot defines eloquence in terms of "sentencis [that] be so aptly compact, that they by a vertue inexplicable, do drawe unto them the myndes and consent of the herers."[7] In a sermon, John Fisher claims, "A corne of mustard sede is veray lytle but it hath a gret vertue compact and gadred in it."[8] *Romeo and Juliet* likewise asks us to see small: through the imaginary experiment of Queen Mab, as we have seen, or the ambiguous promise of the play's "buds" and "infant rind."[9] It also asks us to see through comparative rhetorics of scale: in Romeo's words, "Alack there lies more peril in thine eye / Than twenty of their swords" (2.2.71–72); or in the apothecary's estimation of his poison's power, "if you had the strength / Of twenty men, it would dispatch you straight" (5.1.78–79). Emblematized by the tiny, deadly supply of venom carried in the sting of a scorpion, the operation of poison is a *locus classicus* for making visible the great violence in the very small, as Shakespeare's play does repeatedly.[10]

It is in this ecology of small forms that we encounter the tiny bodies at the center of this lamentable tragedy, buffeted on the flood of something much older and greater than they are. The small and the everyday seem ultimately to pose a *genre* problem in *Romeo and Juliet*. The play's smallness has nagged critics as a problem of generic misfit—a sense that the foibles (however terrible) of two young lovers do not meet the scale of tragedy. As Ruth Nevo has argued, it is a tragedy "at a lower pitch: nearer to the commonplace and ordinary."[11] In harmony with the compact aesthetics of virtue, however, the forces of tragedy in *Romeo and Juliet* work by intensity rather than extension—an intensity charged by the work of latency and action, the rhythms of dormancy and consequence that mark the play of contingency on this (un)remarkable scale.

Mickle Grace

> I must upfill this osier cage of ours
> With baleful weeds and precious-juiced flowers.

Friar Laurence's words in 2.3, spoken while gathering herbs, are woven from a practical familiarity with plants and their uses: from the scene's quotidian rhythm, as he rises with the sun to perform the manual ritual of gathering slips; its springlike image of the full variety of Mother Nature; its memorable evocation of natural potentiality: "mickle is the powerful grace that lies / In plants, herbs, stones and their true qualities"(11–12). These virtues lie dormant in natural things, he tells us a strategy—material intimations of a world of potential action just offstage.

As a guide to the formal patterning in *Romeo and Juliet*, these lines do not so much distill the drama as render it in miniature, allegorizing the extraordinary work of will and fate in an ordinary scene. It is also about miniatures. The Friar organizes his speech according to opposition and oxymoron, which encompasses this paradox of scale: *mickle is the powerful grace* in something as small as an infant rind. His antinomies of proportion are braced by the language and cosmology of "vertue"—a concept that, as we have seen, brings extraordinary force into small, ordinary things. The Friar's lines are usually read as a metaphorical coupling of two kinds of virtue: a literal account of the material virtues housed in the plants before him, which nourishes in turn a meditation on the nature and fate of the moral virtues. As we saw in the previous chapter, this sense of "vertue," though now less common in our current use, names the potential of different kinds of matter to get things done, to fulfill their innate capacities. For all their material resiliency, however, this latency marks them as bearers of contingency. In Shakespeare's play, botanical virtues are not only a metaphor for moral reflection or for the philosophical integuments of the tragedy, a vehicle soon forgotten in the action of the play. Instead, they shape the drama in significant ways, and, by inviting in "vertue" as a keyword, the Friar makes visible alternate patterns in the play's structure—in particular, the outsized force of these small things.

By invoking "the infant rind," Friar Laurence unites the cosmology and compact aesthetics by which virtue operates: its force inheres in the world of material things, where it can be condensed even into the slightest vehicle.[12] Echoing commonplaces of botanical rhetoric, he describes a terrestrial field not just of virtuous creatures but of copious variety—"And from her womb children of divers kind / We sucking on her natural bosom find"(7–8). The syntax in which the Friar captures this diversity echoes the choppy, computational language that characterizes arguments for variety in collections like *The Forrest of Fancy* (1579) and *A Hundreth Sundrie Flowres* (1573): "Many for many virtues excellent, / None but for some, and yet all different."[13] Pictured as a full-bodied mother giving suck, the earth boasts those two qualities: the virtuous force of each individual creature she feeds, and the variety of those creatures when considered as an ensemble. (In the text of the Second Quarto, we have recently learned from Capulet that the earth is also fearsome: a swallower of hope.)[14]

For their handlers, the quotidian world of material virtues represents a practical philosophy of contingency: one according to which virtues' worldly force, their actuation in the sphere of people and things, awaits the right occasion or the right handler. We can hear this rumbling of the mundane and of mechanical procedure in the Friar's language: the warning that, "strained from that fair use," virtue turns vice, "being misapplied."[15] This is the everyday stuff of practical virtuosity. A housewife, drawing simples from her kitchen garden, might also use or misuse, apply or misapply. Skilled handling sought to navigate this everyday contingency: without it, virtue might turn to vice, or vice versa, in the small garden plot as in the castles that are tragedy's more familiar landscapes.

The secrecy associated with nature's store of latent virtues shapes the grammar in which Friar Laurence describes terrestrial power: "O, mickle is the powerful grace that lies / In plants, herbs, stones, and their true qualities." The Friar's attachment to *hidden* virtues suggests both the machinations of the occult and the dangerous secrecy of clandestine marriage. (And, in this context, the double sense of "lie" indexes the moral ambiguity of such secrets in the play.) The skill in natural magic that the Friar's speech implies is rendered more fully in Arthur Brooke's earlier version of the story, where the Friar is introduced as skilled in the secrets of nature:

> The secretes eke he knew,
> 　　in natures woorkes that loorke:
> By magiks arte most men supposd
> 　　that he could wonders woorke.[16]

Like the authority on natural magic Giambattista della Porta, who defines it as an art "full of much vertue, of many secret mysteries [that] openeth unto us the properties and qualities of hidden things," the Friar is introduced as a master of secrets—a role that links his botanical practice to his narrative function, as conveyer of secrets between Romeo and Juliet and as the enabler of their clandestine union.[17] Romeo tells his secrets to the Friar, Juliet to the Nurse; the Friar pries loose the secrets from herbs and stores the secrets of his parishioners; the three of them together make the new secret of their marriage.

The Friar's monologue finds a comic herbal foil in the Nurse's account of Juliet's weaning. On a day coinciding with an earthquake, according to her telling of the tale, she applied wormwood to her nipple to wean Juliet; Juliet, already obstreperous, considers the intervention a misapplication. It is against the landmark of this memory that she and Lady Capulet measure Juliet's age, and the Nurse's telling of the story is a gathering of poorly timed folds: the earthquake, her weaning, her youth (just short of fourteen), the possibility that in marrying she might be "too soon marred," as her father has just said, by being "so early made" (1.2.13).[18] The climax of the story is Juliet's combat with the wormwood-dabbed breast:

> For I had then laid wormwood to my dug,
> Sitting in the sun under the dovehouse wall.
> My lord and you were then at Mantua.
> Nay, I do bear a brain. But as I said,
> When it did taste the wormwood on the nipple
> Of my dug and felt it bitter, pretty fool,
> To see it tetchy and fall out with the dug!
>   (1.3.27–33)

Both the quotidian use of herbs and the image of nursing will be repeated an act later, with the Friar's description of creatures sucking on the bosom of the earth. And, as it does there, an aesthetics of the miniature shapes the scene of combat. In the Nurse's affectionate diminutives, Juliet is both a "pretty fool" and "it," a genderless thing. But here, the combat enters the visible universe of physical comedy, as the Nurse's syntax invites us to join in the open infinitive "to see" this small thing at war with its enemy the dug. Its comedy follows as much from this mismatch of scale as from little Juliet's misrecognition of causality, her confusion of human and herbal agency with the object of the nipple. She is not wrong, though, to resent the sudden bitterness of the small thing to which she had been sweetly cathected. A common use of wormwood reinforces the depreciation of scale: known for its acute bitterness, and used largely as a purgative, the herb also had a special power for repelling insects, controlling household pests like fleas, gnats, and moths.[19] Ridding herself of this other tiny parasite, the Nurse finds herself in an unexpected battle, as Juliet (tetchy and prone to falls) "fall[s] out with the dug." Here, Juliet suggests a militarized version of what Sianne Ngai has described as the aesthetic category of the cute. However, instead of soliciting aggression from the subject who encounters it (as Ngai argues in the case of the cute), this "pretty fool" is endowed with native and dangerous force from the start.[20]

The violent potential energy of the very small haunts the work of miniaturization throughout the play. Juliet takes on herself the compact force of "vertue" when she worries in 3.2 that Romeo has died:

Hath Romeo slain himself? Say thou but "Ay,"
And that bare vowel "I" shall poison more
Than the death-darting eye of cockatrice.
I am not I if there be such an "Ay,"
Or those eyes shut that makes thee answer "Ay."
If he be slain, say "Ay," or if not, "No."
Brief sounds determine of my weal or woe.
             (3.2.45–51)

Juliet, whose first word was "Ay," packs poison into that bare vowel—an abundance of potential force in a small space that also fuels her wordplay (what is a pun if not potentiality packed into a brief sound?). The power of a cockatrice's poison, like that of a scorpion, was notoriously out of scale to its body; John Maplet wrote that despite "beinge in bignesse but as much as a mannes hande" the cockatrice "speedeth so wyth her envenoming that shee . . . doth yet not wythstanding kill all other Serpentes wyth her onely infected & poisonous breath."[21] The ocular workings of that venom tangle Juliet's lines further in the virtuous operations of love, whose force was also thought to enter by the eye—again, through the force of radical miniaturization.[22] Benvolio's prescription to Romeo for ridding himself of his love of Rosaline was to "Take thou some new infection to thy eye, / And the rank poison of the old will die" (1.2.48–49); Juliet, as we learn soon after, will be that new infection, a death-darting "I."

Traffic

In the play, what Friar Laurence calls the misapplication of virtue unfolds according to the misdirection and interruption of the small things in which the play traffics. The potential of virtuous matter to misfire—if mishandled or handled at the wrong time or place—opens the narrative to the distortions of accident.[23] As we know from the prologue, this will be a play *about* traffic, stitched of two-hours traffic onstage. The abrupt movement from the prologue's closed form, delicately balanced within the meter, cross-rhymes, and couplet of a sonnet, to the street brawl of the first scene displays this fall from enclosure to the free violence of its breach. The misdirection of these various objects across the play's topography will continue to pit closed forms against mobile, virtuous force: the wild violence of the streets (through which Romeo and the Nurse both move with relative freedom) against the ostensible calm of the house and eventually the tomb.[24] The plot moves with the transgression of city walls and garden pales, as characters, words, and things breach the enclosures that give Verona its shape. There may be no world without Verona's walls, but there are many worlds and walls within it, and the play's imaginary topography tracks the itineraries of minutiae across and through them.

In the events that follow, no piece of paper reaches its intended destination: small things are left with unrealized (or misapplied) potential. Misdirected letters become even more dangerous than twenty men or twenty swords. As Friar Laurence says of the letter that never reaches Romeo in Mantua, "it was not nice but full of charge"—an epitaph that might be extended to the whole play. That unhappy letter is joined by other paper accidents, all hijacked: the invitation to the Capulet ball that ends up in Romeo's hands; Romeo's letter, read posthumously by the prince. Plant material, too, circulates unhappily—the Friar's vial and the apothecary's poison are both cases where the release of material comes with acknowledged risk, a power out of scale to their humble containers. Even the closed verse forms forged by characters' speech struggle between continuation and interruption—as when Romeo and Juliet seem to be beginning a second sonnet in 1.5 before being interrupted by the Nurse after just a quatrain. All attempts at sequence are interrupted; all Verona's closed forms will be pried open.

As a discourse linking textual and vegetable forms, the power of virtue that the Friar describes is able to travel in small pieces and to operate at a distance. These small pieces of virtuous matter promise to be distinctly capable of transport, of breaching boundaries and walls—a capacity as happily performed by printed books and vegetable slips as by defiant adolescents. Thomas Becon draws on these shared capacities to advertise his *Flour of Godly Praiers* (1550) as "a flower, as if it be ryghtelye used, [which] is of synguler vertue and myghtie in operacyon." Its force reaches out of doors, and "geveth a smel in the stretes to the soule of the faythefull."[25] The volume's mickle grace, which originates in scripture, trails not just into Becon's volume but wherever copies may be carried. Isabella Whitney inscribes her 1573 *Sweet Nosgay, or Pleasant Posye* on similar topography, relying on the portability of its virtues, and on her own and her reader's ability to carry flowers and slips abroad, through London's "stynking streetes, or lothsome Lanes."[26] Becon and Whitney both give their texts' defensive powers a concrete topographical index, projecting itineraries for their flower books across a city ridden with spiritual and physical pestilence. (Whitney is especially canny, as we will see in Chapter 4, to rewrite feminine virtue, usually associated with the enclosures of chastity, silence, and obedience, as something that travels resiliently out-of-doors.)

We can easily imagine the urban topographies conjured by Becon and Whitney projected onto a map of Shakespeare's Verona, another landscape marked by pestilence and across which plant-stuff and paper-stuff are anxiously carried. Like the stinking streets imagined by Whitney and Becon, *Romeo and Juliet* is haunted by plague: in the outbreak that keeps the Friar's letter from reaching Romeo in Mantua; in the language of Mercutio's curse, which in sending a plague "on both your houses" metaphorizes the family lines of Capulet and Montague and precisely evokes the physical terror of plague, that it might breach the walls of a house not yet infected. Mercutio's subsequent image makes small vermin vectors of this danger ("A plague a' both your houses! Zounds, a dog, a rat, a mouse, a cat, to scratch a man to death" [3.1.101–102]). Mice, rats, and cats all scratch to find a way in.[27] Rebecca Laroche and Jennifer Munroe read these small vermin as markers of the insistent permeability of domestic space—the transcorporeality that undermines enclosure of both house and body.[28] Queen Mab is a similarly transcorporeal figure, associated with verbs of motion (she comes, she gallops) and marked by her ability to cross thresholds into close spaces; at night, she "plagues" ladies' lips with blisters (1.4.75). Laroche has also shown the presence of plague in the role of Angelica, the nurse (only named once), who shares her name with the plant whose root was a powerful defense against plague. Held on the tongue as a personal preservative, the virtues of angelica offered protection when going abroad into streets and lanes.[29] Like the paper nosegays that Becon and Whitney tell their readers to carry through London's "noxious lanes," the root of angelica promised a portable forcefield, sovereign protection across mixed terrain and potentially dangerous geographies. Angelica was a small, portable, precious thing.

In the Elizabethan narrative romances of the kind that provided Shakespeare with the events and characters of *Romeo and Juliet*, plants, poems, and people all circulate and change hands, often in hope of being exchanged for one another. A young man writes a sonnet on a slip of paper or on a tree, delivering it—perhaps with a posy of flowers—to the woman he courts, in hopes his poetic or floral labors will be paid back. Often, as they do in Shakespeare's play, those slips go astray. The next paragraphs step briefly away from Shakespeare to consider the erotic traffic in plants, poems, and infection in another Elizabethan narrative. Like Shakespeare, George Whetstone encountered the story of Juliet and Romeo in earlier Elizabethan versions, and, like Shakespeare's play, the story it helped inspire in his *Rocke of Regard* (1576) sees its narrative traffic in poems, plants, and desire tainted by infection. Whetstone's tale presents the indirect but ultimately happy progress of two lovers, Rinaldo and Giletta, whose romance begins at a ball but soon collides with accident, misdirection, and interrupted communication.[30] At a climax of Whetstone's narrative, Rinaldo, ailing and jilted, suffers in the company of Giletta, who offers him a gift of flowers before departing: "vouchsafe this posie of Giliflowers, which carrieth this vertue, that about those whose head they bee bestowed, the same wighte shal not bee much frighted with fearefull fancies."[31] At this moment in the narrative, the posy is a kind of secret message to Rinaldo, to whom Giletta cannot speak freely because she is escorted by another suitor, Frizaldo. Beside the description of Giletta's gift, a printed note appears in the margin: "A secrete vertue in giliflowers." This annotation indexes the posy's hidden message while also treating its force as a general property of gillyflowers. Like the dynamics of virtue in *Romeo and Juliet*, the posy's textual presentation joins herbal and erotic secrecy—a quality that enhances the narrative and the practical value of this piece of knowledge, granting the reader bespoke access into the logistics of floral force and the clandestine communication between lovers.

But, in Giletta's traffic in flowers, not only material virtues are at stake. When Rinaldo responds by denying the flowers' efficacy, complaining "howe much of this vertue faileth in your flowers," he also questions Giletta's virtue. Instead, he makes himself the scene's active trafficker in plant matter and asks her to wear a rosemary branch as an emblem of remembrance. (Juliet's body, too, will be strewn with rosemary.) As they leave, Frizaldo, perhaps having caught a glimpse of the *Rocke*'s marginal note, proves himself a well-trained reader of love lyric and continental romance: he "read the letters of their flowers, and wrested out the sense of their subtile wordes." Under his eye, the interaction has become a study in the physics of betrayal: the branch of rosemary has come to stand for the "subtile" substance of Giletta's contact with Rinaldo, a material conveyance of both memory and contagion, and Frizaldo demands that Giletta chuck it: "Away with this Rosemary (quoth hee) lest it hide some infection (being sometime sicke *Rinaldoes*)." In reading the traffic in flowers, then, Frizaldo suspects a traffic in contagion.

Like Shakespeare's Juliet, Giletta possesses a keen sense of her own place in the traffic in words and things. And she proves a better reader of her own contamination than either male suitor in this triangle. She responds by cutting to the quick of Frizaldo's resistance: "That maye offende you, (quoth *Giletta*) if it were any wayes infected, by this time the open ayre hath purged it, but if before this time, I my selfe am infected, it smally helpes to throwe away this poore braunch, and so your counsel is out of season, and yet for the same I courteously thancke you."[32] Giletta says the silent part of Frizaldo's jealousy out loud: though Frizaldo claims only to object to the branch, she cannot erase, or make uncontagious, her contact with his sexual competition. Giletta's retort acknowledges the continuity between her own substance and that of the rosemary—both, that is, have been in contact with Rinaldo. Like a posy, she has been trafficked and, like the rosemary, exposed to infection. Frizaldo's fear of contagion fails to draw any distinction between the circulation of women, of plants, and of desire. And, he may be right: Whetstone's narrative and contemporary fictions are driven by the fungibility of these different orders of matter. Giletta, too, then—from a position inside these dynamics of circulation—has proved a canny reader of romantic narrative. She knows that both the value she offers and the danger she threatens emerge in traffic.

Buds

Juliet is the figure in the play most bound by sites of layered enclosure: within Verona's walls, within the Capulet compound, in her bedroom, the Friar's cell, the tomb. To catch sight of Juliet, Romeo breaches the garden wall, an entrance that casts Juliet as a *hortus conclusus*, a biblical and medieval walled garden and a conventional figure of virginity.[33] The play's language also repeatedly links her with smallness, registered in the miniaturization that closes both her first name and her family name.[34] In the first two scenes, Juliet and Romeo are both compared by their fathers to buds, images that seem to fix the two children in seasonally overdetermined developmental narratives. But there is something off in each case. Montague worries that Romeo is

> to himself so secret and so close,
> So far from sounding and discovery

As is the bud bit with an envious worm
Ere he can spread his sweet leaves to the air,
Or dedicate his beauty to the same.
                    (1.1.147–151)[35]

This image of Romeo recalls the narcissism of the young man in Sonnet 1, who, the sonnet accuses, "Within thine owne bud buriest thy content"—a paradox that, like the Friar's, joins the antonyms of budding and burying. Montague, like Sonnet 1, accuses the young man of refusing to circulate, or (in an image that ironically suggests Romeo's Petrarchan poetic ventures) to "spread his sweet leaves to the air." In the scene that follows, Capulet promises to circulate young buds, as he invites Paris to enjoy the potential energy of budding young women:

Such comfort as do lusty young men feel
When well-apparelled April on the heel
Of limping winter treads, even such delight
Among fresh fennel buds shall you this night
Inherit at my house.
                    (1.2.25–29)

While Q1 reads "fresh female buds," the Second Quarto calls these "fresh fennell buds"—a reading that lends an even more specific savor of springtime to Capulet's invitation.[36] In these fresh buds, "vertue" and verdancy are packed together.

In Capulet's invitation, Juliet is one among many fresh buds on view—one who, her father worries, remains two summers short of being ripe for marriage. In this context, Capulet's use of "inherit" for the experience of delight he promises Paris is especially striking: in the scene, his word choice posits the act of hospitality as a substitute for the immediate offer of his daughter's hand. But the sense of "inherit" slips easily from its syntactic attachment to "such delight" to an offer that Paris should take possession of the buds themselves; located by Capulet "at my house," this inheritance would amount to a presumptuous act of occupation, a premature breaking open of the Capulet family line. In the Second Quarto and Folio texts, Capulet has said of his daughter just several lines earlier that "Earth hath swallowed all my hopes but she, / Shees the hopefull Lady of my earth"—a phrase that anglicizes a French term meaning "heiress."[37]

Capulet's association of Juliet with earth and with real property makes her later transformation into something more fluid in her father's eyes that much more arresting. Like Friar Laurence's picture of the "infant rind of this weak flower," Juliet promises to body forth the overwhelming force of a tiny form. Capulet echoes this antinomy of scale when he observes the intensity of her tears:

> How now, a conduit, girl? What, still in tears,
> Evermore showering? In one little body
> Thou counterfeits a bark, a sea, a wind,
> For still thy eyes, which I may call the sea,
> Do ebb and flow with tears. The bark thy body is,
> Sailing in this salt flood; the winds thy sighs,
> Who, raging with thy tears and they with them,
> Without a sudden calm will overset
> Thy tempest-tossed body.
> (3.5.129–137)

In Capulet's description of her "one little body," we hear a distinctly paternal combination of condescension, aggression, and tenderness: his shock at that little body carried by this great flood of tears. Naming the smallness of Juliet next to the oceanic tide of her feelings, Capulet reads her "little body" as a kind of materialized poem, a piece of rhetoric in which are blazoned three commonplaces of erotic poetry: bark, sea, wind.[38] These lines further index the body of the actor: the kind of body that counterfeits things, that plays (even within an infant rind) a conduit for greater passion. Finally, we can hear in Capulet's words his horror that she is being carried *away from him* on this flood—a conduit pouring outward from the enclosure of family and home.

As he recognizes Juliet's resistance in the lines that follow, Capulet's anxious fixation on his daughter's scale and circulation increases in violence. He more cruelly derides her smallness: Calling her "Mistress Minion" (151), he threatens to cast her out in the streets, leaving her, like an animal, to graze out-of-doors. He rewrites her fluidity as a property of disposability: "Or I will drag thee on a hurdle thither. / Out, you green-sickness carrion! Out, you baggage, / You tallow-face!"[39] In her disobedience, Juliet seems to her father a diminutive without "dear import" or charge, deprived of childhood latency and dispossessed of the future her feminine virtue seemed to guarantee.

Capulet's imagination, however, does not set the horizon for how Juliet or her body is figured in the play—which, as I have suggested, tends to appraise its mobilia and minutiae not by their status as property but by their capacity for future action. Recall the Nurse's account of tetchy baby Juliet, the small thing (a "pretty fool") at war with the dug touched with wormwood. Or Juliet's own account of her "I" that is not "I" but that still wields the virtuous force of a cockatrice. The play, in the end, shows Verona to be remarkably confused about Juliet's value. When Capulet invites Paris to the party, he suggests that he compare Juliet to other "female buds," but by a metric that has proven something of a crux to editors: in the First Quarto,

> heare all, all see,
> And like her most, whose merite most shalbe.
> Such amongst view of many myne beeing one,
> May stand in number though in reckoning none.[40]

With this instruction, Capulet ambivalently upholds and deflates her value: with her father's allusion to a proverb by which one is not a number, Juliet seems instead one among many, or first among many, but by the same logic also no number at all. The riddle of her appraisal recurs in the final moments of the play, as Montague promises to erect her statue in gold,

> That whiles *Verona* by that name is knowne,
> There shall no figure at such rate be set,
> As that of true and faithfull *Juliet*.[41]

Juliet stands as the value, still uncalculated, against which lesser values are measured—a use of "set" that acknowledges the invention of value by collective agreement. Both fathers, then, assess her meaning by her adjacent surroundings, such that Juliet acts as a kind of zero, a figure that inflates value only when next to another figure, but whose value is otherwise incalculable or unintelligible. In moments like these, we can see how Juliet's *vertue* and Juliet's *value* diverge. While Capulet and Montague figure Juliet's value (her "merite" and "rate") comparatively, by setting her alongside like and unlike things, "vertue" gains force as matter out-of-place, as the small forms of virtue in the play (including Juliet herself) travel across walls and settings.

The play never allows Juliet's value to be set while she is alive; it is only in death, in the mystified form of this statue, that she performs the essential function of the traffic in women, as the object of transaction that binds the two feuding families. Instead, throughout the play, linked to the hyperbolic capacities of conduit and cockatrice, she has resisted being "set" in any number of ways. To this degree, the play's traffic in small things runs contrary to the ends of the traffic in women, especially as those transactions serve to bind kinship and state forms through the telos of heterosexual marriage.[42] But that is not the whole story. In the examples we have considered so far, virtue has had an unstable relation to transactional value: on the one hand, printers and herbalists count on the resilience of virtue as it circulates, as an assurance of the force of plant or book when trafficked to new users. On the other hand, that same indifference to human interests empowers latent virtues to resist the terms and ends that those transactions set. In other words, the very qualities users most want from virtuous things are those capable of most powerfully frustrating them. By this view, up until nearly the end of the play, *Romeo and Juliet*'s traffic in small things dislocates authority, sending these tiny deputies of material power into the streets and out of the house. There, their fates (and rates) are unset, subject to the creaturely world of accident and interruption.

But, despite being indifferent to human ends, virtues are not insulated from human politics. They simply belong to a political cosmology that is not limited to the human—one that, instead, incorporates multiple kinds of power, possessed by a more miscellaneous anthology of animal, vegetable, and literary constituents.[43] As Whetstone's Giletta reminded us, and as Gayle Rubin and Eve Kosofsky Sedgwick forcefully showed for the case of the traffic in women, the traffic in small things is fundamentally asymmetrical.[44] The perks of subject- and objecthood, of activity and passivity, are not evenly distributed across all who participate. On this other field of traffic, we might also ask what asymmetries obtain in the circulation of plants, poisons, poems, girls, boys, words, paper, and power. Just how indifferent are the dynamics of circulation and substitution in *Romeo and Juliet* to the particularities of different kinds of materials and the rates at which they are set? What are the wages of traffic, and for whom?

Part II of *Botanical Poetics* will pose these questions to an important cohort of plant books, poetic gatherings of flowers all published in the 1570s; these case studies give us an opportunity to track the sway of plant capacities in situated accounts of poetic, erotic, and vegetable circulation.

PART II

Scattered, Sown, Slipped

Printed Gardens in the 1570s

CHAPTER 3

Sundry Flowers by Sundry Gentlemen

Among the diverse range of botanically named collections published during Elizabeth's reign can be found a discrete but significant subset of miscellanies from the 1570s: all including poems by members of the Inns of Court, all named for flowers or gardens, and all drawing on a shared set of rhetorical and visual conventions. The most influential of these was George Gascoigne's 1573 *A Hundreth Sundrie Flowres*, which inspired imitations like John Grange's 1577 *Golden Aphroditis*, to which was appended what he or the printer called a poetical garden, Timothy Kendall's *Flowers of Epigrammes* (1577), and George Whetstone's *Rocke of Regard* (1576), composed of sections including a "Castle of delight," "Garden of Unthriftinesse," "Arbour of Vertue," and "Ortchard of Repentance." Gascoigne's collection was preceded by Hugh Plat's 1572 *Floures of Philosophie*, which, like all of these other examples, included a mixture of prose and verse, and advertised to its readers the profitable and delightful variety of its contents.[1]

We can tie each of these poets directly to the Inns of Court and their environs: Gascoigne was a member of Gray's Inn; Plat of Lincoln's Inn. Kendall belonged to Staple Inn, the Inn of Chancery attached to Gray's Inn; Whetstone to Furnival's Inn, the Inn of Chancery attached to Lincoln's Inn; and, though his specific affiliation is unknown, Grange is described in his book as a "student in the common lawe of Englande." With the exception of Gascoigne, who was born twenty years earlier, each of these poets was likely born in the 1550s and saw a humanist education in the schoolroom and university before arriving at the Inns in the 1570s as young men. There, they contributed to a surge in the membership rolls of the all-male legal societies that occurred during the 1560s and 1570s, a period that coincided with a moment of great literary productivity in the Inns and their environs.[2]

The gardens and flowers of these young lawyers draw from a tight set of
rhetorical conventions, including the assortment of material in the volume,
their modes of addressing and inviting the reader, and the centrality of answer poems and other occasional verse explicitly composed in the company
of friends. Their prefatory materials are cast from the same stock figures of
bad readers and—perhaps most strikingly—common figurative topographies:
gardens, arbors, and castles. Even their graphic and material forms draw af-
filiations between these titles, as may be seen in Figures 11–13. To each other
and to potential customers, these volumes' figurative patterns and bordered
title pages signaled bonds of community. Individual volumes, though, were
hardly homogeneous. Their contents are highly miscellaneous, each containing some combination of verse and prose—some offering proverbial wisdom, many including narrative romance. But all feature a gathering of lyric
poems, often set off from its prose surrounds by a divisional title page or separate heading, and often thematically and biographically cordoned as the
product of youthful errancy.

These conventions register in bibliographic and literary form the affilia-
tions that have led scholars to view this generation of Inns men as a distinctive
cohort. As Jessica Winston shows in her comprehensive treatment of the
culture of the Elizabethan Inns, these middle years of Elizabeth's reign represent a highwater mark of the Inns' cultural production, as their literary culture reflected the first full-fledged products of humanist education.[3] Many
of these poets belong to the cohort that Richard Helgerson identifies as the
first generation of Elizabethan prodigals, poets committed to rewriting
the scene of their upbringing within narratives of transgression and waste.
Helgerson understands these literary experiments in light of a finite economy of social roles; shaped by a moment when there simply are not enough
useful places to be putting their useful education, their fictions of literary
production reflect a surplus of educated people with a surfeit of training and
nothing to do with it.[4] The idle pleasures of poetic gardens offer both an outlet
and a figure for that prodigal errancy, a turn from the profitable prescriptions of Tudor governance for self and state to the pleasures of poetry.

For all their performance of social collectivity, however, these collections
were issued in print and made available for sale to readers outside that community, beyond the walls of the Inns and their gardens. This chapter will show
how printed poetic gardens accommodate and stage the competing drives
that result from these textual double lives—toward community and cohesion,
on the one hand, and toward prodigality, errancy, and danger, on the other.[5]

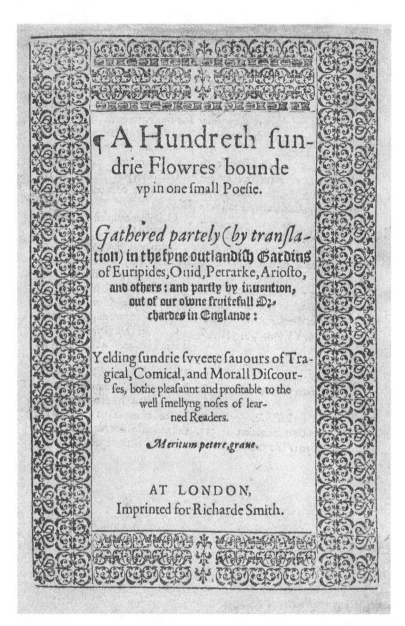

¶ A Hundreth fun-
drie Flowres bounde
vp in one fmall Poefie.

Gathered partely (by tranfla-
tion) in the fyne outlandifh Gardins
of Euripides, Ouid, Petrarke, Ariofto,
and others: and partly by inuention,
out of our owne fruitefull Orchardes in Englande:

Yelding fundrie fvveete fauours of Tra-
gical, Comical, and Morall Difcour-
fes, bothe pleafaunt and profitable to the
well fmellyng nofes of lear-
ned Readers.

Meritum petere, graue.

AT LONDON,
Imprinted for Richarde Smith.

Figure 11. George Gascoigne, *A Hundreth Sundrie Flowres Bounde up in One Small Poesie* (London: Imprinted [by Henry Bynneman and Henry Middleton] for Richard Smith, 1573), title page. RB 59894, The Huntington Library, San Marino, California.

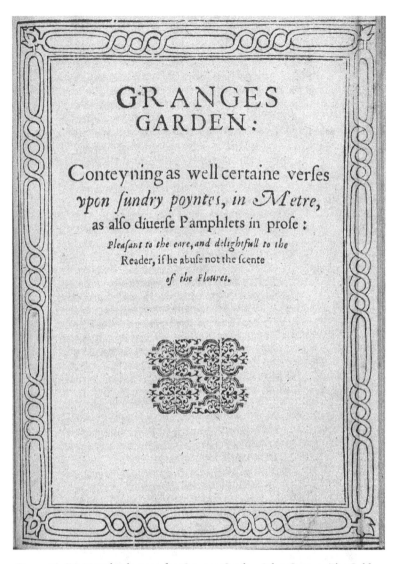

GRANGES
GARDEN:

Conteyning as well certaine verſes
ypon ſundry poyntes, in Metre,
as alſo diuerſe Pamphlets in proſe :

Pleaſant to the eare, and delightfull to the
Reader, if he abuſe not the ſcente
of the Flowres.

Figure 12. Divisional title page for *Granges Garden*. John Grange, *The Golden Aphroditis* (London: Henry Bynneman, 1577) sig. O.iʳ. RB 61156, The Huntington Library, San Marino, California.

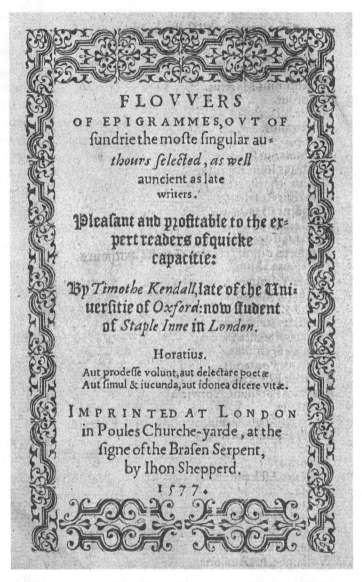

Figure 13. Timothy Kendall, *Flowers of Epigrammes* (London: John Shepperd, 1577), title page. RB 61897, The Huntington Library, San Marino, California.

Winston argues that the Inns' cultural activity in the late sixteenth century worked to mold a collective professional identity, a creative and ideological project served, for example, by the frequency with which poets respond to one another in allusions and answer poems.[6] The close echoes among botanically organized collections represent another way in which such connections are forged, as poets pick up and transform one another's language, signaling affiliation by trafficking in the shared figurative economy of plants. In these extended and infinitely extendable metaphors, botanical forms render the movements of circulation within the friendly gift economy of poetic slips, as poets invite readers into the garden to sample and borrow. They also provide the figurative stuff of these borrowings, their frequent repetitions from poet to poet helping to limn the contours of this imitative literary community. These forms of association turn on questions about the shared materiality of plants and books; and, in these negotiations, what "materiality" means will come down to what it means for matter to survive, to last, or to be eradicated, especially under conditions of mechanical reproduction and collective consumption.

In the cases I consider here, the affiliation between garden and book turns on a tense tug-of-war between figures of enclosure and figures of circulation: of plants, poems, and people, whether within the boards of a book, the gates of a garden, or the walls of the Inns themselves. Each botanical collection within this subgroup shares a set of core rhetorical gestures that straddles enclosure and dispersal. The first is an image of frictionless circulation and free exchange—embodied in the texts by an open invitation to gentle readers, a generosity that accords with the generic expectations and humanist codes of genteel friendships between men. These works link magnanimity to the miscellaneity of the work itself, and the attendant autonomy of individual, borrowable pieces. The second gesture is a recurrent image of danger: each of these poets, as he addresses his readers, worries about the harm that might come to his garden—how its flowers might be plucked, wasted, consumed, or trampled. These images of destruction extend the floral metaphor to the point of abuse, leaving its tenor stubbornly ambiguous: What would it mean for a far-flung reader to "waste" the book? Is it a single copy that a reader might consume or dismember? How would that violence redound against the author—or against the "root" of a text? Precisely what kind of "bad reading" is at stake?

In these collections, botanical metaphor holds out a promise to resolve an implicit but fundamental tension between the enclosure of the book or garden and the circulation of its pieces. Provided a restricted sphere of circulation, the enclosure of the garden and the generative transmission of slips were by no means incompatible: the bibliographical garden and the circulation of texts could be depicted in concert as an idealized version of the homosocial space of the Inns of Court—a universe imagined in terms of lack of constraint, free exchange among equals, circulation without friction or loss. At the same time, the unpredictable itineraries of the printed book—who knows in whose hands it could end up?—challenged the cloistered sphere on which these coteries imaginatively depended. The homosocial world of the Inns of Court, from Googe and Turberville in the 1560s to John Donne in the 1590s to the poetic miscellanies of the 1620s and 1630s, depended on manuscript circulation among friends.[7] And, many publications by Inns men thematize the interaction of manuscript and print, often embedding it within elaborate fictions: in narratives that turn on the circulation of paper slips; in fictions about the genesis of the book in friendly manuscript exchanges; and in doubled addresses to patrons and ordinary readers.[8] However, these lawyer-poets of the 1570s also went into print, and their texts reflect an attunement to the social and imaginative consequences of that venture. My intention here is not to speculate about their motivations for doing so, but to examine the textual forms (and the contortions of textual materiality and poetic subjectivity) to which their encounters with print gave rise.

In a 1951 article, J. W. Saunders influentially argued that Tudor poets, in publishing verse, worried about marring their reputations with what he called "the stigma of print." Saunders's thesis has been significantly challenged and revised in the decades since its publication. But the imagination of reputational harm—and sometimes vivid rhetoric of injury in which it is rendered—is difficult to ignore, even for the poets considered here, whose lives and literary activities were by and large at the periphery of the aristocratic poetic contexts in which Saunders was most interested.[9] For these Inns of Court poets, the imagination of harm is ubiquitous: shaping their apologies for youthful prodigality, the elaborate fictions in which they explain the escape of pages from an author's hand and their illicit path to the print shop, and the floral conceits in which they frame their books. For these poets, stigma operated less as a repressive force than as an occasion for the proliferation of *more*: more conceits, more epistles, more poems, more books. The poets in this chapter suggest an alternate account of textual economy, one that measures literary production not according to regulation but by copious proliferation.

This is not, however, a happy economy of friction-free traffic. The copious and proliferative energy of botanical rhetoric also reinscribes, thematizes, and multiplies the fantasized violence of print publication. The forms in which verse proliferated leave their mark on how we encounter both textual materiality and poetic subjectivity. They shape in turn a complex account of poetic authorship—one marked by risk, injury, uprooting, deracination. Circulation, it turns out, has its costs. As they portray the collision of an imaginary enclosed garden with the circumstances of print circulation, mid-Elizabethan poets confront a complementary act of imaginary violence.

Making Space

Each of these Inns of Court collections from the 1570s is marked by two core gestures. First, an image of free exchange and circulation—embodied in the texts by an open invitation to gentle readers. This version of liberality follows the generic expectations and humanist codes of genteel friendships between men—the virtuous display of hospitality and magnanimity, the invitation to borrow anything, whether language or flowers. These works key this readerly freedom to the work's internal variety. As George Gascoigne's *A Hundreth Sundrie Flowres* (1573) promises, a reader "shall not be constreind" to approach the flowers in any order, or to bother with those they do not care for. The second gesture, coming quickly on the tail of the first, is a recurrent image of danger: each of these poets, as he addresses his readers, worries about the harm that might come to his garden—how its flowers may be plucked, wasted, consumed, or trampled.

At their openings, then, these poetic collections reflect a tension between enclosure and access that echoes the duality I have described throughout these chapters: the form of plant books, I have argued, plays out a dialectic between gathering and dispersal, between the bound book and its scattered pages. In this chapter, this elemental doubleness is rewritten as a social problem: a negotiation of who has access and how. A common motif in books with horticultural titles and in the practice and politics of husbandry, enclosure was both a practical and textual concern in Elizabethan England. Debates over the enclosure of the commons would have been familiar to these young lawyers, as would the series of Tudor laws intended, without great success, to mitigate the force of the social and economic changes associated with it. Instructional works like Thomas Tusser's *Hundreth Good Pointes of Husbandrie* (initially published in 1557, but first including an explicit discussion of enclosure in the edition of 1573) and John Fitzherbert's *Boke of Husbandrie* (published in at least twenty sixteenth-century editions) addressed the enclosure of land for planting and grazing.[10] Even in London, away from the fields that were the subject of these debates, the physical enclosure of gardens and other plots was a growing concern to landowners, including the Inns of Court themselves, whose territory at the center of London seemed ever more encroached upon by the growing city around them.

These dynamics left their mark on each of the books that this chapter considers, but the most assertive boundaries may be found in Hugh Plat's *Floures of Philosophie* (1572). Plat published his *Floures* as a young man just out of university, likely within a year of the time he went down to London from Cambridge and was admitted to Lincoln's Inn. From its invocation of floral pieces to its invitation to freely borrow, its ornamented title page to its combination of advice and poetry, Plat's *Floures* shares many conventions with other flower books published by young members of the Inns. The work is structured around a balance of pleasure and profit: opening with a collection of moralizing Senecan sentences, before turning to a gathering of verse with the running head "The Pleasures of Poetry." When he arrives at this section of verse, Plat shows a special concern with regulating access. Though he opens with an advertisement of its amenities, he concludes with a warning: the final poem is entitled, "For whom this booke was made especially, and whom the Author excepteth from reading it." Those seeking delight or profit ("pleasant" or "wholesome" herbs) are free to gather:

> Of every thing I graunte him some
>   that in my grounde doth growe:
> And him I give free leave likewise,
>   whome hope of gaine doth bring.[11]

Plat's hospitality, however, has a limit; other readers meet a much colder welcome.

In the concluding poem, Plat's gentlemanly liberality is couched within an aggressive fantasy of control. Plat takes a strong stance on the security and enclosure of his garden, enlisting its (apparently enchanted) hardware in his program of selective exclusion: "I have preparde," he writes,

a gate both greate and strong,
    To some it opes, to some it shuts,
        that walkes this way along.

But the gate's insult to hospitality is the less fearsome of the deterrents Plat describes:

A thornie hedge I have preparde
    al craftie theeves to fraye.
And least that no man durst assay,
    for feare of thornie bushe,
And prickles piercing of his fleshe,
    within my grounde to rushe.[12]

Plat's repetition of "I have preparde" frames these features of the gardens as provisions that he—a good husbandman—has made against the possibility of bad readers. As any gardening book would instruct him, he orients his conception of security firmly in the direction of future time, installing measures intended to ward off readers who represent the worst-case scenario of destructive bad faith. But who are those worst-case-scenario readers, and what scenarios do they bring? Such "craftie theeves" are caterpillars or worms, parasites who might "waste the tree." Plat's disarmingly alliterative security measures are also remarkably violent, as he threatens, with his thorny bush, to pierce the flesh of abusive readers.[13] But he also never specifies precisely what act would constitute abuse: if bad readers are parasites, what do they destroy?

A reader approaching Plat's text thus faces a potential conundrum. Plat, as we will also see in the case of John Grange, floats an image of abuse that only ambiguously maps onto possible behavior. How do you waste a tree or a poem that exists in dozens or hundreds of copies? His readers in turn encounter a dilemma of both reference and address: Am *I* a caterpillar, they ask? Will *my* flesh be pierced by prickles? Even Plat's method of discrimination suggests a sameness between good and bad readers: of his gate, he writes, "To *some* it opes, to *some* it shuts" (my italics). Though less vivid than his caterpillar, Plat's repetition of "some" similarly leans on the operation of ambiguity. Like Gascoigne's use of "some" and "sundry" in his prefaces and poems, which will be discussed below, Plat invokes a diversity of readers without ever pinning down their identities. He even names them with the same word. This ambiguity throws the hermeneutic encounter into a dilemma of legitimacy in which readers might wonder whether they belong or whether they should fear "prickles piercing of [their] fleshe." Boasting of the leave he gives a (good) reader, Plat approaches readerly liberty not through practical attempts to constrain, but by inventing disciplinary fictions. In the present tense of Plat's textual address, the threat is the point. The reader is left to ask, *who, me?*

In a quite unmetaphorical sense, the Inns of Court faced the logistical and political struggle of enclosing land with new urgency in the 1560s and 1570s. London grew rapidly in the later sixteenth century, and, in response to the encroachment of nonmembers on their lands, the Inns built up walls around their gardens and upped enforcement of rules about access.[14] As Paula Henderson's analysis of the Inns' records shows, gardeners took on additional responsibility for security during Elizabeth's reign.[15] Lincoln's Inn records a payment to their gardener in 1562 to add a lock to the garden gate—a lock that would have been familiar to Hugh Plat, who was a member of that Inn.[16] At the same time, gardeners were charged with keeping out rogues, bad children, and "sluttish" laundresses. As London became a city with ever-scarcer open space, with access to refreshment and recreation restricted, gardeners became not just cultivators of ground but enforcers of boundaries. Wenceslaus Hollar's map of London (ca. 1660) shows that laundresses would continue to achieve some success in the struggle for available ground: in the more expansive space of Lincoln's Inn Fields, small figures can be seen laying out sheets and garments.[17]

I do not draw on these descriptions of institutional practices and accounts of the use and enclosure of actual gardens to try to offer explanatory ground for the range of metaphors that appear in these texts. As I argued in Chapter 1, landscape architecture, like poetic gardens and printed borders, deploys boundaries to give spaces form, marking off interior and exterior and leading its visitors across patterns of division and differentiation. The Inns during this period were engaged in a project of self-definition that impressed itself on the urban landscape, but which was no less fictive or imaginative for that fact. The legal historian Paul Raffield has described the architectural ambitions of the Inns under Elizabeth in similar terms—as an attempt to give form to a fictive and constitutionally imagined corporate body. Raffield finds this creative world-making at work not just in legal texts and in literary production, but in the material forms of these communities, from the architecture of the Inns to their suppertime rituals. Joined in the project of realizing an ideal commonwealth built on a belief in common law, their utopian impulse,

Raffield writes, was "given permanence and visibility in the physical struc-ture of the Inns."[18] As Laurie Shannon argues, the Inns' literary production enacts a social and imaginative experiment in "horizontal nationhood"—a form of political community organized perpendicularly to the vertical power of the sovereign, one that in itself assembled a kind of "alternative polity."[19]

We can also, as I have suggested above, see the work of enclosure and af-filiation performed by the material forms of printed texts, including the vi-sual substrate of their title pages. Each of the books I have mentioned features an ornamentally bordered title page—a two-dimensional performance of the thingness of the book. As Frances Dolan argues, such borders work like quickset hedges to make the book a space, transforming scattered leaves to a coherent object.[20] They are in this sense as fictional as the narratives the pages contain, or as the elaborate tales of manuscript circulation unspooled in their prefaces.[21] Together, the spatial formation of the page and the metaphor of the garden frame an abstract conceptual field in which reader and text en-counter one another. This is not to say that either refer directly back to *actual* gardens, or that the winding lineaments of printers' ornaments reach out toward worldly vines. All, however, are engaged in the work of enclosure, dis-crimination, and world-building to which these books commit themselves.

The optimism of such a labor, however, is not absolute. The breach repre-sented by publication potentially troubles the utopian enclosure that the Inns might otherwise hold out. Though it seems, on the one hand, to extend the optimism of the Inns' constitutional logic outward to a broader sphere (one can imagine a certain hopefulness about this kind of open-ended address), the fact of publication also breaks the terms of friendship that had cemented that logic in the first place. Even as textual gardens play out this imaginary logic of constitutional polity and free circulation, images of vegetable and po-etic destruction suggest a more pessimistic underside to these same fantasies.

Loose Bindings

Faced with the potentially disquieting anonymity of print publication, col-lections authored by these young male poets boldly advertise license, liberty, or leave: they invite readers to take whatever they like from their garden, to proceed in the order they like, to skip the bits that don't please them and move on to the bits that do. As they imagine possible futures for themselves, each of these examples anticipates a history of its own reading, wrestling along

the way with the internal contradiction that Roger Chartier has identified at
the center of any such history: a dyadic pull between the conflicting forces of
liberty and constraint.[22] How much are readers bound by the demands a text
makes on them (for example, by prescribing the order in which to approach
the contents of the book), and how much are they free to disobey, improvise,
or repurpose the stuff of which the book is made? These fictions are speculative and reflexive, as books elaborately imagine possible futures for themselves
(as we saw in Chapter 1, often in the language of harvest, yield, or redispersal).
They are also explicit negotiations of power, oscillating ambivalently between the performance of submission and the assertion of control. In the
stories these books tell about their own materiality and reception, plant-
thinking sows a persistent concern with the textual survival and proliferation across these unknown landscapes of reception.

Each collection begins by addressing and welcoming in a reader. John
Grange, in his *Golden Aphroditis*, (as we will see at greater length below) offers "free liberty at your wisedomes pleasure to croppe ech floure therin":
"Your choyce is not great, yet chuse what likes you best, the worst turne backe
againe."[23] Hugh Plat grants "free leave" to those who seek profit in his garden, to choose and take the herbs that grow there.[24] George Whetstone makes
a similar note in the preface to his *Rocke of Regard*, reaffirmed in commendatory poems by Abraham Fleming and by John Wytton. Fleming's invitation applies specifically to the "Garden of Unthriftinesse," the section of the
Rocke most like a gathering of short verse:

Who wisheth for vauntage, to vewe and behold,
Unthriftines Garden where weedes do abound,
Hee hath leave to enter, and is not controld,
T'examine the nature of that gracelesse ground:
But so let him medle, with prudence prepard,
That still hee remember the *Rock* of *Regard*.

Wytton echoes the language of "leave" in memorable fourteeners:

And for to vewe this gallant soyle, you freely leave may take,
Roame round about, take what you list, but see no spoyle you make.[25]

These invitations extend the protocols of hospitality to the space of the book:
welcoming the stranger, sharing, offering sustenance and comfort. As acts

of hospitality, they also serve to make the garden a space—specifically, by inviting a stranger to breach its boundary. This often-repeated invitation draws on humanist conceptions of free speech between friends who, as Erasmus's adage goes, hold all things in common. It also calls upon the liberty of speech that was seen as a pillar of good governance, a course of thought that Shannon has traced through the norms of male homosociality.[26] In the garden, this use of liberty bridges two distinct senses: the active generosity and hospitality of liberality, performed by the poet and printer; and the liberty of the reader, understood as a lack of restraint.[27] Poet and/or printer advertise that they cannot, and will not, control the reader's path through the book.

The rhetoric of license, liberty, and leave also calls upon a specifically poetic lineage, a tradition of poetic license that, as Heather James shows, was animated by an engagement with Ovid and his imitators.[28] In a twist on the deployment of the classical ideal of *parrhesia* and the ostensible liberty of poets to speak freely and fictionally, these garden poets emphasize not their own license but that of the reader. The effect remains the same: by placing final responsibility for moral harm on the readers' shoulders, these writers insulate themselves from accusations of immorality. But it is noteworthy nonetheless that these accounts of poetic license—even in their boldest moments—operate not by explicitly claiming their own freedoms, but by granting leave to readers to make their own order and their own meaning. Freedom is exercised at the scene of reception, not of composition.[29]

The most influential and elaborate articulation of this dynamic appears in Gascoigne's *Hundreth Sundrie Flowres*, which includes both a defense of the work's miscellaneous content and a series of letters narrating the manuscript's convoluted course to the printing house. When reissued in 1575 as *The Posies of George Gascoigne Esquire*, the volume was prefaced with an apology for the offense caused by the previous (apparently scandalous) edition.[30] The edition of 1573 is nowhere attributed to Gascoigne (though some individual poems bear his name); rather, the work as a whole is presented as a corporate text, an assemblage of sundry pieces of poetry, prose, and drama, fictionally composed by sundry gentlemen on sundry occasions. As Susan Staub has pointed out, Gascoigne's articulations of variety, pleasure, and artifice closely track the Elizabethan imagination of the garden on which he draws.[31] "Sundry" is the governing term of the collection as a whole, attached both to its formal miscellaneity and to the social world of its production: in the title, naming the "hundreth sundrie flowres" themselves, the "sundrie sweete savours" they yield, and appearing again to name the gathering of

verse within the "divers excellent devises of sundry Gentlemen."[32] The multiplication of preliminaries follows the multiplication of these gentlemen: a
series of letters allegedly tracks the manuscripts' movement from friend to
friend, a path eventually leading (against the will of the initial gatherer)
to the printshop.[33]

The portion of the *Flowres'* introduction ostensibly written by the printer
advertises the work's composite quality according to an aesthetic argument
of liberality: the reader is instructed to proceed in whatever order he or she
likes, gathering whatever flowers the reader most fancies. Inviting the reader
to approach the work in fragments, the epistle from the printer to the reader
promises a piecemeal reading strategy that yields "a greater commoditie
than common poesies have ben accustomed to present." Gathering flowers
as they wish, readers "shall not be constreined to smell of the floures therein
conteined all at once, neither yet to take them up in such order as they are
sorted: But you may take any one flowre by itselfe, and if that smell not so
pleasantly as you wold wish, I doubt not yet but you may find some other
which may supplie the defects thereof." Following the book's mixed formal
composition, the injunction to pluck and gather cedes to the singularity of
readerly taste. "The worke," the epistle concludes, "is so universall, as either in
one place or other, any mans mind may therewith by satisfied."[34] Its "places"
and "flowers" in supplemental relationship, each promises to supply any defect in the other, effectively underwriting an insurance policy for textual
satisfaction guaranteed by the vigor of the book's variety.[35]

This aesthetic advertisement, however, is couched within the frame of a
moral defense, and the *Flowres* slip easily between the two registers and purposes. The printer begins his epistle by addressing the questionable circumstances of its procurement, protesting that he found nothing amiss in the
volume other than two or three "wanton places passed over in the discourse
of an amourous enterprise"—a reference to *The Adventures of Master F.J.*, in
which (he goes on) the words are "cleanly" even if "the thing ment be somewhat naturall." Second, the printer argues, even such "naturall" moments are
not entirely frivolous, since "the well minded man may reape some commoditie out of the most frivolous workes that are written." If a reader fails to reap
in this way, the burden of failure rests entirely on his or her shoulders, just as
the venomous spider sucks poison from "the most holesome herbe" and the
industrious bee gathers honey "out of the most stinking weede."[36]

Gascoigne's herbal lexicon of scent and savor echoes the preface to *Songes
and Sonettes* (1557) but puts these figures to new uses. Tottel's preface makes

demands on those unprepared to properly read the book, asking "the un-learned, by reding to learne to bee more skilfull, and to purge that swinelike grossenesse, that maketh the swete majerome not to smell to their delight."[37] Its sociological outlook entails (most optimistically) a practice of assimila-tion, with the volume itself standing as exemplary model of literary and lit-erate citizenship. While Tottel prescribes a course of purgation to those readers who do not find a smell to their liking, the epistle to *A Hundreth Sun-drie Flowres* invites readers to simply move on to another sample they might enjoy more. Turning from the didactic frame of Tottel's epistle, the variety of Gascoigne's work obviates Tottel's more directive suggestion of self-correction and improvement.

In promising a lack of constraint between text and reader, the first epis-tle compels neither an order of reading nor a single moral message. This for-giving liberality in turn removes agency from the book itself, rendering its bouquet of sundry flowers a storehouse from which the reader might pluck at will. The result is a vision of the text in pieces—first, in the arbitrary (or at least nonbinding) arrangement of textual parts in the volume, and, ultimately, in its centrifugal piecing out by individual readers. The structure of the work does not merely enable but actively demands a set of nonidentical readings, of diverse approaches and departures. The "sundrie" of the volume's title, given hierarchical precedence on the title page above the "posie" that binds the flowers, names the scattered origins of its pieces as well as the scattered versions into which it will be sundered in readers' consumption.

This open-ended invitation has its costs, however, as becomes clear in the series of letters introducing the volume.[38] These documents, each signed only with initials, tell the story of the contents' path to press, registering the cir-culation of poetic slips and scraps within a closed homosocial circle: written by men, compiled by men, and circulated within a community of men like Gascoigne and his fellow members at Gray's Inn. Like other printed gather-ings of poetry, the collection is introduced as written slips or leaves lent to an intimate friend, who bears responsibility for delivering them to the printer against the wishes of the initial gatherer.[39] This once trusted friend, the man-uscript's initial procurer, notes that in choosing to publish he is counting on public good—the "common commodity"—at the expense of friendship. He makes explicit the terms of his potential loss: if the volume is successful, he writes, "I may then boast to have gained a bushell of good will, in exchange for one pynt of peevish choler." "But if it fal out contrary to expectation," he goes on, "I may then (unlesse [readers'] curtesies supplie my want of discretion)

with losse of some labour, accompt also the losse of my familier friendes."[40]
The very premise of the edition—the fiction of frisson it generates with publication—is this promise of the loss of friends, a deferred betrayal that can be
initiated by any reader who purchases the book. In this sense, the printed
book itself marks the abrupt dissolution of the bonds that generated its
contents—the intimate traffic of manuscript slips within the proverbial enclosed garden of the Inns of Court. Held in a reader's hands, the artifact of
the book stands as witness to and agent of this dissolution.

Circulation, in other words, has its costs—a reality from which the
Flowres' initial vision of liberality and freely circulating flowers and slips is
insulated. Gascoigne tracks the wages of circulation elsewhere in the volume—
most extensively in *The Adventures of Master F.J.*, which assembles and sets
in motion a lively army of slips and poems. As Alan Stewart and Susan Staub
have each argued, *The Adventures of Master F.J.*'s narrative progress turns on
the dangers and dynamics of exposure, in ways that merge sexual and textual politics. *A Hundreth Sundrie Flowres*, Stewart argues, invents a nostal-
gic version of manuscript culture—a fictional intimacy manufactured in
counterpoint to the rupture represented by print publication. Stewart ties
Gascoigne's anxiety about textual circulation to a fixation on "gelding," a term
that aligns lexically and thematically with pruning and plucking, both images central to the bibliographical conceits of the flower books of the 1570s.[41]
Staub argues that *The Adventures of Master F.J.* yokes the reader's role as
voyeur to the role of Lady Frances, who acts as both watcher and castrator in
the narrative. Gascoigne thus articulates in imaginary form his worries
about the loss of control represented by public circulation in the marketplace
of print.[42] By imagining injury alongside fantasies of control, *The Adventures of Master F.J.* gives narrative form to the dynamic that this chapter
tracks across printed gardens: the drive, that is, to imagine those enclosures
according to their breach and transgression.

In Gascoigne's *Flowres*, the potential for injury emanates from the outsized role the poet grants his readers. John Kerrigan describes Gascoigne's
tendency to deflect responsibility and defer to the readers in terms of the
"reader's share"; as he argues, it reflects the condition of print publication at
a moment of increasing circulation and anonymous consumption.[43] Perhaps
the most widespread idiom in which readerly diversity is evoked is through
the word "sundry" and its allies ("divers," "some," and so on). When it appears, it is often doubled: that is, sundry poems or sundry savors are soon
followed by the sundry gentlemen who might read them, or by the sundry

occasions on which they were composed. "Sundry," in other words, is likely to find another "sundry" in its vicinity, as we see in the full title of Gascoigne's 1573 collection. The title performs with great efficiency the "sundryness" that characterizes much printed literature of the middle years of Elizabeth's reign—its condensation from many and sundry to the singular and small(er), the mixture of nations, eras, authors, and genres, the final conversion to a literary language of taste and savor. One epistle promises a collection of "divers discourses and verses, invented uppon sundrie occasions, sundrie gentlemen (in mine opinion) right commendable for their capacitie."[44] Later in Gascoigne's volume, the short verse is gathered in a section called "Devises of Sundrie Gentlemen"; several poems are introduced as "such things as he wrote upon sundrie occasions"; another notes that a poem to a lady is written in "a booke wherein she had collected sundry good ditties of divers mens doing"; another introduces a series of poems by Gascoigne by observing the variation in his identifying mark: "his word or posie he hath often changed and therfore I will deliver his verses with such sundrie posies as I received them."[45]

With their tendency to anatomize the variety of readers, uses of "sundry" and "divers" seem atomistically precise about variety. Nonetheless, both terms pose a problem for the imagination: how do you actually *count* readers? That is, while "sundry" and "some" seem to offer a textured account of particularity, and they indeed gesture toward the existence of particularity in the world, they provide no texture in themselves. Instead, on their own, they accomplish a profound vagueness.[46] The multiplications of "sundry," "some," and "divers" that recur in Elizabethan collections render in everyday English the Erasmian principle of the diversity of human opinion: "Quot homines, tot sententiae." However many men you have, that's how many opinions you'll have. But we are never told how many of each. Though the language of computation seems to suggest that someone, somewhere, is counting, it tells us only about relations: instead of a measurement of quantity, Erasmus offers a more open-ended picture of balanced variety.[47]

This vocabulary enables an elasticity of scale when it comes to the matter, forms, and audiences of printed books. Instead of specifying a population, clustered uses of "sundry," "some," and "divers" lineate relationships among classes of particulars: sundry flowers, sundry gentleman, sundry poems, sundry occasions. George Whetstone advertises the variety of his *Rocke of Regard* by placing repetitions of "divers" in parallel play: the master of a feast should "provide divers dishes, to please the divers appetites of his divers guestes." To paraphrase the proverb: so many guests, that many appetites, and so that many dishes. The well-fittedness of guests to appetites to dishes encompasses a strategy that Whetstone calls "*Decorum* in my doings, as everie desire may be satisfied."[48] A trio of "sundries" introduces a poem in the "Devises of Sundrie Gentlemen" attributed to Gascoigne, but credited to the insistence of "five sundrie gentlemen." It is given this extended title: "I have herde master Gascoignes memorie commended by these verses following, the which were written uppon this occasion. He had (in middest of his youth) determined to abandone all vaine delights and to retourne unto Greyes Inne, there to undertake againe the study of the common lawes. And being required by five sundrie gentlemen to wrighte in verse somwhat worthy to be remembred, before he entred into their felowship, he compiled these five sundry sortes of metre uppon five sundry theames whiche they delivered unto him."[49] As Laurie Shannon points out, the scenario depicts a scene of composite authorship, evidence of the capacity of horizontally organized collectives to "devise." And, it is the symmetric multiplicities of "sundry" that assemble the body of this corporate author: its achieved capacity to form composite bodies, to reach across literary, social, and horticultural registers.[50]

Gascoigne takes his trials of "sundry" into the garden in two other poems included in the "Devises of Sundry Gentlemen." These poems extend the link between his aesthetic of sundry mixture and the social and horticultural terms of the garden. They also make clear how "sundry" inevitably carries the possibility of sundering within it; the pleasures of intermingling also mix in the potential violence of separation. Both poems are introduced as inscriptions found in Gascoigne's garden; as site-specific verse, they renew the invitation to pluck now familiar from the *Flowre*'s prefatory materials. Their physical inscription adds an artifactual reality effect to the voyeurism that often characterizes lyric collections: through the medium of the printed book, the reader has been invited into Gascoigne's garden. At the same time, the nature of that inscription implies that the poet himself may well be absent. The two poems appear in apparent juxtaposition: "Gascoignes gardnings, whereof were written in one end of a close walke which he hath in his Garden, this discourse following," and, immediately following, "In that other ende of his sayde close walke, were written these toyes in ryme."[51] Less occasional verse than found poetry, the poems facing each other across this "close walke" are further opposed by the terms with which they are announced: a "discourse" and "toyes in ryme," a single extended argument and a collection of small pieces. Adjacent on the page and in the garden, these poems place the reader on the path of the "close walke" that cuts between them, a landscape element that was itself associated with intimacy and retreat.[52]

The first, "Gascoignes Gardnings" announces and then elaborates an extended comparison between the garden and the mortal world of humans. The poem is bracketed by "sundry," which anchors the first and last stanzas (and does not appear in the four intervening). In the first, "sundry" is aided by its sidekick, "some," which, scattered through the fifth and sixth lines, punctuate the progress of its exemplary logic:

> The figure of this world I can compare,
> To Garden plots, and such like pleasaunt places,
> The world breedes men of sundry shape and share,
> As herbes in gardens, grow of sundry graces:
> Some good, some bad, some amiable faces,
> Some foule, some gentle, some of froward mind,
> Subject like bloome, to blast of every wind.

Here, "sundry" takes the side of growth: it names the fertile diversity of qualities and virtues that make visible the operation of divinity in the world. The repetitions of "some" effectively sunder garden and world in the syntax of the poem, piecing its "discourse" into a partitioned list. Both words return in the final stanza, to invoke, in a vivid twist on *memento mori*, the "sundrye wayes" that plants and humans might meet their end:

> As for the reste, fall sundrye wayes (God wote)
> Some faynt lyke froathe at every little puffe,
> Some smarte by swoorde, lyke herbes that serve the pot,
> And some be weeded from the fyner stuffe,
> Some stande by proppes to maynteyne all their ruffe.

By the sixth stanza, variety has turned from the first stanza's generative promise to the scythe of mortal contingency. Through the language of falling, Gascoigne links miscellaneity to the workings of accident and occasion: their sundering takes sundry forms, as plants fall (and more precisely here, are felled) in myriad ways.[53]

Gascoigne plays with further variations on the "sums" of these "somes" in the poem that follows, which poses another challenge to the happy liberty of vegetable diversity. In "Gascoignes Gardnings," in which the poet begins by invoking the "figure" of the world, the terms of this comparison are largely visual and detached, its moral message largely contemplative. The "toyes in ryme" of the following poem bring the collection's variety ready to hand. As its inhabitation of the garden moves from a *vita contemplativa* to *activa*, the verse entangles the reader in earthly and fleshly consequences:

> If any floure that there is growne,
> Or any herbe maye ease youre payne,
> Take and accompte it as your owne,
> But recompence the lyke agayne:
> For some and some is honeste playe,
> And so my wyfe taught me to saye.[54]

The stanza repeats the invitation of the prefatory materials to cull and gather at will, but with a different outcome. Imagine accepting an invitation to freely borrow from his garden, and then finding—engraved in the midst—a couplet that sounds an awful lot like threatened payback. Here, Gascoigne's apparent endorsement of textual and floral liberality meets its limit, as a reader may have already discovered delving into the dangerous vagaries of textual circulation in *The Adventures of Master F.J.* or reading further into the poems attached in the "Devises of Sundrie Gentlemen."[55]

The refrain replaces the principle of liberality espoused in the collection's frame with a primitive tenet of economic liberalism: take whatever you like, as long as you pay for it. The *Oxford English Dictionary* lists two senses for the phrase "some and some," the first meaning piecemeal, and the second (attributed first to this poem and then to what is likely a direct quotation from 1583) as denoting an exchange (like "tit for tat"). The "somes" of this refrain (repeated in each of the poem's three stanzas) echo the "somes" of the previous poem, where they mark out the partition of sundry plants and herbs. In the second poem, however, the lexicon of commerce casts a shadow over the idiom, so that we also hear "sum for sum," a quantity exchanged for a quantity, an emphasis less on the piecemealing of the borrowed part than its cumulative (and accumulable) value. "Some" does not only solicit an echo; it anticipates a payment. While the instances of "some" in the previous poem partition identity and difference, the lexicon of difference here shifts to a scene of sexualized commerce. As it assembles an erotic triangle of reader/plucker, poet, and poet's wife, the poem folds all three into multiple economic registers: of sexual relations; credit relations (the debt incurred between friends); and commercial exchange (the amount paid by the owner for the book). Gascoigne will be at pains, in his 1575 apology for the 1573 edition, to insist that he received no payment for the earlier printing: he "never receyved of the Printer, or of anye other, one grote or pennie for the firste Copyes of these Posyes," and should not, therefore, be accused of being "not onely a craftie Broker for the utteraunce of garishe toyes, but a corrupte Merchaunte for the sale of deceyptfull wares."[56] In his own voice, Gascoigne disavows any claim for compensation or payback.

But the intrusion of a quid pro quo is not the only challenge to homosocial liberality that the poem suggests. In this circuit of obligation, it is the wife who is the lawgiver and source of precept, the authority who defines "honeste playe" between the poet and his reader, and between the garden and its visitor. As the enforcer of proverbial economic law, the "wife" of this poem takes on the castrating force that Staub attributes to Lady Frances in *The Adventures of Master F.J.* In Gascoigne's poem, the figure of the wife acts as a scapegoat for the logic of compensation—the force that cuts off and cuts short the pleasures of free traffic. In the framing materials of *A Hundreth Sundrie Flowres*, it is the turn to publication that (as Stewart argues) gelds the poems; here, it is the intrusion of huswifely accounting. In both cases, Gascoigne shows us how the garden's ideal of liberality emerges only in contrast with its other, as a fiction projected backward from a site where that liberty has become impossible.

The Common Weeder: Uprooting Poets

In Chapter 1, we saw how the language of husbandry helped tell a speculative story about textual reception. Like the poets and printers considered there, the subjects of this chapter frame the responsibility of the reader according to their management of the cultivated environment. In this poetic context, however, wildness haunts the central horticultural fiction: the danger that the poetic garden might be unwieldy, overgrown, untamed. Specifically, the image of weeds—which appear frequently in these collections—acts as a kind of ensign, announcing both the freedom of readers to stray and their responsibility to purge. However, the mechanics of weeding bring with them the specter of another kind of violence against text and author. In the botanical idiom in which these books of poems present themselves, the violence that Stewart and Staub describe as "castration" goes instead by the name of "uprooting." As they worry that their flowers might be uprooted, wasted, or consumed, the makers of poetic gardens offer a counterpoint to the more optimistic offers of "liberty" and "leave." While this is as much a rhetorical performance as the hospitable invitation to borrow at will, we should also take seriously the vulnerability of such a posture, alongside the performance of authorial submission that it enacts. Publication always seems to come with the possibility of injury—something these poets and printers do not just acknowledge but advertise. The circulation of poetic flowers follows the structure of this paradox: while license might seem to ensure a free flow of borrowing and recirculation, injury is never far off.

The motif of uprooting was not invented whole cloth by Elizabethan poets. Framing texts as weeded or unweeded was a topos of humanist pedagogical writing, in which, as Mary Thomas Crane shows, readers' practice of skilled weeding ensured the safe importation of pagan classics into the English classroom.[57] It remained commonplace in defenses of poetry that virtuous use is the responsibility of the reader, and abuse a product of reading badly—lasciviously, unskillfully, or otherwise boisterously. (We encountered a specifically pharmaceutical version of this defense in Chapter 2, in Plutarch's account of poetic reception.) In his discourse on English poetry, William Webbe exempts poetry "as it is of it selfe" from claims of unprofitability. Instead, he attributes misuse to the "the ill and undecent provocations, whereof some unbridled witts take occasion by the reading of lacivious Poemes." He concludes with an analogy set in a familiar landscape: "this might be sufficient, that the workes themselves doo not corrupt, but the abuse of the users, who undamaging their owne dispositions by reading the discoveries of vices, resemble foolish folke who, comming into a Garden without anie choise or circumspection tread downe the fairest flowres, and wilfullie thrust their fingers among the nettles."[58] Unable to tell a nettle from a flower, and void of choice and circumspection, willful, finger-thrusting readers harm both the garden and themselves. They fail at the basic exercise of prudential judgment.

In poetic settings, "weeds" therefore can stand for the untended parts of a landscape, those that place a greater burden on the reader's skill and circumspection. Gascoigne's *Posies* (1575), revising the 1573 *Hundreth Sundrie Flowres*, introduces a section of "weeds," using this new division to place the burden of proper use on the reader's shoulders. As I argued in Chapter 2, this strategy of authorial deflection builds on the logic of "vertue": accessing weeds' virtuous operation relies on the know-how of the handler, thereby projecting both practical and moral responsibility onto the scene of reading. A garden does not fully determine its use—and, indeed, cannot be held responsible for abuse or misuse.[59]

Not all books are as loose as Gascoigne's: some come prepruned, including others published by members of the Inns of Court in the 1570s and 1580s. Timothy Kendall, for example, promises that he has carefully weeded out potentially noxious examples from his translations of Martial's epigrams—a process of selection suggested by the title, *Flowers of Epigrammes* (1577). Kendall writes that he has "left the lewde, I have chosen the chaste: I have weeded away all wanton and woorthlesse woordes; I have pared away all pernicious patches: I have chipt & chopt of all beastly boughes and branches, all filthy and fulsom phrases: Which I thinke none will mutter at and mislike, but suche as delight more to drawe of the dregs, than drinke of the delicate liquour. I do give them unto thee by the name of *Flowers of Epigrammes, out of sundrie most singular authours selected*." Facing the especially perilous works of Martial, Kendall has performed this service in advance of his reader's arrival, modeling the humanist weeding that Crane describes and condensing the rest in his delicate octavo collection.[60]

Humphrey Gifford makes a similarly alliterative promise for his *Posie of Gilloflowers* (1580): he has applied circumspection and "simple skill" so that "the beauty of my flowers be not blemished with the weedes of wantonnesse, that commonly grow in such gardens." Gifford is not entirely confident about the outcome, however, and hopes that "ye shal finde them rooted out in such sort, that if there remayne any, my trust is they shall not fall out, to be many."[61] Gifford's admission of his limits as a weeder are also an advertisement: beyond the scope of his circumspection, some weeds may have slipped in. Several decades later, Thomas Lodge makes a similar suggestion for weeding in his translation of Seneca, which he calls "a Garden, wherein . . . thou maiest find many holesome Herbes, goodly Flowers, and rich Medicines." The residual burden to cull still falls on the reader: "yet can it not be but some weedes may ranckly shoote out, which may smoother or obscure the light and lustre of the better. Play the good Gardner I pray thee, and pulling up the weedes, make thy profit of the flowers." Readers, however, should still be considerate and skillful in their correction of those stragglers, "lest in pretending to roote out one, thou commit many errors."[62]

Lodge's final note echoes a concern also commonly expressed in horticultural texts: the danger that unskillful weeding might uproot indiscriminately, killing vulnerable plants along the way. Thomas Hill's instructions for weeding depict plant life as profoundly vulnerable to the efforts of weeders and pruners, especially before plants have matured. Offering instruction on how to protect and strengthen seedlings, he writes that tender young plants are threatened by weeds and even by some tools for their removal. Weeding thus requires special care: "After the Seedes beeyng workemanly bestowed in the Beddes, the Gardeners next care must bee, that he diligently pull uppe, and weede away all hurtfull and unprofitable Herbes, annoying the Garden plantes comming up." While the weeds are an annoyance, so too, potentially, is the act of weeding them. The tenderness of plants just "comming up" means that a gardener should weed by hand and not with a tool: "In thys pluckyng up, and purging of the Garden beddes of weedes and stones, the same about the plants ought rather to be exercised wyth the hand, than with any Iron instrument, for feare of feebling the yong plantes, yet small and tender of growth."[63] Hill's picture of care is intimately tactile, articulated with optimism that the exercise of the hand in weeding might— by meeting the tenderness of plant and earth with the tenderness of human touch—encounter these new plants with appropriate delicacy. Like a nostalgia for manuscript circulation, Hill's picture of manual weeding requires the human touch and abjures the violence of mechanized procedure. It is the vulnerability and youth of seedlings that demands such careful attention. Hill goes on, "the Gardener must diligentlye take heede that he doe not too boysterously loose the Earthe, nor handle muche the plantes in the plucking away of the weedes, but the same purge so tenderly, that the rootes of the yong plantes be not loosed and feebled in the soft earth: for occasion will move the carefull Gardener to weede daintie Herbes, being yet yong and tender, least grosse weedes in the growing up with them, may annoy and hinder their increasing."[64] Free of the condescension we usually associate with it, "daintie" here acts as a diminutive, closer to its etymology of "dignity," as a mark of the worthiness of this small thing. Hill's gardener is responsible for the work of interpretation and discrimination that precedes weeding and for the careful handling that does not harm the "daintie Herbes." Throughout these passages, Hill returns to this core vocabulary: these herbs are young and tender; small and tender; the gardener must "purge so tenderly." His language solicits the kind of care he describes, yoking the value of tiny herbs to their vulnerability to boisterous uprooting.

In plant books that include poems, the boisterous harm that threatens young plants comes not from the husbandman-poet but from the guest/reader, who, like Hill's weeder, is the one responsible for care and tender judgment. John Grange renders these dangers especially vividly in the poetic garden appended to his *Golden Aphroditis* (1577). Grange's volume reflects the direct influence of Gascoigne, echoing his language at times, and describes its author as, like Gascoigne, Plat, and other flower-poets, a "student in the common lawe of Englande."[65] The *Golden Aphroditis* consists of an allegorical prose romance, to which, the title page advertises, is "annexed by the same authour aswell certayne metres upon sundry poyntes, as also divers pamphlets in prose, which he entituleth his Garden: pleasant to the eare, and delightful to the reader, if he abuse not the scente of the floures." Here, introducing the poems, Grange balances the liberal hospitality of the lyric collection against the anxiety inspired by unknown readers. The warning against abuse (and the attendant promise of its possibility) is thus tantalizingly posed at the very outset.

At the beginning of the poetical annex that forms the second part of the volume, as Grange invites his dedicatee (along with other gentle readers) to freely cull from his lyric garden, he joins Hugh Plat in voicing an anxiety about waste and destruction. Reader and dedicatee are granted "free liberty at your wisedomes pleasure to croppe ech floure therin." Though Grange trusts the gentleness of his noble dedicatee, he is more worried about less generous readers: "But yet, thus much I doe conjecture, that if they were the sweetest floures of all, yet would they be mislyked of some, and, those of the greater sorte, whiche maketh some in deede for feare of their *Zoilus* mouthes to refrayne their learned pen."[66] These Zoiluses, to whom Grange alludes three times in these few pages, along with the "curious carping Knights" whom he warns off later, are stock figures of late sixteenth-century print. As Heidi Brayman argues, the frequent appearance of Zoilus (infamous for his attack upon Homer) in late sixteenth-century printed prefaces registers anxieties about "unauthorized access" to the book, voicing a perception that an author has somehow lost control over his readership.[67] They indirectly acknowledge, as Brayman notes, that the "bad reader" may be already *inside* the book, forcing readers to question their own access and identity, whether such warnings welcome them in or lock them out.

In the dedication of his garden, Grange concludes by raising and then dismissing the most horrifying possibility, that his reader might take these young flowers up by the root: "But seing this phrase (*Boni est pastoris tondere pecus non diglubere*) is not unknowen to your Honour, I lesse regard or feare the pulling of them up by the rootes, so boldly doe I builde upon your Honors curtesie."[68] The Latin sentence ("It is the duty of a good shepherd to

shear the sheep, not to skin it") cuts through the conceit of the garden to vividly project textual harm onto the author's body, a gentle plea in effect that
he not be "skinned" for his poems. The tenor of this extended metaphor, however, is unclear: what skin might such a reader remove? Grange's figure of
uprooting emerges from a fissure between the condition of the printed book
and the social fantasy of male intimacy it imagines: between his confidence
in the stewardship of his gentle reader and his doubts about the potential bois-
terousness of a common consumer. The figure suggested by the proverb is a
remarkable catachresis, one that asserts the value of the poet only by projecting him backward in the image of uprooting, an otherwise empty vessel defined by its vulnerability. Nonetheless, it is in this image that Grange takes
most forceful ownership of his poems. What it means to be the author of a
printed book is rendered with deep ambivalence, given ideational content only
in the form of this young plant—the slender spray easily plucked by an ungentle reader.

The proverb appears in Erasmus's *Adages*, where it is gathered from Suetonius, a fair corroboration for Grange's assumption that it is familiar to his
patron. There, Erasmus's unfolding of the proverb includes the more topically
relevant "And I hate the herbalist who pulls out the herb root and all"—a sentiment he attributes to Alexander the Great.[69] Erasmus writes that *Boni est
pastoris* may have originated with Tiberius Caesar, who is said to have uttered it as he declined to raise taxes in the provinces, the same context that
occasioned Alexander's denunciation of the bad herbalist. *Deglubere* in Erasmus's gloss is a strikingly violent word, associated not just with the treatment of animals but with the castrating power of women: "*Deglubere* means
to remove the skin, and the expression is derived from peasants who say
deglubere for 'to tear open a shell or pod' and 'to strip the peel from a seed.'
Because of this Catullus gave it an obscene sense, saying that a man is 'skinned'
by a woman; and Fotis in Apuleius says she is accustomed to 'skin men alive.'"
Erasmus's following remark, however, might also serve as a gloss for textual
strategies traced throughout this chapter: "Those who 'shear' therefore strip
in such a way that they leave a portion from which growth can occur; those
who 'skin,' leave nothing. For fleece that has been shorn grows again; when
the skin is torn off there is nothing that you can subsequently remove." It is
this reflection that brings Erasmus to the herbal analogue, his disdain for
cutting short (nipping at the bud, say) the vegetative faculty of growth—the
closing off of possible futures.[70] When Ben Jonson echoes this passage from
the *Adages* in *Timber*, it is to elaborate a pastoral vision of the character of a

prince—one who does not frightfully skin or uproot his subjects, but who cherishes the commonwealth "as his own body." He also slips quickly from the skinning of sheep to the image of uprooting, agreeing with Erasmus and Alexander the Great, who "was wont to say, he hated that gardener that plucked his herbs or flowers up by the roots."[71]

The anxiety about being pulled up—"root and all"—colludes with the stock figures of the "curious carpers," repudiated by Grange, Whetstone, and Gascoigne and appearing alongside Zoilus in countless other prefaces as prototypical "bad readers." In this context, "carping" evokes not just the proximate etymology of slander, but the primary sense of *carpere* in Latin—to pluck, cull, or gather plants, flowers, and fruits, or, by extension, to tear off or tear away.[72] It shares an etymology with "excerpt" and with "discerpt," John Maplet's word for botanical borrowing. The harm here is not just to pluck, but to pluck "curiously"—that conflux of singularity and libido so damning to the judgment of any reader. A curious carper indiscriminately cuts short.

With these visions of good governance, Erasmus and Jonson give voice to what we might think of as a custodial environmental ethic—the gentlemanly privilege, like the textual access offered by Grange, to freely enjoy a resource without diminishing it. This version of stewardship, as a kind of governmental oversight, builds on the logic of virtue discussed in Chapter 2. As Julia Reinhard Lupton writes, the role of the husbandman is ecologically collaborative; the job of this "animal husband" is to alight upon the virtues of his capons or fruit trees, to bring them to maturity and the realization of their offices—in other words, to have them grow according to their own course. Husbandman and housewife, Lupton writes, both exercise "his or her own virtue or practical knowledge by actualizing the virtues of the natural world."[73] Early modern figures of stewardship evoke a version of "right handling" that interacts with and cultivates those virtues without perverting or diminishing them. The ever-expanding economy it presumes and encourages is the condition of possibility for the fantasy of liberality expressed in the floral utopias these gardens represent.

The vulnerability of Grange's poetic shoots to uprooting reflects their freshness and novelty. In his epistle, the reference to pulling flowers up by the roots follows an avowal of their youth: "But (woe alas) a peece of wilde ground lately taken into the gardiners hands, and edged in, being but new set, can not, or very hardly delight any man." Of the flowers he freely offers, he admits, "as yet they have hardly taken roote."[74] The ground is only *lately* planted and edged in, and the flowers have only *hardly* taken root. By apologizing for his "rude garden" and "unsavory floures," Grange undercuts the value of the work as a whole; these violets and primroses, he writes, are "of the worser and meaner sorte, by reason of their firste planting." Early-blooming primroses and violets emphasize the youth of his poetic flowers—reinforced by the lexical firstness of the primrose.[75] We are not yet at the heat of summer, Grange reminds us; winter has just begun to thaw into spring. These are the tender young sprays that Thomas Hill also worries about: roots newly set are especially vulnerable to boisterous weeders. Poems and the poet share this vulnerability, the tender novelty of plants barely rooted.

We can now better understand the dynamics at work in Grange's image. The vulnerability of poet or poem only becomes salient within the horizon of stewardship we see defined by the proverb and by the protocols of horticulture: Why not uproot? Because of what an herb, a taxpayer, a sheep, or a young poet might offer later. John Keper mobilizes the same promissory logic to praise Thomas Howell's *Arbor of Amitie*, as we saw in Chapter 1. In asking not to be plucked too soon, Grange inverts the logic of the *carpe diem* poem: instead of imminent mortality, his sense of timing joins the arc of a poetic career to the course of botanical increase. The harm imagined by Grange matters because of that promise of future growth. Like Howell and his *Arbor*, Grange and his *Garden* are authorized by what Patricia Akhimie calls the ideology of cultivation, the assumption that they are capable of improvement and worthy of care.[76] Text and author accrue value not because of what they are but because of what they will be. In Grange's rendering, the poet inherits the promising latency of plant life, the possibility of growth, the potential of greater things to come. He thus turns the reader's concern from the text to the poet, who becomes a site of incompletion, vulnerability, and potential; his capacities, in turn, demand care, investment, and indulgence. In the words of the Carpenters, we've only just begun.

Wild Oats

Grange is not alone in keying the promise of his poetic garden to his youth. This framework recurs across poetic collections from the middle years of Elizabeth's reign, taking on special force in plant books in general and in these publications by Inns men.[77] References to weeds cluster in works of avowed juvenilia—traces of the stage of life that Roger Ascham called "that most slip-perie tyme."[78] Many poetic gardens frame their contents as products of a period of past prodigality, bracketed in printed editions by divisional breaks and even title pages, and soliciting a reader's special attention and discre-tion.[79] With claims of youthfulness, poets both embrace and estrange the po-tential prodigality of their verse and present it under the guise of humility.

Their primacy places these works of poetry within a robustly developmen-tal frame, as a "green" season in the course of a longer career. Figures of weeding and apologies for immature verse call upon the rhetoric of cultiva-tion that shaped humanist schooling, as Rebecca Bushnell has described, and places poetry on the path of errancy and correction identified by Richard Hel-gerson as part of the script of prodigality.[80] Presenting their poetic careers as the misspent work of youth, mid-Elizabethan poets standardly ascribe to them either the noxiousness of weeds or the sourness of first fruits. If the prodigal story is structured in three parts—advice, digression, return— poetry is suspended in the space of digression, written during the prodigal's period of disobedience and presented to the world as if in quotation marks. Lyric is thus generated—and excused—as the product of that safe space of suspension. A wide swath of English vernacular lyric appeared in print under the mark of this erasure—a promise that the vanity and license that these poems represent had already been squashed, and a rhetorical strategy that secured the authenticity of youthful experience under the shadow of preter-ition.

Prodigality scripts enframe poetry and pleasure as phases on a grander progress. As we have seen, George Whetstone, an acquaintance and eulogizer of Gascoigne, stages his *Rocke of Regard* (1576) in four progressive regions: a castle of delight, garden of unthriftiness, arbor of virtue, and orchard of re-pentance. Whetstone's "Garden of Unthriftinesse" houses his lyric poetry— including material he admits might satisfy his reader's expectation of "a number of vaine, wanton, and worthlesse Sonets." However, the volume's movement through the arbor and orchard that follow restricts poetic un-thriftiness to the garden and does not consume the substance of the poet's (or reader's) character. Poetry (it should perhaps not surprise us) is fleeting.[81]

> Some there be, that having eyed my former unthriftinesse, doe gape (percase) to viewe in this booke, a number of vaine, wanton, and worthlesse Sonets, in some respectes I have satisfied their expectation, moved to suffer the imprinting of them, not of vaine glorie, but of two

good considerations: the one to make the rest of the booke more profitable, and (perhaps) lesse regarded, the better saileable. The other &
chiefest, in plucking off the visard of self conceit, under which I som-
times proudly masked with vaine desires. Other yong gentlemen may
reforme their wanton lives, in seing the fond & fruitles successe of my
fantasticall imaginations, which be no other then Poems of honest
love: and yet for that the exercise we use in reading loving discourses,
sildome (in my conceit) acquiteth our paines, with any thing benefi-
ciall unto the common weale, or verie profitable to our selves, I thought
the *Garden of Unthriftinesse*, the meetest title I could give them.[82]

The trials of the prodigal deliver him to a thriftier maturity. Whetstone
hopes his narration may do the same for the reader. The *Rocke's* allegorical
progression echoes the progressive course of "fashion[ing] a gentleman"
around which Edmund Spenser organizes the 1590 *Faerie Queene*, and we
might further compare the staged structure of Whetstone's volume to the
specific allegorical landscapes through which Guyon moves in the latter
part of book 2.[83] In both cases, the process and progress around which the
books take form also serve to refashion the reader.

By the end of the 1570s, the rhetoric of youthful apology was conventional,
especially among poets linked to the Inns, and was conventionally linked to
the rhythms of plant life. Though it seems not to have made much of a splash
upon publication, and is little read by scholars today, Austen Saker's *Narbonus: The Laberynth of Libertie* (printed by Richard Jones in 1580) aims to
capitalize on this errant, youthful energy—in its author, narrative content,
and imagined readership. Saker and Jones astutely link the prodigal story to
the immaturity of both text and author. Youth provides its audience and its
subject: the *Laberynth*'s title advertises it as "Very pleasant for young Gentlemen to peruse, and passing profitable for them to prosecute," with a story
that follows "the lust of a mans will, in youth: and the goodnesse he after
gayneth, being beaten with his owne rod, and pricked with the peevishnesse
of his owne conscience, in age." Saker, who was a member of New Inn, deploys the work's immaturity to defend its unsavoriness; a reader should not
be surprised by the sourness of the fruit, but instead have faith that "this Tree
yeelding the firste fruite bare but Crabbe, which serveth but for Verges, which
if it be not bitten with the blastes of backebiters, and scorged with the Sunne
of unshamefastnesse, may by the ende of Sommer give that whiche shall be
more pleasant to the toung, and more profitable in tast."[84] The language of

"first fruits" also offers John Florio a title for his *Florio his Firste Fruites* (1578), a collection of proverbs and sayings in English and Italian. The phrase marks the book as the product of youth, and so offers some insulation against criticism; it also advertises it as a ritual offering to its dedicatee, Robert Dudley (to whom Florio "yeld[s] these my simple first fruits"), and to his friendly readers, who he hopes will forgive the fruits' unripeness.[85] As Florio's request for Dudley's protection suggests, solicitations of patronage offered one horizon in which to rewrite the script of youthful prodigality: by depicting the poet as soil that needs improvement, or as a young plant in need of cultivation, they ask the reader to step in as a good steward. Nonetheless, as Saker and Jones's more open address to potential readers shows, any good reader might be a patron to the soil, a contributor to future, sweeter fruit.

These dynamics of youthful transgression and aesthetic deferral take an especially provocative form in the first publications by Nicholas Breton, who, though not a member of an Inn, was the stepson of George Gascoigne, whose influence is especially reflected in Breton's early poetic publications.[86] Breton's *Workes of a Young Wyt*, published in 1577, follows its epistle to the reader with a verse "Primordium" that extends an elaborate agricultural analogy. Breton begins by describing a husbandman's approach to a new plot of land. The initial question is one of epistemic uncertainty: the farmer that "newe breakes up a ground" does not know "what fruit, the soyle will yeelde." To hedge his bets, the poem goes on, he therefore sows the cheapest seed he can find "for tryall": "by proofe of that, how better graine wil proove." According to the poet, these cheap grains are oats:

> a grayne which every man dooth knowe:
> Which prooving yll, his losse can be but small,
> if well, such gaynes as he may lyve withall.[87]

Breton thus frames the poetry in the pages that follow within the horizon of this questionable soil, depicting farmer's and poet's labors as experimental: faced with the risk of unknown future harvests, he affirms instead the probative value of this first casting of seed on new soil.

The *Workes* may well have been Breton's first venture into print (it was published in the same year as his *Floorish upon Fancie*), and his analogy to oats both undercuts the gravity of the present volume and advertises a potentially significant *future* poetic career.[88] This turn toward the future seems to immunize him from criticism in the present. But here, Breton's account of his small labors begins to undermine this innocence.

> What sayd I? Otes? Why, Otes there are I see,
>   of divers kyndes, as some are counted wylde:
> And they are light: and yet with them some be,
>   in steed of better many tymes beguyld.
> And sure I thinke that wylde lyght kynde of grayne,
>   my selfe have sowne, within my barren brayne.
>   (sig. A.iii^r)

Wild oats, any farmer will tell you, are not oats at all: they are another species entirely, one that easily passes for oats but keeps the real seed from flourishing.[89] "Wild oats" number among the "the cheefe weedes, and baggage that requireth to be plucked up," writes Levinus Lemnius in *An Herbal for the Bible* (1587). There, they appear alongside cockle and darnel as those weeds that are "vicious, noisom and unprofitable graine, encombring & hindring good Corne." Thus "choaked and despoiled of convenient moisture," profitable grains either suffer or are "utterly killed and commeth to no proofe at all."[90] Few would agree that the "divers kyndes" of oats extend far enough to include wild ones. In Breton's poem, then, his harvest's unexpurgated variety—an aesthetic selling point!—threatens to let in a more dangerous kind of seed.[91] The reference to wild oats—in Latin, *avena fatua*—may also contain an allusion to pastoral poetry, seen as the fittest home for youthful poetic production in Renaissance understandings of the poetic career. Often translated as "oaten pipe," *avena* names the first musical instrument that appears in Virgil's *Eclogues*, and becomes an emblem of pastoral song.[92] As *avena fatua* (meaning foolish, or futile), the oats of youthful poetry are better for lyric than harvest.

"Wild oats" was already an idiom by the late sixteenth century, though not precisely in the sense we use it now. Though it had long been a moniker for certain destructive and obstructive seeds, it had also come to designate a particular category of person, according to the *OED*, a "dissipated or dissolute young fellow." A "wild oats" was a species of the familiar prodigal son, part of an overlapping economic and agricultural vocabulary that found its way into city comedies, as in Thomas Heywood's *How a Man May Chuse a Good Wife* (1602): "Well goe too wild oates, spend thrift, prodigall"; in *Westward Ho!* (1607): "O God let him not come up, tis the swaggringst wild-oats";

and in *The London Prodigall* (1605): "and for this wilde oates here, young *Flowerdale*, I will not judge."[93] An early example of this character type appears in Thomas Becon's *A Pleasaunt Newe Nosegaye* (1543), where Becon decries the "foolyshe desyre of certayne lyghte braynes & wylde Otes" for changeable fashions.[94] Becon's depiction of youthful vanity shares a number of qualities with the wild oats of Breton's poem: the diversity of fashions, the novelty ("newe fanglenes") of the scene in question, and the pairing of lightness and wildness in his description. In this passage, Becon ties wild oats' "lightheadedness" to the activities of cogitation, invention, and imagination—like seeds scattered abroad by a gust of wind, the mind's airiest operations are those most subject to the influence of changeable fashion.[95]

Unlike these moralizing examples, the twenty-first-century meaning of "sowing wild oats" asserts a position of defensive neutrality. Today, classifying transgressions as "wild oats" immunizes them against consequence and significance, naturalizing immoral or immoderate behavior as the honest purge of youthful energies. Earlier uses of the idiom, however, reflect a familiarity with agricultural labor: wild oats are dangerous to the cultivars around them. The contemporary, neutralizing sense suppresses the interaction of seeds and their neighbors, as it suppresses the consequences of sowing wild oats both for the soil and for the surrounding plants. Nonetheless, like modern uses of the phrase, Elizabethan associations of "wild oats" with youthful unthriftiness attempt to litigate just how consequential the vanities and missteps of youth ought to be. Does youthful expense and misbehavior eat away at the core substance of character and career, or might it be effectively contained and corralled in the safe space of youthful experiment? What happens to the youthful spray *at the root*? As remains the case today, it makes all the difference who is doing the spending or the sowing.

Breton was not oblivious to the threat posed by wild oats. Instead, by slyly introducing a morally treacherous grain, Breton admits the thrill of weeds under the cover of triviality. He here participates in a style of doublespeak common among mid-Elizabethan poets, underselling the significance (positive or negative) of his own labor or responsibility, while signaling the moral and social danger his writing potentially incites. This strategy preserves deniability while affirming an in-crowd's interest in transgressive verse. In Breton's poem, the cultivation of wild oats may be unprofitable, but it is not harmful. And yet, both agriculturally and idiomatically, wild oats choke and stifle other, profitable grains from growing. This ambivalence cloaks two distinct critiques of poetry: that it is ornamental, extraneous, and inert—

something that *makes nothing happen*—or that it is a morally pernicious expression of vanity. Is poetic prodigality merely wasteful, or does it lay waste to the fields growing around it?

Later in Breton's collection, wild oats appear in a different guise: as part of a dialogue in verse between two rustic characters named Simon and Susan, entitled "An odde gretinge, and as madde a wooing betweene a clowne of the country, and his sweete harte." As Breton imports wild oats from the prelude to this new setting, voiced by country people in the structure of a dialogue, their value becomes more ambiguous. Simon, the country clown, assumes a position closer to that articulated in the "Primordium," excusing "young husbandmen" for mistakenly intermingling them with good seed: "Among good Otes perhaps they sowe some now and then"; "Perhappes too unawares, they sow some heere and there." His position gradually weakens, however, in face of Susan's canny interrogation:

> *Sim.* What say you then of Otes? they must be latest sowne.
> *Sus.* But some will sowe them first of all, and mowe them scarce
>   halfe growne.
> *Sim.* Wel, but Otes sowne in time, wil prove a pretty graine.
> *Sus.* But who doth seeke to sowe wild Otes, shal reape but little
>   gaine.
> *Sim.* In deede I thinke wilde Otes, are scarcely woorth the mowing.
> *Sus.* And yet I see young husbandmen, doo thinke them woorth the
>   sowing.
> *Sim.* Among good Otes perhaps they sowe some now and then.
> *Sus.* But who doth sow the good with badde, is no good
>   husbandman.
> *Sim.* Perhappes too unawares, they sow some heere and there.
> *Sus.* How they are sowne I know not, but they come up every where.
> *Sim.* When they are sowne with Rye, they ranckest growe in deede.
> *Sus.* Well it is pity for to sowe such trashe, among good seede.
>
>   (sig. I.i^r)

Simon appears outmatched in this audition for a role as Susan's "good husbandman," as her responses leave little room for Simon's forgiving equivocations. In this sense, she presents a jocular version of Gascoigne's huswifely accountant. Susan's position adjusts a more severely moralizing argument—one articulated, for example, by the figure of the Minister in the

Puritan Christopher Fetherston's *A Dialogue Agaynst Light, Lewde, and Lascivious Dauncing* (1582). Taking a strong position against letting ill seeds
grow from any age, the Minister resists proverbial rationalizations for youthful misconduct. We should not, in fact, "have our swindg while we be yong,"
since "age wil come soone ynough, and it will make us forsake all these
sportes."[96] Lifelong virtue is cultivated by habitual virtuous action, and so
cannot be deferred. You cannot procrastinate when it comes to being godly.[97]
As Amy Tigner points out, the spiritual association of weeds with lust, and
with sins that need to be weeded out, deeply shapes these horticultural
metaphors—as Calvin writes of God's intention "to weede out ye naughti-
nesse and vice out of our Heartes."[98]

Breton, however, takes a different approach to the significance of youthful dissipation. Instead of uprooting wild oats, he turns them into a cover
crop. At the end of the "Primordium," Breton suggests that the ostensibly
fruitless sowing of oats might actually *feed* the soil for future seasons.[99] Like
other young poets, he maps his current vanity onto the shape of a career in
print, arguing that, in fact, the loss of first oats is actually profitable—as long
as you're willing to wait:

> But tis no matter, smal hath been my cost:
>   and this is first tyme that I sturd my brayne,
> Besydes, I have, but little labour lost,
>   in idle tyme to take a little payne.
> And though, I loose, both payne, and grayne in deede:
>   my ground, I trowe, will serve for better seede.
>
> For as the Farmer, though his croppe be yll,
>   the seede yet lost will fatten well the grounde.
> And when he seekes for better grayne to tyll,
>   and sowes good grayne, then is the profit found.
> For, all the first, that good was, for no grayne,
>   will beare good fruite, but with a little payne.
>   (sig. A.iii[r])

The labor of this ill crop, its wasted seeds in time fattening the ground, will
make the next harvest more profitable. This is a remarkable rewriting of the
Onan story: Breton has not spilled his seed in vain because, in a kind of so-
lipsistic crop rotation, his wild oats have helped fatten the ground for future

harvests. While the developmental horizon Breton describes echoes the conventional path of a Virgilian *rota*, he extends it to sketch out a fallow-field theory of poetic career. He transforms the oats from a test of the soil to a cover crop—a different kind of investment entirely. Here, he is able to argue not just that an idle field is morally neutral but that it is in fact profitable—*just not yet*. Breton concludes by craning his reader's neck around toward the future, compelling the reader's investment in Breton's delayed development as poet and citizen. To do so, he allies himself not with a young plant, or even with the husbandman, but with the soil itself.

After beginning with a question about access to poetic gardens, this chapter has traced motifs of planting, tending, and uprooting as they come to figure the composition of poetry and the life cycle of the poet. The horticultural conception of poetic authorship we have encountered in these collections emerges in dialogue with a concern about what harm might happen to the book: How do you destroy a printed poem? What kinds of loss are acceptable and what kinds are remediable—of poetic substance, of labor, of reputation, of personhood? A consideration of the consequences of circulation in print has led us back to a discussion of *roots*. Perhaps surprisingly, though, it is not commerce and print publication that represent acts of uprooting; it is the labor and intervention of readers, consumers who might return to the site of cultivation to destroy either poem or poet at the source.

These examples suggest a distinct approach to the concerns shared by Saunders's notion of stigma and Helgerson's account of prodigality: What kind of permanent damage can poetry actually do? What kind of loss can it bring about? Saunders and Helgerson's accounts of poetic production emerge from distinctive models of loss. While stigma represents a loss of identity, a kind of social death, Helgerson's account of prodigality reframes that damage within a story, by placing the loss of reputation and material substance in a narrative framework that admits the possibility of recovery and return. A natural economy underwrites and informs the life course of the prodigal: the substance of these young poets is not exhausted or consumed by youthful indiscretion—namely, for most of these young men, the writing of poetry. Breton's wild oats suggest that future growth might in fact be *increased* by a period of idleness. The liveliness of the soil, with its cyclical capacity for recovery, underwrites the prodigals, poetic optimism.

By rewriting the terms on which a poet claims the *ground* or *plot* of a garden, Breton and Grange suggest an alternate account of how mid-Elizabethan writers conceive poetic authorship. Toying with the relation of vegetables to the soil, they suggest a poetic subjectivity predicated on possible loss: of substance, self, friends, reputation. To this extent their botanical fictions are explicitly economic, built from an *oikos* proper to the home and the natural world. As we saw in Chapter 1, Elizabethan writers and printers joined horticulture and print publication through a shared scenario of risk. In the account of poetic authorship revealed by the examples in this chapter, the ecology of the poetic garden exposes text and author to more explicitly violent outcomes. Recent criticism, including the work of Catherine Bates and Stephen Guy-Bray, has shown how early modern verse often turned on a poetics of vulnerability.[100] The examples I consider here extend and confirm this trend, further embedding poetic risk within vegetable patterns of growth and decay. They ask us to rethink poetic vulnerability by asking just what kind of vulnerable bodies poets have. The Inns poets considered in this chapter suggest a model of coterie poetry that does not attempt to lock the garden gate or to keep strangers out. In fact, it is the openness to multiple paths of reception that defines the textual condition of printed poetry, an openness on which Isabella Whitney will invent further variations, as Chapter 4 will explore. Instead, these collections redefine poetic property as that which is subject to injury, or against which a poet might claim damages against future yield. Within the horizon of plant books' botanical imagination, the vulnerability of young men to uprooting—their tender susceptibility— is also what makes their poetic futures imaginable.

CHAPTER 4

Isabella Whitney's Dispersals

Isabella Whitney's *Sweet Nosgay, or Pleasant Posye*, published in 1573, shatters the conceit of the enclosed garden. Quite literally, Whitney takes a garden to pieces. The *Nosgay*'s epistle from "The Auctor to the Reader" describes the poet's process of literary invention, as she reads through a range of genres before taking a walk that leads her to a garden: "*Plat* his Plot," "where fragrant Flowers abound."[1] This horticultural encounter is also another textual encounter: Plat's plot, we deduce, names Hugh Plat's *Floures of Philosophie*, published a year earlier, in 1572, 110 sentences of which Whitney will rework in the numbered, rhyming verses that follow. Whitney begins a series of daily visits, taking "slips" with her "to smell unto," eventually assembling a bundled nosegay of fragrant flowers. With these visits to Plat's plot, Whitney rewrites the enclosure of another printed garden, transforming its rooted stuff into a powerfully mobile and reusable object. She will also go on to imagine a future for her own nosegay, projecting a multiple and dispersed field for its use and reception. Whitney's *Nosgay* offers a rare situated encounter with the class of male-authored garden books addressed in Chapter 3. And she helps us envision one kind of reading they make possible, a model of readerly engagement and reuse that turns on the flexibly innate capacities of plants—their "vertues," a way of thinking about vegetable life introduced in Chapter 2. Responding explicitly to the imagery and ideology of the collections explored in the previous chapter, Whitney develops a practice of what we might call "slippery reading," a textual encounter that recedes as it engages, that gathers without diminishing its source.

By engaging with Plat, Whitney exploits the openness of botanical figure to challenge the genteel terms of enclosure by which the Inns operate. Hugh Plat was a new member of Lincoln's Inn when his book was published, and, though Lincoln's Inn Fields had not yet been formally established, its gardens (in Holborn, just north of Temple Bar) were well known. Though

Whitney may not have known Plat personally, she would have been familiar
with his social milieu through her (likely) brother Geoffrey; and, as a resi-
dent of London, she would have been intimately familiar with the spatial
politics of enclosed gardens.[2] As we saw in Chapter 3, the poetic collections
by those members of the Inns all grapple with the problem of access, as
they turn to the world and lexicon of vegetables to proliferate possible futures
for their texts in the hands of unknown readers. Those futures turn peril-
ously on the doubled logic of hospitality: the potential of any act of generosity to enclose the garden, as a discrete form with inside and outside, and to
expose it to harm or invasion by a bad reader. In printed books, this doubleness also structures the operation of address: the ambivalent coexistence of
a text's stated orientation toward a known, friendly reader, and its wider availability to an anonymous audience. With her actions as reader and writer,
Whitney pries open these two dimensions, asserting a claim to the status of
legitimate invitee. Once out of the hands of its creator, the matter of the
book, like the stuff of language, becomes indiscriminately available for proliferation, recycling, and reuse. The imaginary terms by which these garden
enclosures are built also offer Whitney the figurative tools—here, herbal
slips—with which to dismantle them. Her legitimacy, however, turns not on
any invitation the text might offer but on the skill she brings to it.

Slipping, taking, and cutting emerge in Whitney's *Nosgay* not as destructive or diminishing procedures but as generative—even generous—forms of
practice.[3] By going to a garden and coming away with a nosegay, Whitney
rewrites the spatial politics of reading and textual form as they are rendered
in Plat's *Floures* and in other enclosed gardens. While Plat consistently gives
causal force to the *space* of his garden, Whitney bequeaths force to the mobile virtues of slips. Rewriting Plat, the *Nosgay* consistently emphasizes the
virtues of circulation above the territorially bound powers of spaces. Her first
visit, she writes, "I mee reposde one howre," before being called away by a
lack of leisure. She takes a sovereign souvenir, however:

> Though loth: yet at the last I went,
>   but ere I parted thence:
> A slip I tooke to smell unto,
>   which might be my defence.
> In stynking streetes, or lothsome Lanes
>   which els might mee infect.
>   (sig. A.vi^v)

Exiled from the garden, Whitney meets an apparently fallen world outside its walls. Facing the noxious air of streets and lanes beyond, her slips' preservative virtues accompany those pieces as they travel outside the walls and hedges of Plat's garden. They will eventually wander farther, as her nosegay ventures into the hand of new readers. Whitney depicts herself as similarly mobile—unbound by the walls of either Plat's garden or a household—as she moves across city streets and garden gates unchecked and unprotected by either enclosure or belonging. With this practice of piecing out, Whitney treats Plat's plot as a commons, borrowing its fruits without consuming its store so that the garden itself, with all its virtues, might continue to flourish.[4] Careful to take only slips, Whitney warns her readers, should they repair to the original garden, not to damage any plants by the root. This sense of collective stewardship extends even beyond Plat and his garden, as Whitney offers her nosegay to readers as a personal preservative and mobilizes it as a resource for new iterations of readers and pedestrians. The lively mobility of the garden's component parts thus underwrites the distribution of a resource and its affordances.

Helping to place both the author and her text in motion, "slip" stands as the key term for Whitney's textual strategies. The name with which she characterizes her borrowings from Plat's garden, "slips" appears capitalized in the volume's dedication to George Mainwairing, where its typographical distinction helps link a concrete set of material practices. Whitney Trettien has shown how Whitney's use of "slip" merges the fractional logics by which embroidery, texts, and gardens were assembled—all part of the piecemeal and makeshift aesthetics that shaped Elizabethan printed books like Whitney's, especially those published by the *Nosgay*'s printer, Richard Jones.[5] "Slip" is a noun constantly trying to become a verb. From the Middle Flemish or Middle Low German *slippen*, to cut, the substance of "a slip" carries in its name the procedure by which it was formed. The slip as a thing captures this slicing movement, the evasive maneuver of slipping away. Whether a segment of fabric, a sprig cut from a greater plant, or a fragment of text, a slip preserves its source while casting off from it. As such, botanical slips boast distinctive capacities for preservation and proliferation: a skilled husbandman or huswife will not harm the plant from which he or she takes a slip and might even create a new one. This model of engagement ultimately helps empower a fantasy of proliferation and nondiminishment, in which the redistribution of goods (slips) need not consume the source. Recalling the distinctive capacity of vegetables to multiply from fragments, the term's associations assemble a model of resource exploitation in which both copies and originals sustainably proliferate and renew. Introducing the collection as a whole under the sign of this essentially mobile—*slippery*—thing, Whitney prefigures the fugitivity of both poet and verse that the rest of the collection will explore. The poet herself seems throughout the *Nosgay* to be slipping away: leaving Plat's garden, sending letters to family members from afar, and, finally, in the "Wyll and Testament," leaving London under the guise of leaving the earthly plane.

The world of Whitney's slips thus seems centrifugally drawn, its pieces moving ever outward from a central point. But the pieces of the *Nosgay*—poems or flowers—only increase in force for this fact. All of the forms in which she writes—proverbs, advice, epistles, a last will and testament—act most powerfully in the absence of their author, taking effect once she has withdrawn. When skillfully shared, vegetable slips, as gardeners and herbalists well know, carry their virtues with them, acting with generative potential or sovereign therapeutic force at a distance from their source. By unfolding Whitney's interest in these portable virtues, this chapter takes a distinctly vegetable perspective on what has been a central question in scholarship on Whitney's work: her ambivalent authorial presence in her own text.[6] The previous chapter argued that George Gascoigne's adoption of a botanical idiom serves a version of authorship in which the poet seems to recede behind the virtues of his flowers; for Gascoigne, this strategy insulates him from the moral and social consequences of his published verse. Whitney likewise invests her herbal slips with agency, taking seriously their force as sovereign actors whose force carries well beyond her sphere of influence. Like Gascoigne, she posits a distinctly botanical account of poetic authorship—here, as a compiler of virtues. In both cases, the poet cedes to the more active trajectories of vegetative increase and virtuous force.

This practical understanding of botanical-textual virtue fuels Whitney's distinctive account of slipping, redistribution, and dispersal. Whitney weaves a language of virtue through the volume, from her admiring dedication to George Mainwairing (praising "the Garden of [his] godly mind," which is "full fraught with vertuous Flowers" [sig. A.iv^v]), her advertisement of the medicinal and preservative virtues of the slips borrowed from Plat's garden, and the virtuous conduct prescribed both in the proverbial flowers themselves and in the epistolary poems addressed to friends and family. Throughout, Whitney's engagement with virtues recognizes these latent capacities as multiple and mobile. Her interest on distributing virtues departs from readers' expectations in two key ways. First, by emphasizing the virtues of her slips, Whitney resists the proverbial vanity of flowers, their tendency to wither and fade. Drawing on knowledge of herbal medicine and on common tropes from devotional books, she captures what is essential and resilient about the nosegay as a piece of matter. The *Nosgay*'s material consistency and implied moral purposiveness thus seem to respond to what may otherwise appear threatening or transgressive about both poetic language (its superfluity, vanity, and effect on the passions) and printed matter (its fugitive multiplicity and indifferent transgression of social boundaries).

Second, by keying virtue to mobility (both her own and that of her slips), Whitney turns the association of feminine virtue with enclosure (and of fallenness with vagrancy) inside out. Acting as a woman to break these slips free from Plat's enclosed garden, Whitney inverts the conventional gendered understanding of the *hortus conclusus*, the enclosed garden associated with paradise and with the Virgin Mary. Building on images of Eden and the landscape of the Song of Songs, the *hortus conclusus* was a common motif both in medieval devotion and in romance; its renewed associations with Elizabeth in the second half of the sixteenth century ensured its symbolic flourishing.[7] By showing the herbal-textual virtues of her *Nosgay* in circulation, Whitney effectively mounts a counterargument to conceptions of feminine virtue that turn on enclosure. As she and her nosegay move outward through London's lanes, Whitney shows how her slips might survive and even increase their force through circulation and reuse. This is a radical claim for a woman facing the reputational and material danger of her personal departure from the respective enclosures of city and household.[8]

By placing her nosegay and its virtues in this lively cosmos of distributed sovereignties, Whitney strategically recodes the dangers of circulation. As Wendy Wall and others have noted, cultural anxieties about women's circulation meant that the conventional "stigma of print" placed a special burden on female poets—one that Whitney manages in part through these strategies of withdrawal.[9] Like Gascoigne, Grange, and the other male poets who appeared in the previous chapter, however, Whitney finds the morally and reputationally treacherous conditions of print publication wildly aesthetically productive. She does not, however, narrow the horizon of her text to hedge this danger; she broadens it, and, in a strategy that relies on her botanical conception of textual potential, she generates a newly imagined field of textual reception. Just as she slipped out of Plat's garden, the nosegay slips out of her hands and—ever farther from her—into the hands of new and distant readers.

Along the way, this chapter will pause to place Whitney's *Nosgay* in conversation with, first, contemporary polemics in popular print about common access to textual and environmental virtues; and, second, other printed nosegays that, like Whitney's, draw on the gathering's distinctive capacities as a gift, a mnemonic device, and a surprisingly evergreen kind of matter. The concluding section of this chapter argues that Whitney's account of mobile virtues posits a conception of distributed sovereignty—one in which material power operates through the dispersal of deputies, her textual and floral slips, that carry it across space and time to new fields and audiences. This understanding of distributed force allows Whitney to imagine reading, circulation, and reception as phenomena both collective and distant, deferred in time and space from a scene of composition or publication, but where slipping, borrowing, and transfer are infinitely repeated and rewritten. As she negotiates the obedient and fugitive capacities of both readers and slips, Whitney achieves a distinctively social imagination of the book.

Slippery Readers: Whitney, Plat, and Redistribution

Hugh Plat concludes the preface to his *Floures of Philosophie* with a posy, appearing all in capitalized letters: "OF A LITTLE TAKE A LITTLE."[10] The phrase is both an imperative and an invitation, as Plat assumes the role of the garden's hospitable proprietor, humbly welcoming readers and inviting them to borrow—as long as those borrowings are likewise humble. As we saw in Chapter 3, however, there are limits to his textual hospitality. In Plat's *Floures*, those limits emerge explicitly when the collection turns from its series of Senecan sentences to Plat's gathering of original verse, "The Pleasures of Poetry." There, he concludes with a warning: "For whom this booke was made especially, and whom the Author excepteth from reading it." Though he gives "free leave" to those seeking to gather for pleasure or profit, he threatens "craftie theeves" with attacks by a "thornie bush."[11] Whitney's encounter with Plat will turn on precisely what it means to *take*—socially, economically, and materially. What is the boundary between a good reader, who takes a little, and a thief, who takes too much? Plat's proverb suggests that the invitation relies on the cultivation of balance: a symmetry between the source, taken, and the borrower, taking.

As a reader and taker-of-slips, Whitney enters Plat's text at this ambiguous site. She is careful not to violate the explicit terms of his invitation, and her account draws on the same lexicon that shapes the gardens of Plat, Gascoigne, and other poets who appeared in Chapter 3: she joins them in describing her leisure, her choices, the sweetness of flowers. But even as Whitney acknowledges and accedes to these conventions, we can hardly be confident that Plat would think her a friend and not a caterpillar, or one of the other disorderly intruders who plague the gardeners of the Elizabethan Inns of Court. She is perfectly aware, presumably, of the difference when license is exercised by a woman.[12] And she would not be the first to transgress the bounds of hospitality in a garden—like Eve, or like those sluttish laundresses who, as we saw, threaten to take more than a little even while taking only space. Nonetheless, Whitney takes her host at his word, accepting the "leave" he offers readers seeking pleasure and profit. As she admits, she is "bolde" to let her will guide her path into and through the garden as she "fill[s]" her "fancy."

And yet, the license that Whitney claims leaves her invisible and illegible to the garden's keeper. The reader continues to visit, slip, and withdraw back into city streets, without ever encountering the gardener. This disconnect reflects the two books' distinct spatial politics. Though drawing extensively from Plat, in both figurative frame and proverbial content, Whitney renders her collection in a dramatically different form. While Plat emphasizes space, Whitney emphasizes movement. Plat's verse epistles sustain an association between his name and the plot of the garden, both of which are linked (and sometimes confused) with the verb "to plat." The author throughout seems to be platting his plot: framing and devising his scheme or project. As Crystal Bartolovich argues, Plat's attention to spatial enclosure sketches a nascent form of possessive authorship; while he leans heavily on a language of personal possession, Whitney frequently downplays the value of her own labor of gathering and collection.[13] Plat's hedge, meanwhile, draws on the iconography of land enclosure to give form to his book, in setting a social and spatial boundary: its pricking thorns keep out whatever visitors it wishes, however needy they may be.[14]

Whitney concludes her address to the reader with a coy acknowledgment of the spatial politics of Plat's landscape forms:

One word, and then adieu to thee,
   yf thou to *Plat* his Plot

Repayre: take heede it is a *Maze*
to warne thee I forgot.
(sig. A.viii^v)

This "maze" refers to one of the controlling spaces defined by Plat in his garden—though Whitney extends the designation to the entire plot, a description of his unordered *sententiae* that is not entirely unapt. Plat writes that the swerves and corners of his maze are designed to manipulate, frustrate, and (he promises) eventually satisfy women's desire:

A maze there is for Ladies all,
with Lords to walke their fill.
It brings them farre with crooked pathes,
and turnes them straighte againe,
That going much, they thinke themselves
but little grounde to gaine.
But yet in fine, to hoaped ende
their restlesse feete aspire,
And open gappe bewraies it selfe,
to fill their long desire.[15]

Plat's interest in the maze's control over "Ladies all" at first singles out women as its subjects, subordinating them to the agency of the garden's design. The passage's syntax actively performs this subjection, as the maze acts upon its guests, "bring[ing] them farre" and "turn[ing] them straighte againe." The maze's mixture of seduction and suspense, culminating in the "open gappe" to fulfill "long desire," reflects the power of the labyrinth as a conventional site of erotic danger, in which a visitor might be lost, or entrapped, or both.[16] As we saw in Chapter 1, garden mazes could serve as emblems of a visitor's subjection to the designer's whims: while ladies are limited to a partial view of turns and crooked paths, it is Plat who sees the full plot. Whitney seems to have responded negatively to Plat's glimmer of sadism. Echoing his coy line breaks, Whitney's enjambment ("yf thou to *Plat* his Plot / Repayre: take heede it is a *Maze* / to warne thee I forgot") breaks her warning off from the previous lines, giving them the knowing, supplemental quality of an aside— the rhetorical analogue to a scribble of feminist solidarity on the door of a bathroom stall. By giving the end of the maze before a reader has begun, she has defanged its mechanism of constraint: there is no suspense, no error, no need to wander.

While Plat's maze controls people by controlling space, Whitney locates agency in matter that is essentially mobile. The version of "wyll" that Whitney elaborates in her own collection lays claim to a liberty at odds with Plat's enclosure:

> And for my part, I may be bolde,
>   to come when as I wyll:
> Yea, and to chuse of all his Flowers,
>   which may my fancy fill.
>   (sig. A.vii^r)

Here, Whitney assumes the lack of constraint—of sequence, timing, and choice—that Gascoigne promises the readers of his *Hundreth Sundrie Flowres*. While Plat seems to claim his *Floures* as an emergent form of textual property, Whitney resists this tendency in her source. Instead, she takes seriously the gestures of hospitality and gentility by which Plat invites readers in. In this way, Whitney treats this garden not as a space subject to personal property but as a space open to collective use.

Reclaiming common rights to the garden, Whitney takes Plat's plot as a renewable common resource, available to any who do it no harm. Accordingly, Whitney's determination of access follows not who readers are or what they want but the level of skill they possess. By her own account, she is an experienced artisan—one whose legitimate encounter with Plat's text turns on her ability to engage skillfully with the innate virtues and vitality of plants. That is, in the vocabulary descended from Roman law, Whitney claims a right to *usus* and *fructus*, use and enjoyment, but no right of abuse: she promises not to waste the source.[17] In order to achieve this usufructual relationship to Plat's property, to enjoy its fruits without consuming its store, the earth and its fruits must be capable of regeneration. This is, after all, what a slip is: a fragment to be replanted somewhere else, that takes only part and not whole from its site of origin. To succeed in her "slipping" of Plat, and achieve this double-edged legitimacy as a reader, Whitney makes a claim about the kind of matter of which both books and plants are composed. Textual and floral slips can be repeated, multiplied, and recirculated without loss to any original ground. This is a generous and copious version of textual and vegetable economy, an account of nature's stuff—even in its smallest fragments—as resilient and prodigious.

While Whitney assumes these prerogatives as a reader, they may not in fact have been granted to her. Thus, the first crisis we face in the *Nosgay* is Whitney's legitimacy as an interloper into Plat's textual garden. However, whether or not Plat's invitation is addressed to her, Whitney doesn't need it to enter his printed garden. As Romeo and Benvolio prove when they read aloud Peter's copy of Capulet's guest list, a misdirected invitation, a single slip of paper, is all you need to get in. As reader and visitor in his unattended garden, Whitney is invisible to Plat, her entrance unremarked and unrecorded until the dramatic exposure performed by the *Nosgay*'s publication. The many forms of invisibility she plays with in the volume are tangled in this ambiguous freedom. As we saw in the previous chapter, the male poets of the Inns built on the openness of botanical figure to generate community. By picking up and extending a metaphor, Whitney appropriates those same rhetorical and poetic techniques of socialization and community-building— despite being materially excluded from the worldly spaces and symbolic bonds those poets enjoy. Whitney's intervention thus teaches us something essential about how botanical collections work. According to the laws of hospitality that govern these volumes—and that likewise subtend the openness of books to new scenes and new users—you don't have to be on the team to play the game. The materiality of botanical figure, like plant materiality, persists in a form stubbornly available for displacement and reuse, bearing promise and capacity that extend beyond the will and eye of its maker or assembler.

In this way, Whitney assembles a theory of reading that makes room for a mobile and fleeting version of readerly practice. Book historians and historians of reading often remark that modern, private forms of reading—the ability of readers to wander and borrow, to read silently and pilfer with impunity—has made writing its history very difficult indeed: we only rarely find traces of those encounters, and the printed matter or bound form of a book can never fully govern readerly use, reuse, or abuse.[18] Here, what is an epistemological problem for both speculative publishers and retrospective book historians becomes for Whitney the condition and occasion of textual engagement. However, the story she tells about reading, including the anticipation of her own text's consumption, turns less on a modern version of privacy than on a repeated gesture of privation, as the author imagines the traces left by the *Nosgay* in her absence. A similarly wayward understanding of both reading practices and social identity governs the various pieces of Whitney's text, as her itinerary—in theory, a mark of illegitimacy for reader and subject—becomes the core of the *Nosgay*'s aesthetic and thematic substance.

Anticipating Roger Chartier's claim that the history of reading, "by definition, is rebellious and vagabond," her account of her own reading is resolutely mobile and centrifugal, moving ever outward from its points of origin.[19] As we'll see, the same is true of the speculative history she tells of the *Nosgay*'s reception: it is essentially outward bound, slippery, and mobile, like both Whitney and her slips. In this, Whitney's account of textual engagement further anticipates the itineracy that informs Michel de Certeau's understanding of readers' capacity to remake and repurpose their material—an account with which Chartier's formulation is in dialogue. Drawing an analogy between readers and poachers, de Certeau writes: "Far from being writers— founders of their own place, heirs of the peasants of earlier ages now working on the soil of language, diggers of wells and builders of houses—readers are travellers; they move across lands belonging to someone else, like nomads poaching their way across fields they did not write, despoiling the wealth of Egypt to enjoy it themselves."[20] Comparing readers to the Israelites who, in Exodus, "spoil" the Egyptians of gold and silver as they escape, de Certeau defines reading as a tactic of a dispossessed and dispersed population.

I want to pause for a moment on de Certeau's analogy, to account for how it does and does not match Whitney's understandings of reading and textual property. De Certeau's poacher shares Whitney's relationship to land and to soil, as he travels across territories without laying roots—a nomadic role Whitney likewise inhabits, opposed to the textual and social enclosure she encounters in Plat's plot. However, though an itinerant gatherer, Whitney is not a "despoiler," in de Certeau's terms, or caterpillar or thief in Plat's. Plat defines these interlopers according to their intention to diminish and attack the garden. But Whitney makes clear that her skillful handling of slips has done no harm to Plat's plot. Her reading practice turns on a refusal to "spoil": she gathers only slips and spoils neither crops nor soil; she even instructs readers who find Plat's garden in the future to not admit any animals that might "pluck rashly by the root."[21] Whitney assiduously observes Plat's command—"of a little take a little."[22]

Nonetheless, de Certeau's reference to Exodus suggests an ambivalent answer to the question of when *taking* amounts to *spoiling*. While the Israelites seem at first morally and politically righteous in their plundering of the oppressive Egyptians (e.g., in Exodus 3:22), the biblical account is morally questionable enough to have troubled millennia of readers. As one argument runs, expressed in commentaries by both Calvin and ibn Ezra, these riches never belonged to the Egyptians in the first place: they were God's and left to God to seize or redistribute. Saint Augustine refracts this scene through the lens of textual politics in chapter 40 of *On Christian Doctrine*, where he writes that Christians should not shrink from pagan philosophy, but instead claim pagan texts "for our own use, as it were from owners who have no right to them." The people of Israel were right, in this reading, to despoil Egypt, taking their vessels and ornaments, under God's command, "to make better use of them."[23] Augustine's argument for textual expropriation turns not on ownership but on turning them to Christian *use*—an argument that Erasmus will echo and expand by explicitly defending the Israelites against accusations of theft.[24] The spoils were never earthly properties—in our modern sense of human dominion—to start with.

These reflections on spoiling highlight two issues central to Whitney's strategies. One is legal and moral: when is it right to borrow, copy, and recirculate? When it is legitimate to share or to refuse to share? And who is endowed with either privilege? The other is descriptive, elaborating a physics that takes both book and plant as renewable resources. On both issues, Whitney relies on the merging of book logic and plant logic. Whitney's presentation of her encounter with Plat's flowers and her projection of their circulable virtues presume humanity's rights of common property in creation. To whom do these slips belong? Not, ultimately, to Whitney or Plat or any buyers of Richard Jones's little book. The slips, like the virtues carried in them, are implanted by God and belong to him. The resilience and inexhaustibility of virtues authorizes their multiplication and dispersal. The following section will show how an understanding of the virtues of books and plants suggests a radical vegetable model for the redistribution of printed matter.

Virtues Against Enclosure

The language of "vertue" in Whitney's *Nosgay* taps into a broader polemic about access and enclosure, part of an ongoing conversation in early modern England about the enjoyment of nature's store and the purposiveness of creation. For Whitney and other authors of plant books, the power of a text depends not on the agency of the author but on the force of these innate virtues. To some degree, authorial deferrals to native virtue participate in a humility topos, conventional in sixteenth-century writing, that marginalizes the role of the author in asserting the value of a text. But it also suggests an alternate understanding of what property might mean in the context of literary production, one that relies not on containment and control but on the innate capacities of small, circulating forms, available to anyone with skill or training to cultivate them.

In Elizabethan print, an understanding of distributed virtues sustained arguments for access that joined textual, territorial, and medical politics. A brief detour through John Northbrooke's *The Poore Mans Garden* (1571), which also joins together arguments for access to nature and to texts, helps us understand the stakes of this rhetoric in Whitney's *Nosgay*. In Chapter 2, Northbrooke's collection offered an example of how books and gardens could both serve as storehouses of virtues. Here, I observe how, in *The Poore Mans Garden*, the preternatural productivity of scripture and nature justifies a social agenda opposed to the enclosure of land as well as text.

Collecting useful sentences on doctrine from scripture and the church fathers, *The Poore Mans Garden* presents itself as an open resource from which even indigent readers might borrow freely.[25] The volume's commitment to the commonness of nature and text is most fully articulated in an epistle by Thomas Knell Jr., which opens with a broad cosmological narrative setting out the provisions made by God for assuaging human suffering.[26] Knell's picture of creation describes the endowment of the earth with "virtue" to "bring foorth every hearbe of the fielde, that might beare seede in him selfe, after his owne kinde, without gardening, digging, sowing, plantyng, weeding, or any other travayle of man."[27] After the fall, as humanity comes to grapple with its own frailty, the medicinal virtues of herbs (like the virtues of salvation) are accessed only with labor and pain. Emblems and exemplars of divine provision, virtues link the graces implanted in the earth to the storehouse of Northbrooke's book, which is likewise provisioned with examples of virtuous force (in this case, commonplaced sentences of religious doctrine).

The distribution of divine virtues across the vegetable kingdom justifies an argument against vegetable and textual enclosure, as Knell commits the *Garden* to the public commodity. It also provides an occasion for a polemic against superfluous private gardens. Knell contrasts the "operation and subtill vertue" of herbs and flowers to gardens he sees in his contemporary landscape, "so much sumptuousnes bestowed in waste, onely for the vaine delight of the eye"—plus "vaine expences and wasted money." In the moral language of husbandry, such gardens are unthrifty—"neither the bestowers thereof are the healthier, neither anie profit or corporall util obtained"—and only undermine God's provision of comfort, healing, and nourishment.[28]

Though an attack on walled gardens may itself seem superfluous in the introduction to a collection of theological talking points, Knell sees an essential link between the two spheres, as he argues for access and against hoarding and vanity. The critique of superfluous gardening recalls the work for which Northbrooke is now more famous—what may be the earliest attack on the public theaters, in his treatise against "Diceplaying, Dauncing, and vain playes or Enterluds."[29] Knell anticipates Philip Stubbes's polemic about garden architecture and garden use, in which he complains, "In the fieldes and *Suburbes* of the Cities they have Gardens, either palled, or walled round about very high, with their Harbers, and bowers fit for the purpose." The secrecy these luxuries afford becomes both occasion and shield for sin: as Stubbes writes, "least they might be espied in these open places, they have their banquetting houses with *Galleries, Turrets,* & what not els therein sumptuously erected: wherin they may (and doubtlesse do) many of them play the filthy persons."[30] The garden itself in Stubbes's imagination becomes a kind of stage, one inviting visitors to—like actors—"play the filthy persons" as they indulge in pleasures specifically enabled by the privacy of high walls.

Knell and Stubbes's attacks on superfluous gardening set the physical enclosures of those gardens center stage, as they critique the social effects of making private those resources that should be common commodity. Knell's specific indictment of gardens with "huge walles, and high pales" (like Stubbes's allusion to gardens "palled, or walled round about very high") directly invokes the lexicon of anti-enclosure polemics, which thematized the physical infrastructure of enclosing land.[31] Knell thus praises Northbrooke for refusing to enclose this spiritual garden; he "neither hath walled it about with great Bricke walles, nor hedged it about with quick thornes, neither paled it in." Instead, by providing a rich variety of "Slippes, Seedes & Plantes" to all manner of men, Northbrooke has created a "common Garden for the poore."[32] We cannot say how Knell or Northbrooke might have responded to the thorny hedge of Hugh Plat's *Floures,* but we can observe how Whitney's rhetoric builds on their project of common commodity, and how she does so specifically through the same discourse of botanical-textual virtues.

A parallel argument shaped the case made by popular medical books for common access to knowledge and materials of healing. Rebecca Laroche has shown how Whitney's *Nosgay* signals its affiliation with genres of cheap print that likewise promised the poor access to healing and salvation, and likewise merged the virtues of textual and herbal access.[33] Henry Lyte, for example, in his translation of Dodoens's *A Niewe Herball* (1578), advocated for popular access to both plants and to medical knowledge, writing that "even the meanest of my Countriemen," like those who cannot read foreign texts or afford a physician, may still find help closer to home—and "may yet in time of their necessitie, have some helpes in their owne, or their neighbours fieldes and gardens at home."[34] Lyte embeds the distribution of virtuous herbs within a traditional moral economy of neighborliness, signified here by open boundaries between adjacent fields.[35] Plague handbooks especially advertised open access on behalf of the poor to their store of preservative techniques.[36] William Bullein's *Dialogue* (1564), for example, censures "the mercilesse rich, whose whole trust is in the vaine riches of this world, entangled as it were emong Briers."[37] Like the quick thorns of Knell's epistle and the thorny hedge of Plat's *Floures*, Bullein's briars invoke the enclosure of land through the violent pricks that were its emblem in the popular imagination. We can thus hear both the rhetoric and moral universe of Knell's epistle—as it argues for the poor's access to textual and vegetable virtues—in Bullein's advertisement for popular medical knowledge about plague. Both, in politically powerful ways, tie the dispersal of herbal virtues to textual dissemination. Recalling Cordelia's invocation of the "unpublished virtues of the earth," Knell and Bullein reinvigorate the work of making virtues visible as a process of publication in its own right. Medical virtues were buried not just in the earth but in the treasuries of learned men.[38]

Like Bullein and Northbrooke, Whitney promises to set in motion a world of enclosed virtues, distributing sovereign force beyond the walls of Plat's garden and into the hands of a dispersed and miscellaneous readership. In dialogue with this print discourse of virtues, Whitney's model for redistribution pushes energetically out from any center point. (Her only hope for both herself and her nosegay is that a reader wish them "speede" [sig. C.v^v].) The conspicuous mobility of the *Nosgay* and its author is not necessarily an intuitive textual strategy. Introducing herself as "Harvestlesse, and servicelesse also," the poet enters her own book as a woman out of place, cut loose from the ties to household, family, and employment that had previously shaped her identity. The *Nosgay* is, as Laurie Ellinghausen writes, born of and informed by Whitney's "newfound lack of enclosure"—a condition of material precarity that nonetheless fuels Whitney's poetic production.[39]

As published by Richard Jones in 1573, the volume leaves the impression of a dispersed and expanding universe.[40] The *Nosgay's* three sections layer a series of withdrawals, each reliant on the receding figure of the author herself. In the first section, the titular nosegay, Whitney shows herself leaving the garden and eventually recirculating her book in her absence. The author's absence also forms the premise of the poems that compose the second section—a series of verse epistles that repeatedly emphasize her family's distance and unfamiliarity. Her first two letters, for example, remind each of her brothers that she has not heard from them by emphasizing her uncertainty about their location and condition—she is not even sure how her letter will reach her brother G.W. ("nor know I how to send; / Or where to harken of your health" [sig. C.vi^r]).[41] Whitney thus extends the absence that conditions letter-writing in general to a more acute experience of ignorance and alienation.

The collection's third and final section performs the most dramatic departure by assembling a mock "Wyll and Testament." In it, Whitney plays on the multiple senses of "leaving" to show herself bequeathing London to itself at the moment that she retreats from it, driven out by debt and unemployment. The textual situation of the "Wyll" offers a model for the situation into which Whitney issues the printed text of the *Nosgay*. In her breakdown of the disbursement of London properties, Whitney plays with the language of redistribution:

> Now London have I (for thy sake)
> within thee, and without:
> As coms into my memory,
> dispearsed round about
> Such needfull thinges, as they should have
> heere left now unto thee:
> When I am gon, with consience
> let them dispearced bee.
>   (sig. A.vii^v)

Whitney's double use of "dispearsed"/"dispearced" (from the Latin *dispergere*, to scatter) does not so much reappropriate as de-appropriate, scattering rather than regenerating London's purse. (The spelling also calls up "disappeared," as well as "pierced" and "speared," visually and phonetically suggesting the presence of violence.) The passage's doubled dispersals, how-

ever, introduce a new difficulty, as they open up a gap between the time of
the poem (in which Whitney *has* "dispearsed round about"), and the future
time of the will's consummation (let them be "dispearced," Whitney says,
"when I am gon"). In the intermediate period between two dispersals, it is as
if the text is held in probate, suspended between the subject's utterance of
the will and the execution of its terms. The suspense fits snugly onto the
strange temporal disjuncture of reading written poetry: the first dispersal,
indexing the time of poetic utterance; the second, the time of reading. It is only
once the second condition has been fulfilled (once the poet is "gon") that the
trigger is pulled on the final illocutionary prescription: "let them dispearced
bee." Each figure of future textual dispersal offers a reminder of the absence
of the author—a vehicle for expressing her own dispersal.[42] The temporality of
the will offers another version of materiality understood as store, a conception that Whitney at other times applies to written texts, endowed with capacities to be actuated later.[43]

The nosegay as an imagined object shares in the expanding universe that
defines the *Nosgay* as a printed book. And Whitney draws itineraries for it,
sketching out the contours of its possible movement in time and in space. This
begins the moment she leaves Plat's garden. As we have seen, she writes that

> but ere I parted thence:
> A slip I tooke to smell unto,
>   which might be my defence.
> In stynking streetes, or lothsome Lanes
>   which els might mee infect.
>   (sig. A.vii[v])

Linking the spatial imagination of her slips' dispersal to the geographical distribution of plague, Whitney inscribes both on the map of the city. Both
slips and plague are most forceful (for good or ill) as they travel out-of-doors:
a distinctly public and environmental danger, the circulation of plague threatens to turn people sick and environments noxious.[44] Whitney's virtuous
slips, on the other hand, promise a portable environment, a bubble of sweet
air to encompass the bearer who carries them abroad through city streets.

This slipperiness is both a literary tactic and a site of social and material
vulnerability—a twin capacity emblematized by the "slips" that are Whitney's
chosen lexicon for the elemental materials of textual and botanical traffic. The
possibility of "giving the slip" is never far from Whitney's borrowings: in

the period, the phrase could mark the mobility of loose women, the slipperi-ness of the fall, or the untrustworthiness of fair-weather friends.[45] In one of the earliest idiomatic uses of "giving the slip," Edward Hake in 1567 tied "slipping" to the mobility and untrustworthiness of working women—in particular, to the danger that serving maids might "pilfer, filch, and . . . purloyne" from their masters and then "give the slip."[46]

The diffusive capacities of "slip" conspire in the *Nosgay* with lexical force of "abroad," a term that also links textual, geographic, and botanical imagi-naries according to a common model of outward movement. For Whitney and her contemporaries, the word joined the spatial scope of distribution (its breadth) to openness and access, the public status of a text, person, or piece of gossip.[47] To be either a woman or a text "abroad" was to be out of the house, available, and circulable. "Slip" and "abroad" carry with them the potential violence of scattering and fragmentation, the danger of circulation in public. To scatter abroad is also to tear asunder—and we should recall the signifi-cance of "sundry" for Gascoigne as well as the mythic scattering of the Sibyl's leaves, which offered a conventional model for textual fragmentation and re-collection. To be "abroad," then, is not just to be in public or out-of-doors but to be multiple and scattered. Gerard's *Herball* (1633 edition) uses the word to name the propulsive scattering of seeds: one danger of darnel, a chokeweed, is how easily and forcefully its many seeds are "scattered abroad"; or, as Gerard writes suggestively of a variety of lady's smock sometimes called *Noli me tangere*, "if you touch but the cods when the seed is ripe, though you do it never so gently, yet will the seed fly all abroad with violence."[48] Empha-sizing the violence of the seeds' flight, the herbal reminds us of the sudden force of such centrifugal movements, their transgressive capacity to break out and break in.[49]

It is in this context that Whitney links her slips' virtues and their circu-lation: these material virtues travel in small pieces, dormant in slips but un-altered and unweakened by relocation. In this way, they share some of the appeal—but none of the contingency or perishability—of the New-World vir-tues cataloged by Nicolás Monardes in his *Historia medicinal* (1565), trans-lated into English in 1577 as *Joyfull Newes Out Of the Newe Founde World* (which we last encountered in Chapter 2). Advertising "the vertues of diverse and sundrie Hearbes,Trees, Oyles, Plantes, and Stones," the English edition of Monardes's book offered readers access to the healing powers of plants and other materials from the Americas, detailing not just how to find and use them but how to transport them while retaining their medicinal virtue.[50] In

plant books, references to virtue regularly accompany images of textual circulation, giving worldly imaginary form to the distributed force of the printed
book. We find one example in the spiritual semiotics espoused in Thomas
Becon's midcentury devotional books, where a practical metaphysics of textual virtue also assumes vegetable form. In his dedicatory epistle to his *Flour
of Godly Praiers* (1550), Becon extends the rhetorical exemplarity of the
"flower" to an herbally infused account of its worldly power. The "flour" of
godly prayers suggests the very best wheat refined and winnowed from the
chaff, but also refers explicitly to flowers, as when Becon elaborates the book's
distinctly herbal virtues in the book's dedication to Lady Anne, Duchess of
Somerset. In his elaboration of the *Flour*'s portable herbal virtues, Becon
shares in Whitney's cartographic imagination of the printed book's distributed force: "It is a flower, I graunte. Notwithstandynge suche a flower, as if it
be ryghtelye used, is of synguler vertue and myghtye in operacyon. No evyl
ayer can hurte where the savouer of thys flower commeth. Yea the devil the
world & the flesh can not abide the ayer of thys flower, so mighte is the spiritual operacion therof. The flower geveth a smel in the stretes to the soule of
the faythefull, as Cimamone and Balme, that hathe so good a savoure, yea a
swete odoure doth it gyve as it wer mirre of the best."[51] The fruits of the
prayers follow transitively from the fruitfulness of scriptural fields, an efficacity that trails in turn not just into Becon's volume but wherever (he seems
to be suggesting) copies may be carried, as the flower "geveth a smel in the
stretes to the soule of the faythefull." In Becon's case, virtue's singularity has
a spiritual source: the prayers are drawn, he boasts, from scripture whenever
possible. Using as few words of his own as he could, he tried instead "to
glene oute of the frutieful fyelde of the sacred scryptures." Like Whitney's,
his process of composition represents a labor of gleaning. The multiplication
of these virtues is represented by the book itself but—as long as it is
"ryghtelye used"—realized in the repetition of the prayers it contains.

The virtue of Becon's *Flour* joins two themes that shape printed books of
flowers. On the one hand, the unmanning of the text, by which a botanical
logic of virtue endows the book with a nature and agency other than the
author's. Like later plant books, he also imagines the *Flour*'s material circulation, its consummation in a dispersed form of textual use and consumption.
In this way, Becon's geography closely anticipates the "stynking streetes, or
lothsome Lanes" (sig. A.vi^v) through which Whitney carries her nosegay.
Across the imagined geographies of a pestilent city, Whitney and Becon
invoke botanical dispersal to give the text's defensive powers a concrete

topographical index. Both imbue the physical book—carried in hand, pocket, or satchel—with talismanic force, as virtue abides in the distinctly portable form of the thing itself.

Through a discourse of botanical virtue, Whitney links slipping not with the violence of scattering but with preservation and conservation. As it travels, the force of the nosegay remains sovereign, its seat of power multiplied or relocated along with it. This energy generates the recipe that concludes her series of 110 rhyming flowers:

¶*A soveraigne receypt.*

*The Juce of all these Flowers take,
   and make thee a conserve:
And use it firste and laste: and it
   wyll safely thee preserve.

       *By Is. W. Gent.
        (sig. C.v^r)

Whitney frames the text on the model of a medical recipe, one that—if the reader forms a conserve of the flowers—promises to preserve them from illness or danger. Within the logic of the book, that textual virtue is the force of advice: like the recipe, or the flowers, it should also be received, taken, made a conserve. (With this prescription "to take," Whitney offers a medicinal alternative to Plat's imperative to "take a little.") But the recipe is neither a single object nor a single event: the reader is instructed to use and reuse, without any worry that the flowers' virtue (in the form of a "conserve") might diminish. The temporality of the receipt in this way enacts the strange temporality of the proverb, which, as Stephanie Elsky shows, reflects the "time out of mind" of commonplace and custom.[52] This capacity to speak across times and occasions is part of what empowers both proverb and recipe to be held in common. The virtuous logic of use and application empowers the sovereignty of the sovereign receipt: the latent powers implanted by God in the soil (with herbs as his deputies) and the latent powers implanted in texts (with Whitney's slips as deputies). Whitney's "sovereign receipt," then, helps us see in a new light the operation of power at the scene of reception. A reader must still *take, make,* and *use,* transforming the nosegay's slips to juice as they receive the text.[53] Both recipes and slips promise the force of repetition wherever they travel.

There is some irony that, in the midst of the *Nosgay*'s several withdrawals, Whitney is constantly giving advice, from the Senecan *sententiae* of the nosegay's flowers to the monitory theme of her epistles. With each withdrawal, Whitney generates a substitute that speaks for her in her absence: the nosegay, the epistles, and the "wyll" all become prosopopoeic objects that amplify the collection's voice. The entire volume turns on the presumptuousness of absent command. The logic of virtue encapsulates this double movement: as a kind of portable sovereignty, it governs outcomes wherever it travels, however far from any voice that may have initially legitimated it. This strategy gives a distinctive status to how the *Nosgay* frames each of its sections as an object, as each emerges as Whitney recedes and bears the mark of this melancholy pull. While this absence forms a condition for inscription in general, Whitney draws our attention to the pathos of that gap: the excruciation of delay, the anxiety of transport and handoff. This is also the irony that drives her "sovereign receipt": the recipe's sovereignty is realized in the absence of human authorization; and the apocalyptic echoes of alpha and omega in its sovereign instruction to "use it first and last" mark the deadness of the letter that seems nonetheless to speak to her reader with sovereign force.

Theses on Nosegays

In describing her poetic collection as a nosegay, Whitney advertises it as a composite object with healing force. She also declares it a social transaction. The following pages place Whitney's *Nosgay* in the context of other Tudor nosegays, which likewise link their composite form to the social field of their circulation. Floral or literary, nosegays suggest this horizon of expectation: that the object will be borne by new users and readers, an imagination of social exchange that will prepare us to turn in the final section of this chapter to the distinctive way in which Whitney figures her own potential readership. In sixteenth-century England, printed nosegays formed a mini-genre of their own, examples of composite forms defined by Elyot's description of "nosegay" and "fascicle" as "any thynge knytte togyther." But these nosegays also reflect additional affordances of small, bundled forms: nosegays are carried, presented, and held close to the body. While a garden or a growing plant is connected to the earth, the nosegay is keyed to the human body—through nose, hand, or bosom—and moves wherever its bearer travels. As tokens that shore up erotic and devotional relationships, nosegays are transactional and intimate: their power depends on physical proximity, the closeness of the nosegay's scent to its bearer's nose, its ambivalent incorporation as bodily supplement. The nosegay's association with the body is reinforced by its regular Latin translation, *fasciculus,* often alternately translated as "handful"—or, in Elyot's words, as we've already seen, "a grype, or thyng bounden togither," or that "whiche maye be borne in a mannes hande."[54] As bound or knit things, nosegays, fascicles, and handfuls are all scaled to the human grip and suitable for transport.

As conceits of small-scale gathering, titles like "handful" and "nosegay" announce not just a text's multiple sources but its status as a physical object, often in terms that ambiguously toe the line between metaphor and literal reference. Consider, for example, Anne Wheathill's *Handfull of Holesome (Though Homelie) Hearbs* (1584), the duodecimo binding of which ergonomically scales the prayer book's figurative conceit to the literal hand of its reader. Or N.B.'s dedication of his *Smale Handfull of Fragrant Flowers* (published by Richard Jones in 1575) to Lady Sheffield, in which his "simple gift" of a "litle *handful of Flowers*" literally compels her body into the fold of the book—and the book into the fold of her hand.[55] These conceits call the form of the text into being, but they also call into being a readerly relationship, demanding an attendant set of corporeal, interpretive, and memorial practices.

Socially and generically, the nosegay operates within a mnemonic system of gift exchange—a world of associations and expectations that emerge especially in erotic and in devotional contexts. Whether presented as a New Year's gift, or framing the dedication of an otherwise humble pamphlet, nosegays imply rituals of presentation and transaction. Even Plat, in his dedication to Lady Anne, Countess of Warwick, presents the *Floures*—otherwise rooted in his plot—in the form of loose flowers ("I do heere offer unto your Ladyship, a small handfull or two, of loose flowres, to be disposed at your discretion, either in garlands to were on your head, or els in nosgaies to beare in brest aboute you") before treating them throughout the rest of the volume as a securely enclosed garden.[56] The scene of dedication, acting through an almost occult magnetism, has reshaped his garden into a nosegay.

Jacques Bellot's phrase book, *The Englishe Scholemaister* (1580), follows its examples of French and English usage with a guide to another kind of translation: a bilingual gathering of flowers and their meanings, entitled in

English, *The Posye or Nosegay of Love.*[57] It contains, he promises, "the Posies of sondrye Flowers, Hearbes, and Plantes. That are put commonlye in Nose-gayes," which Bellot goes on to present in the form of an inventory of plants and their meanings as romantic gifts. Lest there remain any doubt as to their purpose, Bellot introduces this bouquet with the proverbial note that love conquers all—first, by flowers and fruits, then by favors and writings, and "above all, by presentes."[58] The delivery of nosegay as gift extends the project of translation and transaction that shapes the rest of Bellot's phrase book—forging translations and relations between languages, between lovers, between human and nonhuman.

As an olfactory mnemonic, nosegays encourage their bearers to remember the one who gave the gift. This memorial function stands potentially at odds with traditional moral and material concerns about the ephemerality and vanity of flowers, epitomized by the verse from Isaiah: "All flesh is grasse, the Scripture saith, and vadeth like a flowre."[59] Whitney, though she worries about the possible abuse of her nosegay, does not mention the possibility of it wilting or going obsolete—as we have seen, a central concern to herbalists and apothecaries, for whom the shelf life of a given virtue in a given form was a standard datum in an herbal or distilling manual. These virtuous nose-gays, on the other hand, might be used and reused, their force undiminished by readers' engagement. Both devotional and erotic nosegays are remarkably—even miraculously—evergreen.

One of the earliest "nosegays" printed in England, Thomas Becon's *A Pleasaunt Newe Nosegay* (first edition, 1542), begins by hailing its imagined devotional readership in the voice of the nosegay itself. Appearing on the verso of the title page, a poem called "The Nosegaye speaketh" directly addresses the reader as a friend, figuring the scene of reading and consumption as a space of intimate companionship. The poem begins:

> What meanest thou my frende to gather
> Floures, which sone perysh and decaye,
> Theyr savours wyll not laste ever
> As by experience se thou maye.

The following two stanzas extend this commonplace monitory advice, amplifying its picture of transitory things, and conclude with this same refrain: "As by experience se thou maye." Then, in the fourth stanza, the nosegay's tone takes on greater urgency, as it asks the reader:

Receave me into thy bosome
If thou doste desyre a nosegaye,
My floures are full of delectacion
As by experience se thou maye.

To knowe thy selfe thou mayst learne here
God and thy kynge truely to obeye,
And to thy neyghbour to be dere
As by experience se thou maye.

Take me nowd unto the therfore
Beare me in thy bosome alwaye,
Much pleasure have I for the in store
As by experience se thou maye.[60]

The book presents a storehouse of wisdom into which the reader is summoned
and welcomed—one that can in turn be incorporated back into the bosom
of the reader to be enjoyed in future time. As memento, the book/nosegay
thus offers a solution to the ephemeral vanity of the worldly bouquet evoked
by the first stanzas. In the final three stanzas, the nosegay's promises about
the future map onto the more immediate future of reading; the pleasures "in
store" await just past a turn of the page. The "experience" of the refrain becomes the experience of reading the book, which replaces the opening stanzas' experience of gathering ephemeral flowers. In the prose dialogue that
follows, Becon knits the composite form of the codex to the bouquet of virtues that its text contains (in this case, patience, chastity, and so on), a gathering that will be echoed in other collections of wisdom and devotional
literature, like John Larke's *The Boke of Wisdome Otherwise Called the
Flower of Vertue* (1565) and N.B.'s *Smale Handfull of Fragrant Flowers* (1575).

The nosegay's placement in the bosom takes its biblical cue from a verse
in the Song of Songs: as given in the Bishops' Bible, "When the king sitteth
at the table, he shall smell my Nardus: a bundell of myrre is my love unto
me, he wyll lye betwixt my brestes."[61] The storage of myrrh in the bosom
becomes a figure for the enduring faithfulness of the church—a token of
future insurance that will be echoed by the rhetoric of other printed nosegays. In early modern England, the "bundell," or bouquet, *fasciculus* in
the Vulgate, is sometimes glossed as a nosegay, echoing the association
in Elyot's dictionary cited above.[62] For example, the title page of *The Godlie*

Garden of Gethsemani (1576) renders the verse in a couplet: "A nosegay of myrrh is my true love to me: / Betwene my brestes his dwelling shalbe."[63] Drawing on a typological resonance with the draft of myrrh before the crucifixion (Mark 15:23), recusant texts, like this one, are more likely to emphasize the nosegay's bitterness, held close as a reminder of the passion. Saint Bernard had written influentially that, since his conversion, he had taken care "to gather up this bundle of myrrh and to place it in my breast, a bundle gathered together out of all the anguish and sorrows of my Lord," and would "proclaim the memory of the abundant sweetness of this myrrh as long as I live."[64] In all of these translations and elaborations, the nosegay signals both an intimate relation to the body of the reader and a mnemonic endurance in future time: the bridegroom, like the bundle of myrrh, *will* abide (*inter ubera mea commorabitur*).

When they appear in plant books, nosegays carry a typological affinity with the book itself, performing in emblematic miniature the printed volume's complicated status as composite material and as giftable object. Becon's speaking nosegay plays this role, as the metaphorical bundle of flowers becomes the voice of the book, and the same strategy shapes Whitney's *Nosgay* and other volumes published by Richard Jones. Over the course of Elizabeth's reign, Jones used images of nosegays more than any other printer, and he became an especially enthusiastic exploiter of their rhetorical capacity to convey a text's composite qualities. Their bundled variety promised readers both moral profit and sensory pleasure.[65] Other handfuls and nosegays printed by Jones in the years just preceding and following Whitney's include the broadside attributed to John Symon, *A Pleasant Posie, or Sweete Nosegay of Fragrant Smellyng Flowers* (1572) and N.B.'s *Smale Handfull of Fragrant Flowers* (1575), as well as *A Handefull of Pleasant Delites*, a collection that exists in an imprint of 1584 though likely first dates to at least a decade earlier.[66]

Though a very different book in its content and stated audience, Jones's edition of *Smale Handfull of Fragrant Flowers* recalls the framing of Whitney's collection.[67] Its title page announces its status as a New Year's gift and stages the reader's receipt of the text as part of a voyeuristic extension of that original event. An introductory poem from the book to the reader indexes its title to the moment of reception, as it arrives in the reader's hand: "Since I poore booke am put into thy hand, / although the tome or volume litle bee."[68] Another preliminary poem advertises the *Handfull*'s lasting freshness, granting that "although this booke be small," the flowers may still delight the

reader "because they are continuall greene." The *Handfull*'s pedagogical ambition further echoes the conceit of Whitney's text, as it asks readers to
"Searche therfore suche a Honycombe," of which the author promises, "The
joyce whereof beyng pleasant sweete, / Is for a curteous Matrone meete." In
this case, however, it specifically addresses women, instructing them to
"Learne as he teacheth you to doo, / That framde this Posie for your sake."[69]
Most of the rest of the brief text is structured as an inventory of feminine
virtues, the fragrant flowers a virtuous lady is meant to gather into a small
handful she can carry with her. As we saw in Chapter 2, this structure reflects the capacity of "virtue" to link moral and material qualities, especially
as both muster force collectively. However, by asking that the book be
"throughly scand / with zelous minde," this small volume withholds the liberty that Whitney claims in her visit to Plat's plot and that she offers to her
own readers. While the *Handfull*'s instructions aim to defend against the loss
of feminine virtue represented by the scattering of herbs, Whitney's dispersed
slips resist this enclosure.

In another anthology, Jones's edition of *A Handefull of Pleasant Delites*
(1584), the first poem following an address to the reader is presented as a nosegay, and similarly does double duty as textual content and epitome. A catalog of emblematic flowers, the poem stands in as the bouquet itself (a bundle of
flowered verses) and as an account of its presentation to a lover: "A Nosegaie
alwaies sweet, for Lovers to send for Tokens, of love, at Newyeres tide, or for
fairings, as they in their minds shall be disposed to write."[70] Immediately
following the dedication from the printer, the "Nosegaie" carries additional
phatic force: it helps bring the imaginary book into being, giving form to
scattered leaves or slips. The nosegay, perhaps like the book itself, is meant
to be a gift ("for Lovers to send for Tokens"), just as other nosegays like
Whitney's are framed as participants in a gift economy. Composed in rhyming poulter's measure, like the volume's opening poem from "The Printer to
the Reader" and like much of Whitney's verse, the "Nosegaie" appears with
no tune associated with it, which further marks it as inscription, linked to
the materiality of book and gift rather than the potentially performed verse
or song that characterizes the rest of the volume.[71]

Like Whitney's nosegay, and like Becon's, the *Handefull of Pleasant Delites*'s nosegay demands to be remembered. Usually attributed, along with the
volume, to Clement Robinson, the poem compiles a gathering of emblematic flowers: "*Lavander* is for lovers true," "*Rosemarie* is for remembrance,"
"*Violet* is for faithfulnesse." Most famous for being echoed by Ophelia in act

4, scene 5 of *Hamlet*, the catalog of the "Nosegaie" closely follows the commonplaces of flower symbolism systematized in writers like Bellot. However, it questions the static seasonality of that code:

> A Nosegaie lacking flowers fresh,
> > to you now I do send.
> Desiring you to look thereon,
> > when that you may intend:
> For flowers fresh begin to fade,
> > and *Boreas* in the field,
> Even with his hard conjealed frost,
> > no better flowers doth yeeld:
> ¶ But if that winter could have sprung,
> > a sweeter flower than this,
> I would have sent it presently
> > to you withouten misse:
> Accept this then as time doth serve,
> > be thankful for the same,
> Despise it not, but keep it well,
> > and marke ech flower his name.[72]

More black than green, this New Year's gift of winter flowers overcompensates for the barrenness of the season with a display of semantic and erotic constancy, one that distinguishes it from the ephemerality of regular flowers.[73] The negative construction of the first sentence, however, undersells this appeal: "A Nosegaie lacking flowers fresh, / to you now I do send." The opposite of "fresh" is not "immutable" (the virtue upon which the poem's apology eventually lands) but "rank," leaving open the threat that the offering is more bitter or rotten than sweet—a possibility that quietly haunts the poet's address to an absent lover in the lines that follow. These lines also arguably place the verse within the scope of a *carpe diem* poem, in which reminding a lover of the rankness of old flowers makes the case for erotic consummation in the fleeting present.

As the first poem in the volume, Robinson's "Nosegaie" takes on the additional responsibility of welcoming the reader into the book, a doubling of office reinforced by the close association between "nosegay" and the titular "handful." The trace of this double address, in which the reader (the recipient of the book) is also hailed as the poem's second-person subject (the recipient of the nosegay), subtly queers the poem's floral and bibliographical economy. Consider the following lines, for example, in the voice of the book, or uttered in the style of Becon's personified nosegay:

> *Peniriall* is to print your love,
>   so deep within my heart:
> That when you look this Nosegay on,
>   my pain you may impart,
> And when that you have read the same,
>   consider wel my wo,
> Think ye then how to recompence,
>   even him that loves you so.[74]

The nosegay, like a book, is a mnemonic device—one that recalls, when breathed in or looked into, not just affection for an absent friend, but the debt incurred by the gift itself. Erotic compensation is one obligation marked on the nosegay's gathering of chits—in a libidinal economy stuck in anticipation. With their mood of unhappy erotic investment, these lines recall George Gascoigne's rendering of erotic economy in his *Hundreth Sundrie Flowres* (1573), where he tells those who borrow flowers from his garden to

>   recompence the lyke agayne:
> For some and some is honeste playe,
> And so my wyfe taughte me to saye.[75]

Whitney taps into a similarly mixed economy when she asks her distant readers to give her some credit, hoping,

> And that when I am distant farre,
>   it worne be for my sake:
> That some may say, God speede her well
>   that dyd this Nosegay make.
>   (sig. C.v^v)

For Whitney, this backward relay of credit is predicated (naturally) on her own absence, the condition under which her nosegay might be borne in the bosom as a reminder of the debt she is due. Each of these debts represents a curb on the free flow of license, an admission that the freedom of a nosegay to circulate still needs the ballast of due compensation—Whitney's slips, it seems, never fully slip away from their gatherer or from this mnemonic economy. However far it may travel, and into however many hands or bosoms, a nosegay remembers who bound it.

Dispersals: New Geographies of Reception

As she projects the *Nosgay*'s reception forward in time and outward in space, Whitney imagines an ever more far-flung secondhand economy for her book, sketching out expanding itineraries and topographies of reception. At several points, Whitney asks readers who dislike the nosegay to pass it on rather than destroy it, entreating "That thou my Nosegay not misuse, / but leave it to the rest" (sig. A.vii^v), and hoping for the nosegay's continued redistribution: "But if thy selfe doo lothe the sent. / geve others leave to weare them" (sig. C.v^v). Whitney asks her readers to reproduce the gesture of generosity and hospitality by which the book was originally assembled and shared by repeating the granting of *leave*, or license, to a new cohort of readers. (In the context of the rest of the *Nosgay*, the language of "leave" newly links the freedom of textual reception to *leaving* and *leave-taking*, echoing the collection's persistent melancholic note of departure.) In this future textual economy, nosegays circulate as clothing circulates—literally, as the nosegay becomes a garment, worn in the bosom before being passed on to second- and third-hand bearers. Built from this iterative model of leave-giving, the future that Whitney imagines is less a rehoming than a kind of relay, a future path assured by the potential diversity of her readership. Whitney's virtues thus imply two distinct models of collective identity. One, as we have seen, understands herbal virtues as something held in common, part of a traditional moral economy in which textual and natural resources are goods meant for common use. The other, following these more scattershot paths of the printed book, links its multiple readers—of variable class, gender, complexion—by an accident of commercial transaction. Both models, as limned by botanical virtue, shape Whitney's imagination of the *Nosgay*'s circulation and reception.

The dispersed and plural future that Whitney imagines would be impossible without an analogously multiple conception of the *Nosgay*'s materiality. Whitney's various prescriptions for redistribution might be recursively repeated, as the nosegay is handed off from one differently complected reader to another. There is no limit to its future travels. Whitney's nosegay, in other words, is a very strange gift—its transactional and material qualities decisively shaped by the multiplicity with which Whitney imagines it as an object. A reader holding the nosegay in her hand knows perfectly well that it is not singular, that other copies are held in other hands, in other rooms or lanes. As Lorna Hutson shows, by modeling the *Nosgay*'s reception on scent, Whitney fashions her book as a substance undiminished by consumption, a convenient capacity for the multiple occasions that Whitney regifts the nosegay throughout the volume. Hutson argues that the distinct material resilience of scent—and the nosegay's capacity to be smelled and resmelled indefinitely—helps bridge the otherwise incommensurate economies of gift-giving and commercial transaction.[76] The result is an account of multiple readership that would be impossible without a conception of the nosegay's form and matter as iterable: it can be reused, and the plants in Plat's garden can be infinitely reslipped—as long as the procedure is performed skillfully.

The elasticity and resilience of plant virtue, which Hutson identifies as a distinctive affordance shared by scent and by print, subtends Whitney's imagination of a more broadly and diversely distributed field of readers.[77] For Whitney, this social imaginary often takes the form of geographical dispersal. In the farewell to the reader that follows the 110 flowers, Whitney elaborates the nosegay's possible futures, folding them into the trope of her own departure:

> Yf he for whom I gathered them,
>   take pleasure in the same:
> And that for my presumption,
>   my Friends doo not mee blame.
> And that the savour take effecte,
>   in such as I doo know:
> And bring no harme to any els,
>   in place where it shal goe.

Whitney follows this image of the nosegay's physical dispersal—at a distance, in whatever "place where it shal goe"—with a reminder of her own imminent withdrawal and the request, as we have seen, that "when I am distant farre, / it worne be for my sake" (sig. C.v^v). In the first part of this passage, the series of conditions gradually scales up from the most familiar—a single person, the dedicatee—to "Friends," "such as I doo know," and, then, most anonymously, "any els, / in place where it shal goe." Whitney's readers in turn understand that they belong to a loosely choreographed collective—linked by the text's distinctive virtues but distinguished by their conditions, constitutions, and locations.

It has been a theme of previous chapters that tropes of books as plants empower poets and printers to imagine futures for their texts, to script scenes of textual reception and the gathering, scattering, and proliferation of textual pieces in time to come. In doing so, they face what is simultaneously an epistemological inquiry, a mathematical problem, and a poetic adventure: How do you know who your readers will be? How do you count them? And, how do you picture them? The remaining pages in this chapter show how Whitney approaches this set of problems equipped with the styles of dispersal and redistribution we have seen so far. While she shares some strategies with other poets whose work appeared in print in the middle years of Elizabeth's reign, her modes of collective imagining also break from her contemporaries, guided by the *Nosgay*'s entanglement in this botanical poetics of dispersed virtues.

Speculating about multiple audiences places both poet and printer in the position of making a fiction, one that—by figuring readers as disparate pieces composing a greater whole—effectively blazons them, fixing them as entries in an inventoried list. Richard Jones habitually explored these dynamics of address and tended to take a position that was, as Michelle O'Callaghan observes of Jones's address to the reader in *A Handefull of Pleasant Delites*, "speculative rather than prescriptive."[78] Rather than predict or prescribe, Jones conjures multiple possible readers to whom he could make a sale, using variety to ground his case for winning many potential customers. Promising something for everyone, Jones's emphasis on variety allows him to hedge his bets: he imaginatively generates multiple readers for the text, and with the copiousness of the book's miscellaneous form, offers something to entice each of them. This form of speculation operates not by discerning or predicting but by multiplying.

Before returning to Whitney, I'd like to briefly discuss two other speculative inventories of textual reception. The first case returns to Nicholas Breton's 1577 *Workes of a Young Wyt*, where, before sowing his wild oats, the young poet inventories human diversity through an extended comparison of books to cheese. Both kinds of matter, Breton explains, display the variety of human taste: "I Have both heard & read oft tymes, that Bookes and Cheeses may very well be likened one to the other, in this poynt: for the diversitie of mens judgementes given of them. For they are wares both, to be looked on for love, and bought for money. The Cheese once out of the Presse, shortly after comes to market to be solde: where (perhaps) it is tasted of many, before it be bought. And bookes once imprinted, are presently in shoppes, where many peruse them, ere they be solde." For several pages, Breton enumerates a series of allegedly common opinions on both books and cheese, repeating the phrase "Some wyl say" well over a dozen times.[79] Anaphora transforms the passage into an inventory of human kinds, with each "some" marking out an *item* in the properties of English society.

In other cases, a rhetoric of extended enumeration assembles a more ambitious taxonomy of potential readers. In his 1581 *Short Inventory of Certayne Idle Inventions: The Fruites of a Close and Secret Garden of Great Ease, and Litle Pleasure*, C. Thimelthorpe responds to his anxiety about appearing in print by elaborating a taxonomy of readerly types. Drawing an extended comparison with falconry, the author sends his wits out into the world on a surveillance mission: by their return, they have "bestowed some time in travayling and wandering toe and froe, and have not only traverst the large and wyld field of this world, but as neare as wee coulde, have also beaten every little scrubbe and bushe." Their mission is to return with an accounting of the diversity of human taste and opinion (of "pennes and tongues").[80] Thimelthorpe's fantasy generates a rich survey of dispersed intellectual society, articulating along the way what he also wants out of his book: that it should obediently report back, having surveyed a landscape of human folly while remaining untouched by it. Like well-trained falcons, neither his book nor his readers should give him the slip. While Gascoigne compares human diversity to the sundriness of herbs and flowers, and Breton likens it to variable taste in cheese, Thimelthorpe imaginatively procures himself a falcon to survey open fields of possible readers. While Thimelthorpe shares with Whitney an interest in dispersed geographies of textual reception, he generates a stance both more anxious and more satirical than Whitney, whose imagination of her readership is both remarkably vague and remarkably forgiving.

Unlike Breton or Thimelthorpe, Whitney broaches the vagaries of reception through a conception of herbal virtue, one that understands readerly variation through the medical logic of human complexion. Like these other poets, she acknowledges human diversity as she attempts to sketch out possible itineraries for reception:

And for thy health, not for thy eye,
    did I this Posye frame:
Because myself dyd safety finde,
    by smelling to the same.
But as we are not all alyke,
    nor of complexion one:
So that which helpeth some we see,
    to others good doth none.
            (sig. A.vii^r)

Whitney treats the differential taste of her audience with remarkable neutrality, even as she pictures a displeased or even disgusted reader—an indifference that she maintains with some consistency:

I shall no whit be discontent,
    for nothyng is so pure:
But one, or other will mislyke
    therof we may be sure.
            (sig. C.v^v)

Whitney does not dismiss these readers as swine averse to the sweetness of her marjoram; her sense of the variety of readers' responses admits—even requires—that her nosegay might not smell as sweet to every nose. An analogous sense of fit between remedy and patient was fundamental to early modern medical practice, which sought to match the elemental constitution of herb or simple (whether hot and wet, or cold and dry, for example) to a patient's temperament.[81]

Whitney's turn to a language of complexion smuggles in a more expansive picture of readerly diversity, one that—however vague in the *Nosgay*—would have invoked for readers more vivid inventories of human types. As the Galenic model taught, humans possessed a range of complexions, born of the collusion of embodiment and environment, and those complexions determined each body's interactions with drugs and disease. Works that describe the diversity of human character merge the physiology of complexion with an aesthetics of copiousness emblematized by the fecundity of vegetable life. For example, Lemnius's *De habitu et constitutione corporis*, Englished by Thomas Newton as the *Touchstone of Complexions* (1576), surveys the variety of human complexion on the same Galenic model. The resulting picture of human variety links it to the fertile variety of nature's virtues; as herbs and flowers are part of nature's copious provision, he writes, so is the variety of human character and complexion.[82] Like the vegetable kingdom, the great variety of human beings boast their own proper virtues and peculiar effects, due to "the Humours and Elemental qualityes which doe constitute the complexion of humayne body, and cause divers sorts and sondry differences of Natures and maners." Lemnius's prose echoes the repetition of "some" and "sundry" that we heard in Gascoigne's poetry in Chapter 3 and that resounds through the prefaces of Breton and Thimelthorpe. This rhetorical structure reaches a climax in an exemplary inventory of the diversity of human kinds:

> And in this sorte, doth this constitution whereof wee now speake, breede and bring foorth into the Theatre of this world, some that be stout Braggers and shamelesse praters, some Parasites & clawbackes, some Dolts and cockscombs, some selfe pleasers, which thinke more of themselves then all the rest of the Towne besyde doth, some Mynstrelles and Pypers, some gracelesse Ruffians and Spendalls, ryotously wastyng and consumyng their Patrimony: Some Dycers and Gamsters, some Trencher frends and Coseners: Some Counterfaiters, Skoffers, Tumblers and Gesturers, some Jugglers, & Legier du maine players, wyth a great rablemente of other lewde Lubbers of other sorts besyde.[83]

Like Whitney's "Wyll," and like the passages from Breton and Thimelthorpe, Lemnius relies on an inventory to paint a picture of a broad social field. In assembling this account, Lemnius places the copious variety of both gardens and people within a robust cosmology: one that links the colors of herbs and flowers, the arrangement of planets and stars, and the staggering diversity of humoral complexion. Each particular, he explains, has its own complexion or virtue, its own sparklingly stubborn way of being.

Lemnius's rhetorical strategy turns on the power of display: all of these kinds, he writes, are bred and brought forth into "the Theatre of this world." Whitney displays a dexterity for this kind of inventorying in the "Wyll," where she endows the variety of London's places and kinds with vivid poetic energy. However, she offers us no such images here. Despite the significance of human particularity to her understanding of her text's reception, she offers no pictures or examples of her potential readers. Instead, Whitney suggests a more open-ended pattern for the text's future circulation, asking poorly matched readers to pass it on. Though she invokes the period's fundamental discourse of human classification, her account of the *Nosgay*'s circulation refuses to perform those very classifications.

> Or if that thy complexion,
>   with them doo not agree:
> Refer them to some friend of thine,
>   tyll thou their vertue see.
> And this I pray thee, whether thou
>   infected wast afore:
> Or whether with thy nature strong,
>   they can agree no more.
> That thou my Nosegay not misuse,
>   But leave it to the rest:
> A number may such pleasure finde,
>   to beare it in their brest.
>   (sig. A.vii^v)

To a point, we can understand this passage in the context of other speculative attempts at imagining audience: it suggests a variety of readers, an open field of circulation. But Whitney seems both remarkably optimistic and surprisingly incurious about this potential multitude. References to "the rest" and "a number" suggest an unknown quantity of readers ("leave it to the rest: / A number may such pleasure finde, / to beare it in their brest"). Instead of the taxonomic and anatomizing "somes" of these other inventories, Whitney's use of "some" serves only to de-specify: "Refer them to *some* friend of thine," whomever that may be. The temporality is equally openended: "Refer them to some friend of thine, / till thou their vertue see," Whitney writes. The "till" of this command enlists the reader in a project without a timeline; these future, uncounted others will be satisfied at the end of an unspecified period. The unknowns of reception are couched within the conditional horizon of Whitney's verbs: A number *may* find pleasure. And yet this putative scene, however vaguely posited, is remarkably intimate: that vague number may find pleasure "to beare it in their brest." Summoning readers' bodily experience, she names the potential pleasure they find in the nosegay's intimate incorporation. The pleasures she invokes—like the geography of the scenes at which we imagine it realized—are dispersed and diffuse.

The openness that marks Whitney's description of her readership translates the intimate address of Becon's nosegay to a broader social field. As we saw above, his 1542 printed nosegay concludes its introductory poem with a stanza that promises a store of pleasure but first demands, "Take me nowd unto the therfore / Beare me in thy bosome alwaye." The direct command of this nosegay's "take me" translates into the conditional mood of Whitney's "may"; the temporal immediacy of "Take me *nowd* unto the" is deferred by Whitney's "*till* thou their vertue see"; the promise of pleasure "in store" is distributed instead across a wide field of potential future experience. Even the apparently specific reference to "thy bosome" becomes the vaguely multiplied image of "their brest." Becon's voice of second-person necessity becomes a third-person condition of possibility in Whitney. Whitney's rendering transforms Becon's scene by multiplying it, scattering it across a constellation of potential encounters. The *Nosgay's* diffuse geography, traced by the paths of its future consumption, accords with what Michael Marder calls the "bad infinity" of plant growth: it strives toward no final form or telos.[84] The bad infinity of textual circulation, in turn, breaks the intimate dyad of Becon's lyric address.

And yet, Whitney is not quite so easygoing as her shrugging deferral to differently completed readers suggests. Despite the conventional humility and ostensible flexibility of Whitney's authorial position, the *Nosgay* is a remarkably bossy text, each of its sections framed by an imperative and often didactic orientation. As I have suggested, each of Whitney's deputies— the slips of rhyming sentences, the epistles, the "wyll"—becomes a kind of miniature sovereign. How, then, should we understand Whitney's imagination of the *Nosgay's* future? Like the social formations that scholars have described as reading publics in later periods, the imagined readership limned by Whitney's slips conjures a dispersed social body organized by dispersed printed copies. It represents a form of imaginative gathering in the face of textual dispersal, and, in its open-ended apostrophes, an energetic performance of the world-making *poiesis* that Michael Warner identifies as one of the core qualities of publics.[85]

But the vagueness of Whitney's account leaves this hypothetical collective in suspense. We might better understand this social-textual-botanical imaginary not as a public but according to the protocols of virtue. I suggested above that the *Nosgay* distributes virtue's sovereign force across the overlapping geographies of London and of the text's reception. Whitney assembles her receptive cartography as a field across which "vertues" circulate, as tiny pockets of efficacity that accompany books and slips and advice. But these virtues bring a certain tension with them: as bossy little deputies, they enforce memory and textual continuity at a distance. But they are also agents of the kind of looseness that has generated those distances in the first place. Like a spell, or a slipknot, they bind and unbind at once. For Whitney, though, any collective identity achieved by this body of readers follows their shared gestures of taking leave and giving the slip. They may be slippery together, but are always, inevitably, slippery apart.

How to Read Like a Pig

Swinelike Grossenesse

In the preface to the *Songes and Sonettes* (1557), publisher Richard Tottel exhorts the lyric anthology's readers to purge themselves of that "swinelike grossenesse, that maketh the swete majerome not to smell to their delight." They should, in other words, flush out the piggishness that keeps them from appreciating the poems that follow. Key to Tottel's exhortation is his confidence that unlearned readers are not fated to remain swinelike and gross: the central step of this process is "by reding to learne to bee more skilfull." Promising to place privately held poetry into public hands and to make those new hands more skillful, Tottel's preface to the reader offers a picture of access and assimilation, a suggestion that the reader—by the act of reading itself—might acquire the skill of discernment, the capacity to unlock the sweetness of the poetry.

For all the fluidity of readerly capacity and social role in this scene, Tottel's image turns on a resolutely immovable object: the swine. As studious readers learn and purge, and horded texts are published, the signifier of "swinishness" remains statically locked. So incalcitrant a bad reader is the swine that we see it recur in a range of early modern scenes of textual reception, its bad judgment the timeless stuff of both proverb and natural history. It was a truism that the sweetness of marjoram is repellant to swine, and the proverb on which Tottel draws finds its antecedents in Lucretius and earlier. In the *Adages*, Erasmus writes that the herb's sweetness is "inimical to the swinish tribe."[1] The pig's inability to savor sweet things also figures as one of the animal's basic properties in Edward Topsell's *Historie of Foure-Footed Beastes*, where Topsell notes that "sweet savours" are in fact "very hurtfull to swine, especially the sweet oyle of Marjoram."[2] The same proverb had special literary significance. It will return in visual form on the title page of Philip

Sidney's 1593 *Arcadia* (Figure 14), where it serves less as an invitation to self-improvement than as a Cerberus guarding the door to the volume.[3] "I breathe," the marjoram says in scrolling text, but "not for you."[4]

The swine frequently emerges at these moments of contested gatekeeping, with its role as an arbiter of worthy and unworthy readership finding its canonical endorsement in Matthew 7:6, which reads in the King James Version: "Give not that which is holy unto the dogs, neither cast ye your pearles before swine: lest they trample them under their feete, and turne againe and rent you."[5] The verse had long been taken to bear on the distribution and reception of texts. Augustine writes that swine are "despisers of truth," while the verse's pearls stand for those "spiritual things" on which we set such a high value because they lie hidden, "in shells, one might say," in the wrappings of allegory.[6] Boccaccio cites the same verse in a defense of allegorical reading in vernacular poetry, and—like Augustine—considers the damage

Figure 14. Philip Sidney, *The Countesse of Pembrokes Arcadia* (London: [by John Windet] for William Ponsonby, 1593), title page (detail). RB 69478, The Huntington Library, San Marino, California.

done by granting access to the wrong readers. We easily forget, however, the verse's dramatic ending, with its image of trampling and rending: Matthew and his exegetes and echoers remind us that the pig and the dog are not only unrefined consumers but destructive ones.[7]

By not appreciating the *scent* of the marjoram, the pig fails unskillfully at a kind of extractive reading at which Renaissance readers practiced and trained. According to humanist teachers and scholars, as we have seen, a skillful reader proceeds in the fashion of a bee, gathering sweetness from a range of sources without diminishing the sources themselves. Smelling the marjoram, to turn back to the initial analogy, allows one to enjoy the sweetness of a scent without consuming it. As Isabella Whitney showed us, smell is iterable in a way that eating is not, and so poses a promising analogy for the strange materiality of the printed book, which offers itself to diverse readers in multiple locations, to be tasted and retasted but (ideally) never consumed. The pig uproots this fantasy: living obstinately in the present, by compulsively tearing things out of the ground, it destroys both present enjoyment and future use (a distinctly swinish capacity that will prove central to its cultural identity). The pig represents a bone in the throat of the long history of literary taste.

The stakes of garden-gatekeeping, then, are high. Granting access to the wrong audience poses a mortal danger to the text, the plot, the single stem. I argued in Chapter 3 that the bad reading that John Grange imagines when he conjures the uprooting of his flowers threatens to do more than misconstrue or underestimate the text. The reader-uprooter challenges poetry's survival and the possibility of its productive future. This position might be reduced to the maxim "Don't read like a pig." Specifically, the image of uprooting alights upon a complex of associations around the figure of the swine as an archetypal bad reader—not only lacking in taste but inclined to violently uproot rather than merely savor or sample. This version of stewardship structures an understanding of "good reading" that turns on a nonconsumptive version of taste—something at which pigs, it turns out, are notoriously bad. Indeed, with their strong inclination to dig, uproot, and destroy, they are the worst possible stewards.

Pigs have something to teach us, I believe, about how printed books encounter and imagine their readership. I would like to attend, then, to their recurrent appearance as a figure of the bad reader at moments when sixteenth-century English books struggle to tell the story of their own reception and consumption. The destruction threatened by a bad reader produces a paradox when the valuable thing being trampled is a *textual* thing—to what, we might ask, does trampling or rending pertain when the value of a text is not necessarily attached to any given example?[8] The setting of the early modern traffic in printed books lends this question a special significance: What happens to the possibility of destruction when the thing of value is many things, dispersed among readers, and so redundantly present in a range of locations? The worry about defouling and trampling expressed by Augustine, Boccaccio, and others is transformed in the context of print. What does it mean to destroy a printed poem?[9]

The swine that haunt Elizabethan printed poetry venture an answer to this question. By tracing a series of pigs through early modern English printed books, the following pages reflect back on the previous two chapters by reconsidering the poetic garden from the perspective of its worst enemy. While imagining a pig nosing its way into a volume of poetry may verge on the preposterous, this threat performs a necessary conceptual labor. When it appears in printed preliminaries, the figure of the swine accommodates an immaterial imagination of distant and dispersed reception to a materialist account of textual composition. In other words, the pig participates in two procedures that might seem to be in tension: first, helping authors and publishers conceive of the strange fact of print publication, by making imaginable a world in which a single thing might be in multiple places at once; and, second, giving material form to the imagined text as a robust sensory object, perceived as sweet, bitter, honeyed, salty. In its encounter with the swine, the printed poem joins the abstract text to the particular page, indefinitely iterable and circulable but still subject to mortal injury. These figural conventions will lead us to conclude with the period's most notorious scene of uprooting: Guyon's destruction of the Bower of Bliss at the conclusion of book 2 of *The Faerie Queene*. We may not be surprised to find a pig present at the scene of this crime. However, in Spenser's inversion, it is not the swine who is responsible for the act of uprooting.

Pigs Against the Future

As Swine are to gardens and orderly plantations, so are tumults to Parliaments, and Plebeian concourses to publick Councels turning all into disorders and sordid confusions.

—Charles I, *Effata regalia: Aphorismes divine, moral, politick*

The sign of the pig indexes not just an absence of taste, but the possibility and even imminence of harm: of trampling, razing, uprooting. However unclean and undiscerning it may be, the swine is most dangerous when it uproots—which is after all what pigs do, whether digging for truffles or trampling the harvest. This capacity, recorded in Matthew 7 and in millennia of pig-lore, motivates the proverb in the epigram above attributed to Charles I.[10] An agent of filth, disorder, and uprooting, the swine can serve as a figure of class transgression, as it is for King Charles, and as an emblem of the operation of destructive passion, which is how the phrase appears in George Whetstone's *The Honorable Reputation of a Souldier* (1585), where it describes the danger that envy poses to an army: "the common Envy, wher she hath passadge, is like a swine in a garden, a destroyer without regarde, and in a Campe, a very subvertion."[11] As figures of class transgression, lasciviousness, and destructive consumption, swine invoke the danger and possibility of "passage"—the consequences of more open access to gardens, camps, books, Parliament.[12]

In this way, the swine stands as a limit case to the liberties offered by Elizabethan printed gardens. As we saw in Chapters 3 and 4, it was conventional for poetic gardens to promise readers license to proceed at will, inviting them to progress in an order or a manner unconstrained by either author or printer. Those same poets also imagined the disruptive or even violent turns those liberties might take—and worried not just about the limits of authorial control but about the vulnerability of the text and its maker to injuries like uprooting. Both poet and poem become subject to serious—even fatal— harm. (There is a reason, after all, that we say we *submit* a piece of writing.) And here the mal-literate pig enters the garden, at the limit of textual hospitality, as the sharp edge of submission.

With this possibility of destruction in mind, warnings against piggishness conscript the reader into a project of textual conservation. Bartholomew Chappell, in the epistle to his *Garden of Prudence* (1595), asks his dedicatee's help to "take upon you the keeping of this litle sweete Garden, that neither the wilde Boare destroy it, neither carping Knights, or any of *Momus* wightes devoure it, but that it may have free passage (by your Honourable assistance) amongst all godly Christians."[13] The book's free passage among the godly turns on cutting off passage for wild boar and carping knights. In Whitney's *Nosgay*, swine threaten to rush in at the moment she opens Plat's book (and her own) to new readers. Here, she vividly imagines her source text's hypothetical destruction. Having invited her reader to visit Plat's garden, she advises an approach to etiquette that turns on stewardship:

> In any wise, be chary that
> > thou lettest in no Swine:
> No Dog to scrape, nor beast that doth
> > to ravin styll inclyne.
> For though he make no spare of them,
> > to such as have good skyll:
> To slip, to shere, or get in time,
> > and not his braunches kyll:
> Yet barres he out, such greedy guts,
> > as come with spire to toote:
> And without skill, both Earb & Flower
> > pluck rashly by the roote.[14]

The passage begins with a problem of admission and inclusion: "be chary that / thou lettest in no Swine." The pig is, once again, first in a list of those to be kept out of the garden, joined (as in Matthew) by the familiar company of the dog, to which Whitney adds an open-ended category of beasts inclined to "ravin styll."[15] Porousness itself poses a danger: the very fact of a gate that opens makes the garden-text vulnerable to injury, as even a skilled reader might expose it to a destructive stowaway. "Ravin" here designates a predatory, beastlike quality—specifically, the voracious appetite of a predator, its desire to consume. The "ravin" reader is ravenous. The word also suggests a crime against property (from the Latin *rapina*)—a synonym for plunder, theft, or ravishment.[16] By the end of these lines, however, the "ravin styll" of beasts has turned to the lack of skill of a rash reader, whose animalized "greedy guts," alongside the beastly qualities of uprooting, have been displaced onto a hypothetical human consumer of the book.

It is in this sense the kind of consumption that is at stake in the image of the pig: a swine's bad taste cannot easily be severed from its proclivity to uproot, to cut off the harvest of future generations. As Whitney's language makes clear, good readers share with the skilled gardener a sense of timing: they know how "To slip, to shere, or get in time, / and not his braunches kyll." An unskilled reader, meanwhile, plucks *rashly* by the root. These examples project the opposite of swinelike consumption as the better practice of taste—one that cultivates rather than consumes. And it reiterates the association of good taste with restrained stewardship, the qualities of the good herbalist and well-governing prince.

Their inclination to uproot exposes pigs to an exceptional violence in book 15 of Ovid's *Metamorphoses*, where Pythagoras explains that the swine became the first animal sacrifice after having been found guilty of uprooting corn (here in Golding's translation):

> Wheras there was no sacrifyse beforne,
> The Swyne (bycause with hoked groyne he wrooted up the corne,
> And did deceyve the tillmen of theyr hope next yeere thereby)
> Was deemed woorthy by desert in sacrifyse too dye.[17]

The swine is charged here not just with consuming the grain, but with ruining a *future* year's harvest. He has deceived the tillmen both of present profit and of "theyr hope next yeere." This is a task toward which swine, with "hoked groyne," are morphologically predisposed.

Ovid intensifies and elaborates this fable in the *Fasti*, where Ceres herself performs the first animal sacrifice, killing a sow for ruining next year's harvest and for—with her obsessive rooting—erasing the footprints of her daughter just as she is trying to trace her disappearance to the underworld. In the fable, Ceres's path forms an allegory of reading, as she tracks and deciphers clues across the landscape, until the unfortunate sow becomes an agent of deletion, erasing writing and destroying the traces that gave the goddess some path toward hope. When the figure of razing returns in the Bower of Bliss, below, it will again be yoked to inscription and forgetting.

In Ovid's accounts, the pig's crime consists not just in its own present pleasure but in its violence against future time. Like a bad gardener or careless weeder, as we saw in Thomas Hill's weeding instructions in Chapter 3, swine pose a special danger to young and tender plants. Topsell warns that they are especially destructive in springtime, when hogs take extra pleasure in young herbs. He infuses this dimension of their appetite with an especially vivid dose of wantonness—citing Columella, Topsell warns readers to give them "some sodden drinke, wash or swill" in the spring, "before your Hogs go abroad to bite at the sweet and fresh-growing-hearbes, least they provoke them to loosenesse."[18]

Scholars of folklore and anthropology have long tried to account for the association of swine and boar with death in Western symbolism and theology. R. P. Knight in 1836 speculated that the "symbolical use of the boar to represent the destroying or rather the anti-generative attribute" is likely the origin of religious abhorrence of pork.[19] The Mishneh Torah forbids the breeding of swine and dogs (in most circumstances) "because the damage they do is substantial and frequent."[20] In Ovid's fable, these foundational acts of erasure are countered with the iterative ritual of animal sacrifice—a punishment for this violence against future reproduction, in a repetition that, in its observation, extends past violence indefinitely into future time.

The power to uproot, however, is not always a bad thing. Or so modern-day homesteaders who employ pigs for plowing their fields might tell you—so long as you don't need to rely on their judgment of where and what to plow. A poem called "Losse of hurtfull thinges is gayne," in Francis Thynne's *Emblemes* (1600), takes the groining boar as a purifying force. For earth that has run rank with weeds, the warlike boar brings a hygienic purge:

> Producinge earth inrich'd, makes rich againe
> the toylinge laborer hopinge fruitfull gayne;
> but yf neglect, it unmanurde growe,
> corruptinge weedes and harmefull plants do flowe.
> with wrootinge groyne, [the] feirce and warlike bore,
> turnes up and betters that bad lande before,
> destroyeng those unprofitable springes,
> to frutefull land which such annoyance bringes,
> which is not losse, but bettringe to the feilde,
> more holsome frute then redie for to yeilde.
> wherfore from thee, yf taken bee the thinge
> *which* needlesse is, and doth not profitt bringe,
> nor losse nor greife, let that be unto thee,
> for weedes pluck'd up, hurt not the ground, wee see.[21]

Offering us one more "pig against the future," again by specifically targeting youth in their "unprofitable springes," Thynne rewrites uprooting not as loss but as bettering—to the field, if not to individual plants. The violence of weeding effects a form of moral and agricultural improvement of the kind resisted by Nicholas Breton's wild oats in Chapter 3. Thynne's rooting boar echoes what Stephen Greenblatt will identify as the regenerative violence of

Guyon's destruction of the Bower, as well as the power of cyclical regeneration insured by the boar preserved in Spenser's Garden of Adonis. There is a kind of destruction, Thynne writes, "which is not losse."[22]

The association of *Suidae* with death touches the core of the legacy of Adonis, whose story links seasonal death and regeneration in Shakespeare's poem and in the eponymous garden in *The Faerie Queene*'s book 3. In *Venus and Adonis*, at the moment of Adonis's fatal wound, the wild boar transforms into a swine: "And, nuzzling in his flank, the loving swine / Sheathed unaware the tusk in his soft groin."[23] Here, Shakespeare echoes the "hoked groyne" described by Ovid's Pythagoras, and anticipates Thynne's "wrootinge groyne," using a word that denotes both the passive site of Adonis's wound and the penetrating weapon of the boar's tusk. Shakespeare's poem lexically displaces this fatal power onto the complementary body part, in turn confusing concave and convex, subject and object, the hard stuff of the tusk and the soft stuff of the thigh. Always a pun when pigs are in the picture, groin goes both ways.[24]

Dunghill Kind

> Saide *Guyon*, See the mind of beastly man,
> That hath so soone forgot the excellence
> Of his creation, when he life began,
> That now he chooseth, with vile difference,
> To be a beast, and lacke intelligence.
> To whom the Palmer thus, The donghill kinde
> Delightes in filth and fowle incontinence:
> Let *Gryll* be *Gryll*, and have his hoggish minde;
> But let us hence depart, whilest wether serves and winde.

In his edition of *The Faerie Queene*, A. C. Hamilton glosses this final stanza of book 2 with the observation that, in concluding the episode of the Bower with an obstinate pig, Spenser may have been influenced by the moral quoted above: in the version attributed to Charles I, "As Swine are to gardens and orderly plantations, so are tumults to Parliaments." It is, Hamilton helpfully notes, "here very appropriate."[25] And yet, it is not; or, at least not for Gryll, who has done nothing to harm the Bower. He is its residue and survivor, avatar of its spirit of materialist pleasure in the future beyond the canto's last line. It is instead the hero Guyon who is the swine in the garden, uprooter and waster of beds and bowers.

This reordering of the conventional relationship between pigs, gardens, and poetry offers another twist in the scene's difficult place at the end of book 2, which has long troubled its readers with the Knight of Temperance's paradoxical intemperance. This final section will suggest that Guyon's destruction of the Bower of Bliss rewrites the scenes of rash lyric uprooting conjured by mid-Elizabethan poets. Presenting us with another garden in mortal danger of being uprooted, Spenser engages with the figurative conventions described in my previous two chapters, as book 2's extended battle with prodigal temptations culminates in a distinctly vegetal scene. From this angle, seen in conversation with those earlier collections, the destruction of the Bower seems not just a spiritual purification, a purge of temptation in the name of greater prudence, but a specific destruction of media forms.

When the poem arrives at the Bower, canto 12 has already traversed a landscape hewn by patterns of prodigality and expenditure. In stanzas 8 and 9, as Guyon and the Palmer approach the Rock of Reproch, the Palmer presents its visions of excess in terms that recall George Whetstone's framing of the "Garden of Unthriftinesse" in his *Rocke of Regard* (1576): by the "lustfull luxurie and thriftlesse wast" that mark the youthful excesses of younkers and prodigals. The economic vocabulary of self-management returns as they arrive at "the quicksand of *Unthriftyhed*" (2.12.18), and extends to the "plentifull dispence" (2.12.42) poured forth by the Bower. The image of the Bower as an outpouring of expense invokes the ideals of aristocratic hospitality and liberality that informed lyric collections of the 1570s—"lost credit and consumed thrift" that the Palmer ascribes to "looser daies."[26]

The poem encounters Verdant, the canto's central example of youthful prodigality, as he is already caught in Acrasia's thrall in the Bower. Like the young poets in Chapter 3, Verdant joins vegetal images of youth to the pleasures and dangers of "plentifull dispence." And, like them, Verdant comes close to the edge of fully submitting to idleness, passivity, and pleasure before being pulled back into narrative progress.[27] As Garrett Sullivan observes, Verdant's languor takes a distinctly vegetal hue. His face lays out its own verdant landscape, bearing the marks of early spring, and his name, springgiving, marks him as doubly green: *vert* and *Ver*-dant, and the source of springing "vertues," though they have receded into latency in the Bower.[28] The colorway of Verdant's youthful prodigality places him in the company of "green" poets like Kendall, Grange, Breton, and Spenser himself, who, in the *Fowre Hymnes*, apologizes for the products of "greener times."[29] Kendall, introducing his *Flowers of Epigrammes* (1577), ascribes the reading of poetry to his "greene and growyng yeares"; Gascoigne identified in a number of poems with a "greene knight" who was a figure of wasted youth.[30] The rhetoric of greenness helps imagine a literary career that brackets poetic production as part of a passing developmental phase—discourses, George Pettie writes, "devised by a greene youthfull capacitie."[31]

We might also, across the landscape of canto 12, find a few books. Across this terrain, Spenser disperses the lexicon of botanical poetics. Arriving at "the most daintie Paradise on ground" (2.12.58), a reader might mistake this landmark for the *Paradise of Dainty Devices* (1576), already issued in multiple editions by 1590. And the list of the objects taken by Guyon's destructive fury (2.12.83) might also inventory the titles of Elizabethan printed books:

"But all those pleasaunt bowres and Pallace brave, / *Guyon* broke downe, with rigour pittilesse" | *Brittons Bowre of Delights* (1591); Pettie's *A Petite Pallace of Pettie His Pleasure* (1576); Painter's *The Palace of Pleasure* (1566); *A Poore Knight his Pallace of Private Pleasures* (1579).

"Their groves he feld" | "A grove of graces," printed by Henry Denham with Fleming's *The Diamond of Devotion* in 1581.

"Their gardins did deface" | Grange's "Garden" (1577); Guicciardini's *The Garden of Pleasure* (1573); Peacham's *The Garden of Eloquence* (1577); the "close and secret garden of great ease, and litle pleasure" in Thimelthorpe's *A Short Inventory of Certayne Idle Inventions* (1581).

"Their arbers spoyle" | Howell's *The Arbor of Amitie* (1568); or the "arbour of vertue" in Whetstone's *Rocke of Regard* (1576).

"Their banket houses burne" | Elyot's *Banquett of Sapience* (1557); the "banquet of comfettes" in Breton's *The Workes of a Young Wyt* (1577); *The Banquett of Dainties* (1566).

The landscape of the Bower reads like a graveyard of printed volumes, each title an epitaph for a once fashionable mode of inscription. Meanwhile, Guyon's repertoire of destructive techniques joins ways of gardening to ways of reading: he rigorously breaks down, spoils, defaces, and burns. Cabinets are suppressed—a strategy of censorship. And, finally, their buildings are razed—a mode of architectural demolition, but more commonly a technique for the obliteration of written traces.[32] Verdant's shield has already, stanzas earlier, been subjected to a complementary erasure, being "fowly ra'st, that none the signes might see" (2.12.80). Guyon, like Ceres's swine in the *Fasti*, becomes an agent of violent forgetting. (Guyon will soon after accuse Gryll of the same crime: that he "so soone forgot the excellence / Of his creation.") As we saw in Chapter 3, uprooting was itself an established metaphor in humanist models of reading, the responsibility of a prudent reader facing a classical text.[33] To the degree that Guyon's uprooting of the Bower represents an allegory of reading, it is a practice in the hermeneutics of extirpation: a style of reading committed to ensuring it is a text's final interpretation.

Scholars have suggested that the scene Guyon discovers in the Bower reflects a specific engagement with lyric poetry, especially as the suspension of lyric time resists the movement of narrative progress.[34] I would suggest we further consider the degree to which Spenser might be engaging specifically with *printed* lyric, by wrestling with earlier Elizabethan collections that—as we have seen in previous chapters—articulated their own conceptions of time and the waste of poetic matter. The bowers and groves that provide the objects for Guyon's eradication had been implicated in debates about the prodigality of poetic production and consumption. Through a robust botanical imagination, those printed poetry collections grappled with extinction and proliferation—a set of questions on which Spenser reflects throughout book 2's dynamic of ruin and monument.

As Wendy Beth Hyman argues, Guyon brings the violence of time into the Bower, breaking its suspended seasonlessness, and personally introducing (and accelerating) the ravages of its passage.[35] As we saw for Isabella Whitney, slipping must be timely; "to slip, to shere, to get in time" is the core of horticultural skill. Guyon, however, seems in an incredible rush. He and the Palmer must act quickly lest Acrasia catch their drift and "slip" away: in stanza 81, action begins as "suddein forth they on them rusht." Guyon here becomes the bad reader who Plat worries will "rush" into his garden—or, like the raven beasts who Whitney knows, if they sneak in the gate, will "rashly" uproot. Like those other beasts, Guyon has already intruded. With this rush, Guyon breaks from the remarkable passivity that has characterized his action in the final cantos of book 2; as Harry Berger observes, this passivity allies him with the *modus patiendi* of Verdant, which extends up until the dramatic action of extirpation at the end of canto 12, when his patience breaks into the abrupt "now" of action. Action happens incredibly quickly once it happens, as the Bower is destroyed in a stanza, and "of the fayrest late, now

made the fowlest place" (2.12.83). In this context, Guyon's violence is an assault on a vegetable style of temporality and not merely an assault on vegetables. He resists the imperative patience of gardener and husbandman, just as
the Book of Temperance abhors the latent passivity of vegetable life.

As we have seen, however, it is usually swine who are rushers and ruin-
ers, joined by the occasional dog. What should we make then of Gryll, the
hog who at the end of the canto remains unreformed, unweedable, and in no
rush at all? The entire episode of the Bower's destruction, I have suggested,
is framed by a reversal of role, in which Guyon takes on the swinish task of
uprooting, leaving Gryll only to persist. Gryll's crime, according to Guyon,
is forgetting—and not merely forgetting, but forgetting "so soone" the excellence of his creation. And yet it is Guyon who has been the rash extirpator of
memory and Gryll who insists on remembering the Bower and countering
Guyon's refusal to acknowledge what he has destroyed.

Readings of Gryll tend to take him as a figure of resistance to book 2's
narrative and hermeneutic progress, his hoggishness a stubborn refusal to
get with the narrative program. In this sense, he extends what the lyric force
of the Bower had also threatened: to be a drag, or a stay, on epic progress—
an agent of suspension. Gryll also proves remarkably resistant to allegorical
reading. Book 2's final stanza concludes with a circular declaration from the
Palmer and then an abrupt departure. "Let *Gryll* be *Gryll*, and have his hoggish minde" is not quite a lesson: though technically in the imperative it prescribes no action; and his possession of a "hoggish" mind, as it calls back in
rhyme to the "donghill kinde," repeats that act of classification but does not
in itself convey any knowledge. Instead, Guyon and the Palmer depart to a
contingent world of changing weather, while Gryll remains safely and circu-
larly contained within his own mind and kind.

It's not entirely right to say, though, that Gryll hasn't been read. Both
Guyon and the Palmer *have* read him. It is in making Gryll an example that
Guyon takes on the Palmer's role as teacher: "See the mind of beastly man,"
he instructs us, "That hath so soone forgot the excellence / Of his creation."
The Palmer also reads Gryll, though not according to his allegorical meaning, but according to his class in the world of creatures. As the Palmer says
of Gryll's preference not to recover from his enchantment:

> The donghill kinde
> Delightes in filth and fowle incontinence:
> Let *Gryll* be *Gryll*, and have his hoggish minde.

The Palmer's observation imitates the tropes of natural historical general-ization and proverb, performing the fixity of classification by the natural orders of "kinde."[36] In this articulation, we might hear the voice of Topsell, whose *Historie of Foure-Footed Beastes* promises to relay creatures' "Names, Conditions, Kindes, Vertues."[37] Its present-tense voice ("Delightes") carries the timeless mood of proverb—like the one in Geoffrey Whitney's *Choice of Emblemes* (1586) that promises that "Goats delight in the woods, pigs in the mud."[38] Gryll in turn becomes the kind of slippery reader known not by the contents of his mind but by the contours of his kind. By taking up space and being useless, Gryll assumes a poetic force much like that which Heather James ascribes to the long catalogs of flowers that appear elsewhere in Spens-er's poetry: by not "surrendering to allegorical interpretation," he resists the demands of utility that usually guide industrious bees through the flowers of rhetoric, refusing to be transmuted into profit.[39] A pocket of inutility in the course of the poem, the only kind of action that studying Gryll prepares you for is walking away.

In these various ways, then, it is not Gryll who teaches us to read poetry like a pig, but Guyon. Or, at least, like the kind of pigs who are usually found reading Renaissance poetry. In framing the conclusion of book 2 in this way, Spenser re-asks the question that shaped so much literary production during Elizabeth's reign: what does poetry have to do with waste? As we have seen, prodigality narratives redeem the wastelands of youthful poetry by imagining a future that proceeds otherwise—in which poets have returned from erotic poetry, and from eating husks with swine in foreign fields (as the Prodigal Son does, in the biblical account), to a productive, virtuous, and temperate life in the commonwealth. In this sense, the scene of the Bower returns Spenser to a set of topoi and concerns that had dominated poetic discourse in the previous decade. But he breaks from the model of pleasur-able division that those other poems embraced.[40] For Whetstone, the purpose of his "Garden of Unthriftinesse"—as for Gascoigne, with his "Weedes," and Grange, with his "Garden"—is not to uproot but to incorporate as lessons the poetic products of youthful prodigality. This containment—by figura-tive conceit and by printed division—is a technology of preservation. I sug-gested in Chapter 3 that the developmental logic displayed by the youthful verse of Grange and Breton represents an inversion of the gendered logic of *carpe diem*: instead of seizing the day, and plucking young women before they fade, they argue *against* uprooting young men before they have a chance to grow. Guyon, clearly, takes the path of plucking—a strategy of violent forgetting to which Gryll offers material resistance simply by surviving.[41]

This superfluous survival of plants, stuff, and poetry will be the subject of the following and final chapter, through a consideration of Thomas Tusser's rhyming husbandry, William Shakespeare's sonnets, and the uncanny capacity of fragments to persist.

PART III

An Increase of Small Things

CHAPTER 5

Richard Tottel, Thomas Tusser, and the Minutiae of Shakespeare's *Sonnets*

Thomas Tusser's *A Hundreth Good Pointes of Husbandrie* (1557) begins with the proverbial assurance that "small things grow in harmony," a promise of increase and accumulation that the ensuing pages of couplets do their rhyming best to fulfill.[1] In Tusser's immensely popular handbook, husbandry emerges as a practice of memory and accumulation, one that links the small things of harvest to the small forms of poetic advice, and offers prescriptions for their joint storage and preservation. As such, Tusser's *Pointes* reflects the piecemeal styles of botanical poetics that previous chapters have explored; in its experiments with small verse forms and with the passage of time, it extends the questions of poetic and vegetable survival raised by images of uprooting and the circulation of virtues. Tusser's husbandry suggests a version of memory that rests not on singular monumentality but on fragmentation and dispersal. Taking its cue from this alternate account of poetic posterity, this final chapter reads Tusser's *Pointes* alongside the poetic collection published in 1609 under the title, *Shake-speares Sonnets. Never before Imprinted.* Shakespeare's *Sonnets*, I argue, are indebted to an alliance between agricultural labor and rhetorical condensation that had been forged in mid-Tudor printed books like the 1557 *Pointes* and the expanded Elizabethan editions that followed. For at least a hundred years, critics have looked for "life" in Shakespeare's poetry in whole poems, as a property of complete organic form. It has been a theme of the preceding chapters, however, that vegetable life resides in fragments, most energetically available in piecemeal form for recycling, reordering, and reuse. The following pages suggest that the *Sonnets'* minutiae—which have at times frustrated and disappointed readers—signal their indebtedness to the pedagogical traditions of husbandry, shaping the poems' famous engagement with the work of memory according to a piece-meal logic of practical cultivation. I will, like Tusser, begin with the couplet.

The Break of the Couplet

John Crowe Ransom begins a 1938 essay on Shakespeare's sonnets with a warning: "I will not hold back from throwing a few stones at Shakespeare, aiming them as accurately as I can at the vulnerable parts."[2] For Ransom and his successors, as often as not those vulnerable parts are Shakespeare's couplets, which, as Yvor Winters writes, so often fail to "rise to the occasions which they invoke."[3] The structure of more than half the sonnets, according to Ransom, is "seriously defective."[4] To many of his midcentury critics, Shakespeare's couplets seem abrupt, pat, or flat-footed, ill-suited to the lines preceding them and a threat to the organic form of the sonnet. Winters found himself unable to forgive their regular "evasion" and "cliché," writing that "the element of genius which goes into many of these sonnets raises one's expectations to the point that one cannot take this sort of triviality with good grace." He confessed to finding them "more and more disappointing."[5]

It may seem an irony that Shakespeare should stand accused of so miscarrying the distinguishing feature of the peculiarly English sonnet form that now bears his name. Nonetheless, these confessions of critical disappointment respond to something significant in the poems. Ransom and Winters are disappointed not just by the expectations raised by the name of "Shakespeare" but by the expectations generated in a sonnet's first twelve lines. Its several movements compacted into the space of fourteen lines, the English sonnet is a finite engine of anticipation, with poet and reader managing the expectations suggested by genre and form along with those generated within the poem itself—of imminent turn, escalation, or resolution. Much of this burden of satisfaction, in and at the end, falls on those final two lines.

The disproportionate pressure put on the couplet makes the Shakespearean sonnet a distinct challenge. Unlike the Petrarchan form, whose final six lines can counterbalance the eight preceding the volta, the English form can only work with two. As Paul Fussell writes, "the very disproportion of the two parts of the Shakespearean sonnet, the gross imbalance between the twelve-line problem and the two-line solution, has something about it vaguely risible and even straight-faced farcical: it invites images of balloons and pins."[6] In the case of Shakespeare's sonnets, the danger of disproportion is intensi-

fied by one of their most distinctive features: the regular syntactical indepen-
dence of the final two lines, which makes them seem superfluous and easily
detached, a part that does not belong to the organic poem.[7] Against those critics who see this autonomy as a failing, Rosalie Colie argues that a common
sense of critical disappointment should instead alert us to something fundamental about the *Sonnets*: the rhetorical force of the tradition of epigram in
shaping those final lines.[8] As she notes, many of these couplets could as happily pose as freestanding distichs, syntactically complete and semantically
sufficient, their short form offering an invitation to piecemeal reuse and repetition. The characteristic fragmentary quality that Colie so astutely per-
ceives marks these sonnets' allegiance to a different aesthetic dispensation
from that of those formalist critics, a source of frustration to readers struggling to find their integrated, organic form.

The conceptual disunity of the sonnet is given striking visual form in
the quarto of 1609, where the couplets have been indented and set off from the
rest of the poem at the margin—a layout that has now become so standard
for sonnets as to be unremarkable. This arrangement, however, did not appear widely in print before the 1590s and was still not standard by the time
of Thomas Thorpe's 1609 edition. Coleman Hutchison has pointed out
the fragmentation of the sonnets in Thorpe's edition, which breaks many of the
poems across multiple pages, arguing that this layout challenges visual closure and distinguishes the quarto from most earlier published sequences.[9]
In Hutchison's analysis, powers of memorability and monumentality are associated with those sonnets that appear unbroken on a single page; these
whole poems, he argues, are better remembered and more often anthologized.
What has gone unremarked, however, is that the spatial distinction of the
couplet provides the strongest force of visible fragmentation in the printed
book. Every sonnet in the sequence (including the twelve-line Sonnet 126,
with its indented empty brackets; see Figure 20) is broken in pieces by this
final indentation, a memorial strategy that works not by preserving the whole
but by fragmenting it, freeing the couplet as gloss or condensation to be stored
separately and efficiently.[10] The indentation of the couplet breaks the unity
of the sonnet both visually and conceptually, often registering a discursive
shift from present to future, or particular to general. It punctuates what precedes, but also often stands in for *the point*, condensing into portable form
what Philip Sidney calls the "handle" of the knowledge preceding it.[11]

In this sense, the very fact of indentation runs counter to the monumentality and closure that Wendy Wall has attributed to sonnet sequences of the

1590s, many of which rendered poems on autonomous pages, in formal borders, and with authorial inscription.[12] For both Wall and Heather Dubrow, these fixities of form represent strategies for shoring up the authority of the poet in print against the backdrop of a manuscript culture that routinely broke up, reordered, and recirculated poems.[13] The indentation of the couplet, on the other hand, embeds the printed sonnet firmly within these manuscript practices. It acts as what Dubrow calls a "hint of dispersal," which by pointing out the autonomy of a piece of language marks its availability for transport and transfer.[14] Reinforcing the formal cues observed by Colie, these hints are also invitations and incitements to readers, with either their memory or commonplace book at the ready, to repeat and recirculate the small form. Anticipating the anxieties of twentieth-century formalists, George Puttenham in his *Arte of English Poesie* (1589) recognized that the couplet itself could incite this piecemeal view of a poem. Warning that the closure offered by a rhyming distich potentially undermined a stanza's unity, Puttenham found it to exemplify one of several ways in which a "staffe" might "fall asunder and seeme two staves"—a defect for which Puttenham faulted Chaucer, who "shut up the staffe with a *disticke*, concording with none other verse that went before, and maketh but a loose rime, and yet bycause of the double cadence in the last two verses serve the eare well inough."[15] In other words, though a couplet closes the stanza, it simultaneously intensifies the risk of its dissolution. Prosody and visual form thus combine to incite the pieces of the sonnet to "fall asunder," opening up couplet and quatrains to divergent textual futures.

This chapter proposes an alternative genealogy for the fragmentary "poetry of statement" that Colie identifies in Shakespeare's couplets, less distinguished perhaps than the epigrammatic traditions she describes: the rhyming "pointes" of husbandry published by Thomas Tusser in 1557 and regularly reissued and expanded in the century following. Though scholars have long noted the significance of themes and imagery of husbandry, especially in those poems early in the sequence, *Shake-speares Sonnets* shares more than a well of images and practices with Tusser's manual of household management. Husbandly technologies of production and reproduction are indeed central to the "procreation sonnets," the first seventeen poems in the sequence, so called because of their exhortations to generation and increase. But while husbandry leaves a strong thematic imprint in the sonnets, it also carries with it a set of rhetorical patterns and hermeneutic expectations—expectations that are condensed in the form of the couplet and the work it performs. As Thomas Greene has shown, the burden that husbandry bears to prepare against future time in Shakespeare's sequence is often condensed in the couplet—what we might consider the sonnet's stylistic and conceptual "point."[16] Husbandry thus provides theme and content to both Shakespeare's *Sonnets* and Tusser's *Pointes*, but also it carries with it a style of reading and writing, practices exemplified and explicitly prescribed in Tusser's handbook.

As an attention to Tusser and other contemporary publications shows, knowledge of husbandry was itself the stuff of verse in the sixteenth century, affiliated with the epigrammatic tradition invoked by Colie while also carrying strong aesthetic and stylistic attachments to the density and portability of small forms. Tusser's *Pointes* represents a particularly popular example of this growing body of literature in the mid-sixteenth century, as printed books attempted to guide men and women in the management of their homes and fields and the increase of their property and properties.[17] Tusser's practical collection addresses itself directly to the householder, compressing wisdom on the management of self and household into memorable pairs of rhyming couplets—and, occasionally, other verse forms. In fact, the various sixteenth-century editions of the *Pointes* include some of the earliest "sonnets" printed in England and display a range of experiments with poetic and visual form. Tusser's *Pointes* yokes the couplet's fragmentary style to the promise and possibility of its practical use. Advising his readers that points "be taken in hand," Tusser's verse takes up as an aesthetic strategy the danger of "fall[ing] asunder" against which Puttenham warns.

The couplet performs an essential interpretive labor for Tusser, looking forward and backward at once to make provision for future time. The "points" include themselves in those husbandly preparations: they are to be "taken in hand," stored, remembered, and repeated. Both provisions themselves and tools of provision, they turn the eye of the husbandman forward to provide against winter, old age, or some other coming dearth. Often, these poetic prescriptions carry a specifically manual connotation, endorsing Sidney's claim that poetry is "best for memorie, the onely handle of knowledge"[18]—another tool, like the plow and the cart, among the "husbandly furniture" that Tusser describes. The detachability of the couplet that has so troubled Shakespeare's critics is explicitly prescribed in the *Pointes*, as these small forms encourage repetition, memory, and reinscription, whether in a copy book or on walls or vessels. In this sense, they enact a form of memory markedly distinct from the "monumentality" of the whole poem—one that relies specifically on this fragmentary quality to make them available for mnemonic recirculation and repetition.

The compact portability that defines a "point" helps explain what may be Tusser's most surprising claim to posterity: as author of the first indented couplet in a printed English sonnet.[19] The earliest such example likely appears in the first edition of the *Pointes* in 1557, where a year's calendar of household advice leads into a poem entitled "A sonet, or brief rehersall of the properties of the twelve monethes afore rehersed."[20] The poem runs through these properties line by line before turning in the indented thirteenth line to a general conclusion about household prudence and the need to prepare against cosmic mutability. With its rambling anapests and series of seven paired rhymes, the quatorzain does not fit all of our expectations of a sonnet. Nonetheless, its confident turn into the couplet would make it at home among poems by Wyatt, Surrey, and others in *Songes and Sonettes*, the better remembered lyric miscellany brought out by Tusser's publisher, Richard Tottel, in the same year.[21] Moreover, as I will discuss at greater length below, this final prospective turn is closely echoed in the sonnets of Shakespeare, where sums distilled from the passage of days and months are likewise registered in indented, rhyming distichs, visually distinct turns from the time of the calendar to a practical or speculative commentary upon it. This is an important corollary to the couplet's portability: as a traveling piece of wisdom, it must, like a proverb, speak to various times and places—carrying with it an abstract of knowledge not bound to the moment or site of its origin.[22] The commentary does not belong to the calendar, just as the couplet does not fully belong to the sonnet; both are made to travel beyond it.

I do not intend to suggest that Tusser himself indented this couplet, any more than I mean to imply that Shakespeare himself is responsible for the formatting of Thorpe's 1609 edition of the *Sonnets*. Though such textual arrangements may have appeared in manuscript, they could easily have been introduced in the printshop by a compositor who was reading astutely.[23] In either case, the couplets' indentation marks a specifically editorial and hermeneutic function: it *reads* the poem that precedes it. Whether that role is inhabited by the specific body of poet, scribe, compositor, or stationer, it is marked on the page by the couplet's indentation. Whoever was responsible for introducing the indentation, it will be my claim that Shakespeare's and Tusser's couplets participate in the same formal, hermeneutic, and textual economy. Moreover, this mark—or, rather, the empty space where the mark of a signifier would be—is less the bearer of poetic or practical content itself than a form of action within the poem. A break in syntactic and rhythmic progression, it commands and reorients a reader's attention, redirecting the time and space of reading.

Taken in sum, the 1557 "Sonet" and several later poems by Tusser—in addition to the sonnet of 1557, a second in 1570, and another two sonnets in 1573—are the earliest print examples I have found of sonnets that conclude with indented couplets, each decades prior to the more regular indentation of couplets in many sonnet sequences of the 1590s.[24] Close in form but distant in genre from what we now take to be the mainstream of English poetry in this period, these short poems have been lying in plain sight, among the earliest printed examples of the lyric form—the sonnet—now fundamental to our understanding of the English lyric canon. Tusser's immediate model in this respect, however, is neither Petrarchan love poetry nor the epigrammatic tradition discussed by Colie, but the pedantic epitome we also see in a range of other midcentury publications, including a number by Tusser's publisher, Richard Tottel: a summation, often in divergent typeface, of preceding matter, whether in books on the conduct of everyday life or moral wisdom. These couplets are not only detachable but are almost separate poems, close morphological cousins of the monthly abstracts and figures that Tusser instructs his readers are "points of themselves, to be taken in hand."[25] In Tusser's *Pointes*, this typographically realized process of abstraction and condensation is registered not just in the sequential points themselves but in the mixture of matter, summation, and gloss that is presented with increasing complexity in successive editions of the *Pointes*. Part of their rhetoric of practicality, in other words, consists in this performance of epitomization, as the points generate increasing—and increasingly pithy— offspring. The couplets that end Tusser's sonnets, then, do not just close what comes before; they bring with them expectations of a future of iteration and detachment—a hermeneutic and material practice that links the provision of husbandry with the sonnet form.

As I will argue here, Shakespeare's sonnets draw not just on the rich ideological associations of husbandry or on a material knowledge of particular technologies, like tilling, perfume-making, or grafting. As a juxtaposition with Tusser's *Pointes* helps to show, the sonnets specifically reflect the poetic techniques of practical instruction. As in Tusser's case, this rhetoric of practicality is no less rhetorical: spurning the ends of "practice," practical condensation becomes a stylistic impulse on its own terms. Like the second-person address of practical instruction or lyric apostrophe, summation and indentation work to mold the reader's attention. One function of these sums is to modulate the time of reading: the closed form of an end-coupleted sonnet generates its own expectations—of development, turn, and closure, but also storage and dispersal. In the procreation sonnets, these expectations are saturated with the techniques of husbandry and the anxieties about dearth and deprivation that drive them, figures of knowledge and uncertainty precariously balanced on the empty space opened between quatrain and couplet. For Tusser, such uncertainty and mutability turn his gaze toward future harvests and future uses of his book; his couplets are, he writes, "things nedefull in time for to come," intended for the reader's piecemeal recirculation and reuse.[26] Shakespeare's sonnets likewise imagine being read in future times— as in the poet's wish, in the couplet of Sonnet 60, that "to times in hope, my verse shall stand"—along with the techniques of preservation and increase that might provide for such a future.[27] However, as their affinities with Tusser's piecemeal poetics suggest, one of the expectations generated by Shakespeare's *Sonnets* is not just a future reading, as many individual sonnets make explicit, but of a life outside the poem, a future for the couplet that does not belong to—and indeed might threaten—the sonnet itself.

Tusser's Sonnets

There is some irony in reading Shakespeare's *Sonnets* alongside Thomas Tusser's *Pointes*, rather than the other famous collection published by Richard Tottel in 1557: *Songes and Sonettes, Written by the Right Honorable Lorde Henry Haward late Earle of Surrey, and Other.* For all of his importance in the early history of the Stationers' Company and as a printer of legal and literary titles, Tottel's name now survives largely as the common title to *Songes and Sonettes*, known to literary history as Tottel's Miscellany, the first printed collection of the courtly verse of Wyatt, Surrey, and others, and model for the many collections of songs and sonnets brought out in the decades that followed.[28] Published in the same year, Tusser's *Pointes* and Tottel's Miscellany would go on to become the sixteenth century's two most popular works of nonscriptural verse, each spawning myriad editions and imitators.[29] Nonetheless, Tusser's *Pointes* in many ways feel like an interloper in the distinguished tradition represented by the lyric of Tottel's Miscellany. Even among the so-called "Drab Age" poets, C. S. Lewis wondered whether, in Tusser, he had found "one of those works before which the literary critic hesitates, doubtful whether his commission extends so far."[30] John Thompson gives the *Songes and Sonettes* a central place in his account of the "founding of English metre," but explicitly excludes Tusser, whose rambling anapests, he writes, "provide chiefly metrical curiosities."[31] They seem somehow outside the time of literary history, proverbial echoes from the proverbially timeless countryside rather than crafted or authored pieces of verse.[32] This chapter takes a different approach to Thomas Tusser, arguing that this *other* publishing event of 1557 offers us more profitable insight into Shakespeare's *Sonnets*. In particular, the formal affinities with Tusser's pedantic versifying help defamiliarize that most familiar of verse appendages: the final couplet that appears first in the sonnets of Thomas Wyatt, a nearly unprecedented genetic mutation in the sonnet form, but one that became the characteristic feature of English sonnets and would eventually offer a formal invitation to countless experiments with closure and condensation.[33] A reading through and alongside Tusser ultimately suggests that Ransom and Winters were right, on some level, to be disappointed by Shakespeare's couplets: a couplet's loyalty, in this reading, is not directed toward the integral or monumental poem, but—fragmentarily—to some future provision, as a seed of something outside of the poem.

Like Shakespeare's *Sonnets*, the first edition of *A Hundreth Good Pointes of Husbandrie* begins with a figure of increase, here in the form of a Latin epigram: "Concordia parvae res crescunt, / Discordia maximae dilabuntur."[34] Immediately preceding the first numbered point, the distich seems to govern not just the household economy but the economy of the text, as its own "small things" set off on their pattern of increase across the ensuing pages. This literary meaning may not have been the precise sense of *res* that Tusser or Tottel had in mind with the epigrammatic superscription: the maxim usually circulated in political contexts, such that it might be translated to suggest that "Small *states* grow in times of peace."[35] In its place, the maxim offers a benediction on the microcosmic state of the householder and the world of things that he governs: that his small possessions, if he reads well and follows instructions, should grow, like the small points of the book itself, which would increase in the following pages from one to one hundred and beyond.[36] In the agricultural context of Tusser's work, the image of growth alights upon a vibrant imaginary and practical world in which the growth of small things names precisely the business of cultivation with which husbandmen are engaged. Bridging national affairs and household politics, husbandly accumulation and bibliographical augmentation, the motto condenses, onto the modest back of the *res parva*, the worldly and symbolic investments that drive Tusser's work.

Tusser's first point situates this growth squarely within the conjugal polity:

> Where couples agree not, is rancor and poysen:
> where they two kepe house than, is never no foysen.
> But contrary, lightly where couples agree:
> what chaunseth by wisdom, looke after to see.[37]

In the fourth point, Tusser returns to the power of concord: "Provision thy cator, and all shall goe well: / for foysen is there, where provision doth dwell." Provision, the thriftiness that is the hallmark of the good husbandman, ensures foison—the thriving of field, household, and store. All, finally, turn on the concord and agreement of couples, which Tusser lexically exemplifies hundreds of times over through the repetition of rhyming couplets. A preface added to the edition of 1570 introduces the points themselves in a similar "provisionary" frame:

> What lookest thou then at the last?
> Good lessons for thee and thy wyfe?
> Then kepe them in memorie fast,
> From youth, to the last of thy lyfe.
>
> What looke ye for more in my booke?
> Things nedefull in tyme for to come?
> Else misse I of that I do looke,
> If pleasant thou findest not some.[38]

From these first pages, the book's orientation is toward future time, as it looks forward not only to its future reading (as Shakespeare will in the *Sonnets*) but toward its future use, for which it will be extracted and relocated for "fast keeping" in the memory (mental or material) of the reader. In the edition of 1573, the "things" of the latter quatrain become "points," a hint of how Tusser sees the point's distinctly utilitarian time—that is, as a crucial tool in the husbandman's toolbox, to be kept and increased in preparation for "tyme for to come." The practice of husbandry anticipates and absorbs these future readings.

The "point," as Tusser uses it, participates in a rich semantic field in which its form and its function—its distinct smallness and its ability to point out, teach, index—are complexly intertwined. In a range of contexts, "point" names a unit within a series: a rhetorical segment of argument, a point of law, one lesson among others. In 1551, the mathematician Robert Recorde defined the basic geometrical unit both theoretically, as "*A Poynt or a Prycke*, . . . that small and unsensible shape, whiche hath in it no partes, that is to say: nother length, breadth nor depth"; and practically, as the small imprint of a pen, pencil, or other instrument, likewise without length or breadth because not "moved, nor drawen from his fyrst touche." A line, in turn, is just a "great numbre of these prickes," a concept that Recorde visually assembles on the page with illustrations of both terms.[39] Tusser's points are not only minimal discursive units but points in time, compact lessons sequentially distributed across the span of the year. Interpellating a reader or listener as the subject of the prick, these points imply its imperative force: a point is something to obey, learn, and internalize.

Tusser's use draws not only on the force of the point as a periodic mark within the progress of discourse but on its power to mark something out as noteworthy. To point at something is to draw attention to it, to demand that a reader attend to it.[40] In this sense, the numbered and pilcrowed points of Tusser's edition echo the typographic and hermeneutic function of the marginal pointing manicule: the imperative to "note me," "remember me," or "repeat me."[41] Like the other examples of "gnomic pointing" described by G. K. Hunter (such as marginal quotation marks, fleurons, asterisks, and italics), these marks direct the attention of the reader toward what is worth remembering: those points, in Tusser's phrase, to be taken in hand.[42] The form itself contains an imperative, commanding the reader's attention and response. The composition of the page thus gives visual form to Colie's observation about the epigrammatic extractability of the distich in the sonnet: its very indentation marks it for extraction and repetition. The seriality of Tusser's maxims, however, results in a sharp contrast to this economy of readerly attention, potentially undermining the function that gnomic pointing performs. How do you pick what to extract from a work that might be dismissed—fairly—as one damned point after another?

The visual punctuation of verse on the page collaborates with typographic pointing to make a point a point: completed by a full stop, or point, and broken by the space between lines and stanzas. As Malcolm Parkes notes in his history of punctuation, the visual layout of a poem on the page is its first layer of punctuation, binding its language and giving it point and shape.[43] When Petrarch's sonnets appeared in print, they were composed with hanging indents off of the quatrains and tercets—that is, with the first, fifth, ninth, and twelfth lines at the left margin and the following lines indented. Manuscripts of Thomas Wyatt's sonnets follow this layout, punctuating quatrain and tercet even when the rhetorical periods of the verse do not, as do the sonnets appended to different editions of Sidney's *Arcadia*. The short poems in *Songes and Sonettes* break from this visual tradition, rendering each poem, as Parkes notes, "a simple stichic structure."[44] Throughout the 1557 editions of both Tusser's *Pointes* and the *Songes and Sonettes,* the basic stanzaic units are made autonomous islands within the continuous sea of the book, with generous white space committed to separating and distinguishing them.[45] Printed in black letter, flush left, each stanzaic block of text visually literalizes the "small parcelles" that Tottel advertises in the preface to his miscellany.[46]

In other midcentury publications by Richard Tottel, stanzas are broken down into substance, fragment, and gloss—a compositional pattern that complicates any expectation of the stanza's fixity in print. In William Baldwin's *Treatise of Moral Philosophy,* which Tottel brought out in a series of at least eight editions beginning in 1555, a reader finds at least 103 short poems mixed into the mostly prose work, dispersed pieces of monitory or sententious verse that display close visual and rhetorical affinities with the disposition of text in Tusser's *Pointes.*[47] Though Baldwin is now best known for compiling and composing much of the *Mirror for Magistrates*, the *Treatise* was in fact his most reprinted work in the sixteenth century, going through more than twenty editions from multiple publishers by 1600, each of them expanding what was essentially a commonplace collection of pithy maxims following brief narrations of the "lives and answers" of their classical authors.[48] Including a discrete section of "Piththie Metres" as well as dozens of short poems distributed throughout the work, the *Treatise*'s range of didactic poetry is intensely engaged in what Chloe Wheatley in her work on the early modern fascination with epitome has called the "compact economy" of verse.[49] Each chapter of sayings concludes with a seven-line stanza, appearing in either roman type or italic instead of in black letter and broken off from the preceding matter by a pilcrow and the heading, "The summe of all." These verse condensations digest and concisely sum up the prose *sententiae* that precede them.[50] The third chapter, "Of the world, pleasures, and daungers therof," summarizes its commonplace reflections on worldly vanity with the following lines:

❡ The summe of all.
The world is a region, divers and variable,
Of god created in the beginning:
To conteyne his creatures of kyndes innumerable
Wherein eche one should live by his winning.
Whose many pleasures are cause of gret sinning.
Wherfore all that gladly, as vayn dooe them hate,
Shall after this world have permanent estate.[51]

The poem itself is already a pointed "summe," or summit: it narrows from the preceding sentences, a shift accentuated by the change to the airier typeface.

Even within the stanza, the final couplet is pointed. In the turn of its "Wherfore," the sixth line breaks from a summation of the world and ubiquity of sin to a promise for future time, one that implicitly guides moral behavior. The "summe" both abstracts and condenses the previous precepts, drawing on the language of those classical counsels to generalize a creed that encompasses but reorients the utterances of Seneca, Pythagoras, and others within an appropriately forward-looking Christian context. An analogous effect is achieved by one of the major editorial innovations of the 1557 *Songes and Sonettes*, absent from its manuscript models: the black-letter parcels of individual poems are given titles, printed in roman type, that abstract a sum from the verse below. These titles are often in dialogue with the conceptual work performed by the poems' couplets. The collection's first fourteen-line sonnet, for example, is printed with the title, "Description of Spring, wherin eche thing renewes, save onely the lover." Echoing "spring" and "thing," and likewise abstracting from the poem's more particular seasonal inventory, the title draws directly on Surrey's couplet: "And thus I see among these pleasant things, / Eche care decayes, and yet my sorow springs."[52]

A similarly pointed visual differentiation characterizes the pairing of condensation and indentation throughout editions of Tusser's *Pointes*. In the first edition of 1557, as we have seen, the progress of the months is followed by a fourteen-line poem abstracting their appointed properties, titled "A sonet, or brief rehersall of the properties of the twelve monethes afore rehersed" (Figures 15 and 16).[53] The poem is composed as a series of seven rhyming couplets, with each month apportioned a single line and a proverbial summation provided in the final couplet. This last couplet, which is slightly indented at the left margin, steps out of the time of the calendar in

99 Then welcome thy haruest folke, seruauntes and all:
with mirth and good chere, let them furnish thyne hall:
The haruest lorde nightly, must geue the a song:
fill him then the blacke boll, or els he hath wrong.

100 Thy haruest thus ended, in mirth and in ioye:
please euery one gently, man woman and boye.
Thus doing, with alway, such helpe as they can:
thou winnest the name, of a right husband man.

Finis.

Nowe thinke vpon god, let thy tonge neuer cease,
from thanking of him, for his mighty encrease.
Accept my good wil, finde no fault tyll thou tryes:
the better thou tryuest, the gladder am I.

¶ A sonet, or brief rehersall of the properties
of the twelue monethes afore rehersed.

As Ianeuer fryse pot, bidth corne kepe hym lowe:
And feuerell fill dyke, doth good with his snowe:
A bushel of Marche dust, worth raunsomes of gold:
And Aprill his stormes, be to good to be solder:
As May with his flowers, geue ladies their lust:
And Iune after blooming, set carnels so iust:
As Iuly bid all thing, in order to ripe:
And August bid reapers, to take full their gripe.

                                   D.h.   Septem

A hundreth good poyntes of husbandry.

September his fruit,biddeth gather as fast:
October bid hogges:to come eate vp his mast:
As dirtie Nouember, bid thresheat thine ease:
December bid Christmas,to spende what he please:
So wisdom bid kepe,and prouide while we may:
For age crepeth on as the time passeth away.
Finis.

Thinges thriftie ,that teacheth the thriuing to thriue:
teache timely to trauas, the thing that thou triue.
Transferring thy toyle,to the times truely tought:
that teacheth the temperaunce,to temper thy thought.
To temper thy trauaile,to tarrye the tide:
this teacheth the thriftines,twenty times tride.
Thinke truely to trauaile,that thinke it to thee:
the trade that thy teacher taught truely to the.
Take thankfully thinges,thanking tenderly those:
that teacheth thee thriftly,thy time to transpose.
The trouth teached two times,teache thou two times ten:
this trade thou that takest,take thrift to the then.

❧ ¶Imprinted at London in flete strete
within Temple barre ,at the sygne of the
hand and starre ,by Richard Tottel
the third day of Februarp.An.1557.

*Cum priuilegio ad impri-
mendum solum.*

Figure 16. Thomas Tusser, *A Hundreth Good Pointes of Husbandrie* (London: Richard Tottel, 1557), sig. D.i^v. By permission of the British Library. Shelfmark C.31.c.26.

order to make a general claim about the passage of time: "So wisdom bid kepe, and provide while we may: / For age crepeth on as the time passeth away." This indentation is an anomaly among contemporary printed fourteen-line stanzas, and, on the tail of six earlier couplets, seems to mark not so much a prosodic shift as a break in kind. The couplet is not just more of the same, but of a different order. Dympna Callaghan has noted that Tusser's 1557 "Sonet" abstracts from the temporal year to reach the central prescript of husbandry: the need to thriftily shore up in the present to prepare for the barren winters of both calendar and old age—a conceit, as Callaghan notes, that gives it a basic affinity with Shakespeare's Sonnets 5 and 6, which also describe techniques for preparing against the ravages of winter.[54] This reorientation aligns the couplet with the "provision" endorsed in Tusser's opening points, perching the imperative for store at the end of the year, where it encompasses the previous months while gazing provisionally forward. It thus digests the passage of the year, offering a reading of the passage of time itself from this provisional, visionary perspective. As it appears within the volume, the poem is introduced as a double condensation—according to the title, a rehearsal of the rehearsal just completed—extending and complicating the volume's stalled conclusion, which carries on after the hundredth numbered point in the form of an additional point, a "Finis," this "sonet," another "Finis," a twelve-line poem in which each word begins with a "T," and, finally, the colophon. Tusser here performs the difficulty of ending that the couplet so often aspires to solve.

In the edition of 1570, the "sonet" has been transformed. The properties of each month are arranged in a table, where each is rewritten as a dimeter couplet, appearing next to its proper month and numbered with a pilcrow (Figure 18). The typography is much more complex: the title ("The kindely propertie of every moneth.") is first in italic and, on its second line, in black letter. The couplets themselves are printed in black letter, like the points on the preceding page, while the names of months, appearing with number and a pilcrow, are in roman type.[55] The modulation of typeface here echoes the work performed by Baldwin's "summes," formally registering the work of condensation and commentary and hierarchizing the matter of the page.

What was the sonnet's couplet has been partially preserved on the previous page (Figure 17), where, amplified to a stanza of three couplets, it helps conclude the full calendar of points instead of their condensed "rehersall" in the sonnet. Its title there (a couplet in itself) echoes Baldwin's "summes of all":

¶Of all thing this seemeth the summe,
   one going, another to come.

World lasting looke never to lin,
yeare ended againe to beginne.
Who looketh to wealth to attaine,
must travaile againe and againe.
Good therefore it is (as I say)
providyng for age, while we may.[56]

"Seemeth" here serves a double purpose, naming the visual perspective from the summit of the year, while undermining that promise of closure with the relentless repetitions of worldly time. It is the summit of the year, but also the summation of wisdom that applies to all years and resists their decay, instructing the reader to collect a "summe" of all things—future provision undiminished by the coming and going of months and ages. The multivalence of "summe" leaves it both inside and outside the movement of time.

The edition of 1573 continues the breakup and dispersal of the months and their kindly properties: these brief couplets have been redistributed, so that they appear at the beginning of each month as introductions to a series of equally pithy couplets that condense and introduce the full four-line points that follow (Figure 19, showing the month of October). Puttenham's worries about the coupleted poem being torn asunder are here enthusiastically consummated, as the "kindely properties" are restored to their proper months, the final step of their decoupling from the 1557 "sonet" and calendrical table of the 1570 edition. Thoughtfully, Tusser opens the book with instructions on how to manage this variety, with language that emphasizes their removal and handling. On the verso of the title page, we read, under the heading "A lesson how to conferre every abstract with hys moneth":

In every month, er in aught be begonne,
Read over the month, what availes to be donne,
So neyther this travel, shall seeme to be lost:
Nor thou to repent, of this trifeling cost.

The figure of abstract, & month do agree,
Which one to another, relations bee,

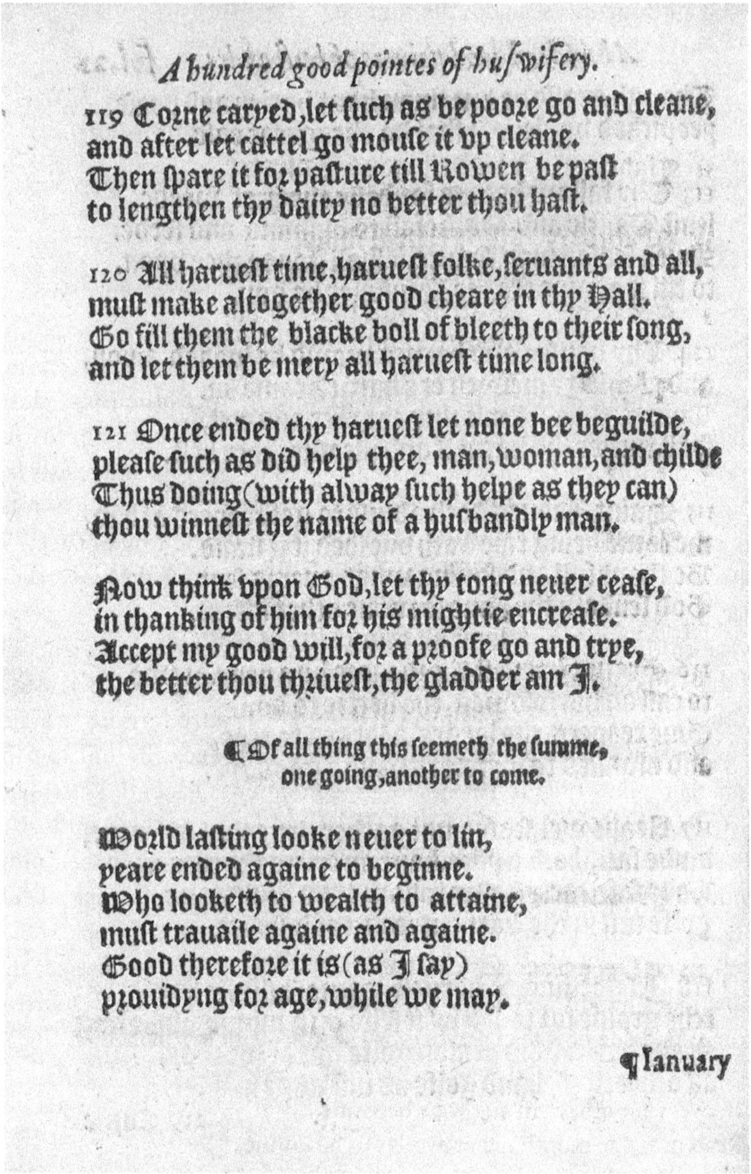

A hundred good pointes of huswifery.

119 Corne caryed, let such as be poore go and cleane,
and after let cattel go mouse it vp cleane.
Then spare it for pasture till Rowen be past
to lengthen thy dairy no better thou hast.

120 All haruest time, haruest folke, seruants and all,
must make altogether good cheare in thy Hall.
Go fill them the blacke boll of bleeth to their song,
and let them be mery all haruest time long.

121 Once ended thy haruest let none bee beguilde,
please such as did help thee, man, woman, and childe
Thus doing (with alway such helpe as they can)
thou winnest the name of a husbandly man.

Now think vpon God, let thy tong neuer cease,
in thanking of him for his mightie encrease.
Accept my good will, for a proofe go and trye,
the better thou thriuest, the gladder am I.

¶ Of all thing this seemeth the summe,
one going, another to come.

World lasting looke neuer to lin,
yeare ended againe to beginne.
Who looketh to wealth to attaine,
must trauaile againe and againe.
Good therefore it is (as I say)
prouidyng for age, while we may.

¶ Ianuary

Figure 17. Thomas Tusser, *A Hundreth Good Pointes of Husbandry, Lately Maried unto a Hundreth Good Poynts of Huswifery* (London: Richard Tottel, 1570), sig. F.i^{v}. RB 49623, The Huntington Library, San Marino, California.

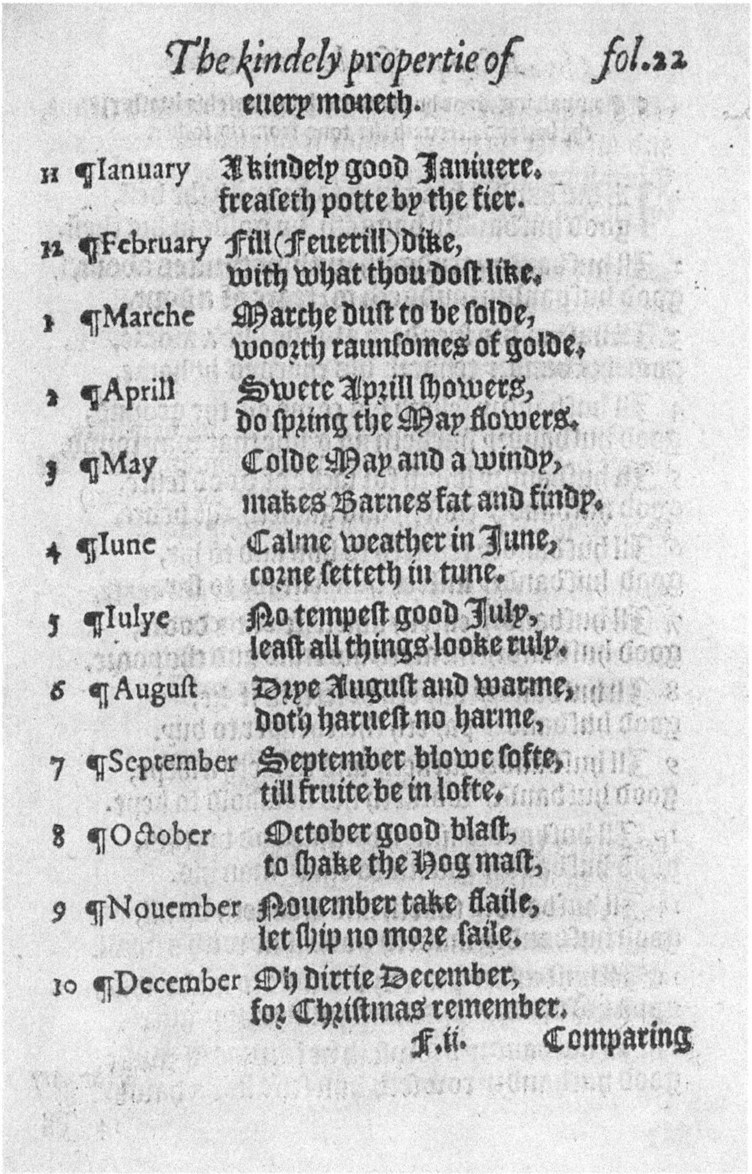

The kindely propertie of *fol.*22
euery moneth.

11 ¶Ianuary A kindely good Ianiuere,
freaſeth potte by the fier.

12 ¶February Fill (Feuerill) dike,
with what thou doſt like.

1 ¶Marche Marche duſt to be ſolde,
woorth raunſomes of golde.

2 ¶Aprill Swete Aprill ſhowers,
do ſpring the May flowers.

3 ¶May Colde May and a windy,
makes Barnes fat and findy.

4 ¶Iune Calme weather in Iune,
corne ſetteth in tune.

5 ¶Iulye No tempeſt good Iuly,
leaſt all things looke ruly.

6 ¶Auguſt Drye Auguſt and warme,
doth harueſt no harme.

7 ¶September September blowe ſofte,
till fruite be in lofte.

8 ¶October October good blaſt,
to ſhake the Hog maſt.

9 ¶Nouember Nouember take flaile,
let ſhip no more ſaile.

10 ¶December Oh dirtie December,
for Chriſtmas remember.

F.ii. Comparing

Figure 18. Thomas Tusser, *A Hundreth Good Pointes of Husbandry, Lately Maried unto a Hundreth Good Poynts of Huswifery* (London: Richard Tottel, 1570), sig. F.ii^r. RB 49623, The Huntington Library, San Marino, California.

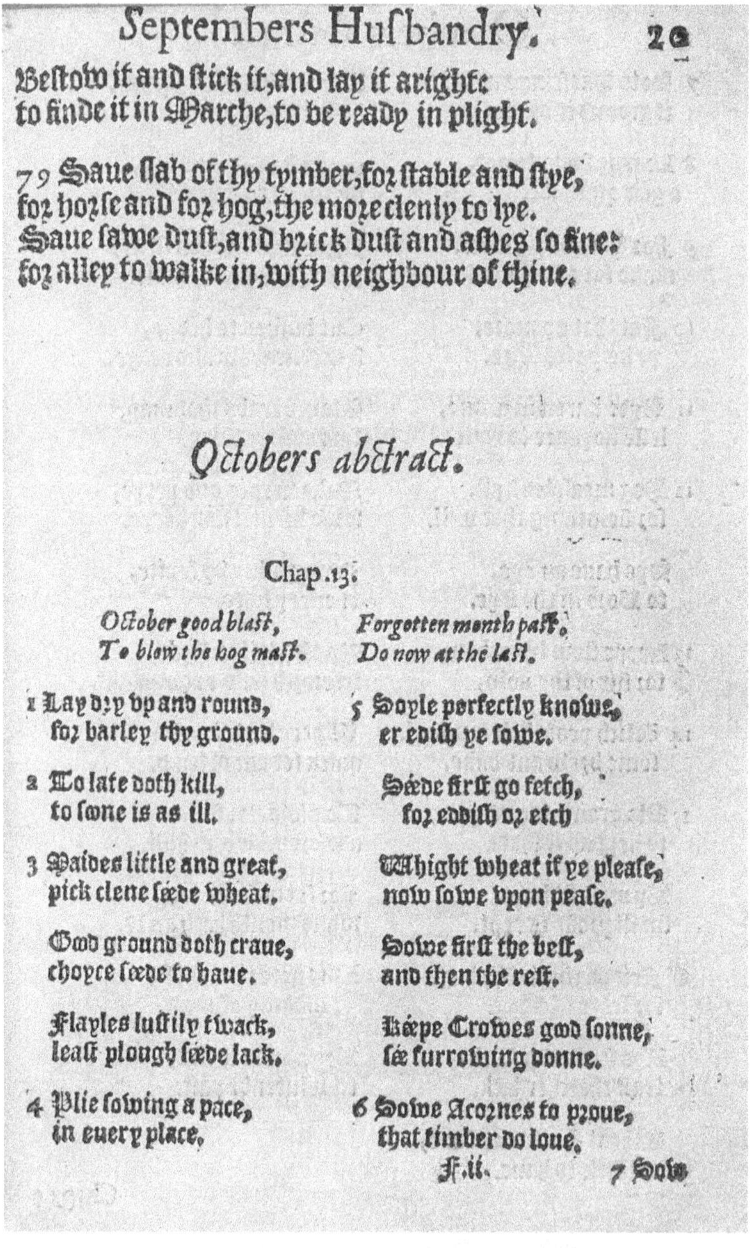
Septembers Husbandry. 20

Bestow it and stick it, and lay it arighte
to finde it in Marche, to be ready in plight.

79 Saue slab of thy tymber, for stable and stye,
for horse and for hog, the more clenly to lye.
Saue sawe dust, and brick dust and ashes so fine:
for alley to walke in, with neighbour of thine.

Octobers abstract.

Chap. 13.

October good blast,
To blow the hog mast.

Forgotten month past,
Do now at the last.

1 Lay dry vp and round,
for barley thy ground.

2 To late doth kill,
to soone is as ill.

3 Maides little and great,
pick clene seede wheat.

Good ground doth craue,
choyce seede to haue.

Flayles lustily twack,
least plough seede lack.

4 Plie sowing a pace,
in euery place.

5 Soyle perfectly knowe,
er edish ye sowe.

Seede first go fetch,
for eddish or etch

Whight wheat if ye please,
now sowe vpon pease.

Sowe first the best,
and then the rest.

Keepe Crowes good sonne,
see furrowing donne.

6 Sowe Acornes to proue,
that timber do loue.

F.ii. 7 Sow

Figure 19. Thomas Tusser, *Five Hundreth Points of Good Husbandry United to as Many of Good Huswiferie* (London: Richard Tottel, 1573), sig. F.ii[r]. RB 69672, The Huntington Library, San Marino, California.

The lessons that after those figures do stand:
Be points of them selves, to be taken in hand.[57]

The passage provides the reader a range of instructions. The heading, "to conferre," describes the labor of bringing back together each abstract with its
month—a way to carry them by the handle across the intervening pages
between them. The "lessons," meanwhile are "points of them selves" to be
stored and accumulated for future use—that is, "taken in hand." Tusser prescribes these reading practices under the heading of a prudential economy:
a proven method by which the labor of reading will be redeemed and not
repented. These abstracted points, which sharpen the points of the points,
are lessons that, in turn, generate another lesson on how to read them. The
abstracts thus extend the work begun in the quatorzain of 1557, confirming
the distinction we saw first represented in that couplet, unhooking and
amplifying its single abstract condensation into an army of miniaturized
abstracts.

Though the "rehersall" of the 1557 edition does not survive in its quatorzain form in later editions, additional poems called "sonnets" do appear,
which also make use of the pointing of the page.[58] The edition of 1570 includes
"A sonet to the Lady Paget," a quatorzain in tetrameters, of three cross-rhymed
quatrains and a final rhyming couplet—again indented, though more conspicuously than the 1557 couplet. The poem's logical organization proceeds
in pairs, with a series of images of prodigality that are both extended and
broken by the turn into the couplet: "Even so must I for pleasures past, / still
wishe you good while life doth last." Here, the poet's performance of praise
aims to offer some compensation for the ravishings of debt tallied in the lines
above. The time of the couplet ("while life doth last") breaks from the preceding census of debtors, extending the poet's performance of praise into an
indefinite future—a debt that, as we saw in Tusser's yearly "summe" above,
cannot be acquitted on earth. In the edition of 1573, the same poem has been
arranged by the compositor to fill the whole page. Twelve lines are broken in
half and arranged into three narrow staves. The couplet however, retains both
its lineation and its indentation, standing out as a conspicuous base to the
column teetering above it.[59]

An even more marked typographic turn is evident in two poems called
"sonets" in the 1573 edition, each printed with an indented, rhyming couplet:
"A Sonet against a slaunderous tongue" and "A Sonet of the Authors first vii.
yeares service."[60] Prosodically, both follow the notes of instruction published

by Gascoigne in the same year, proceeding in iambic pentameter and with cross-coupled lines. In both cases, the special status of the couplet is confirmed not just by indentation but by its composition in roman type instead of black letter—a distinction that, by visual affinity, makes it seem as much a second title as part of the poem. While this sharp typographic break likely served to keep the second sonnet from running onto the next page, the compositor nonetheless understood the difference between poems to be less important than the internal structural distinctions they shared—that is, between quatrains and couplet.

In both poems, the couplet turns toward abstraction, though deployed to different ends. In "A Sonet against a slaunderous tongue," the final couplet breaks from the serial exempla of the quatrains, drawing a sententious answer from the preceding rhetorical questions. Moving from species (literally) to genre, the couplet names what these wasteful examples (including darnel, thistles, hornets, and toads) have in common before drawing a moral precept from those natural percepts. The serial instances of cankerous waste might be continued indefinitely (such is the exemplary bounty of nature) were it not for the turn initiated in the eleventh line, as it introduces the final and encompassing example: "Now once for all, what good (shew who so can) / Do stinking snakes, to this our common welth?" An emblem continuous with those preceding but also a substitute for them ("now once for all"), these stinking snakes begin the couplet's climb toward generality by invoking the synecdochic logic of the commonwealth. With the couplet, the poem's mode conclusively turns from observation to law: "No more doth good, a pevish slaunderous tong, / But hurts it self, and noyes both old and yong." The conclusion to the poem immediately following, "A Sonet of the Authors first vii. yeares service" likewise marks out a distinction in time: the seven annual cycles of the quatrains are sublated by the move into the couplet, which absorbs and negates the worldly time of the calendar. Its examples of annual rites and events—from individual months and seasons, to seasonal weather, moons, and the habits of birds—might be indefinitely extended were the couplet not there to break the series and turn retrospective inventory to future promise: "Still yours am I, though thus the time hath past, / And trust to bee, so long as lyfe shall last." Like the couplet of the 1557 "Sonet," it extracts a rule that legislates throughout the year and beyond, protecting its subject from the daily ravages of mutability.[61]

Each of these sonnets uses the couplet to stage a resolution to a problem of seriality and transience, making good on or closing a catalog of time's waste and decay with a turn to a new kind of utterance differently bound to present and future. In the sonnet "rehersall" of 1557, the monthly structure of the first twelve lines stakes an implicit limit on their continuation, while the sentiment of the couplet ventures to ideologically contain the mortal stakes of that seriality. In all three later poems, the examples and their "kindely properties" could be infinitely cataloged, or could end with the "et cetera" of the ever increasing natural historical catalog—a mode of enumeration and description from which the couplet nonetheless turns, acceding to the constraints of the sonnet form.[62] The closural force of the couplet breaks out of the scrolling temporal progress of the poem to a law of time management within which it—and to which the reader—is bound.

Shakespeare's Points of Good Husbandry

Images of husbandry are shot through Shakespeare's *Sonnets*, and, though found most conspicuously in the first seventeen poems, commonly called the "procreation sonnets," they equip the sequence as a whole with a vocabulary that knits together horticultural, economic, sexual, and literary increase. That the sonnets' layered metaphors draw from practical manuals is not surprising, but, as I am arguing here, Shakespeare's distinct stylistic strategies are also shaped by a debt to practical genres. In their attempts to persuade, command, praise, instruct, and exhort, Shakespeare's sonnets are much more likely than their contemporaries to use second-person pronouns and to articulate verbs in the imperative mood.[63] Perhaps most important, the couplets that conclude the sonnets—where these instances of second-person address are most likely to be found—are frequently easily severable from the twelve lines preceding them. Drawing rhetorically and conceptually from the ideology of husbandry, they are indebted to practical "points" like Tusser's and are structurally bound to the possibility of their extraction and reuse.

Agricultural instruction is not the only pedagogical context engaged in the *Sonnets*. Scholars have long noted that the first seventeen sonnets in the sequence lean heavily upon Erasmus's "Epistle to perswade a young jentleman to Mariage," widely available to Shakespeare and others in Thomas Wilson's translation in his *Arte of Rhetorique* (1553).[64] The series of poems shares with the epistle two central features: the language of horticulture and husbandry woven through both, and the basic conceit of an exhortation to marry. In this sense, they carry a double instructional valence: the imitative scene of the humanist classroom, addressed by Wilson's exemplary epistle; and the exhortation itself, to produce more by tilling, grafting, and printing.[65] In addition to these two forms of imitation and increase, the modes of practical instruction we see in Tusser's *Pointes* represent a third instructional discourse in the *Sonnets*, in which the lessons of husbandry are forcefully yoked to their formal condensations and summations.[66] We saw earlier how the disunity threatened by the couplet seemed to pose a danger to the organic lyric identity of the sonnet; here, another aspect of their identity as lyric is reoriented, as the traditional second person of the poetry of praise is thus given new force through the pedagogical address of instruction.

In what follows, I will focus on the place of the couplet in several sonnets early in the sequence, before considering, in conclusion, how these dynamics are rewritten in Sonnet 126—a poem in just six couplets, usually considered the last of sequence addressed to the young man.[67] Though Shakespeare's couplets rarely employ a simple generalization or a turn from example or illustration to an abstract lesson, a significant number of sonnets switch modes between the quatrains and the couplet from a figure or series of figures to a prescription or promise. The formal and stylistic tension between the third-person figuration of a process, natural or artificial, and second-person command or exhortation is likewise at the heart of the rhetorical work performed by Tusser's *Pointes* and other practical books as they navigate between objective descriptions of method and instructions addressed directly to an unknown reader. These rhetorical techniques thus take up the central question of any instruction in husbandry—How will a technique or direction translate to the world and time of the reader? Will the reader comply?—and respond, in each case, with rhetorical modes of action and address that are well suited to such transfer between times, places, and persons. In Sonnet 10, for example, this translation is voiced as a second-person exhortation; in Sonnet 11, a prescription ventriloquized through nature's intentions; and in Sonnet 15, as a promise or threat articulated in the poet's first person singular. Each of these detachable distichs legislates toward some future time, turning from the quatrains and converting their store to a glimmer of future action.[68] Their relation to a future beyond the poem is partly due to the epigrammatic quality that Rosalie Colie has detailed. That is, the couplets seem tokens or comments easily detached—indeed, one might argue, already detached—from the rest of the poem and able to speak to occasions outside of it. Often this capacity is enabled by the extended reach of the couplets' verbs beyond the worldly time of the quatrains, into a prospective or provisionary stance.

Like the conclusions of Tusser's sonnets, Shakespeare's couplets are caught up in an anticipatory dynamic of compensation and recuperation, which is initiated in the biological and economic language of the procreation sonnets but continues throughout much of the sequence.[69] The senses of accumulation and condensation captured simultaneously in the "summes" of Tusser and Baldwin exemplify this overlap of rhetoric and economy. By the reparative logics shaping the couplets in Sonnets 29, 30, and 34, for example, the young man becomes a source of value that ransoms the quatrains' despair. With these redemptive turns, the couplets state and perform a "summe of all" that echoes the condensation, cancellation, and abstraction modeled by Baldwin's verse summations and by Tusser's concluding couplets. Seen together, they help show the economic logic of value and substitution at work in these various senses of "sum." In each case, a sum replaces the mutable time of the year with a portable message.

It is precisely this turn away from the sonnets' subjection to mutability and toward a different kind of utterance—one inessentially tied to its site in the poem—that Thomas Greene blames for the lifelessness of so many couplets. Still the most substantial treatment of husbandry in the *Sonnets*, Greene's 1985 essay, "Pitiful Thrivers: Failed Husbandry in the Sonnets," reiterates and rewrites the midcentury sense of critical disappointment with which I began and that we see in Ransom, Winters, and others. Greene argues that the first seventeen sonnets in particular, figuratively embedded as they are in husbandry's calendar of seasonal transformation, exhibit an economic anxiety that far exceeds any real sense of agricultural risk or mortal peril. Against the consuming sense of dread and decay generated in the quatrains, the assurances of the couplet seem to offer themselves as a kind of insurance policy, articulating a promise about future time or recommending a technique for its management. For Greene, these couplets inevitably fail, however, because they "tend to lack the energy of the negative vision in the 12 lines that precede them." The "energy" of that mutability, and the anxiety that attends it, is always in excess—an affective and cosmic constant unmet by the couplets' best compensatory efforts. Greene continues, "The final affirmation in its flaccidity tends to refute itself; the *turn* fails to reverse the rhetorical momentum adequately, as the language loses its wealth and potency while asserting them."[70] Like the language used by Ransom and Winters, this accusation of flaccidity, with its attendant loss of both wealth and potency, takes up the emasculating vocabulary of persuasion elaborated in the sonnets themselves, such that the couplets appear to participate in the linguistic economy of husbandry but share none of its biological force. The plain statement diagnosed by Colie, which she associates with the genre of epigram, here becomes a symptom of the kind of work the couplets are trying to do: in turning from lively substance to abstract condensation, they become metacritical and lifeless.

Part of the problem, Greene suggests, may be the nature of the "affirmation" itself, which voids poetic language of the figurative and associative "energy" that usually drives it—often replacing it with precisely the kind of prescription and prediction we saw at work in Tusser.[71] Shakespeare's couplets in this sense appear an essentially conservative (and inevitably unsuccessful) gesture, an attempt to give stable form to and bank (or sum up) lasting value from the shifting fortunes the quatrains describe. As Greene writes, "The turn toward restoration can be read as a desperate bourgeois maneuver, struggling to shore up the cosmic economy against the mutability which instigates true verbal power."[72] For Stephen Booth, this translates into a mode of psychological compensation, as the gnomic simplicity of the couplets provides some readerly comfort, resolving the tension and friction of the quatrains much like the speeches of political restoration at the end of a tragedy.[73] As we have seen, Tusser's sonnets are constructed according to a similar double logic, their first twelve lines generated as if by the foison of the earth (literally and otherwise), while their couplets constrain thriving with thrift: they turn away from worldly plenitude—the vibrant store captured by the distinctly natural historical genre of the catalog—with a change in mode that closes the preceding series through the language and practice of provision. For Greene, this lifelessness is implicitly the danger of criticism itself—of cashing out the mutability of language for a "point" to be taken "for all time."

Edward Hubler, in *The Sense of Shakespeare's Sonnets* (1952), also identified the problem with the *Sonnets* as a failure of "generation" and "development," and he likewise turns centrally to the procreation sonnets (with their own interests in problems of generation) to make his point. Too often, Hubler writes, Shakespeare pours his energies into the quatrains "and the couplet fails to share the power in which the quatrains were conceived. In such instances the couplet is poetically, but not intellectually false." It seems, as Hubler borrows Shakespeare's words to convey, to have been "begotten in 'the ventricle of memory . . . and delivered upon the mellowing of occasion.'"[74]

The concluding partial citation from *Love's Labour's Lost* paints Shakespeare as a bumbling rhetorician, whose words are drawn from an ill-kept store and subjected to an ill-timed performance. As Hubler helps us see here, the occasion of the couplet is always belated: it comes after the body of the sonnet itself, but it also threatens to be indefinitely repeated, off-site and away from the occasion of its inception.

On the other hand, Hubler argues, Shakespeare was most successful when his *dispositio* followed a strict architecture; he finds every sonnet beginning with "When" structurally successful because this temporal hook leads into a series of logically ordered subordinate clauses. The problems begin when the poet breaks from this mold before reaching the end: "if the pattern did not reach to the end of the sonnet, or if there was no 'so' or 'for' notion to follow the logical sequence, the couplet, as in the fifteenth sonnet, stood in danger of seeming to be tacked on."[75] As it happens, the couplet of Sonnet 15—Hubler's central example here—is about tacking on: the insertion of a branch from one tree into the bark of another, for the additive production of future copies. It names and performs an intervention. To Hubler, however, its promise to "ingraft you new," like the couplet itself, seems an arbitrary technological supplement, a prosthetic afterthought inessentially attached to the poem's soaring consideration of "every thing that growes." The "conceit of this inconstant stay" that it finds there offers a particularly powerful instance of the outsized anxiety diagnosed by Greene. This is also the first site in the sequence where the technical intervention promised by the couplet is performed in the poet's first person, and where, through the pun on grafting/graphing, the preservatives of husbandry are figuratively tethered to the power of writing. The poet's failure in these lines thus comes to stand for the failures of poetry in general to follow through on its promises. Grafting is, like writing, a technology of repetition, but the figure's force is undermined by the repetition and belatedness implied in the literary technology of the couplet itself.

It may be, though, that these feelings of critical dissatisfaction misrecognize the kind of fecundity actually at stake in these sonnets—which, as both images and instances of craft, advocate a version of piecemeal proliferation that I have described in these pages as early modern England's botanical poetics. Like the image of grafting, this botanical poetics breaks from patrilineal models to imagine a more dispersed future for both poem and fruit. Sonnet 15 conjures just this kind of proliferative optimism through the image of engrafting, as the couplet promises a technological solution to the problems posed by the quatrains. We might also compare Sonnet 11, where the methodical management of future time is conveyed through the figure of the seal and the attendant concluding injunction, "Thou shouldst print more, not let that coppy die."[76] These technological interventions both appear in the couplets, which perform a sharp break from the previous lines. As tools of art posed against the inexorable sweep of nature, they seem to Hubler and other modern readers as lifeless prostheses. In Sonnets 11 and 15, the specificity of their artifice is less an abstraction than a contraction, zooming in from the inconstancy of the cosmos to the precision of manual technique. In an account of Shakespeare's "preservation fantasy," Aaron Kunin observes that the "final moves" of many of the sonnets command or suggest a particular technology of preservation—gestures that turn toward future time through the specificity of practical technique.[77] Such methods likewise instantiate and effect "the repeated disavowal of change in favor of repetition" that Margreta de Grazia has identified at the core of these sonnets' poetic project.[78] The techniques named in the couplets, and—crucially—the formal techniques *of* the couplets, manage these anxieties about time and change, disciplining the forms and deformations of future time.

These two "technological" sonnets also rely on one of the procreation sonnets' characteristic gestures, those moments where Shakespeare evokes the "double time" of loss and decay. This effect is most precisely rendered in the first line of Sonnet 11, "As fast as thou shalt wane so fast thou grow'st," but we might also compare the rates of change in Sonnet 12: "sweets and beauties do them-selves forsake, / And die as fast as they see others grow" (12.11–12). These paired pacings choreograph a kind of cosmic equipoise, the metrical elegance of which here veils the ruthless economy of sacrifice and substitution behind it. The world's store is finite, these moments suggest; you cannot have your posterity or your perfume and eat it too—a stark contrast to Tusser's commitment to the premise of increase and incremental accumulation, sanctioned by the fecundity of nature herself.[79] We hear this doubleness again in the "Cheared and checkt" of Sonnet 15 and in the simultaneous movements of the final line's "As he takes from you . . ."

Both couplets pose their technological interventions within an ambiguous temporal frame. Though the poet claims to engraft "as he takes from you," the nature of Time is *always* to take, suggesting the possibility that the poet must also *always* be engrafting, keeping pace (as it were) with Time. This problem of pacing and closure is further complicated when we read the couplet through its pun on writing, which seems to initiate the performance of engrafting in the present moment of poetic utterance, but to continue that action indefinitely, its lyric iterations keeping pace with the passage of time. We saw this double time expressed earlier in Tusser's sonnet of 1557: "So wisdom bid kepe, and provide while we may: / For age crepeth on as the time passeth away." A similar double movement shapes the rhyming title under which it was rewritten in 1570: "Of all thing this seemeth the summe, / one going, another to come." The couplet performs, in the contrast between "summe" and "come," the tension between the time of accumulation and the cyclical time of the calendar. Each of these cases is complicated by the potential of "as" to signify both simultaneity and similarity. As Joel Fineman suggests, "In the procreation sonnets the theme of biological repetition regularly invites poetic devices that stress verbal repetition, and these together regularly call up images whose point is to figure these formal relations in ways that embody the immediate experience of temporal loss."[80] The play of the couplets themselves—both in their relation to the quatrains, as similar and different, and in the rhyme they contain—extends this pattern of loss beyond the verbal and lexical frame in which Fineman describes it. They repeat and reflect the lines that precede them but also leave them behind.

This dynamic reaches a climax in Sonnet 126, the twelve-line poem generally taken to be the last of the poems addressed to the young man. Ironically, though critics have singled out Shakespeare's couplets as his sonnets' distinctive defect, many have found more satisfying closure in this unusual poem, a sonnet whose quatrains are couplets and whose couplet is blank. Because of the poem's unusual composition, Sonnet 126 almost seems to be making a joke about the problem of closure: with six couplets, all playing on repetition and paradox, and indented rounded brackets where a final pair of lines would be, it is all couplet and no conclusion (Figure 20).[81] Despite uncertainty about the sequence's ordering, and despite what may be even greater uncertainty about the origin or meaning of these parentheses, it has often been considered an envoy to the 125 sonnets that precede it—according to Northrop Frye, "a masterly summary of the themes and images of the beautiful-youth group."[82] Operating like the "soveraine misteres over wrack" of its fifth line, the abbreviated poem seems to condense and "detaine" the mutability of the preceding sequence. The "masterly" poem, as Frye calls it, seems to various critics to husband the preceding poems, summing them up and drawing them into a coherent economy.[83]

But the ostensible good husbandry of Sonnet 126 begins, as Tusser does, with anxieties about the ravages of time. Each of the first three couplets repeats the paradox of temporal give-and-take described above. At the

Or layd great bafes for eternity,
Which proues more fhort then waft or ruining?
Haue I not feene dwellers on forme and fauor
Lofe all,and more by paying too much rent
For compound fweet;Forgoing fimple fauor,
Pittifull thriuors in their gazing fpent.
Noe,let me be obfequious in thy heart,
And take thou my oblacion,poore but free,
Which is not mixt with feconds,knows no art,
But mutuall render,onely me for thee.
    Hence,thou fubbornd*Informer*, a trew foule
    When moft impeacht,ftands leaft in thy controule.

126

OThou my louely Boy who in thy power,
    Doeft hould times fickle glaffe,his fickle,hower:
Who haft by wayning growne,and therein fhou'ft,
Thy louers withering,as thy fweet felfe grow'ft.
If Nature(foueraine mifteres ouer wrack)
As thou goeft onwards ftill will plucke thee backe,
She keepes thee to this purpofe,that her skill.
May time difgrace,and wretched mynuit kill.
Yet feare her O thou minnion of her pleafure,
She may detaine,but not ftill keepe her trefure!
Her *Audite*(though delayd)anfwer'd muft be,
And her *Quietus* is to render thee.
            (   )
            (   )

127

IN the ould age blacke was not counted faire,
    Or if it weare it bore not beauties name:
But now is blacke beauties fucceffiue heire,
And Beautie flanderd with a baftard fhame,
For fince each hand hath put on Natures power,
Fairing the foule with Arts faulfe borrow'd face,
Sweet beauty hath no name no holy boure,
But is prophan'd,if not liues in difgrace.

H 3

Therefore

Figure 20. William Shakespeare, *Shake-speares Sonnets. Never Before Imprinted* (London: by George Eld for Thomas Thorpe, 1609), sig. H3ʳ. STC 22353. By permission of The Folger Shakespeare Library.

beginning of the poem, the "lovely Boy" holds time in his hand, so that, at first, it is the poet on the other side of the temporal comparison ("Who hast by wayning growne, and therein shou'st, / Thy lovers withering, as thy sweet selfe grow'st"). Next, it is nature's power that holds back the effects of time ("As thou goest onwards still will plucke thee backe"), a symmetry to which the poem soon poses a limit. Nature "may detaine, but not still keepe her tresure": her possession of the young man is itself subject to a debt that comes due.

With this progression, the first couplets have followed the temporal and provisional course of husbandry: the poem shifts from the natural rhythms of growth and decay to the problem of profit. However, in the sonnet's unsatisfied economy, Tusser's optimistic rewriting of Ecclesiastes—in which the "keeping" of household thrift counters the takings of worldly vanity, just as the young man's conjectural husbandry should counter the wastes of time— is surrendered. The poem's concluding *Audite* and *Quietus* extend and complete the economic accounting performed by couplets earlier on in the sequence, freezing the processive give-and-take of the poem's earlier lines. In this sense the *Audite* of Sonnet 126 seems to demand a long-delayed answer to the audit first requested in Sonnet 4, where the word is likewise capitalized and italicized: "Then how when nature calls thee to be gone, / What accepable *Audit* can'st thou leave?" (4.11–12). Uncoupled, the lovely boy leaves the blank space that follows, the punctuated white of the page. Rejecting the "comfort of the couplet" suggested by Booth and the bourgeois reparation identified by Greene, Sonnet 126 leaves the lovely boy neither author nor begetter of this economic rendering but its victim; not he, but nature, is the keeper of this household account. There is no comfort or redemption here.[84]

At stake in all of Tusser's "summes" is the latent danger that those thrifty condensations might replace the worldly description or experience that precedes them, in the way that the distillation of Shakespeare's Sonnet 54 turns on the "sweet deaths" of the roses from which it draws. To the Sonnets's disappointed critics, the autonomy of Shakespeare's couplets seems to threaten something similar—to effect not just the deadening but the erasure of the language in the twelve preceding lines. In its inorganic relationship to the rest of the poem, a couplet threatens to forget the organic life the sonnet had seemed to possess. And, in the couplets of Sonnet 126, the mutable vitality of the lover is eventually cashed in, sacrificed in the payment of a debt. The "thee" of Sonnets 1–125 is thus effectively mourned, an imaginary object of instruction and praise dissolved in an apparently conclusive transaction. The

1609 *Sonnets* thus rewrites the terms of Tusser's pedagogical relationship. In replacing Tusser's foison and thrift with the zero-sum game of temporal decay, the *Sonnets* deprive provision of the optimism with which Tusser had endowed it; like the distilled perfume of Sonnet 5, the abstraction of the sum condenses and preserves language but loses its vitality. The practical work of memory, operating through the repetition of fragments, contains loss in its very performance.

Though empty brackets did not normally in the period designate missing text, they did designate text that was in one way or another removable. The parentheses, like the indentation to which they are joined in Thorpe's edition, mark division and divisibility—in the case of Sonnet 126, reiterating the separability of the absent couplet. Richard Mulcaster in his *Elementarie* (1582) writes that parentheses should "enclose some perfit branch," one that "breaketh" the sentence.[85] Puttenham called parentheses the "Insertour," used (in arboreal language, again evoking the "tacking on" of Sonnet 15) "to peece or graffe in the middest of your tale an unnecessary parcell of speach."[86] Reflecting this sense that parenthetical language does not quite belong to the body of text surrounding it, Rayna Kalas reads the empty brackets of Sonnet 126 as the marks of a "non-proprietary" poetics. They draw the reader's attention to the form of the poem and to the materiality of its paper and ink, placing the poem in a contrapuntal relationship to the play on identity that drives much of the sequence to this point, and offering "a series of physical properties" that "belong to no one."[87] In offering this view of textual property, this configuration echoes the meditation on "taking" that emerges from Isabella Whitney's encounter with Hugh Plat. In the case of Shakespeare's *Sonnets*, a nonproprietary poetics extends from the dramatic emptiness of these typographical markers to the visual indentation and formal detachability of couplets throughout the sequence. Their openness and emptiness, at this point, should not be a surprise. But this is also what is strange about the indented parentheses: while indentation marks the significance and utility of a piece of language, parenthesis marks, as Puttenham puts it, "an unnecessary parcell." Whether by utility or inutility, both kinds of parcel belong only precariously to their surroundings.

Indeed, what may be most remarkable about the compositor's inclusion of the curved brackets at the end of Sonnet 126 is not the empty space within them but the empty place to their left: the space of the indentation, preserved there in a kind of symbolic and spatial observance. I have argued that the movement across this white space performs the work of speculation, turning toward future agricultural and genealogical time but also to the time of the text's reception. The space is not in itself a signifier, but an empty mark that repoints the reader's attention. As a formal invitation to dispersal, the couplet opens to the reader and to its own future recirculation—leaving us, perhaps, to read the curved brackets as a pair of empty quotation marks from which a sentence has already been removed, the open bark from which a branch has been detached. The space of the parentheses therefore both satisfies and disappoints: it fills out the expected space of the sonnet, but fails to deliver the closure we want from the couplet. In this sense, we might say Sonnet 126 finally satisfies the disappointment of Ransom and Winters, consummating a reader's sense that the indentation is in fact a hinge on which the couplet might swing, by which the poem itself might be opened or closed.

Heaps of Experiment

In 1608, soon before his death at a little over the age of fifty-six, Hugh Plat published *Floraes Paradise*, a collection of two hundred horticultural experiments that was, according to its title page, "Beautified and adorned with sundry sorts of delicate fruites and flowers, By the industrious labour of H.P. Knight." The volume was motivated, Plat wrote, by his own experience and by his old age: with the end of his days in sight, he was prepared to "unfolde my *Napkin*, and to deliver my poore talent abroad." In the years leading up to 1608, Plat had not kept his napkin entirely closed: in broadsides, pamphlets, and books like *The Jewell House of Art and Nature* (1594) and *Delightes for Ladies* (c. 1600), Plat had published tips, recipes, and remedies for a wide range of social ills and household inconveniences. This commitment to sharing the wisdom of his experience extended to the form of *Floraes Paradise*. Its series of numbered experiments favored substance over hierarchical method, he explains, which he leaves "at this time to Schoolemen . . . whose labours have greatly furnished our Studies and Libraries, but little or nothing altered or graced our Gardens and Orchards." Instead, in offering readers the fruits of his labor and skill, Plat asks them to "give me leave to write briefly & confusedly, with those that seeke out the practicall, and operative part of Nature."[1] His paradise was, in essence, a loose heap of experimental fruits and flowers—one whose very looseness qualified it for readers' use.

We last encountered Hugh Plat in Chapter 4, when he was a young man just out of university and a new member of Lincoln's Inn. In 1572, his *Floures of Philosophie* was published by Henry Bynneman—a gathering of prose sentences and original verse that he had also written "briefly & confusedly," though not yet on the subject of what he calls in 1608 the "operative part of Nature." By this later date, Plat had become the experimentalist and prolific intelligencer of natural knowledge as which he remains best known today—a producer and publisher of hands-on wisdom whose persona seems a far cry from the humanist student who kept busy gathering textual flowers. Nonetheless, there are continuities between Plat's first and last publications, not least his framing of their textual contents in the lexicon of vegetable life. Like his early work, Plat's later publications favor mixed composition and serial literary forms, which reflect his elaborate manuscript practices of note-taking and information retrieval. These compilations also invite readerly imitation and reuse, pragmatic examples of the dynamics of vegetable recycling and recirculation I have described throughout the preceding pages. Published thirty-six years after the *Floures of Philosophie, Floraes Paradise* thus forms something of a capstone to his career in print, allowing us to see how his experimental persona built on the habits and vocabulary of his greener years—as he continued throughout to generate and circulate small forms available for reuse, eventually in the form of written experiments.[2]

A little under two decades later, Francis Bacon would just predecease his final publication, though he too first gave it a name from the world of plants. The *Sylva Sylvarum* was published soon after Bacon's death in 1626 at age sixty-five, in effective exile from the political power he had enjoyed for much of his adult life. Edited and introduced by his literary executor William Rawley and published alongside the utopian fable *The New Atlantis*, the *Sylva Sylvarum* was a long and rangy collection of ten centuries of experiments. Its title alluded to the double Latin meaning of *silva* as both "forest" and "matter"—so that Bacon's title might translate as a "forest of forests," or, more aptly, a "forest of stuff." The collection presents itself as a gathering of raw, or unformed, matter; Rawley, evoking the primal chaos of creation, called it an "Indigested Heap of Particulars."[3]

To historians of science, Plat and Bacon have traditionally represented related but distinct tracks in the emergent practices of experimental science: one, a vernacular peddler of popular but sometimes useful recipes, and the other a natural philosopher and systematizer of what would later triumph as the scientific method. In this view, Bacon's epistemic program breaks from the work of popular experimentalists like Plat and the tradition of books of secrets. Bacon himself hinted at this story, and sometimes suppressed the influence of the more commercial and (in Bacon's view) superstitious work of figures like Plat.[4]

More recent scholarship, however, has suggested that Bacon may have been protesting too much. Deborah Harkness has shown how Plat and Bacon, along with the programs of natural knowledge they endorsed, actually had quite a bit in common, from their social milieu around London's Inns of Court to their interest in experimental philosophy—however much Bacon was sometimes at pains to disavow these commonalities. Angus Vine has illuminated the manuscript practices by which both gathered, copied, and ordered information—textual habits of compilation indexed in the serial form and vegetable titles of the *Paradise* and *Sylva*.[5] Later in the seventeenth century, a related repertoire of textual practices shored up the epistemic communities around the midcentury reformer Samuel Hartlib and, later, the Royal Society. Members of the latter, in concert with an international Republic of Letters, assembled a scientific project that relied on the circulation and storage of small textual forms and the social networks those paper fragments sustained.[6] From this perspective, despite their differences, Plat and Bacon's piecemeal textual practices anticipate the social and epistemic transformations that later came to be known as the Scientific Revolution.

The textual and natural imaginary uncovered by *Botanical Poetics*, however, suggests that we might as easily see both figures not as early pioneers but as belated participants in an aging discourse—aftershocks from a way of thinking about textual matter and the natural world that reached a heyday in their youth. *Floraes Paradise* and *Sylva Sylvarum* still grapple with dynamics of textual circulation and reception that were negotiated in plant books of the 1560s and 1570s: the borrowing of detachable slips, the piecemeal composition of text and cosmos, the freedom of readers to reorder and reuse. Plat's practical *Paradise* may have broken from the moral content of his earlier *Floures*, but it held close to the textual practices that composed it. Bacon's rhetoric may be more ambivalent, and his natural philosophy more complex, but his "Heap of Particulars" still reflects that collective work of gathering and reordering.

In giving their collected experiments figurative titles, Plat and Bacon turn to what I have suggested is a distinctly poetic labor of imagination and self-presentation; these figures give names to hard-to-name forms, making intelligible each book's mixed composition and open invitation to future readers. And, fashioned in this way as another loose binding, Bacon's *Sylva Sylvarum* shares quite a bit with the earlier *Forrest of Fancy*. The 1579 *Forrest*, as we saw in Chapter 1, leads with its formal looseness, apologizing for its "disordered placing of every perticuler parcel thereof, being rudely and dispersedly devided."[7] Faced with this disorder of particulars, the collection endorses a path of trial, experiment, and accident. The *Forrest*, in turn,

promises to supply enough variety that readers should not find themselves
"addicted" to the order of the book. It leaves the reader free to wander. *Sylva
Sylvarum* also yokes its formal mixture to the reader's liberty. Rawley's
epistle promises that the work's "Indigested Heap of Particulars" is productively miscellaneous, meant "to unloose Mens mindes," which are otherwise
"bound" to the charms of rhetorical order and method. Like the authors of
mid-Elizabethan poetic gardens, who offered their readers license and leave
to gather, Bacon intends the loose binding of the text to unbind readers,
freeing them up to repeat, try for themselves, and find their own order. As
Gascoigne wrote of his *Hundreth Sundrie Flowres* (1573), readers "shall not
be constreined to smell of the floures therein conteined all at once, neither
yet to take them up in such order as they are sorted."[8]

In Bacon's literary and scientific project, it is premature judgment that
brings on that bondage, but deferral that unlooses men's minds, fueled by an
extended process of collection and observation. This effect of dilation requires short literary forms—like the "Indigested Heap" of the *Sylva's* experiments, or like the "short and dispersed sentences" of aphorism, which
(Bacon writes) represent a "knowledge broken" that leads men on to further
inquiry rather than shutting it down.[9] As he writes elsewhere, aphorism
"doth leave the wit of man more free to turn and toss, to make use of that
which is so delivered to more several purposes and applications."[10] Other
reflexive titles under which Bacon gathered notes and observations also emphasize their textual looseness, like his *Commentarius Solutus*, or his early
manuscript collection of formularies or prose sentences, which he called
"Promus."[11] Drawing on the language of domestic economy, "promus" refers
to a butler, or the layer-out of goods in a household, and was opposed to
"condus," a steward, or layer-in of goods. Bacon's use of the term alludes
to one of Erasmus's adages, *Promus magis quam condus*, which, by accusing
someone of being more of a butler than a steward, serves as a diagnosis of
over-liberality. It refers to those who take more out of a storehouse than
they put in. As Alan Stewart notes, however, Bacon inverts its message; for
him, laying-out is a virtue.[12] While Bacon filters his sense of textual order
through the lexicon of housekeeping, it is hospitality and gentlemanly liberality (rather than husbandly thrift) that shapes his view of the sociability of
knowledge.

And yet, a *Sylva Sylvarum* is hardly a *Forrest of Fancy*. Even Bacon's title
seems to forcefully revise the premise of the earlier poetic collection, classi-
cizing its vernacular alliteration and replacing its mess of fancy with a mess

of matter—a *copia rerum* instead of a *copia verborum*. As Rawley explained in his epistle, Bacon aimed to break from earlier natural histories that "being gathered for Delight and Use, are full of pleasant Descriptions and Pictures; and affect and seeke after Admiration, Rarities, and Secrets." Rejecting this conventional pairing of profit and delight, Bacon instead wants to lay the groundwork for future interpretation, gathering materials "Fundamentall to the Erecting and Building of a true *Philosophy*."[13] We might, then, expect all the trees and flowers in these collections to be the fleshy kind: the living things addressed in their experiments and not the figurative conceit of each book's self-imagination. In their writing, Plat and Bacon both advertise plainness of speech, disavowing the conspicuous materiality of the earlier period's style, with its mountains of similes and affinity for alliteration. For Plat, a plain style served the common circulation of vernacular knowledge, while, for Bacon, it broke with the fecundity of a copious style, which, as he famously wrote, abandoned the "weight of matter" in order to "to hunt more after words, than matter."[14]

While Plat is far more open than Bacon to hunting after delight, he takes the fundamentals of building even more seriously: every experiment in his *Paradise* leads a reader to an actionable method. Its words tend toward the making of things. Nonetheless, the reflexive title of Plat's *Paradise* makes a different kind of generic promise than a rhetorical forest—one that values the formed conceit of the codex alongside the terrestrial conceits that Plat suggests for home or garden. Despite the raw seriality that both forms share, Plat presents the commodified book as an already formed and enclosed object—the paradise, like the well-honed "jewel house," that in reality reflects a lengthier and more tangled process of experiment, reading, overheard intelligence, and ordered and reordered notebooks. As Isabella Whitney perceived in 1573, Plat was keenly attuned to circulation's costs and benefits: he figuratively enclosed his flowers against the possibility that a reader might lay waste to them. In the later parts of his career, he also carefully stage-manages sharing and withholding knowledge, granting curated access to nature's "operative parts" by mixing useful experiments with teasers for instructions available only to those who seek him out.[15] The *Paradise*'s concluding sentences suggest that the present offering is just a hint of what is in store: "And thus I have culled out a few choice flowers, out of a large ground," Plat writes, but he is "readie to second them with a new supply of fresh Inventions."[16] Like Thomas Howell or Nicholas Breton, he promises another harvest from the greater storehouse of a "large ground"—one that, exceeding the well-formed walls of the *Paradise,* might look something like his neighborhood in Bethnal Green, which was a hub of London plant cultivation and incubator for the growing trade in market gardening. Here, Plat's idea of "profit" joins the word's commercial sense with a rhetorical and practical commitment to the common good, which he pursued through a range of inventions that included projects for improving soil and crop yield. Despite holding some things back, Plat presents his experiments as available for "common use."[17]

Just what kind of "use," though, do these collections invite or allow? And how does their affiliation with the longer tradition of plant books shape those models of utility? From the perspective of ecology, *use* is a loaded and powerful concept—especially when we are asking about the use of books that are themselves about the use of nature to human ends, and when one of those books is by Francis Bacon. During the twentieth century, Bacon came to stand as a notorious origin point for modernity's exploitive and instrumentalizing view of nature—a prophet of the disenchantment of the world and the triumph of a violent human dominion.[18] Martin Heidegger described this viewpoint, originating in the seventeenth century, as the tendency to approach the stuff of nature as mere resources, what he called "standing-reserve" (*Bestand,* in German).[19] Both plant matter and textual matter seem, from this view, *merely useful,* their existence meaningful only insofar as they remain ready-to-hand for human ends. The idea of a reserve is hinted at in the ancient vocabulary for forests: the Greek *hulē* and the Latin *silva,* while referring to actual forests, also came to refer to raw matter—the kind awaiting imprint of form or adoption for human use. Those same etymologies inform the *silva* as a literary genre characterized by raw disorder: forests were full of material for use, ready for store and provision.[20] With his "new supply of fresh Inventions" ready just off-stage, Plat implies access to a similar kind of textual reserve. As these images of textual supply suggest, plant books sometimes seem to promise a similarly ever-ready fuel source; this kind of resource-thinking reclaims the qualities that I have described as latency instead in the name of readiness.

But this is not the whole story that we have seen unfold across these chapters. As often as not, plant books paint themselves as ostentatiously unready; far from wholly passive or subsumed into human ends, they have demanded patience, handling, and help. We have seen plants and texts cling to their own timescales: they are immature or overripe, newly set and still sour, wilting or stubbornly evergreen. The resulting collaborations of human and herb follow Isabella Whitney's gloss on skill: "To slip, to shere, or get in time, / and not his braunches kyll."[21] Getting "in time" means taking slips in season—in the time of the plant—but it can also mean slipping just soon enough (in the urgency of *carpe diem*) or not yet: living with plants is living with waiting. But the intransigence of these seasonal patterns was a matter of contention. Early modern debates about art and nature turned on altering not just the forms of creatures but their schedules, as practitioners hoped to grow roses in winter, for example, or accelerate a harvest of cherries or plums. Many experiments in the *Paradise* and *Sylva,* as in earlier books of instruction, investigate just this kind of alteration. For these techniques, which seek out the "operative" part of nature, to use a plant is to remake vegetable rhythms to fit the dissonant time scheme of human purposes.

In gardens and forests, the practice of use follows from the possibility and exercise of transport: the borrowing, rearranging, and recycling of slips at new times and new settings. At times, in these pages, the transport and traffic of small forms has structured a fantasy of free circulation, an open network across which texts, plants, and human desires and identities circulate without friction or loss. This imagination of borrowing without diminishing—of taking without taking away—implies a particular environmental economy. An herbalist or shepherd, confident that the culled herb will recover and that the sheared sheep will regain its wool, trusts in the spontaneous fecundity of nature, its prodigious capacity to grow back (and even beyond) what we remove.

But some poets also set limits to these capacities, and they reclaimed their printed poetry not as an immaterial and infinitely transmissible text, but as a mortal substance—subject to harm and worthy of cultivation and care. As they imagined being uprooted, these poets defended the distinct value of both themselves and their poems. In doing so, they struggled to articulate an ecology of printed poetry: was mechanically reproduced writing a ready reserve, or a precious and depletable substance? Just how bottomless a well could the printed book or the fertile field be? And how indifferent to the use or abuse to which it was subjected? Often, the answer turned on who was doing the borrowing, and how. As Whitney writes, only a reader with the necessary skills might slip in time and "not his braunches kyll." With the right handling, however, or with regular maintenance, a garden or anthology might be available for repeated harvesting. The gardens of both nature and book, however, have since come to seem largely indifferent to handling—achieved sites of preservation and endless tanks of fuel, impervious to abuse or depletion. This image, of course, is also a fantasy—one whose optimism has fueled centuries of colonial extraction and bioprospecting and fed a fetishism of unlimited growth still only meekly countervailed by present-day calls for economic "de-growth." This picture of growth presumes that there is a kind of taking that does not take away, of using that does not use up. But transport and borrowing can never be free. Neither texts nor plants circulate or propagate without friction loss or the ravages of slow decay; all require logistics, collective infrastructure, and good timing.

Instead of "pointes," "flowres," or "slips," Plat and Bacon gather small forms that they give the name of "experiments." Like the poems or *sententiae* gathered in other gardens and forests, these small, portable forms of experience build a bridge from the particularity of occasion to something beyond it. [22] In this way, they create a place—like Taverner's Henrician garden of *loci communes*—that provides a common resource precisely because it might obtain in any number of times and places. Each of these forms is essentially iterable: a point, recipe, slip, poem, and experiment can happen and then happen again. The slips comprising the *Sylva* and *Paradise* belonged to an environment of profound textual mobility: as Vine has shown, Bacon and Plat copied recipes and intelligence from notebook to notebook and expected for their experiments a future of copying, testing, reorganization, and recirculation through networks of readers and practitioners. The printers of both titles have preserved space for readers on the space of the page, where an enclosing frame marks off the text of experiments from generous adjacent margins. Aside from scattered notes, numbers, and headings, these framed columns are mostly blank space: open-ended invitations to annotation and further inquiry. As Ayesha Mukherjee shows, Plat was himself an assiduous annotator, and used marginal flowers and trefoils much like those used by Ben Jonson (Figure 4). For Jonson, these symbols are small vegetable icons of the nectar-gathering humanist bee, marking out passages worthy of copying or remembering. For Plat, they note recipes he has tried, with marks appearing multiple times for those he repeatedly tested: the kind of copying at work here is practical, embodied, and buoyed by repeated attempts.[23] Plat's marks quietly align the replicability of recipes and experiments with practices of culling and excerpting cultivated by plant books across the period. In doing so, he models a rhetorical approach to one of the great problems faced by the early Royal Society: the capacity of experiments to pertain in general, though only ever executed at particular times and places. In the coming decades, the orchestrated environment of the experiment house would authorize the lessons drawn from those experiences to travel—like proverbs, couplets, or flowers—from occasion to occasion.[24]

Over the course of the previous chapters, we have seen a vein of textual and botanical traffic that bears increasingly abstract fruit: like the "summes" of Tusser's months, following a textual model of summation and condensation; like the perfume of Shakespeare's Sonnet 5 and the grafted fruit of Sonnet 15, both of which extract and capture material from the passing seasons, as the couplet does from the poem's quatrains; like the "violl" of Milton's *Areopagitica*, by analogy to which books preserve "the purest efficacie and extraction of that living intellect that bred them."[25] At times, this generalization has taken the abstract form of exchange value, admitting the dynamics of a monetary economy into the space of the garden: what "sum", as Gascoigne asks, might be made of the exchange of "some" and "some" that plays out there? In this light, if we want to ask what kind of knowledge is produced by Bacon's or Plat's experiments, we might also ask what kind of knowledge is produced by the couplet to Shakespeare's Sonnet 15, or what kind of survival.

The remaining pages of this Epilogue turn to a moment of plant morphology that has appeared only occasionally in the previous chapters, but that is central to how Plat and Bacon understand the utility of nature and of experiments: the fruit. The very name we give to these fleshy, seed-bearing structures posits them as the end of a process rather than a moment in a cycle, framing them by the bounds set by human use: they are something enjoyed. As marketable products (or produce), the "fruits" of labor often seem extractable from the seasonal cycle of growth and decay. But they are themselves exceptionally vulnerable to rot: a product of preservation and extraction, an agent of proliferation, but also a precarious object that solicits (and does not always reward) exceptional care.

For Elizabethan writers and gardeners wondering if their labors would bear fruit, the imperatives of use were filtered through the oft-repeated pairing of profit and delight—a literary qualification that, as we saw, Rawley rejects on Bacon's behalf in his epistle to the *Sylva*. Less ambivalently, Plat reminds us of this traditional framing of use with an epigraph on the *Paradise*'s title page: *Hiis fruere, & expecta meliora*. Enjoy (or use, or profit from) these things, but look out for better (or more pleasant) ones. The epigraph splits its view across present and future, concluding with what is both spiritual advice and a specific literary promise: the next supply of experiments and inventions will be even better. Like the styles of husbandly *pro*-vision we saw in Chapter 5, "expecta" is an enjoinder to optimism that relies etymologically on vision—here, *spectare*.[26] Perhaps most important, *fruere* is a pun: the deponent Latin verb *fruor* was also the origin of *fructus*, or fruit. (*Fructus sum* could mean both "I enjoyed" or "I am a fruit.")[27] Plat's title, we might recall, promises a store of "delicate fruites and flowers"—in forms both rhetorical and vegetable, as a reader would soon learn. The epigraph thus suggests a robust model of readerly use, an invitation that the reader holding the volume enjoy the fruits of the book, many of which are literally *fruits*, like the especially delicate quinces suggested by one experiment, or the early-fruiting strawberries described in another.[28] In this way, the phrase encapsulates the economic and cornucopian impulse that drove Plat's recipes for improvement; witness to devastating seasons of dearth and suffering, he now promises his readers increase and—in the epigraph's agriculturally productive sense—fruits.[29] Handing the *Paradise* over to the reader's use, Plat's invitation to "enjoy" promises an indefinitely renewable resource. Drawing on this sense, *Floraes Paradise* grants a reader-practitioner the power to use and to enjoy the fruits of the book, ground, or plant, but not to waste or deplete those resources—a condition that Whitney understood very well when she accepted the invitation offered by Plat's 1572 *Floures*. To achieve this capacity, Whitney and Plat both understood, demanded the constant labor of skilled cultivators.

The language of fruit crops up again at the heart of Bacon's experimental program, which famously distinguishes between two kinds of experiments: *experimenta fructifera* and *experimenta lucifera*—"of *Use*, or of *Discovery*," as he describes this division in the *Sylva*.[30] As their Latin names suggest, they bring either fruit or light. Fruit also subtly finds its way into the experimental practices of Salomon's House in the *New Atlantis*, the description of an imagined society published with the *Sylva Sylvarum*. There, among the many figures involved in carrying out, ordering, and interpreting experiments, is a subset known as "Inoculators." The Inoculators are responsible for the execution of experiments—but the word itself is a synonym for grafting, from the Latin word for bud, or "eye." While these Inoculators stand at a crucial point in the process, Bacon places more value on the role of the Interpreters of Nature, whose labors follow those of the Inoculators, and who raise discoveries to the level of axiom.[31] The Inoculators are emblematic of what the philosopher Michèle Le Doeuff argues is the shaping force of gardening-thought in Bacon's philosophy. Against interpretations of Bacon as a precursor of modern industrial science, we should instead, she suggests, look to gardening as a paradigm for Bacon's understanding of the relation of man and nature. In Bacon's leveling of art and nature, the bounded power of the Inoculator is something like the orchardist's, whose sole power over nature lies in bringing bodies together or apart—the rest, Bacon writes, "is done by nature working within."[32]

Consider one of a series of techniques for grafting that appears in the *Sylva*'s fourth century of experiments. Bacon describes an alleged method for accelerating fruit production—"a Conceit that sheweth prettily," he writes, that "if you graft a *Late Coming Fruit*, upon a Stocke of a *Fruit-tree* that *commeth early*, the Graft will beare *Fruit Early*, As a Peach upon a Cherry." The contrary is also allegedly effective. But Bacon dismisses both versions of this hearsay as "but Imaginations, and untrue." His reasoning relies not on experience but on principle: "The *Cause* is, for that the Cions overruleth the Stocke quite; and the Stocke is but passive onely, and giveth, Aliment, but no Motions to the Graft."[33] Bacon begins here with a procedure, a "conceit" as he calls it, which he has in this case drawn from Giambattista della Porta's *Magia Naturalis*, but which a reader might as easily associate with recipes circulated by practitioners or printed in a book like Plat's *Paradise*. However, transforming the recipe from della Porta, he ends with a general law, one legislated by the grafts themselves: "the Cions overruleth the Stocke."[34] Moving with the scion as it travels, this law of governance is both mobile and ostensibly universal in its applications. Like the couplet of Sonnet 15, it "overrules" and guarantees the continuation of kind.

Bacon's experiment has here borne a very different kind of fruit. Rawley's epistle describes the process of generating axioms as an "Extraction"—a word that, appropriately, can name either a textual or botanical method of drawing out. While della Porta's technique erred (Bacon argues) in setting the grafter at war with the time of the fruit, Bacon's axiom of "overrule" has won its own kind of war with time and contingency, as a law that extends indifferently across time and place. Meanwhile, as Bacon extracts axioms from the neutral ground of the experiment, Plat extracts more fruit. Plat is as concerned as Bacon about the ability of particulars to travel, but his response is not to plot those particulars in rows and columns but to inscribe on the landscape an actual plot. Plat's first experiment lays out instructions for an alchemically informed "Philosophicall Garden," which "wil receive any Indian plant, and make all vegetables to prosper in the highest degree,

& to beare their fruites in England, as natural as they doe in Spaine, Italie, or elsewhere."[35] Though turned to a more expansive geography, Plat here reimagines the model of national improvement that fueled stories like that of the first pippin grafted on an English tree, allegedly brought by Henry VIII's royal fruiterer.[36] The utopian idea of a ground in which anything might grow would come in the decades following to inspire numerous philosophical gardens and physic gardens, which became earthbound collections in their own right. In the late seventeenth century, the physician and natural philosopher Hans Sloane began collecting an immense range of specimens from around the globe, including more than three hundred herbaria volumes of dried plants and more than twelve thousand boxes of what he called "vegetable substances." Each with a small window and encased in marbled paper, these boxes "make nature discrete, and so ownable," James Delbourgo argues.[37]

Sloane's boxes and the networks that supplied them give infrastructural reality to the fantasy for which Sebastian taunts Gonzalo, after they have just been shipwrecked in *The Tempest*: "I think he will carry this island home in his pocket and give it his son for an apple" (2.1.91–92). In their optimism, Sloane's boxes might remind us of the compartmented books and gardens of the previous century, though they serve a massive project of transporting and relocating plants, people, and texts—in Sloane's case, a project partially funded by his marriage to the heiress of a sugar plantation. It would not seem so impossible by the end of the century to carry home an island in vegetable form—as long as you didn't need it to be ripe.

The logistics of plant transport depend on fitting the rhythms of plant life to the demands of transoceanic travel: fruit rots, a slip loses is freshness, roots and seeds lose their virtue. European collectors and natural philosophers proposed methods for preserving specimens as they were transported across long transoceanic journeys, on ships shared with rats, cats, and mildew. John Evelyn suggested the roots of specimens be coated with honey. John Woodward instructed that roots be "wrapt up in a lump of *Clay or Loame* and then put in a Box with Moss, and so sent over."[38] The collector-apothecary James Petiver published a broadsheet called *Brief directions for the easie making, and preserving collections of all natural curiosities* (1709?), asking specimen collectors to gather the pieces of plants in a book, or *hortus siccus*. For large fruit, he recommended preservation: "All large pulpy moist *Fruit*, that are apt to decay or rot, as *Apples, Cherries, Cowcumbers, Oranges*, and such like, must be sent in *Spirits* or *Pickle*, as *Mangoes*,

&c. and to each Fruit, its desired you will pin or tye a sprig of its *Leaves*, and *Flowers*."[39] Collecting a specimen, either dry or wet, means re-gathering its leaves and flowers, pinning or tying it pieces together. Another way to collect a mango—not exactly pickled—is represented in Hans Sloane's collection. Sloane had in his collection a bezoar stone, calcified matter formed inside the body of an animal, "form'd round the Stone of that great Plum, which comes pickled from thence, and is called *Mango*."[40]

Petiver's reference to "*Mangoes*, &c" may be to the fruit or to a pickle: by the end of the seventeenth century in England, "mango" had come to mean a kind of pickling from vinegar and salt, with no reference to the fruit, so that Evelyn could give a recipe for "Mango of Cucumbers."[41] Though reputed for their lusciousness, mangos largely traveled—and were likelier to en-counter Englishmen—in the form of achar; the name in turn was detached from the fleshy kind of mango and attached to this more general method of preservation. The logistics of transporting and preserving remade the force of the word; a jar of mango might have no mango in it at all.

I have not landed randomly on Sloane and Petiver's mangoes. One mile from where I live, in the Coconut Grove neighborhood of Miami, are some of the oldest mango cultivars in the continental United States, first planted early in the twentieth century. At the base of branches, grafted seams are still visible where bark of stock and scion grew together decades ago. The trees were introduced by David Fairchild, botanical prospector and for many years director of the USDA's Office of Seed and Plant Introduction, who used the eight-acre bayside property as a home and agricultural experiment station. There, he tested and cultivated hundreds of tropical plants, including more than fifty varieties of mangoes.[42] Like Petiver, and like Sloane, Fairchild's vegetable career took shape alongside expanding colonial ambitions; and, like them, his collection brought global specimens—quite literally—home. Like Sloane's boxes of vegetable substances, Fairchild's orchard is a strange archive. Originally housed and maintained in domestic spaces, both collections have served public projects of national improvement. And, like any archive, it is as notable for what it leaves out as what it includes, including details on the Bahamian gardeners who planted and grafted with Fairchild. At the seam of branch and stock, though, the trees carry the trace of that earlier labor.

The couplet of Shakespeare's Sonnet 15 sets the poet, arm in arm with the fruit tree, against the ravages of time: "And all in war with Time for love of you / As he takes from you, I ingraft you new." Because the scion (in Bacon's words) overrules the stock, grafting ensures the fruit's endurance. However, as I have suggested, this is a procedure for preserving abstractions; the fruit identity it cherishes is a form shared between fruits, not the fleshy substance of any particular example. But we might also read a competing pull in these lines, a kind of undertow against that version of preservation. In the doubled pacing of the poem's final line, the poet's "I ingraft you new" struggles to keep up with the workings of Time; as Time continues to take (as it inevitably does), the poet must continue to graft anew. With this recursive procedure, preservation looks less like an achieved task than the continuous and uncertain work of survival. The poet commits to the ongoing labor of maintenance, the kind of unremitting caretaking that unfolds in time rather than trying to find a way out of it.

Fairchild's mango trees are "in war with Time" and with the rising saltwater of Biscayne Bay. In 1992, following Hurricane Andrew, while dozens of other trees were pulled down, most mango and avocado trees survived, in part because they had been grafted and their crowns cut down: their cultivation (inadvertently) shaped them for survival. In their war with time, these mango trees are keeping pace. But time is moving faster: their posterity depends on a limestone shelf that keeps stock, scion, and fruit about seven meters above Biscayne Bay on a calm day, at low tide.

NOTES

Introduction

1. Unless otherwise noted, all citations from the *Sonnets* refer to William Shakespeare, *Shake-speares Sonnets. Never before Imprinted* (London: by George Eld for Thomas Thorpe, 1609). I have also relied on *Shakespeare's Sonnets*, ed. Stephen Booth (New Haven, CT: Yale University Press, 1977).

2. On these dynamics, see the work on grafting by Rebecca Bushnell, Jean Feerick, and Vin Nardizzi: Rebecca Bushnell, *Green Desire: Imagining Early Modern Gardens* (Ithaca, NY: Cornell University Press, 2003), esp. 132–160; Jean E. Feerick, "The Imperial Graft: Horticulture, Hybridity, and the Art of Mingling Races in *Henry V* and *Cymbeline*," in *The Oxford Handbook of Shakespeare and Embodiment*, ed. Valerie Traub (Oxford: Oxford University Press, 2016), 211–227; Vin Nardizzi, "Shakespeare's Penknife: Grafting and Seedless Generation in the Procreation Sonnets," *Renaissance and Reformation* 32.1 (2009): 83–106. I will return below to how the botanical poetics I describe here departs from other models of textual creation and legitimacy.

3. Here I lightly paraphrase Andrew Marvell's "The Mower against Gardens" (see Elizabeth Story Donno, ed., *Andrew Marvell: The Complete Poems* [London: Penguin, 1985], 105).

4. Thomas Howell, *The Arbor of Amitie, wherin is comprised pleasant Poëms and pretie Poesies* (London: Henry Denham, 1568), sig. A.v^r.

5. This version of the olive tree was used by Robert Estienne the elder as early as the 1528 Bible, and on larger books from that point on; members of the family used differently sized versions of an olive tree as printer's marks at different times. See Nos. 291–307 in Philippe Renouard, *Les marques typographiques parisiennes des XVe et XVI siècles* (Paris, 1926). On the changing use of these marks and their meaning, see Elizabeth Armstrong, *Robert Estienne, Royal Printer: An Historical Study of the Elder Stephanus* (Cambridge: Cambridge University Press, 1954), 10, 234; and Fred Schreiber, "The Estiennes," *American Book Collector* 3 (1982): 2–10. Grafton's marks may be found in R. B. McKerrow, *Printers' & Publishers' Devices in England & Scotland 1485–1640* (London, 1913), Nos. 95, 104, 114. At least one version of Grafton's rebus shows the tree growing from the barrel without the visible incision (McKerrow, No. 90). English copies of the Estienne olive tree by John Wolfe and John Norton are included in McKerrow, Nos. 310–311 and 348–350. Compare also the notes on grafting and the materiality of the printed text in Random Cloud, "FIAT *f*LUX," in *Crisis in Editing: Texts of the English Renaissance*, ed. Randall M Leod (New York: AMS Press, 1994), 61–172.

6. Contemporary philosopher Michael Marder identifies a strain in Western metaphysics that classifies the vegetable kingdom as "ontologically deficient," a judgment that fixes plants

as passive matter and thus condemns them to exploitation. *Plant-Thinking: A Philosophy of Vegetal Life* (New York: Columbia University Press, 2013), 21–23.

7. This version of Genesis counts animals, as Laurie Shannon puts it, as "herb-entitled subjects." *The Accommodated Animal: Cosmopolity in Shakespearean Locales* (Chicago: University of Chicago Press, 2013), 42. According to Richard Hooker's account of the orders of life, plants "though beneath the excellency of creatures endowed with sense, yet exceed them in the faculty of vegetation and of fertility." Richard Hooker, *Of the Laws of Ecclesiastical Polity*, ed. Arthur Stephen McGrade (Cambridge: Cambridge University Press, 1989), 68. On these orders of being, see Feerick and Nardizzi's introduction, "Swervings: On Human Indistinction," in *The Indistinct Human in Renaissance Literature*, ed. Jean E. Feerick and Vin Nardizzi (New York: Palgrave Macmillan, 2012), 1–4. For classic articulations of this interconnected view, see E. M. W. Tillyard, *The Elizabethan World Picture* (London: Chatto and Windus, 1943), 80–83; A. O. Lovejoy, *The Great Chain of Being* (Cambridge, MA: Harvard University Press, 1936).

8. John Maplet, *A greene Forest, or a naturall Historie* (London: Henry Denham, 1567), fol. 28$^{r–v}$.

9. Ibid, fol. 28^v. We might compare this emphasis on segments to the metaphorics of rootedness described by Christy Wampole, *Rootedness: The Ramifications of a Metaphor* (Chicago: University of Chicago Press, 2016).

10. *The Complete Works of Aristotle: The Revised Oxford Translation*, vol. 1, ed. Jonathan Barnes (Princeton, NJ: Princeton University Press, 1984), 746. On lifespans and morphology of plants and insects, see R. A. H. King, *Aristotle on Life and Death* (London: Duckworth, 2000), 92. On fragmentary propagation, which was described at length in Theophrastus, see Bruce E. Haissig and Tim D. Davis, "A Historical Evaluation of Adventitious Rooting Research to 1993," in *Biology of Adventitious Root Formation*, ed. Tim D. David and Bruce E. Haissig (New York: Plenum, 1994), 275–332. As Garrett Sullivan argues, the nutritive or vegetative soul does not only distinguish vegetable life from animal and human existence; it also connects these orders of being; see Garrett A. Sullivan Jr., *Sleep, Romance, and Human Embodiment* (Cambridge: Cambridge University Press, 2012).

11. On the posy, see Juliet Fleming, *Graffiti and the Writing Arts of Early Modern England* (London: Reaktion, 2011), 20.

12. Maplet, *A greene Forest*, fol. 28^v. The circulating small forms of husbandry and horticulture in this way represent a vernacular and artisanal analog to the varieties of atomism described in Gerard Passannante, *The Lucretian Renaissance: Philology and the Afterlife of Tradition* (Chicago: University of Chicago Press, 2011). As Passannante shows for the legacy of Lucretianism, these quotidian practices of detachment and reattachment in Elizabethan England also informed a literary culture that valued scattering, recombination, and accumulation.

13. Historians have shown the significance of traffic in plant materials to the growth of European empires in the sixteenth, seventeenth, and eighteenth centuries. See Londa Schiebinger and Claudia Swan, eds., *Colonial Botany* (Philadelphia: University of Pennsylvania Press, 2007); Daniela Bleichmar, *Visible Empire* (Chicago: University of Chicago Press, 2012); and, more broadly, H. A. Curry, N. Jardine, J. A. Secord, and E. C. Spary, eds., *Worlds of Natural History* (Cambridge: Cambridge University Press, 2018).

14. As M. H. Abrams writes, "It is astonishing how much of Coleridge's critical writing is couched in terms that are metaphorical for art and literal for a plant; if Plato's dialectic is a wilderness of mirrors, Coleridge's is a very jungle of vegetation." M. H. Abrams, *The Mirror*

and the Lamp: Romantic Theory and the Critical Tradition (Oxford: Oxford University Press, 1953), 169. See also Denise Gigante, *Life: Organic Form and Romanticism* (New Haven, CT: Yale University Press, 2003). Abrams's and Gigantes's perspectives are complicated by the picture of Lucretianism developed by Amanda Jo Goldstein in *Sweet Science: Romantic Materialism and the New Logics of Life* (Chicago: University of Chicago Press, 2017).

15. Cleanth Brooks, "Irony as a Principle of Structure," in *The Critical Tradition: Classic Texts and Contemporary Trends*, ed. David H. Richter (Boston: Bedford/St. Martin's, 2007), 799.

16. William Eamon calls practical handbooks "one of typography's most important contributions to sixteenth-century literature." William Eamon, *Science and the Secrets of Nature* (Princeton, NJ: Princeton University Press, 1994), 113. On profit and delight, see Robert Matz, *Defending Literature in Early Modern England* (Cambridge: Cambridge University Press, 2000). On the phrase's importance for gardening literature, see Bushnell, *Green Desire*, 93–107; and Jill Francis, "Order and Disorder in the Early Modern Garden, 1558-c. 1630," *Garden History* 36.1 (2008): 22–35.

17. Thomas Tusser, *Five hundreth points of good husbandry united to as many of huswiferie* (London: Richard Tottel, 1573), sig. A.iii^v.

18. Philip Sidney, *The Defence of Poesie* (London: for William Ponsonby, 1595), sig. C2^v.

19. Botanical poetics in this sense is consonant with Colleen Rosenfeld's account of "indecorous thinking," an approach to poetry that values "the member over the corpus, the part over the whole." (Colleen Ruth Rosenfeld, *Indecorous Thinking: Figures of Speech in Early Modern Poetics* [New York: Fordham University Press, 2018], 75). On Renaissance poetics as craft knowledge, see Patricia Parker, *Shakespeare from the Margins* (Chicago: University of Chicago Press, 1996), 43–82; and Rayna Kalas, *Frame, Glass, Verse: The Technology of Poetic Invention in the English Renaissance* (Ithaca, NY: Cornell University Press, 2007).

20. Maplet, *The greene Forest*, fol. 28^v.

21. For this reason, my subject in the following chapters is not pastoral poetry, or the presence of plants in other genres of escape (though the pleasant seclusion of both garden and pasture will figure at times) but the poetic practices of everyday life. I am inspired in this approach by Frances E. Dolan's rich account of the imaginative energies of seventeenth-century agriculture in *Digging the Past: How and Why to Imagine Seventeenth-Century Agriculture* (Philadelphia: University of Pennsylvania Press, 2020).

22. William Shakespeare, *Romeo and Juliet*, ed. René Weis, Arden Shakespeare, 3rd ser. (London: Bloomsbury, 2012), 2.3.11–12.

23. Some of these differences are captured in the early modern spelling of "vertue," which is used with regularity in early modern English printed books (a fact explored more fully in Chapter 2). This account of "vertue" dovetails with Holly Crocker's argument that premodern senses of "vertue" are less attached to the masculine dynamics of *vis* and *vir*. Holly A. Crocker, *The Matter of Virtue* (Philadelphia: University of Pennsylvania Press, 2019).

24. Shannon, *Accommodated Animal*, 44.

25. See "The Princelye pleasures, at the Courte at Kenelwoorth," in *John Nichols's The Progresses and Public Processions of Queen Elizabeth I: A New Edition of the Early Modern Sources*, vol. 2, *1572 to 1578*, ed. Elizabeth Goldring et al. (Oxford: Oxford University Press, 2014), 322–332.

26. See Bushnell, *Green Desire*, esp. 84–107. These instructional books are described in the classic monographs by Eleanour Sinclaire Rohde: Eleanour Sinclair Rohde, *The Old English Herbals* (London: Longmans, Green, and Co., 1922); and Rohde, *The Old English Gardening*

Books (London: Martin Hopkinson, 1924). Works on husbandry are surveyed in G. E. Fussell, *The Old English Farming Books from Fitzherbert to Tull, 1523–1730* (London: Crosby, Lockwood & Son, 1947). A more recent bibliography may be found in Blanche Henrey, *British Botanical and Horticultural Literature Before 1800*, 3 vol. (Oxford: Oxford University Press, 1975).

27. Classical antecedents include texts by Xenophon, Virgil, Columella, and Varro. See Joan Thirsk, "Making a Fresh Start: Sixteenth-Century Agriculture and the Classical Inspiration," in *Culture and Cultivation in Early Modern England: Writing and the Land*, ed. Michael Leslie and Timothy Raynor (Leicester: Leicester University Press, 1992), 15–34. Thirsk and Andrew McRae argue that increasing numbers of books on husbandry were the result of structural changes in access to land, learning, and capital, especially following the dissolution of the monasteries. See Andrew McRae, *God Speed the Plough: The Representation of Agrarian England, 1500–1660* (Cambridge: Cambridge University Press, 2002), 135–168; Joan Thirsk, ed., *The Agrarian History of England and Wales*, vol. 4, *1500–1640* (Cambridge: Cambridge University Press, 1967). On transformations in agricultural practice, in addition to Thirsk, see Mark Overton, *Agricultural Revolution in England: The Transformation of the Agrarian Economy 1500–1850* (Cambridge: Cambridge University Press, 1996), esp. 10–62.

28. Barnabe Googe, trans., *Foure bookes of husbandry, collected by M. Conradus Heresbachius* (London: Richard Watkins, 1577), sig. A6^r. Andrew McRae argues that this resignification of husbandry asserted a model of increase that would newly authorize a defensible place for profit within the moral economy (*God Speed the Plough*, 142–143). Important Tudor works of husbandry prior to Googe's translation include Fitzherbert's *Boke of Husbondrye* (London: Robert Pynson, 1523) and Thomas Tusser's *A hundredth good pointes of husbandry* (London: Richard Tottel, 1557), both frequently reprinted through the century; in the 1580s and 1590s, farming books grew in number and also grew more specialized, as in the case of Leonard Mascall's trio of titles on (respectively) grafting, poultry, and livestock. See Leonard Mascall, *A Booke of the Arte and maner howe to plant and graffe all sortes of trees* (London: Henry Denham for John Wight, 1572); *The Husbandly ordring and Governmente of Poultrie* (London: Thomas Purfoote for Gerard Dewse, 1581); and *The first booke of Cattel* (London: John Wolfe, 1596).

29. My account of the husbandry of print in this Elizabethan moment is indebted to, and in dialogue with, Wendy Wall's account of "Renaissance national husbandry," a project that linked the cultivation of the land to the business of print in establishing a distinct English identity. As I discuss further in Chapter 1, the link between printing and planting at this earlier moment takes a more hesitant relation to the solidity of the land and the nation, and relies instead on more provisional practices of projection and anticipation. See Wendy Wall, "Renaissance National Husbandry: Gervase Markham and the Publication of England," *Sixteenth Century Journal* 27.3 (1996): 767–785.

30. Meeker and Szabari develop a rich account of what "speculation" means when it comes to thinking with plants, including the important role of vegetables in the histories of financial and philosophical speculation. Natania Meeker and Antónia Szabari, *Radical Botany: Plants and Speculative Fiction* (New York: Fordham University Press, 2019), 6, 17.

31. Marder, *Plant-Thinking*, 104; see also Joshua Calhoun, *The Nature of the Page: Poetry, Papermaking, and the Ecology of Texts in Renaissance England* (Philadelphia: University of Pennsylvania Press, 2020), 2, 7. This book builds on a rich body of work produced by the community of scholars publishing on plants and gardens in early modern England: see especially Bushnell, *Green Desire*; Rebecca Laroche, *Medical Authority and Englishwomen's Herbal Texts,*

1550–1650 (Farnham: Ashgate, 2009); Jennifer Munroe, *Gender and the Garden in Early Modern English Literature* (Aldershot: Ashgate, 2008); Vin Nardizzi, *Wooden Os: Shakespeare's Theatres and England's Trees* (Toronto: University of Toronto Press, 2013); Amy Tigner, *Literature and the Renaissance Garden from Elizabeth I to Charles II: England's Paradise* (Farnham: Ashgate, 2012). See also John Slater's work on the "Phytological Aesthetic," focused on early modern Iberia, which draws important connections between plants and humanist textual practices, including between botanical catalog and rhetorical copia. I am grateful to Professor Slater for sharing his work with me in draft form.

32. Calhoun, *The Nature of the Page.*

33. Unlike Tilney's *Flower*, neither text implies authorial involvement in the title. Maplet's prefaces refer to his "Aegemonie," and the first part of the *Forest* was entered between 22 July 1566 and 22 July 1567 as "a boke intituled *Aegemonie or the chefeste and pryncipall vertues of stones.*" Edward Arber, ed., *A Transcript of the Registers of the Company of Stationers of London, 1554–1640 A.D.*, 5 vols. (London: Privately printed, 1875–1894), 1:340. The *Arbor* is entered the next year to Denham as "a boke intituled *the myrror of amytie*" (1:364).

34. Randall Anderson, "Metaphors of the Book as Garden in the Renaissance," *Yearbook of English Studies* 33 (2003): 248–261, at 260. Anderson offers a useful inventory and important framing of these titles.

35. The calculations in the paragraphs that follow derive from a data set drawn from the ESTC, which has shaped the project as a whole. The full dataset is available online at http://jmrosenberg.net/botanicalpoetics. I am indebted to Virginia Schilling at the ESTC project at the University of California, Riverside, for her willingness to share this data and her assistance in gathering it. The terms represented in this data set (including variant spellings) are: flower, flowers, fiore, flour, flours, floure, floures, flores, florum, flovver, flovvers, flower, flowres, flovvre, flovvres, flovres, flovre, bower, bovvre, bowre, bovver, garland, garlande, posy, posie, posies, posye, poesies, nosegay, nosgay, nosgaye, blossom, blossomes, blossoms, blossome, forest, forrest, arbor, arbour, fruit, fruite, fruits, herbs, hearbes, herbes, hearbs, herb, hearb, hearbe, honisuckles, honeysuckles, gilloflowers, gilloflovvers, gillyflowers, myrrhe, myrrh, garden, gardens, jardin, gardyne, gardin, gardeine, grove, groue, orchard, ortchard, ortyard. After gathering a spreadsheet of these examples, the data was cleaned by myself and a research assistant, Ruth Shannon Trego, removing duplicates and false positives, and each element of the set was classified according to how the term appeared (short title or long title, in running head or internal division, and so on), and further classified according to genre, printers, dedicatees, and elements of book form, including format, title page design, and the presence of an index or table of contents. We also generated absolute number counts and percentages of market share. The central conclusions I have drawn here are based on a subset of examples prior to 1613 in which the botanical term features as a central titular metaphor. In comparing these quantities, I am cognizant of Peter Blayney's warnings about these overall counts, but they do not significantly affect my more general conclusions. Peter Blayney, "STC Publication Statistics: Some Caveats," *The Library*, 7th ser., 8.4 (2007): 387–97. See also Alan B. Farmer and Zachary Lesser, "What Is Print Popularity? A Map of the Elizabethan Book Trade," in *The Elizabethan Top Ten*, ed. Andy Kesson and Emma Smith (London: Routledge, 2013), 19–54.

36. Leah Knight, *Of Books and Botany in Early Modern England: Sixteenth-Century Plants and Print Culture* (Farnham: Ashgate, 2009), 1–38. My own study extends Knight's rich analysis into the context of practical works of horticulture and agriculture with the modes of anticipation and reception they entail.

37. On the influence of Tottel's miscellany, see Steven W. May, "Popularizing Courtly Poetry: Tottel's Miscellany and Its Progeny," in *The Oxford Handbook of Tudor Literature*, ed. Mike Pincombe and Cathy Shrank (Oxford: Oxford University Press, 2009), 418–436; Stephen Hamrick, ed., *Tottel's "Songes and Sonettes" in Context* (London: Routledge, 2013); Arthur F. Marotti, *Manuscript, Print, and the English Renaissance Lyric* (Ithaca, NY: Cornell University Press, 1995), 212–19, 291–302. On later sixteenth-century editions of the miscellany, see Paul A. Marquis, ed., *Richard Tottel's "Songes and Sonettes": The Elizabethan Version* (Tempe: Arizona Center for Medieval and Renaissance Studies in conjunction with Renaissance English Text Society, 2007). On Elizabethan poetic collections, the various editions prepared by Hyder E. Rollins and published by Harvard University Press between 1923 and 1935 remain invaluable. Important recent monographs by Megan Heffernan and Michelle O'Callaghan have significantly reframed these collections, examining the expertise and imagination of printers alongside collections' poetic content, and cautioning against the anachronistic term "miscellany." Megan Heffernan, *Making the Miscellany: Poetry, Print, and the History of the Book in Early Modern England* (Philadelphia: University of Pennsylvania Press, 2021); Michelle O'Callaghan, *Crafting Poetry Anthologies in Renaissance England* (Cambridge: Cambridge University Press, 2020).

38. On the place in the book trade of these collections (which have generally received greater scholarly attention because of their inclusion of Shakespeare), see Alexandra Halasz, "The Stationers' Shakespeare," in *Shakespeare's Stationers*, ed. Marta Straznicky (Philadelphia: University of Pennsylvania Press, 2013), 17–27; and Roger Chartier and Peter Stallybrass, "Reading and Authorship: The Circulation of Shakespeare, 1590–1619," in *A Concise Companion to Shakespeare and the Text*, ed. Andrew Murphy (Oxford: Blackwell, 2007), 35–56.

39. Farmer and Lesser, "What Is Print Popularity?," 41–50. These are the middle two of four total categories they employ: least reprinted are "topical" publications, like almanacs, and at the other end are those categories subject to monopolies, coveted sources of guaranteed income for those publishers who held royally granted patents in particular classes of books.

40. This figure understates the difference insofar as some of the titles included in the second wave were first published during Henry VIII's reign. Though we can be sure that some editions have not survived, it's clear that many of these titles never reached a second edition, while those that did were more likely to be devotional books or ongoing reprints of earlier titles (like Udall's *Terence*). On survival rates, see Alan B. Farmer, "Playbooks and the Question of Ephemerality" in *The Book in History, The Book as History: New Intersections of the Material Text: Essays in Honour of David Scott Kastan*, ed. Heidi Brayman et al (New Haven, CT: Yale, 2016), 87–125.

41. Taverner composed the *Garden of Wisdom* mainly of selections from Erasmus's *Apophthegmata* and was also responsible for an edition of the *Adagia* first published in 1539. On liberties taken by Taverner as a translator and compiler of Erasmus, see DeWitt T. Starnes, ed., *Proverbes or Adagies, gathered out of the Chiliades of Erasmus by Richard Taverner. With New Additions, as Well of Latin Proverbs, as of English (1569)* (Delmar, NY: Scholars Facsimiles, 1977). Erasmus's collections of small textual forms were popular in England throughout the sixteenth century. See Erika Rummel's survey of copies of Erasmus's *Adages* in England, through their appearances in dictionaries and in personal and college libraries. Erika Rummel, "The Reception of Erasmus' *Adages* in Sixteenth-Century England," *Renaissance and Reformation* 18.2 (1994): 19–30. On the Renaissance fascination with proverbs, see Mary Thomas Crane, *Framing Authority: Sayings, Self, and Society in Sixteenth-Century England*

(Princeton, NJ: Princeton University Press, 1993); Margaret Mann Phillips, *The "Adages" of Erasmus: A Study with Translations* (Cambridge: Cambridge University Press, 1964).

42. On commonplacing, see the instructions by Richard Holdsworth, "Directions for a Student in the Universitie," in *The Intellectual Development of John Milton*, vol. 2, ed. Harris Francis Fletcher (Urbana: University of Illinois Press, 1961), 623–655; Ann Moss, *Printed Commonplace-Books and the Structuring of Renaissance Thought* (Oxford: Clarendon Press, 1996); Peter Mack, *Renaissance Argument: Valla and Agricola in the Traditions of Rhetoric and Dialectic* (Leiden: E. J. Brill, 1993), 117–167; Peter Mack, *Elizabethan Rhetoric: Theory and Practice* (Cambridge: Cambridge University Press, 2002), 43–45; and Adam Smyth, "Commonplace Book Culture: A List of Sixteen Traits," in *Women and Writing, c. 1340–c. 1650*, ed. Anne Lawrence Mathers and Phillipa Hardman (Rochester, NY: Boydell and Brewer, 2010), 90–110. Angus Vine draws important distinctions between commonplace books and miscellanies in *Miscellaneous Order: Manuscript Culture and the Early Modern Organization of Knowledge* (Oxford: Oxford University Press, 2020), 30–62.

43. The metaphor derived from a classical analogy, originating in Seneca's Epistle 84, that likened reading to the activity of a bee as it visits a field of flowers; it was reinforced by the etymologies of anthologies and florilegia. For a thorough treatment of this metaphor, see G. W. Pigman III, "Versions of Imitation in the Renaissance," *Renaissance Quarterly* 33 (1980): 1–32.

44. Many of these continental imprints were well represented in English personal and college libraries of the sixteenth and seventeenth centuries. Another important example, relatively common among English readers and in English libraries, is Stobaeus's *Anthologion*, or *Florilegium*, especially in the edition prepared by Konrad Gesner (Basel, 1549) and later editions based on it.

45. R. H. Rouse and M. A. Rouse, "*Ordinatio* and *Compilatio* Revisited," in *Ad Litteram: Authoritative Texts and Their Medieval Readers*, ed. Mark D. Jordan and Kent Emery Jr. (Notre Dame, IN: University of Notre Dame Press, 1992), 113–134; M. B. Parkes, "The Influence of the Concepts of Ordinatio and Compilatio on the Development of the Book," in *Medieval Learning and Literature: Essays Presented to Richard William Hunt*, ed. J. J. G. Alexander and M. T. Gibson (Oxford: Clarendon Press, 1976), 115–141; Mary A. Rouse and Richard H. Rouse, "*Statim invenire*: Schools, Preachers, and New Attitudes to the Page," in *Authentic Witnesses: Approaches to Medieval Texts and Manuscripts* (Notre Dame, IN: University of Notre Dame Press, 1991), 191–220; Jeffrey Todd Knight, "Organizing Manuscript and Print: From *Compilatio* to Compilation," in *The Medieval Manuscript Book: Cultural Approaches*, ed. Michael Johnston and Michael Van Dussen (Cambridge: Cambridge University Press, 2015), 77–95. On compilations and models of textual mixture, see Arthur Bahr, *Fragments and Assemblages: Forming Compilations of Medieval London* (Chicago: University of Chicago Press, 2013).

46. Ann Blair, *Too Much to Know: Managing Scholarly Information Before the Modern Age* (New Haven, CT: Yale University Press, 2010); and Blair's essay, "Le florilège latin comme point de comparaison," *Extrême-Orient Extrême-Occident* (2007): 185–204. See also Moss, *Printed Commonplace-Books*, 24–40, for her account of the prehistory of these Renaissance systems of thought including the many florilegia generated for preaching in medieval Europe.

47. *Ortulus anime the garden of the soule* is the earliest primer (vernacular prayer book) printed in English, first printed in Antwerp in 1529 (the first surviving edition is of 1530), where author George Joye had fled after his arrest in 1527. On *Ortulus anime* and the legacy of primers, see Charles C. Butterworth, *The English Primers, 1529–1545* (Philadelphia: University of Pennsylvania Press, 1953); and Susan M. Felch, "The Backward Gaze: Editing Elizabeth

Tyrwhit's Prayerbook," in *Editing Early Modern Women*, ed. Sarah C. E. Ross and Paul Salzman (Cambridge: Cambridge University Press, 2016), 21–39.

48. Udall's *Floures for Latine spekyng selected and gathered oute of Terence* builds on and expands the model of Cornelius Grapheus's *Ex Terentii comoediis colloquendi formulae selectae flosculi* (Antwerp: Johannes Grapheus, 1529), which was widely reprinted across Europe. Udall, who was an advocate of Erasmian pedagogy while headmaster at Eton from 1534 to 1541, followed up on the *Floures* with his own pedagogically oriented edition of Erasmus's *Apophthegmata*. See Ágnes Juhász-Ormsby, "Nicholas Udall's *Floures for Latine Spekynge*: An Erasmian Textbook," *Humanistica Lovaniensia* 52 (2003): 137–158; and Ágnes Juhász-Ormsby, "Erasmus' *Apophthegmata* in Henrician England," *Erasmus Studies* 37.1 (2017): 45–67.

49. Udall's *Floures* were first published by Thomas Berthelet, and the title was taken on by Thomas Marshe in the latter half of the century. Misha Teramura identifies two editions published by Marshe uncounted in the STC in "The Terence Editions of Thomas Marshe," *Papers of the Bibliographical Society of America* 113 (2019): 69–82.

50. William Webbe, *A discourse of English poetrie* (London: John Charlewood for Robert Walley, 1586), sig. A4^r.

51. John Bishop, *Beautiful blossomes, gathered by John Byshop, from the best trees of all kyndes* (London: [by Henry Middleton] for Henry Cockyn, 1577), sig. ¶.ii^v. On the changing significance of alliteration, see the epilogue to Ian Cornelius, *Reconstructing Alliterative Verse: The Pursuit of a Medieval Meter* (Cambridge: Cambridge University Press, 2017), 147–154.

52. Jason Scott-Warren, *Shakespeare's First Reader* (Philadelphia: University of Pennsylvania Press, 2019), 70. See also Jeffrey Todd Knight, "'Furnished' for Action: Renaissance Books as Furniture," *Book History* 12.1 (2009): 37–73. Leah Knight observes that the titles of plant books offer them a ready-made invitation into domestic life (*Of Books and Botany*, 113–115). See also Vine, *Miscellaneous Order*, 208–223, on the management of information and household management.

53. John Grange, *The golden Aphroditis a pleasant discourse* (London: Henry Bynneman, 1577).

54. In either case, Grange scoured Maplet's collection for moral, literary, and natural historical matter. Hyder E. Rollins also notes references to Chaucer, Skelton, Erasmus, and Becon's *Castel of Comforte*, as well as direct borrowings from *Songes and Sonettes*, Howell's *Arbor*, Gascoigne's *Hundreth Sundrie Flowres*, *A Handful of Pleasant Delights*, and *A Paradise of Dainty Devices*. Phrases in the dedication echo *A smale handfull of fragrant flowers* (1575, attributed by printer Richard Jones to N.B.), but there is no direct evidence that Grange took inspiration from its content. Hyder E. Rollins, "John Grange's *The Golden Aphroditis*," *Harvard Studies and Notes in Philology and Literature* 16 (1934): 177–198. Rollins counts Grange as a significant stylistic precursor to John Lyly's euphuism.

55. Grange, *Golden Aphroditis*, sig. L.iii^v.

56. Scott-Warren, *Shakespeare's First Reader*, 113.

57. Heffernan and O'Callaghan place the work of compiling that generated poetic collections in the context of printers' contributions, an imaginative labor that Heffernan discusses in terms of the material poetics of "stationers' figures" (*Making the Miscellany*, 54–88) and that O'Callaghan calls the "formal work of conjoining" (*Crafting Poetry Anthologies*, 38). For an extended discussion of Jones's strategies, see Kirk Melnikoff, "Jones's Pen and Marlowe's Socks: Richard Jones, Print Culture, and the Beginnings of English Dramatic Literature," *Studies in Philology* 102 (2005): 184–209; and "Richard Jones (fl. 1564–1613): Elizabethan

Printer, Bookseller and Publisher," *Analytical & Enumerative Bibliography* 12 (2001): 153–184. On Jones's editorial and business practices in the context of his collaborations with Isabella Whitney (further discussed in Chapter 4), see O'Callaghan, *Crafting Poetry Anthologies*, 73–113. This work and my own build on the model for understanding stationers as active readers and interpreters proposed by Zachary Lesser in *Renaissance Drama and the Politics of Publication* (Cambridge: Cambridge University Press, 2004).

58. Gérard Genette, *Paratexts: Thresholds of Interpretation*, trans. Jane E. Lewin (Cambridge: Cambridge University Press, 1997). I find useful Genette's articulation of paratext as those elements making a book offerable and presentable to a reader and consumer: "They surround and extend it, precisely in order to *present* it, in the usual sense of this verb but also in the strongest sense: to *make present*, to ensure the text's presence in the world, its 'reception' and consumption in the form (nowadays, at least) of a book" (1). His emphasis on the role of the author in the working of paratext is not helpful in the context of early modern printed books. For a range of responses to Genette's concept and a reinterpretation in the context of early modern book elements, see Helen Smith and Louise Wilson, eds., *Renaissance Paratexts* (Cambridge: Cambridge University Press, 2011); Smith and Wilson offer a useful reassessment of the concept in their Introduction (1–14). On the bibliography of title pages (as an innovation of printed books), see R. B. McKerrow and F. S. Ferguson, *Title-Page Borders used in England and Scotland, 1485–1640* (London: Printed for the Bibliographical Society at the Oxford University Press, 1932); and Margery Corbett and Ronald Lightbown, *The Comely Frontispiece: The Emblematic Title-Page in England 1550–1660* (London: Routledge & Kegan Paul, 1979). Useful interpretations of title page design in early modern print include William Sherman, "On the Threshold: Architecture, Paratext, and Early Print Culture," in *Agent of Change: Print Cultures After Elizabeth L. Eistenstein*, ed. Sabrina Alcorn Baron, Eric N. Lindquist, and Eleanor F Shevlin (Amherst: University of Massachusetts Press, 2007), 67–81; Helen Smith, "'Imprinted by Simeon such a signe': reading early modern imprints," in *Renaissance Paratexts*, 17–33; Lucy Razzall, "'Like to a title leafe': Surface, Face, and Material Text in Early Modern England," *Journal of the Northern Renaissance* 8 (2017): n.p.

59. Here, I adapt Jessica Pressman's definition of bookishness as a quality of contemporary literature, using it to name "an aesthetic practice and cultural phenomenon that figures the book as artifact rather than as just a medium for information transmission." "Jonathan Safran Foer's *Tree of Codes*: Memorial, Fetish, Bookishness," *ASAP/Journal* 3.1 (2018): 97–120, at 97.

60. Piper argues that an attention to its status as a local, finite object is "essential for understanding the medium of the book." Andrew Piper, *Book was There: Reading in Electronic Times* (Chicago: University of Chicago Press, 2012), ix. A plant book, while never singular, is always present in "book-copies," in Joseph Dane's useful formulation, rather than as an "abstract book"; similarly, it resists what David Scott Kastan helpfully calls a "platonic" approach to the book, as distinct from a pragmatic. See Joseph Dane, *What is a Book?* (Notre Dame, IN: Notre Dame University Press, 2012); and David Scott Kastan, *Shakespeare and the Book* (Cambridge: Cambridge University Press, 2001), 117–19. Early modern understandings of books' materiality and immateriality have been explored by James Kearney, *The Incarnate Text: Imagining the Book in Reformation England* (Philadelphia: University of Pennsylvania Press, 2009); Sarah Wall-Randell, *The Immaterial Book: Reading and Romance in Renaissance England* (Ann Arbor, MI: University of Michigan Press, 2013); Daniel Selcer, *Philosophy and the Book: Early Modern Figures of Material Inscription* (London: Continuum, 2010); Lindsay

Ann Reid, *Ovidian Bibliofictions and the Tudor Book* (Burlington, VT: Ashgate, 2014); and Charlotte Scott, *Shakespeare and the Idea of the Book* (Oxford: Oxford University Press, 2007).

61. Subject to open-ended circulation, plant books take on some of the "infinite transmissibility" that Juliet Fleming has argued was resisted by the posy in the period, though they still fail to achieve the "immaterial, abstracted status" that eventually accompanies that version of transmissibility (Fleming, *Graffiti*, 20). Compare the indelible account of similar dynamics in a later period of "technological reproducibility" in Walter Benjamin, "The Work of Art in the Age of Its Technological Reproducibility: Second Version," in *The Work of Art in the Age of Its Technological Reproducibility, and Other Writings on Media* (Cambridge: Harvard University Press, 2008), 19–55.

62. Roger Chartier and Peter Stallybrass, "What Is a Book?," in *The Cambridge Companion to Textual Scholarship*, ed. Neil Fraistat and Julia Flanders (Cambridge: Cambridge University Press, 2013), 188–204. As they argue, the idea of authorship is inseparable from the form of the gathered codex: an author is "someone who is bound with him or her self" (195).

63. Thomas Elyot, *The Dictionary of syr Thomas Eliot knyght* (London: Thomas Berthelet, 1538), sig. H.iii^r, s.v. "fasciculus."

64. John Palsgrave, trans., *The Comedye of Acolastus translated into oure englysshe tongue* (London: Thomas Berthelet, 1540), sig. b.i^v.

65. My approach accords with the call by Allison Deutermann and András Kiséry to join material and formal analysis of early modern books. See their introduction, in *Formal Matters: Reading the Materials of English Renaissance Literature*, ed. Allison K. Deutermann and András Kiséry (Manchester: Manchester University Press, 2013), 1–14; and András Kiséry, with Allison Deutermann, "The Matter of Form: Book History, Formalist Criticism, and Francis Bacon's Aphorisms," in *The Book in History, the Book as History: New Intersections of the Material Text; Essays in Honor of David Scott Kastan*, ed. Heidi Brayman, Jesse M. Lander, and Zachary Lesser (New Haven, CT: Yale University Press, 2016), 29–64. In the context of poetry, these issues are generatively framed in Ben Burton and Elizabeth Scott-Bauman, eds., *The Work of Form: Poetics and Materiality in Early Modern Culture* (Oxford: Oxford University Press, 2014).

66. Jeffrey Todd Knight, *Bound to Read: Compilations, Collections, and the Making of Renaissance Literature* (Philadelphia: University of Pennsylvania Press, 2013), 3. A growing body of early modern book history emphasizes what was piecemeal and provisional about early modern texts: useful accounts of this view are found in Helen Smith, "The Book," in *A Handbook of English Renaissance Literary Studies*, ed. John Lee (Oxford: Wiley & Sons, 2017), 396–410; Adam Smyth, "Poetry and the Material Text," in *A Companion to Renaissance Poetry*, ed. Catherine Bates (Oxford: Wiley & Sons, 2018), 545–556; and Juliet Fleming, William Sherman, and Adam Smyth, eds., "The Renaissance Collage: Toward a New History of Reading," special issue, *Journal of Medieval and Early Modern Studies* 45.3 (2015). See also Heffernan, *Making the Miscellany*; Alexandra Gillespie, "Poets, Printers, and Early English *Sammelbände*," *Huntington Library Quarterly (HLQ)* 67.2 (2004): 189–214; and Alexandra Gillespie, "Caxton's Chaucer and Lydgate Quartos: Miscellanies from Manuscript to Print," *Transactions of the Cambridge Bibliographical Society* 12.1 (2000): 1–25.

67. For an instructive view of a range of these practices, see the essays in Fleming, Sherman, and Smyth, "Renaissance Collage," as well as Whitney Trettien, *Cut/Copy/Paste: Fragments from the History of Bookwork* (Minneapolis, MN: University of Minnesota Press, 2021).

68. On styles of marking books, see William Sherman, *Used Books: Marking Readers in Renaissance England* (Philadelphia: University of Pennsylvania Press, 2008); Lisa Jardine and Anthony Grafton, "'Studied for Action': How Gabriel Harvey Read His Livy," *Past & Present* 129 (1990): 30–78. Princeton's Archaeology of Reading project has made available a wide range of Renaissance annotated books, including Gabriel Harvey's well-annotated copy of the same 1580 edition of Tusser's *Pointes*. Online at https://archaeologyofreading.org. On Jonson's marginal flowers, see Sherman, *Used Books*, 45; and Heather James, "Ben Jonson's Light Reading," in *A Handbook to the Reception of Ovid*, ed. John. F. Miller and Carole E. Newlands (New York: Wiley Blackwell, 2014), 246–61, at 251–252.

69. See also G. K. Hunter on "gnomic pointing" in printed books in "The Marking of *Sententiae* in Elizabethan Printed Plays, Poems, and Romances," *The Library*, 5th ser., 6.3–4 (1951): 171–188; on the manicule, see Sherman, *Used Books*, 25–52. In relation to rhetorical teaching, see Walter Ong, "Tudor Writings on Rhetoric," *Studies in the Renaissance* 15 (1968): 39–69, at 55. For a rich reading of these marks in the context of playbooks, see Claire Bourne, *Typographies of Performance in Early Modern England* (Oxford: Oxford University Press, 2020), 32–76.

70. Thomas Crewe, trans., *The Nosegay of morall Philosophie, lately dispersed amongst many Italian authours, and now newely and succinctly drawne together into Questions and Answers* (London: Thomas Dawson, 1580). On Meurier and the "demand for popular works of gnomic wisdom," see Hugh Roberts, *Dogs' Tales: Representations of Ancient Cynicism in French Renaissance Texts* (Leiden: Brill, 2006), quote at 84; and Claudie Balavoine, "Bouquets de fleurs et colliers de perles: Sur les recueils de formes brèves au XVIe siècle," in *Les formes brèves de la prose et le discours discontinu (XVIe–XVIIe siècles)*, ed. Jean Lafond (Paris: Vrin, 1984), 51–71. Moss groups Meurier's collection with the great number of "vernacular collections of sayings, proverbs, and similitudes, which do not replicate the commonplace-book's arrangement of its material under heads and suggest a much looser pattern of perusal and use" (*Printed Commonplace-Books*, 207 n. 23). See also Crane, *Framing Authority*; and Natalie Zemon Davis, "Proverbial Wisdom and Popular Errors," in *Society and Culture in Early Modern France* (Stanford, CA: Stanford University Press, 1975), 227–70.

71. While this is the most extreme example, other moments in the text also gather multiple brief answers to questions (for example, at Crewe, *Nosegay*, E7^r).

72. Brian Cummings describes this dynamic: "In Erasmus, in particular, copiousness is always a tension as much as it is an ideal, in which *brevitas* fights with *varietas*." Brian Cummings, "Encyclopaedic Erasmus," *Renaissance Studies* 28.2 (2014): 183–204, at 185.

73. Terence Cave, *The Cornucopian Text* (Oxford: Clarendon Press, 1979). See also the practices of textual amassing discussed in Richard Halpern, *The Poetics of Primitive Accumulation* (Ithaca, NY: Cornell University Press, 1991).

74. *The .xv. Bookes of P. Ovidius Naso, entytuled Metamorphosis*, trans. Arthur Golding (London: William Seres, 1567), sig. b.iiii^r.

75. On the quantity of botanical knowledge that Renaissance naturalists faced, see Brian W. Ogilvie, "The Many Books of Nature: Renaissance Naturalists and Information Overload," *Journal of the History of Ideas* 64.1 (2003): 29–40.

76. Leah Knight, *Of Books and Botany*, chap. 1.

77. The investments of English Renaissance rhetoric and poetics in the far-fetched and imported are richly explored in Catherine Nicholson, *Uncommon Tongues: Eloquence and Eccentricity in the English Renaissance* (Philadelphia: University of Pennsylvania Press,

2014); Jenny Mann, *Outlaw Rhetoric: Figuring Vernacular Eloquence in Shakespeare's England* (Ithaca, NY: Cornell University Press, 2012); and Miriam Jacobson, *Barbarous Antiquity: Reorienting the Past in the Poetry of Early Modern England* (Philadelphia: University of Pennsylvania Press, 2014).

78. William Harrison, *The Description of England*, ed. Georges Edelen (Washington, DC: Folger Shakespeare Library; and New York: Dover, 1994), 262. On the significance of denizening crops in this period, see Dolan, *Digging the Past*, 55–9.

79. As Londa Schiebinger and Claudia Swan note in their introduction to *Colonial Botany*, botany was both "big science" and "big business" in the early modern world (1–16).

80. Nicolás Monardes, *Joyfull newes out of the newe founde worlde, wherein is declared the rare and singuler vertues of diverse and sundrie Hearbes, Trees, Oyles, Plantes, and Stones, with their aplications, aswell for Phisicke as Chirurgerie*, trans. John Frampton (London: William Norton, 1577.) Daniela Bleichmar describes Monardes's *Historia medicinal* as "the book that did the most to publicize New World *materia medica* in the late sixteenth and early seventeenth centuries." Daniela Bleichmar, "Books, Bodies, and Fields: Sixteenth-Century Transatlantic Encounters with New World *Materia Medica*," in Schiebinger and Swan, *Colonial Botany*, 83–84.

81. On the imagination of readerly diversity, see Heidi Brayman, "'The Great Variety of Readers' and Early Modern Reading Practices," in *A Companion to Shakespeare*, ed. David Scott Kastan (Oxford: Blackwell, 1999), 139–57; and John Kerrigan, "The Editor as Reader: Constructing Renaissance Texts," in *The Practice and Representation of Reading in England*, ed. James Raven, Helen Small, and Naomi Tadmor (Cambridge: Cambridge University Press, 1996), 102–124. These developments are not entailed by print itself as a technology. Alexandra Gillespie makes the essential point that a number of these phenomena in fact emerged in the context of the large-scale production and sale of manuscripts in the later Middle Ages. Alexandra Gillespie, *Print Culture and the Medieval Author: Chaucer, Lydgate, and Their Books, 1473–1557* (Oxford: Oxford University Press, 2007), 13–16.

82. These conditions of uncertainty and a loss of control are hardly unique to the sixteenth century and are a condition of inscription in general. The situation of the print marketplace does activate these circumstances and attendant anxieties in new and compelling forms, however, as Wendy Wall (on the voyeuristic text in *The Imprint of Gender: Authorship and Publication in the English Renaissance* [Ithaca, NY: Cornell University Press, 1993], 169–226) and Alexandra Halasz (writing on the commodity form of the pamphlet in *The Marketplace of Print: Pamphlets and the Public Sphere in Early Modern England* [Cambridge: Cambridge University Press, 1997]) have both shown. Halasz argues that a "phobic conception of widely circulated discourses" leads authors of pamphlets to compulsively "imagine unknown and unknowable readers" (*Marketplace of Print*, 12–13).

83. Robert Matz has shown how this duality received from Horace significantly framed Renaissance poetic debates. See his *Defending Literature in Early Modern England: Renaissance Literary Theory in Social Context* (Cambridge: Cambridge University Press, 2004), 1–24.

84. Ben Jonson, trans., *Horace, His Art of Poetrie*, in *Ben Jonson*, ed. C. H. Herford and Percy Simpson, and Evelyn Simpson, vol. 8, *The Poems; the Prose Works* (Oxford: Clarendon Press, 1947), 327. In Latin, "Omne tulit punctum qui miscuit utile dulci."

85. This gustatory framework is articulated in J. C. Scaliger's *Poetics* (1560), which divides epigrams into classes of bitter, sour, salty, or sweet. See Rosalie Colie, *The Resources of Kind: Genre-Theory in the Renaissance* (Berkeley: University of California Press, 1973), 68. For an

excellent gathering of recent work on gustatory metaphors in early modern books, see Jason Scott-Warren and Andrew Zurcher, eds., *Text, Food, and the Early Modern Reader* (New York: Routledge, 2019).

86. *Songes and Sonettes* (London: Richard Tottel, 1557), "To the reder."

87. See especially Sherman, *Used Books*; and Bradin Cormack and Carla Mazzio, *Book Use, Book Theory* (Chicago: University of Chicago Press, 2005). Jennifer Richards offers a measured defense of what might be distinct about *reading* in "Useful Books: Reading Vernacular Regimens in Sixteenth-Century England," *Journal of the History of Ideas* 73.2 (2012): 247–271. Calhoun makes an analogous observation about the importance of *use* for an ecology of books in the introduction of *The Nature of the Page*, 12.

88. On scholarly use, see Grafton and Jardine, "'Studied for Action'"; Crane, *Framing Authority*. In a brilliant reading of Spenser's catalogs of flowers, Heather James shows how these moments resist humanist instructions for taking profit from rhetorical flowers (Heather James, *Ovid and the Liberty of Speech in Shakespeare's England* [Oxford: Oxford University Press, 2021], 37–51).

89. On the place of profit and pleasure in debates about poetry, see Matz, *Defending Literature*; and, on Sidney's reworking of these categories, Catherine Bates, *On Not Defending Poetry: On Defence and Indefensibility in Sidney's Defence of Poesy* (Oxford: Oxford University Press, 2017). Russell Fraser surveys the positions of the "anti" camp in *The War Against Poetry* (Princeton, NJ: Princeton University Press, 1970). For a suggestive account of the dynamics of uselessness, opposing the teleologies they suggest, see Corey McEleney, *Futile Pleasures: Early Modern Literature and the Limits of Utility* (New York: Fordham University Press, 2017).

90. This example is discussed in Chapter 2. Gosson's "use" is closer to the sense of custom, or the Latin *usus,* while Gascoigne's image of handling renders the weeds more directly subject to the reader's manipulation. As Catherine Bates shows, though, the idea of "use" in Gosson's argument names a "business model" that draws profit from the poetic transaction (Bates, *On Not Defending Poetry,* 4). See Stephen Gosson, *The Schoole of Abuse* (London: Thomas Woodcock, 1579), sig. A7ᵛ; and George Gascoigne, *The Posies of George Gascoigne Esquire* (London: by Henry Bynneman for Richard Smith, 1575), sig. ¶¶.ivʳ.

91. Richard Helgerson, *The Elizabethan Prodigals* (Berkeley: University of California Press, 1976); Patricia Akhimie, *Shakespeare and the Cultivation of Difference* (New York: Routledge, 2018). The avowed "greenness" of these young poets is illuminated by account of the color's wide-reaching meanings in early modern culture in Bruce Smith, *The Key of Green: Passion and Perception in Renaissance Culture* (Chicago: University of Chicago Press, 2009).

92. Nicholas Breton, *The workes of a young wyt* (London: Thomas Dawson, 1577), sig. H.ivᵛ; John Lyly, *Euphues and his England* (London: Gabriel Cawood, 1580), sig. ¶3ᵛ. Breton is dicussed in the suggestive discussion of page-turning in Craig Farrell, "The Poetics of Page-Turning: The Interactive Surfaces of Early Modern Printed Poetry," *Journal of the Northern Renaissance* 8 (2017), n.p.

93. Edmund Spenser, *Complaints* (London: William Ponsonby, 1591), sig. V2ᵛ. See the reading of this passage in Heather James, *Ovid and the Liberty of Speech*, 37–51.

94. Michel Foucault, "What is an Author?", in *The Essential Foucault*, ed. Paul Rabinow and Nikolas Rose (New York: The New Press, 1994), 377–391, at 390. With their invitations to free circulation, plant books anticipate some of the poststructuralist accounts of writing that Foucault subjects to critique; as he writes, it would be "pure romanticism" to imagine fiction

operating freely "without passing through something like a necessary or constraining figure" (159). As Meredith McGill argues, however, that constraint might be something other than the author (Meredith McGill, *American Literature and the Culture of Reprinting, 1834–1853* [Philadelphia: University of Pennsylvania Press, 2003], 17–19.)

95. Roger Chartier, *The Order of Books* (Stanford, CA: Stanford University Press, 1994), viii. If modern readers are, in Michel de Certeau's memorable formulation, "poachers," then the compulsive attention paid by these botanical titles to enclosure and its breach engages a problem at the core of any attempt to narrate textual consumption. Michel de Certeau, *The Practice of Everyday Life* (Berkeley: University of California Press, 1984), 174.

96. C. S. Lewis, *English Literature in the Sixteenth Century, Excluding Drama* (Oxford: Oxford University Press, 1944), 262. A pioneering counterargument is found in Yvor Winters, "The 16th Century Lyric in England: A Critical and Historical Reinterpretation: Part I," *Poetry* 53.5 (1939): 258–272. There has been exciting recent work on the period; see, for example the essays collected in Mike Pincombe and Cathy Shrank, eds., *The Oxford Handbook of Tudor Literature, 1485–1603* (Oxford: Oxford University Press, 2009), esp. Part 3.

97. On these models of impression, see Margreta de Grazia, "Imprints: Shakespeare, Gutenberg, Descartes," in *Printing and Parenting in Early Modern England*, ed. Douglas A. Brooks (Burlington, VT: Ashgate, 2003), 29–58. As Stephen Guy-Bray argues, long-standing associations of textual composition with heterosexual reproduction have inscribed poetry within those normative and future-oriented structures. Stephen Guy-Bray, *Against Reproduction: Where Renaissance Texts Come From* (Toronto: University of Toronto Press, 2009). And, as Vin Nardizzi shows in an analysis of grafting in Shakespeare's Sonnet 15, the queering of reproduction finds an energetic ally in the procedures of vegetable propagation ("Shakespeare's Penknife," 83–106). On poetic reproduction specifically, see Matthew Zarnowiecki, *Fair Copies: Reproducing the English Lyric from Tottel to Shakespeare* (Toronto: University of Toronto Press, 2014). The most comprehensive treatment of metaphors for the body of the "divulgated" text is Heidi Brayman *Reading Material in Early Modern England: Print, Gender, and Literacy* (Cambridge: Cambridge University Press, 2005), 69–125.

98. Vegetable and reproductive models of propagation also represent the key point in Thomas Greene's challenge to Terence Cave's articulation of Renaissance copiousness in light of deconstructive versions of textual dissemination. In resisting this approach, Greene asserts the persistence of some connection to textual origins, via the model of Otto Rank's understanding of birth trauma. See Thomas Greene, *The Vulnerable Text* (New York: Columbia University Press, 1986), 1–17; and Cave, *The Cornucopian Text.*

99. John Milton, *Complete Prose Works of John Milton*, ed. Don M. Wolfe et al., vol. 2. (New Haven, CT: Yale University Press, 1959), 492. As Mark Rose notes, Milton's following image of a good book as "the pretious life-blood of a master spirit, imbalm'd and treasur'd up on purpose to a life beyond life" (*Complete Prose Works*, 2:493) links bibliography and biology and may echo William Harvey's contemporary argument for the circulation of blood. See Mark Rose, "The Public Sphere and the Emergence of Copyright: The Stationers' Company, *Areopagitica*, and the Statute of Anne," in *Privilege and Property: Essays on the History of Copyright*, ed. Ronan Deazley, Martin Kretschmer, and Lionel Bently (Cambridge: Open Book Publishers, 2010), 75–76. On the domestic ordinariness of Milton's image of the vial, see Katie Kadue, *Domestic Georgic: Labors of Preservation from Rabelais to Milton* (Chicago: University of Chicago Press, 2021), 127–135.

Chapter 1

1. H.C., *The Forrest of Fancy: wherein is Conteined very prety Apothegmes, and pleasaunt histories, both in meeter and prose, Songes, Sonets, Epigrams and Epistles, of diverse matter and in diverse manner* (London: Thomas Purfoote, 1579). Though the volume is sometimes attributed to Henry Constable or to Henry Chettle, the attribution is not certain.

2. Ibid, sigs. A.ii^r-A.iii^r.

3. On this association, see E. R. Curtius, *European Literature and the Latin Middle Ages* (Princeton, NJ: Princeton University Press, 1953), 313–314.

4. Thomas Hill, *The Gardeners Labyrinth: Containing a discourse of the Gardeners life* (London: Henry Bynneman, 1577).

5. The earliest surviving edition was published by John Day for Thomas Hill as *A most briefe and pleasaunte treatise, teachyng howe to dresse, sowe, and set a garden* ([London, 1558?]). Hill's handbook would be issued more than a half dozen times, eventually under the title, *The proffitable Arte of Gardening, now the third tyme set fourth: to whiche is added muche necessary matter, and a number of Secrettes with the Phisick helpes belonging to eche herbe* (London: Thomas Marsh, 1568).

6. Juliet Fleming, "How to Look at a Printed Flower," *Word and Image* 22.2 (2006): 165–166. Fleming builds on Francis Meynell and Stanley Morison, "Printers' Flowers and Arabesques," *The Fleuron* 1 (1923): 1–43. See also Juliet Fleming, "How Not to Look at a Printed Flower," *Journal of Medieval and Early Modern Studies* 38.2 (2008): 345–371; and Juliet Fleming, "Changed Opinion as to Flowers," in *Renaissance Paratexts*, ed. Helen Smith and Louise Wilson (Cambridge: Cambridge University Press, 2011), 48–64. On the use of ornament by particular printers, see Hendrik D. L. Vervliet, *Granjon's Flowers: An Enquiry into Granjon's, Giolito's, & De Tournes' Ornaments; 1542–86* (New Castle, DE: Oak Knoll Press, 2016); Peter W. M. Blayney, "The Flowers in *The Muses Garland*," *The Library* 22.3 (2021): 316–343; Katherine Butler, "Printed Borders for Sixteenth-Century Music or Music Paper and the Early Career of Music Printer Thomas East," *The Library* 19.2 (2018): 174–202.

7. See especially Fleming, "How Not to Look at a Printed Flower," 345–371. See also Stanley Morison, "Venice and the Arabesque Ornament," in *Selected Essays of the History of Letter-Forms in Manuscript and Print*, vol. 1, ed. David McKitterick (Cambridge: Cambridge University Press, 1981), 142–160.

8. Frances E. Dolan, *Digging the Past: How and Why to Imagine Seventeenth-Century Agriculture* (Philadelphia: University of Pennsylvania Press, 2020), 148–151.

9. David Jacques, "The *Compartiment* System in Tudor England," *Garden History* 27.1 (Summer 1999): 32–53. On knots, for which evidence for actual practices is much more rare than references, see Jill Francis, *Gardens and Gardening in Early Modern England and Wales, 1560–1660* (New Haven, CT: Yale University Press, 2018), 182–209.

10. Bynneman's first use of modular ornament may have been for a royal commission, the elegantly printed broadsides announcing the first royal lottery (*A very rich Lotterie generall, without any Blanckes* [London: Henry Bynneman, 1567]); some of the flowers that compose the frame were also in use at the same time by Henry Denham, with whom we know that Bynneman sometimes collaborated. Flowers numbered 17, 18, and 30 in Vervliet's inventory appear on the *Lotterie* and were in use by both Bynneman and Denham (*Granjon's Flowers*, 49, 52, 75). Until the archbishop's death in 1575, Bynneman was one of Matthew Parker's favored printers; soon after that he developed a relationship with Christopher Hatton, later Lord Chancellor. Henry Plomer measures Bynneman's success both by the quality of the

books themselves and by the three presses of which he was in possession. See Henry Plomer, "Henry Bynneman, Printer, 1566–83," *The Library*, n.s., 9.35 (July 1908): 225–244; R. B. Mc-Kerrow, *Dictionary of Printers and Booksellers in England, Scotland and Ireland, and of Foreign Printers of English Books, 1557–1640* (London: Printed for the Bibliographical Society, by Blades, East & Blades, 1910), 59–60; Mark Eccles, "Bynneman's Books," *The Library*, 5th ser., 12.2 (June 1957): 81–92.

11. Leonard Digges, *A geometrical Practise, named Pantometria* (London: Henry Bynneman, 1571); and Digges, *An Arithmeticall Militare Treatise, named Stratioticos* (London: Henry Bynneman, 1579). Woodcuts depicting hunting scenes with hounds and figures in courtly dress introduce his editions, printed for Christopher Barker, of George Turberville's and Gascoigne's *The Booke of Faulconrie or Hauking* and George Gascoigne's *The noble arte of venerie* (both 1575). William Bourne's *A regiment for the Sea* ([1574?]), printed by Bynneman for Thomas Hacket, also features a woodcut.

12. Hill, *Gardeners Labyrinth*, sig. B3r.

13. The detail recalls Leviticus 19:10: "Thou shalt not gather the grapes of thy vineyard cleane, nether gather every grape of thy vineyard, but thou shalt leave them for the poore and for the stranger."

14. Katherine O. Acheson, "Military Illustration, Garden Design, and Marvell's 'Upon Appleton House' [with Illustrations]," *English Literary Renaissance* 41.1 (2011): 146–188, at 173.

15. On geometric diagrams, "plats," and "plots" and their relation to practical knowledge, see Henry S. Turner, *The English Renaissance Stage: Geometry, Poetics, and the Practical Spatial Arts, 1580–1630* (Oxford: Oxford University Press, 2006), 43–81.

16. On the influence of Italian gardens, see John Dixon Hunt, *Garden and Grove: The Italian Renaisance Garden in the English Imagination, 1600–1750,* second ed. (Philadelphia: University of Pennsylvania Press, 1996). "Knot" was first used in this sense early in the sixteenth century. See Francis, *Gardens and Gardening*, 89–90; Jacques, "The *Compartiment* System," 41. See also Robin Whalley and Anne Jennings, *Knot Gardens and Parterres: A History of the Knot Garden and How to Make One Today* (London: Barn Elms, 1998); Roy Strong, *The Renaissance Garden in England* (London: Thames and Hudson, 1979), 52–53, 65, on discussions of the knots in *Hypnerotomachia Poliphili* (Venice, 1499) and at Theobalds and Nonsuch; Paula Henderson, *Tudor House and Garden: Architecture and Landscape in the Sixteenth and Early Seventeenth Centuries* (New Haven, CT: Yale University Press, 2006), 76–77, 85, 122–124. David Jacques argues that English enthusiasm for elaborately woven garden knots did not predate the 1580s ("The *Compartiment* System," 32).

17. The prospect onto the knot featured in both poems and portraits, like the miniature portrait of the More family attributed to Rowland Lockey (Victoria and Albert Museum) or that of young Lettice Newdigate; portraits featuring views onto labyrinths include the portrait of a member of the Delves family (British School, 1577; National Museums Liverpool). On labyrinths in portraiture, see Francis, *Gardens and Gardening*, 186–192; Roy Strong, *The Elizabethan Image* (New Haven, CT: Yale University Press, 2019), 93–97. On the More family portrait, see Roy C. Strong, *Artists of the Tudor Court: The Portrait Miniature Rediscovered, 1520–1620* (London: Victoria and Albert Museum, 1983), 159–161. On the "spatial prodigality" of long galleries in stately homes, especially as a provisional site for private conversation, see Lena Cowen Orlin, "Galleries," in *Locating Privacy in Tudor London* (Oxford: Oxford University Press, 2008), 226–261.

18. As Penelope Reed Doob shows in her survey of the form's long history, a labyrinth operates by this double view. Penelope Reed Doob, *The Idea of the Labyrinth* (Ithaca, NY: Cornell University Press, 1990), 1–2. The gardening writer William Lawson was drawn to the experience of disorientation and dependence a maze could perform, placing its visitor in a position that demands a second figure who already knows the plot: "Mazes well framed a mans height, may perhaps make your friend wander in gathering of berries, till he cannot recover himself without your helpe." Lawson, *A new orchard and Garden* (London: Bernard Alsop for Roger Jackson, 1618), 58. Before the seventeenth century, few garden mazes were hedge mazes; they were planted with herbs well shorter than a man or woman's head.

19. See, for example, J. Hillis Miller, *Ariadne's Thread: Story Lines* (New Haven, CT: Yale University Press, 1992). On the labyrinth as a narrative emblem of "lost direction" in Northrop Frye and elsewhere, see Angus Fletcher, "The Image of Lost Direction," in *Centre and Labyrinth: Essays in Honour of Northrop Frye*, ed. Eleanor Cook et al. (Toronto: University of Toronto Press, 1983), 329–346. On the motif in Petrarch, see Teodolinda Barolini, "The Self in the Labyrinth of Time: *Rerum vulgarium fragmenta*," in *Petrarch: A Critical Guide to the Complete Works*, ed. Victoria Kirkham and Armando Maggi (Chicago: University of Chicago Press, 2009), 33–62; Thomas M. Greene, "Labyrinth Dances in the French and English Renaissance," *Renaissance Quarterly* 54.4 (2001): 1415–1419. In the context of dramatic plotting and "the meander," see Claire Bourne, *Typographies of Performance in Early Modern England* (Oxford: Oxford University Press, 2020), 198.

20. On the significance of this etymology, see Doob, *Labyrinth*, 97.

21. Francis, *Gardens and Gardening*, 199–202.

22. William Lawson, for example, writing several decades after Hill, advertised that his stationer had "bestowed much cost and care in having the Knots and Models by the best Artizan cutte in great varietie"; nothing, he and his printer both hoped, "might be anyway wanting to satisfie the curious desire of those, that would make use of this booke." Lawson, *A new orchard and Garden* (1618), sig. A3^{v}.

23. Thomas Hill, *A most briefe and pleasaunt treatyse, teachynge howe to dress, sowe, and set a Garden* ([London]: Thomas Marsh, 1563), sig. C.i^{r}. On knots and the role of pleasure, see Rebecca Bushnell's argument in *Green Desire: Imagining Early Modern Gardens* (Ithaca, NY: Cornell University Press, 2003), 54, 68.

24. Hill, *Proffitable Arte of Gardening* (1568), fol. 10^{v}.

25. Gervase Markham, *The country house-wives garden* (London: Anne Griffin for John Harison, 1637), 79.

26. By the 1568 publication of the *Proffitable Arte of Gardening*, either Hill or his publisher (then, Thomas Marsh) gives this freedom the force of beautification and suggests whichever knot the reader prefers "as a bewtifiyng unto your Garden" (16).

27. Thomas Hill, *The profitable Arte of Gardening, now the thirde time set forth* (London: Henry Bynneman, 1574), sig. T.i^{v}. In a British Library copy of the 1568 edition, a reader has taken advantage of the "spare roume" provided by the knot's verso to add a recipe (BL General Reference Collection 967.b.3).

28. David Jacques describes it as "one, totally impractical, embroidery pattern" ("The *Compartiment* System," 49).

29. Francis, *Gardens and Gardening*, 201.

30. Francis suggests they may have been lifted from the influential designs of Jacques Androuet Du Cerceau (*Gardens and Gardening*, 203). On Du Cerceau, see Laurent Paya, "Ideal

'Parquets' and 'Parquetages' by Jacques Androuet Du Cerceau: Decorative Mannerism and the Art of Gardens in France, in the Sixteenth Century," *Studies in the History of Gardens and Designed Landscapes* 34.4 (2014): 323–338.

31. This example is described in Fleming, "Changed Opinion as to Flowers," 53. The arguments to each chapter in Harington's translation are printed with borders as well, though the allegory is marked with a single woodcut ornament.

32. In this account of Wolsey's lavish expenditure, it is not ultimately a positive *moral* value. Cited in Strong, *The Renaissance Garden in England*, 24.

33. As Mary Learner and Jennifer Munroe show, patterns of knots in books ostensibly for gardeners recur in pattern books for embroidery and for printers. Jennifer Munroe, *Gender and the Garden in Early Modern Literature* (Aldershot: Ashgate, 2008), 99–103; Mary Learner, "Needlework, Sampling, and Science in Early Modern Pattern Books," paper presented at the Huntington Library and Gardens, San Marino, CA, 4 June 2019. The manuscript *Trevelyon Miscellany* links landscape and embroidery knots through practices of print and manuscript copying—these images were, as Heather Wolfe writes, "part of a common vocabulary." Heather Wolfe, ed., *The Trevelyon Miscellany of 1608: An Introduction to Folger MS V.b.232* (Washington, DC: Folger Shakespeare Library, 2007), 7. On this ensemble of practices, see Juliet Fleming, William Sherman, and Adam Smyth, eds., "The Renaissance Collage: Toward a New History of Reading," special issue, *Journal of Medieval and Early Modern Studies* 45.3 (2015).

34. Chapter 2 will describe an analogous role for the lexicon of formal "compactness."

35. Francis Meres, *Palladis tamia, Wits treasury* (London: Peter Short for Cuthbert Burby, 1598), 276.

36. C. Thimelthorpe, *A Short Inventory of certayne Idle Inventions: The Fruites of a close and secret Garden of great ease, and litle pleasure* (London: Thomas Marsh, 1581). Some versions of well-knittedness more forcefully resisted the "several-ness" at the core of Thimelthorpe's description, most memorably perhaps E.K.'s praise of Spenser's "knitting of sentences" in the *Shepheardes Calender*'s epistle to Gabriel Harvey. Edmund Spenser, *The Shepheardes Calender: Conteyning twelve Aeglogues proportionable to the twelve monethes* (London: Hugh Singleton, 1579), ¶.ii^{r-v}.

37. Visitors to European gardens of the sixteenth and seventeenth centuries especially admired their composite forms, curiously arranged in beds, knots, and parterres. Even the Bower of Bliss, with its walls (however penetrable), is a composite form, made of elements that Spenser will serialize and of which he will index the destruction across a full stanza. Discussed further in "How to Read Like a Pig," below.

38. On discontinuous reading and the codex form, see Peter Stallybrass, "Books and Scrolls: Navigating the Bible" in *Books and Readers in Early Modern England*, ed. Jennifer Andersen and Elizabeth Sauer (Pennsylvania: University of Pennsylvania Press, 2000), 42–79.

39. Those printed with separate dedications may have been intended for separate regifting to (potential) patrons; nonetheless, they were continuously printed. Remarkably little has been written on the use of divisional title pages. An exception, focused on a slightly later moment, is Whitney Trettien, "Copy: Edward Benlowes's Queer Books," in *Cut/Copy/Paste: Fragments from the History of Bookwork* (Minneapolis: University of Minnesota Press, 2021).

40. Nicholas Breton's *A Floorish upon Fancie: As gallant a Glose upon so trifling a text, as ever was written* (London: Richard Jones, 1577) includes a separate title page and preface for the "manie pretie Pamphlets" in his "Toyes of an Idle head" (both are absent from the 1582 edition, though the "Toyes" remain). Breton's other publication of the same year, *The workes of a young wyt* (London: Thomas Dawson, 1577), includes no divisional title pages but does advertise the inclusion of supplements: the works, the title advertised, were "trust up with a Fardell of pretie fancies . . . Whereunto is joyned an odd kynde of wooing, with a Banquet of Comfettes." See also John Florio's 1591 *Florios second frutes . . . To which is annexed his Gardine of Recreation yeelding six thousand Italian Proverbs* (a title in many ways a throwback to the previous decade).

41. On joining and on the significance of craft for understanding print practices of compilation, see Michelle O'Callaghan, *Crafting Poetry Anthologies in Renaissance England* (Cambridge: Cambridge University Press, 2020), 98–100.

42. George Whetsone, *The Rocke of Regard, divided into foure parts* (London: [Henry Middleton] for Robert Waley, 1576), sig. ¶.ii^r–iii^r.

43. I am indebted here to Robert Matz, who links this phrase to Spenser's interest in the containment of poetic superfluity in *Defending Literature in Early Modern England: Renaissance Literary Theory in Social Context* (Cambridge: Cambridge University Press, 2000), 106–110.

44. Richard Helgerson, "The New Poet Presents Himself: Spenser and the Idea of a Literary Career," *PMLA* 93.5 (1978): 893–911, esp. 894–895.

45. Louise Wilson, "'Certaine Hours Amongst My Bookes': Recreation, Time, and Text in 1580s London," *Shakespeare Studies* 45 (2017): 60–67. As Wilson notes, for example, Henry Bynneman retitled his 1576 reissue of James Sanford's translation of Lodovico Guicciardini, *Houres of recreation, or Afterdinners: Which may aptly be called The Garden of Pleasure*; the first edition, in 1573, had been published as *The Garden of Pleasure*. While both versions mark off recreation and pleasure as bounded experiences, the new title (more faithfully to the Italian source) defines that boundary by time of day, rather than by the space of the garden. Compare other annexed gardens of recreation, like the gathering of proverbs that John Florio appends to *Florios second frutes*, cited above, to which, according to the title, is "annexed his Gardine of recreation yeelding six thousand Italian proverbs." For Florio's reliance on Sanford and Guicciardini in his *Firste Fruites* (1578), see Frances Yates, *John Florio: The Life of an Italian in Shakespeare's England* (Cambridge: Cambridge University Press, 1934), 37–39. John Bishop's *Beautiful Blossomes* (1577) was reissued with a new title page the following year as *A garden of recreation plentiously furnished with all kindes of delectable flowers* (London: Henry Cockyn, 1578). Cockyn had licensed "bewtifull blossoms gathered by John Bisshop from the best Trees of all kyndes Divine philosophicall. Astronomical. Cosmographicall. historicall and humaine" on 10 December 1576. Edward Arber, ed., *A Transcript of the Registers of the Company of Stationers of London, 1554–1640 A.D.* (London: Privately printed, 1875–1894), 2:306. Callghan shows how poetic anthologies specifically reflected these "early modern cultures of recreation" in *Crafting Poetry Anthologies*.

46. These titles were a greater focus for Denham's business after he acquired William Seres's lucrative patent for printing psalters, primers, and books of private prayer in the 1570s. Arber, *Registers*, 2:771; Patricia Brewerton, "Denham, Henry (fl. 1556–1590)," *ODNB*.

47. On the use of these borders in printed prayer books, see Kate Narveson, *Bible Readers and Lay Writers in Early Modern England: Gender and Self-Definition in an Emergent Writing Culture* (New York: Taylor & Francis, 2012), 159.

48. William Hunnis, *Seven Sobs of a Sorrowfull Soule for Sinne* (London: Henry Denham, 1583). Hunnis succeeded Richard Edwards as master of the Children of the Chapel in 1566. Though the complete volume was entered to Denham in the Stationers' Register in 1581, the "Honisuckles" were first entered separately in 1579, to Thomas Dawson.

49. Though Hunnis's religious publications are not typically classed among poetic miscellanies of the period, their commonalities of rhetoric and material form suggest an important affinity. For an argument for Hunnis's involvement in an edition of *The Paradise of Dainty Devices*, see Steven W. May, "William Hunnis and the 1577 *Paradise of Dainty Devices*," *Studies in Bibliography* 28 (1975): 63–80.

50. Abraham Fleming, *The Diamond of Devotion, Cut and squared into sixe severall points* (London: Henry Denham, 1581). On the *Diamond*, see Amie Lynn Shirkie, "Abraham Fleming's *The Diamond of Deuotion, Cut and squared into sixe seuerall points*: A Documentary Edition" (master's thesis, University of Saskatchewan, 2006). As Shirkie notes, this was the most popular of Fleming's religious writings, and it went through at least five editions between 1581 and 1608 (1–3). The three extant copies of the *Diamond* include each section (though neither the Huntington nor the Folger copy of the 1581 edition is perfect, the missing leaves do not map onto a complete division.)

51. Abraham Fleming had worked extensively in London printing houses in the 1570s, even before his belated graduation from Cambridge in 1582. Patricia Brace, "Abraham Fleming," in *British Rhetoricians and Logicians, 1500–1660*, ed. Edward A. Malone, *Dictionary of Literary Biography* 236 (Detroit: Gale Research, 2001), 126–139; Cyndia Susan Clegg, "Fleming, Abraham (c. 1552–1607)," *ODNB*. In his first attributed venture in print, a translation in rhymed fourteeners of Virgil's *Eclogues* (1575), Fleming incorporates an intricate density of reference systems, including a lettered system of marginal annotations that links to notes at the end of each eclogue. Robert Cummings rightly attributes Fleming's attention to textual organization to the Ramist environment in which he studied at Cambridge. Robert Cummings, "Abraham Fleming's *Eclogues*," *Translation and Literature* 19.2 (2010): 147–169, at 152.

52. For an example of the complex reference systems contributed by Fleming to editions he indexed or translated, see the index to proverbs that Fleming added to the second edition of Baret's *Alvearie* but did not complete. John Baret, *An Alvearie or quadruple dictionarie* (London: Henry Denham, 1580), sig. Nnnn4^r. See also his indexes to Veron's Latin and English dictionary (1582) and to Arthur Golding's translation of Calvin's sermons on Deuteronomy, introduced as "A Table of All and Singular the Doctrines of Master John Calvin delivered in his two hundred sermons upon Deuteronomie, Gathered and laid together orderlie by the letter in the forme of a Concordance, by Abraham Fleming." Arthur Golding, trans., *The sermons of M. John Calvin upon the fifth booke of Moses called Deuteronomie* (London: Henry Middleton for George Bishop, 1583). On Fleming as editor and corrector, see Elizabeth Story Donno, "Abraham Fleming, A Learned Corrector in 1586–87," *Studies in Bibliography* 42 (1989): 200–211.

53. Abraham Fleming, *Diamond of Devotion*, 249–250.

54. John Grange, *The Golden Aphroditis: A pleasant discourse, penned by John Grange Gentleman, Student in the Common Lawe of England* (London: Henry Bynneman, 1577). Folger Shakespeare Library, STC 12174.

55. Gifford, *Gilloflowers*, sigs. *.2^v and I1^r. Entered by John Perrin, 26 October 1580, as "Giffardes *gyllie flowers*" (Arber, *Registers*, 2:380).

56. J. K. Barret, *Untold Futures: Time and Literary Culture in Renaissance England* (Ithaca, NY: Cornell University Press, 2016), 16.

57. On the importance of these texts for early modern agriculture, see Joan Thirsk, "Making a Fresh Start: Sixteenth-Century Agriculture and the Classical Inspiration," in *Culture and Cultivation in Early Modern England: Writing and the Land*, ed. Michael Leslie and Timothy Raynor (Leicester: Leicester University Press, 1992), 15–34; and Andrew McRae, *Godspeed the Plough: The Representation of Agrarian England, 1500–1660* (Cambridge: Cambridge University Press, 2002), 135–168. On the significance of husbandry for English humanism, see Lorna Hutson, *The Usurer's Daughter: Male Friendship and Fictions of Women in Sixteenth-Century England* (London: Routledge, 1994), 17–51; Jennifer Richards, *Rhetoric and Courtliness in Early Modern Literature* (Cambridge: Cambridge University Press, 2003), 92–101; and Daniel Wakelin, *Humanism, Reading, and English Literature, 1430–1530* (Oxford: Oxford University Press, 2007), 43–45.

58. In the *Georgics*, he writes, "lorde what pleasaunt varietie there is, the dyvers graynes, herbes, and flowres, that be there described, that redynge therin, it semeth to a man to be in a delectable gardeyne or paradyse." Thomas Elyot, *The boke named the Governour* (London: Thomas Berthelet, 1537), fols. 29^v-30^r. On husbandry in the classroom, see Andrew Wallace, *Virgil's Schoolboys: The Poetics of Pedagogy in Renaissance England* (Oxford: Oxford University Press, 2011), 123–177; and Daniel Wakelin, *Humanism, Reading, and English Literature*, 200–201.

59. See Victoria Kahn, *Rhetoric, Prudence, and Skepticism in the Renaissance* (Ithaca, NY: Cornell University Press, 1985); on *phronesis*, prudence, and practical knowledge, see Turner, *The English Renaissance Stage*, esp. 43–50.

60. Hill, *Labyrinth* (1577), sig. D2^r.

61. Francis R. Johnson, "Thomas Hill: An Elizabethan Huxley," *Huntington Library Quarterly* 7.4 (1944): 329–351. There is remarkably little scholarship on Hill.

62. On almanacs, see Lauren Kassell, "Almanacs and Prognostications," in *The Oxford History of Popular Print Culture*, vol. 1, *Cheap Print in Britain and Ireland to 1660*, ed. Joad Raymond (Oxford: Oxford University Press, 2011), 431–442; Adam Smyth, "Almanacs and Ideas of Popularity," in *The Elizabethan Top Ten*, ed. Andy Kesson and Emma Smith (London: Routledge, 2013), 125–134; Tessa Watt, *Cheap Print and Popular Piety, 1550–1640* (Cambridge: Cambridge University Press, 1991), 263–267. On format, see Bernard Capp, *Astrology and the Popular Press: English Almanacs, 1500–1800* (London: Faber, 1979), 30, 42. Classic surveys include Carroll Camden Jr., "Elizabethan Almanacs and Prognostications," *The Library*, 4th ser., 12.1 (1931): 83–108; and Eustace F. Bousanquet, *English Printed Almanacks and Prognostications: A Bibliographical History to the Year 1600* (London: Bibliographical Society, 1917).

63. Hill generally offers proximate natural explanations for these signs; for example, the link between comets and harvests relies on meteorological exhalations. Thomas Hill, *A contemplation of Mysteries: contayning the rare effects and significations of certayne Comets* (London: Henry Denham, 1574), sig. A2^v.

64. Thomas Hill, *The Contemplation of Mankinde, contayning a singuler discourse after the Art of Phisiognomie* (London: [Henry Denham for] William Seres, 1571), sig. ¶¶8^r. On prognostication and sciences of the weather, see Craig Martin, *Renaissance Meteorology: Pomponazzi to Descartes* (Baltimore: Johns Hopkins University Press, 2011).

65. William Fulke, *Antiprognosticon: that is to saye, an Invective agaynst the vayne and unprofitable predictions of the Astrologians as Nostrodame, &c.* (London: Henry Sutton, 1560). It had also been published in a Latin edition in the same year.

66. Thomas Hill, *The moste pleasuante Arte of the Interpretacion of Dreames* (London: Thomas Marsh, 1576), sig. A4ᵛ.

67. On husbandry, governance, and the science of war, see Gentian Hervet, trans., *Xenophons treatise of householde* (London: Thomas Berthelet, 1532), sigs. H.vᵛ-H.viʳ.

68. See Zachary Lesser, *Renaissance Drama and the Politics of Publication* (Cambridge: Cambridge University Press, 2004); Alan B. Farmer and Zachary Lesser, "What Is Print Popularity? A Map of the Elizabethan Book Trade," in Kesson and Smith, *Elizabethan Top Ten*, 19–54.

69. In both cases, it immediately precedes the list of future titles.

70. Hill, *The Contemplation of Mankinde*, sigs. Hh5ᵛ-7ʳ.

71. It is this feature, which Hill frames as part of an adventure in print, that links both examples to the event of the book's publication. On military virtue and action in face of incomplete knowledge, see Lorna Hutson, "Fortunate Travelers: Reading for the Plot in Sixteenth-Century England," *Representations* 41 (1993): 83–103.

72. On the tension between courtly and humanist models of composition in Elizabethan England, see Mary Thomas Crane, *Framing Authority,* chapter 8. On courtly models of grace, see Harry Berger, *The Absence of Grace: Sprezzatura and Suspicion in Two Renaissance Courtesy Books* (Stanford, CA: Stanford University Press, 2000).

73. Hill, *Gardeners Labyrinth* (1577), sig. D2ʳ. See Columella, *On Agriculture, Volume I: Books 1–4,* trans. Harrison Boyd Ash (Cambridge, MA: Loeb Classical Library, 1941), Book II, XX.6.

74. Peter Harrison, *The Bible, Protestantism, and the Rise of Natural Science* (Cambridge: Cambridge University Press, 1998), 206, 239–248.

75. Wendy Wall, "Renaissance National Husbandry: Gervase Markham and the Publication of England," *Sixteenth Century Journal* 27.3 (1996): 767–785.

76. On accident and adventure in Turberville and his contemporaries, see Hutson, "Fortunate Travelers"; Laurie Shannon, "Poetic Companies: Musters of Agency in George Gascoigne's 'Friendly Verse,'" *GLQ: A Journal of Lesbian and Gay Studies* 10.3 (2004): 453–483; on accident and poetry, see Michael Hetherington, "Gascoigne's Accidents: Contingency, Skill, and the Logic of Writing," *English Literary Renaissance* 46.1 (2016): 29–59.

77. George Turberville, *Epitaphes, Epigrams, Songs and Sonets* (London: Henry Denham, 1567) sig. *.8ʳ.

78. George Turberville, trans., *The Heroycall Epistles of the Learned Poet Publius Ovidius Naso* (London: Henry Denham, 1567), sig. X2ʳ.

79. Petrarch's *Phisicke against Fortune* invokes this saying in advice addressed to someone writing for the sake of fame: "As I sayde erewhyle, perhaps it were better for thee to digge, and goe to plough, and thereby to hope for a good Harvest: for it is salfer sowing in the ground, then in the winde. For the studie of fame, and earnest travell in writyng, as it hath advaunced the renowme of many, so hath it sent over innumerable to be fooles and beggers in their olde age, and shewed them bare and babblyng spectacles to the common people." Thomas Twyne, trans., *Phisicke against Fortune* (London: Thomas Dawson for Richard Watkins, 1579), fol. 66ᵛ.

80. George Wither, *A collection of emblemes* (London: [Augustine Mathewes] for John Grismond, 1635), 106.

81. Turberville, *Heroycall Epistles*, sig. N8ʳ. Compare Oenone's "bootelesse Plough" at sig. D6ᵛ. With slightly more optimism, Turberville uses the plowman's painful delay to depict the

lover's alternating experience of hope and despair in "The Lovers must not dispaire though their Ladies seeme straunge": (Turberville, *Epitaphes*, fol. 22ʳ)

The Ploughman eke that toyles
and turnes the ground for graine,
And sowes his séede (perhaps to losse)
yet standes in hope of gaine.
He will not once dispaire,
but hope till Harvest fall:
And then will looke assuredly
to stuffe his Barnes withall.

82. Catherine Bates, "Profit and Pleasure? The Real Economy of Tottel's *Songes and Sonettes*," in *Tottel's "Songes and Sonettes" in Context*, ed. Stephen Hamrick (London: Routledge, 2013), 37–62, at 62. Seth Lerer makes a related argument, linking these images in the collection to cultivation in an explicitly agricultural context, in "Cultivation and Inhumation: Some Thoughts on the Cultural Impact of Tottel's *Songes and Sonettes*," in Hamrick, ed., *Tottel's "Songes and Sonettes" in Context*, 147–161.

83. Examples of related images are found in "The lover forsaketh his u[n]kinde love" (sig. K.iʳ⁻ᵛ), "The lover thinkes no paine to great, wherby he may obtain his ladie" (sig. Q.iiiiʳ), and "The lover dredding to move his sute for dout of denial, accuseth all women of disdaine and ficklenesse"(sig. Cc.iᵛ). *Songes and Sonettes, written by the right honorable Lorde Henry Haward late Earle of Surrey, and other* (London: Richard Tottel, 1557).

84. Turberville and many of his readers would have been familiar with Mantuan from early in their schooling. On the place of Mantuan's *Adulescentia* in the humanist curriculum, see Lee Piepho, trans. and ed., *Adulescentia: The Eclogues of Mantuan* (London: Routledge: 1989); and Lee Piepho, "Mantuan's Eclogues in the English Reformation," *Sixteenth Century Journal* 25.3 (1994): 623–632.

85. George Turberville, trans., *The Eglogs of the Poet B. Mantuan Carmelitan, Turned into English Verse* (London: Henry Bynneman, 1567), 79. Turberville's "ploughmen" renders Mantuan's phrase in Latin, "operas pubes ne rustica perdat," which calls them "rural young men."

86. Catherine Nicholson, "Proper Work, Willing Waste: Pastoral and the English Poet," in *A Companion to Renaissance Poetry*, ed. Catherine Bates (London: Wiley, 2018), 401–13.

87. On monitory verse, see Cathy Shrank, "'Matters of Love as of Discourse': The English Sonnet, 1560–1580," *Studies in Philology* 105.1 (2007): 3–49.

88. Thomas Howell, *The Arbor of Amitie, wherin is comprised pleasant Poëms and pretie Poesies* (London: Henry Denham, 1568).

89. The Bodleian Libraries, University of Oxford, 8° H 44 Art.Seld. This collection predates Selden's death in 1654; its front flyleaf contains notes on legal matters in a sixteenth-century hand that is not Selden's. See Michael David Felker, "The Poems of Isabella Whitney: A Critical Edition" (PhD diss., Texas Tech University, 1990). The *Arbor* is immediately followed by Tilney's *Flower of Friendship* (1571), a dialogue published first in 1568 by Denham and printed (then and in this 1571 issue) with the same bordered title page as the *Arbor*.

90. On Howell's life and publications, see Cathy Shrank, "Howell, Thomas (fl. 1560–1581), poet," in *ODNB*. Elizabeth Pomeroy describes Howell as a "minor" link between Surrey and

Sidney. Elizabeth Pomeroy, *The Elizabethan Miscellanies: Their Development and Conventions* (Berkeley: University of California Press, 1973), 14–15.

91. These two dimensions also reflect a peculiar split in the meaning and etymology of "arbor," which altered what had been the regular spelling of "herber," meaning a lawn or garden of flower or herbs; the *OED* notes that the tendency to distinguish "herber" and "arbor" (linking the latter with trees) begins around 1550 (*OED*, s.v. "arbour | arbor, n."). This double frame will be echoed in a concluding poem by Fraunces Flower, which praises the poet ("Then muse no whit to sée a gift, / ygraft in this my friende: / Whose pleasant verse by natures skill, / to thée doth pleasures lende") and the arbor ("The plunging minde in deepe desires, / may here in arbor rare: / Bereave unrest with pleasures rife, / and rid his soule from care") in parallel terms (*Arbor of Amitie*, sig. G4ᵛ).

92. Keper was a friend of Howell's from university, and his verse appears in answer poems later in the volume and in other publications of Howell's: see his appearances in Howell's *Newe Sonets, and pretie Pamphlets* (London: Thomas Colwell, [1570?]), sigs. A4ʳ, B2ʳ, C4ᵛ, F1ʳ, G1ʳ–G3ᵛ; and *H. His Devises, for his Owne Exercise, and his Friends Pleasure* (London: Hugh Jackson, 1581), sig. M.3ʳ.

93. On Renaissance ideas of a poetic career, see the essays in Patrick Cheney and Frederick A. de Armas, eds., *European Literary Careers* (Toronto: University of Toronto Press, 2002); Patrick Cheney, *Spenser's Famous Flight: A Renaissance Idea of a Literary Career* (Toronto: University of Toronto Press, 1993); Richard Helgerson, *The Elizabethan Prodigals* (Berkeley: University of California Press, 1976); and Richard Helgerson, *Self-Crowned Laureates* (Berkeley: University of California Press, 1983). On the way in which such small-scale forms might empower the liberty of the poet, see Heather James, "The Poet's Toys: Christopher Marlowe and the Liberties of Erotic Elegy," *Modern Language Quarterly* 67.1 (2006): 103–127.

94. One framework for these lines is aspirational. Keper departs temporarily from his imperatives to classify those who "further forth" and "laude" Howell's verse as "learned wits"—a model for readers to behave likewise.

95. As Patricia Akhimie argues, the early modern discourse of husbandry participated in an "ideology of cultivation" that fixed upon improvement of the self and the land. This same ideology, however, came to view certain bodies as capable of improvement and others incapable, such that the capacity for cultivation was itself a mark of class and race. Patricia Akhimie, *Shakespeare and the Cultivation of Difference* (New York: Routledge, 2018), 1–48. Akhimie argues that this ideology "separates those who own land from those who work on it, and those whom husbandry will improve from those who will cultivate vegetable life but not themselves." Patricia Akhimie, "Pinching Caliban: Race, Husbandry, and the Working Body in *The Tempest*," in *Shakespeare/Sense: Contemporary Readings in Sensory Culture*, ed. Simon Smith (London: Arden Shakespeare, Bloomsbury, 2020), 269–290, at 274.

96. Thimelthorpe, *Inventory*, sigs. L1ʳ–L2ʳ.

97. Howell directs a number of didactic poems to friends, including one that fashions itself as a "healthfull phisick note," and prescribes a diet (*Arbor*, fols. 22ʳ–23ʳ).

98. I discuss these dynamics as they relate to the temporality of address in "The Poetics of Practical Address," *Philological Quarterly* 98.1–2 (2019), 95–117.

99. Thomas Tusser, *A hundreth good pointes of Husbandry* (London: Richard Tottel, 1570), fol. 14ᵛ.

100. Wendy Wall, *The Imprint of Gender* (Ithaca, NY: Cornell University Press, 1993), 1–3, 82. My understanding of the social dynamics of poetic and erotic cultivation here is further indebted to Akhimie, *Shakespeare and the Cultivation of Difference*.

101. Quoted from Abraham Fleming's 1589 translation, which uses "strangers" to render "barbarus" in Latin (sig. B2^r). Compare the Loeb translation by H. Rushton Fairclough, revised by G. P. Goold (Cambridge, MA: Harvard University Press, 1999), Ec.1.68–72.

102. See, for example, Bushnell, *Green Desire*, 132–160.

103. See Rayna Kalas's essential discussion of framing in *Frame, Glass, Verse: The Technology of Poetic Invention in the English Renaissance* (Ithaca, NY: Cornell University Press, 2007); and Megan Heffernan's astute reading of this connection in the *Forrest*, especially as it implicates the physical book, in *Making the Miscellany: Poetry, Print, and the History of the Book in Early Modern England* (Philadelphia: University of Pennsylvania Press, 2021), 61.

104. The surging wave also suggests a potentially feminine version of monstrosity; compare Errour's *fluxus* of pamphlets in *Faerie Queene*, book 1.

105. On the ocean as a site of "human activity, risk, and opportunity," see Steve Mentz, *At the Bottom of Shakespeare's Ocean* (London: Continuum, 2009), quote at p. 3; and, from a different angle, Luke Wilson, "Drama and Marine Insurance in Shakespeare's London," in *The Law in Shakespeare*, ed. Constance Jordan and Karen Cunningham (Basingstoke: Palgrave, 2007), 127–142.

106. Compare Neptune's attempted seduction of Leander in Marlowe and Chapman's poem; cf. Judith Haber, *Desire and Dramatic Form in Early Modern England* (Cambridge: Cambridge University Press, 2009), 39–43; James Bromley, "'Let It Suffice': Sexual Acts and Narrative Structure in *Hero and Leander*," in *Queer Renaissance Historiography*, ed. Vin Nardizzi, Stephen Guy-Bray, and Will Stockton (Farnham: Ashgate, 2009), 67–84.

107. On early modern insurance, see Luke Wilson, "Drama and Marine Insurance"; Karl H. Van D'Elden, "The Development of the Insurance Concept and Insurance Law in the Middle Ages," in *The Medieval Tradition of Natural Law*, ed. Harold J. Johnson (Kalamazoo, MI: Board of the Medieval Institute, 1987), 191–200.

108. The mind as much as the body needs variety, just as the stomach "is quickly cloyed with feeding continuallye uppon one kinde of meate." Both "desyreth chaunge" (H.C., *Forrest*, sig. A.4^r).

109. Hetherington, "Gascoigne's Accidents," 31.

110. Another poem set in a forest, in commendation of the robin redbreast (sig. I3^v–I4^r), also turns on the occasion of discovery. In that case, though, having described the Orphic virtues of its song, the poet wants to possess the robin and is unable to part from it.

111. My understanding of addiction in this passage is indebted to Rebecca Lemon, *Addiction and Devotion in Early Modern England* (Philadelphia: University of Pennsylvania Press, 2018).

Chapter 2

1. George Puttenham, *The arte of English poesie: Contrived into three Bookes* (London: Richard Field, 1589), 256. Parenthetical citations refer to this edition. The *Arte* was published anonymously in 1589 but has been generally attributed to George Puttenham since the 1936 edition by Alice Walker and G. D. Willcock (*The Arte of English Poesie* [Cambridge: Cambridge University Press, 1936].) On this attribution, Puttenham's life, and the context and significance

of the *Arte,* see the critical edition by Frank Whigham and Wayne A. Rebhorn, eds., *The Art of English Poesy: A Critical Edition* (Ithaca, NY: Cornell University Press, 2007).

2. These numbers are based on an analysis of 61,318 titles transcribed by the Early English Books Online Text Creation Partnership. Terms included with "vertue" were: vertu, vertus, vertue, vertues, vertuous, vertuouse, vertuosity, vertuositie; and with "virtue": virtu, virtus, virtue, virtues, virtuous, virtuouse, virtuositie, virtuositie. I am grateful to Lindsay Thomas for her help in this analysis and for writing the Python script that analyzed the data.

3. This etymology has had an important role in the genealogy of Renaissance studies, shaping Jakob Burckhardt's understanding of the virility of virtuous force in his analysis of Machiavelli, a reading that influenced Nietzsche, among others. The etymological connection remains a commonplace in discussions of virtue; as the second sentence of the *Oxford Handbook of Virtue* observes, "the term *virtue* comes from the Latin word *virtus,* the root of which is *vir,* or 'man.'" Nancy E. Snow, "Introduction," in *Oxford Handbook of Virtue,* ed. Nancy E. Snow (Oxford: Oxford University Press, 2018), 1. Connections between *vir,* virtue, and virility have been explored at particular length in discussions of Shakespeare's Roman plays. See Colin Burrow, *Shakespeare and Classical Antiquity* (Oxford: Oxford University Press, 2013), 167, 229–230; Phyllis Rackin, "*Coriolanus:* Shakespeare's Anatomy of *Virtus,*" *Modern Language Studies* 13.2 (1983): 68–79, at 72, 75; Bruce Smith, *Shakespeare and Masculinity* (Oxford: Oxford University Press, 200), 42; Coppelia Kahn, *Roman Shakespeare: Warriors, Wounds, and Women* (London: Routledge, 1997), 14–20.

4. Thomas Elyot, *The boke named the Governour* (London: Thomas Berthelet, 1537), fol. 185[r]. Elyot's phrasing closely echoes the *Tusculan Disputations,* the relevant sentence of which is quoted and translated in Thomas Cooper's *Thesaurus linguae Romanae & Britannicae* (London: [Henry Denham], 1578) in this way: "A viris virtus nomen est mutuata. Cic. *Vertue toke hir name first of,* Vir, *that is, a worthie man*" (sig. Llll4[r]); and in John Dolman's translation (*Those fyve questions, which Marke Tullye Cicero, disputed in his manor of Tusculanum* [London: Thomas Marsh, 1561]): "Nowe the name of vertue, is deryved of the name of man, whiche in latine is vir" (sig. L.v[r]). Pierre de La Primaudaye's *The French Academie* (London: Edmund Bollifant for George Bishop and Ralph Newbery, 1586) ties this etymology to the ages of man (570). These associations are productively viewed in light of Holly Crocker's recent discussion of the gender politics of medieval and early modern conceptions of virtue. See Holly A. Crocker, *The Matter of Virtue: Women's Ethical Action from Chaucer to Shakespeare* (Philadelphia: University of Pennsylvania Press, 2019).

5. It reflects in this way the cosmology (discussed in the Introduction) of "scattered microsovereignties and dispersed capacities" described by Laurie Shannon in *The Accommodated Animal: Cosmopoly in Shakespearean Locales* (Chicago: University of Chicago Press, 2013), at 44; and by Julia Reinhard Lupton, "Creature Caliban," *Shakespeare Quarterly* 51.1 (2000): 1–23. See also Elizabeth Spiller's rich account of material virtue and world-making in William Gilbert's *On the Magnet* and Philip Sidney's *Defence of Poesy* (*Science, Reading, and Renaissance Literature: The Art of Making Knowledge, 1580–1670* [Cambridge: Cambridge University Press, 2004], 24–58.)

6. William Shakespeare, *Romeo and Juliet,* ed. René Weis, Arden Shakespeare, 3rd ser. (London: Bloomsbury, 2012), 2.3.19–20; Thomas Becon, *The flour of godly praiers most worthy to be used* (London: John Day, 1550), sig. A7[r]; George Gascoigne, *The posies of George Gascoigne Esquire* (London: Henry Bynneman for Richard Smith, 1575), sig. ¶¶.iiii[r].

7. Julia Reinhard Lupton, *Thinking with Shakespeare: Essays on Politics and Life* (Chicago: University of Chicago Press, 2011), 10.

8. For an anatomy of the range of senses in which Machiavelli uses *virtù*, see Russell Price, "The Senses of *Virtù* in Machiavelli," *European Studies Review* 3.4 (1973): 315–345, which tracks the moral and martial senses of the word in Machiavelli and his contemporaries, including an accounting of the word's connections to the physical sense of force and energy discussed here. This lineage from the language of force has been influential in readings of its (arguably) amoral significance, for example, in Jakob Burckhardt's description of *virtù* as a "combination of force and skill" that is "compatible with villainy" (quoted in Price, "Senses of *Virtù*," 323). Price notes several Machiavellian uses of *virtù* in the ecological sense of natural force or efficacy. On possible medical meanings of *virtù*, see Felix Gilbert, "On Machiavelli's Idea of *Virtù*," *Renaissance News* 4.4 (1951): 53–55. For approaches to the concept in Machiavelli, see also Quentin Skinner, "Machiavelli and the Misunderstanding of Princely *Virtù*," in *Machiavelli on Liberty and Conflict*, ed. David Johnston, Nadia Urbinati, and Camila Vergara (Chicago: University of Chicago Press, 2017), 139–163; Guido Ruggiero, *Machiavelli in Love: Sex, Self, and Society in the Italian Renaissance* (Baltimore: Johns Hopkins University Press, 2007), 85–107; Paul D. McLean, "The Management of Chance in Renaissance Florence," *American Journal of Cultural Sociology* 9 (2021): 460–489. Early English translations of the term were irregular. On manuscript translations of *The Prince* in circulation prior to the printed English edition of 1640, see Alessandra Petrina, *Machiavelli in the British Isles: Two Early Modern Translations of "The Prince"* (Farnham: Ashgate, 2009). John Geerken, in a review of Petrina's book, specifically tracks renderings of *virtù*, finding that in one of the two translations it is regularly given as "vertewe" while in the other "*virtù* becomes *wisdom, valor, courage, excellence, glory, resolution, valiance, worthiness, and discipline*." John Geerken, review of *Machiavelli in the British Isles*, by Alessandra Petrina, *Renaissance Quarterly* 63.3 (Fall 2010): 957–959.

9. Elyot, *Governour* (1537), fol. 45ʳ. Sidney, in his *Defence of Poesie*, writes that "the everpraise woorthie *Poesie* is full of vertue breeding delightfulnesse." Philip Sidney, *The Defence of Poesie* (London: for William Ponsonby, 1595), sig. K1ᵛ.

10. Jenny C. Mann, "The Orphic Physics of Early Modern Eloquence," in *The Palgrave Handbook of Early Modern Literature and Science*, ed. Howard Marchitello and Evelyn Tribble (Basingstoke: Palgrave, 2017), 231–256, at 231–232.

11. Walter Raleigh, *The History of the World* (London: [by William Stansby] for Walter Burre, 1614), 15.

12. Robert Mason, *A mirrour for merchants* (London: [Thomas Creede] for John Browne, 1609), 35.

13. In some accounts, this knowledge followed soon after creation itself, from the moment in which Adam named the creatures *and* knew their virtues and properties. The French surgeon Ambroise Paré, for example, wrote that God taught Adam "the nature, the proper operations, faculties and vertues of all things contained in the circuit of this Universe." Peter Harrison, *The Fall of Man and the Foundations of Science* (Cambridge: Cambridge University Press, 2008), 128. On the legibility of inward virtues in the form of outward signatures, see Harrison, *Fall of Man*, 251–252; and James Bono, *The Word of God and the Languages of Man* (Madison: University of Wisconsin Press, 1995), 129–139.

14. William Warde, trans., *The secretes of the reverende Maister Alexis of Piemount* (London: John Kingston for Nicholas England, 1558), sig. +.iiᵛ. See William Eamon's discussion of

Warde's introduction in "How to Read a Book of Secrets," in *Secrets and Knowledge in Medicine and Science, 1500–1800*, ed. Elaine Leong and Alisha Rankin (London: Routledge, 2016), 23–46. Torquemada introduces his discussion of healing springs and waters with a similar commonplace: "God hath given to many things different force and qualitie, so that few or none are without theyr particular vertues, if wee were able to attaine to the knowledge of them." Antonio de Torquemada, *The Spanish Mandevile of Miracles, or The Garden of curious Flowers* (London: Edmund Matts, 1600), sig. L1^r.

15. The twinned endowment of infused virtue and human skill is invoked in texts as varied as *Bulleins Bulwarke* (1562), Pierre de La Primaudaye's *The French academie* (published in French between 1577 and 1590; the relevant passages translated into English in the third volume in 1601), and in John Parkinson's botanical compendium, *Paradisi in sole, Paradisus Terrestris* (1629), which credits God with the virtues, properties, and variety of plants and with "many good instructions also to our selves." John Parkinson, *Paradisi in sole, Paradisus Terrestris, or A Garden of all sorts of pleasant flowers* (London: Humphrey Lownes and Robert Young, 1629), sig. **3^v.

16. The status of occult virtues will be intensely debated by natural philosophers in the seventeenth century and represents an important topic in the historiography of the Scientific Revolution. For a small sample of this important debate, see Keith Hutchison, "What Happened to Occult Qualities in the Scientific Revolution?," *Isis* 73.2 (1982): 233–253; John Henry, "Occult Qualities and the Experimental Philosophy: Active Principles in Pre-Newtonian Matter Theory," *History of Science* 24.4 (1986): 335–381; and the exchange between Brian Vickers ("The 'New Historiography' and the Limits of Alchemy," *Annals of Science* 65.1 [2008]: 127–156) and William Newman ("Brian Vickers on Alchemy and the Occult: A Response," *Perspectives on Science* 17.4 [2009]: 482–506). In the context of a broader intellectual history, Brian Copenhaver, "The Occultist Tradition and Its Critics," in *The Cambridge History of Seventeenth-Century Philosophy*, ed. Daniel Garber and Michael Ayers (Cambridge: Cambridge University Press, 1998), 454–512. I am further indebted to the formative work of Walter Pagel on Paracelsus. *Paracelsus: An Introduction to Philosophical Medicine in the Era of the Renaissance* (Basel: Karger, 1958; rev. ed., 1982).

17. As quoted in Pamela H. Smith, "What Is a Secret? Secrets and Craft Knowledge in Early Modern Europe," in Leong and Rankin, *Secrets and Knowledge*, 64–65. Quotation from Vannoccio Biringuccio, *The Pirotechnia*, trans. Cyril Stanley Smith and Martha Teach Gnudi (New York: Basic Books, 1943), 114. See also Pamela H. Smith, "Why Write a Book? From Lived Experience to the Written Word in Early Modern Europe," *Bulletin of the German Historical Institute* 47 (2010): 25–50.

18. Smith, "What Is a Secret?," 64.

19. On Dioscorides's use of the term, see John M. Riddle, *Dioscorides on Pharmacy and Medicine* (Austin: University of Texas Press, 1985), 32.

20. Comparing *dunamis* to *energeia* and *entelechia*, Aristotle writes, "so is the waking to the sleeping, and that which is seeing to that which has its eyes shut but has sight." W. D. Ross, trans., *Metaphysics*, in *The Complete Works of Aristotle*, ed. Jonathan Barnes, vol. 2 (Princeton, NJ: Princeton University Press, 2014), 1048b1–2.

21. Diocles's writings do not survive in complete form, which partially accounts for the uncertainty. See Philip J. van der Eijk, *Medicine and Philosophy in Classical Antiquity* (Cambridge: Cambridge University Press, 2005), esp. 293–295. See also Philip J. van der Eijk, ed., *Diocles of Carystus: A Collection of the Fragments with Translation and Commentary* (Leiden: Brill, 2000);

Alain Touwaide, "Le médicament en Alexandrie: De la pratique à l'épistémologie," in *Sciences exactes et sciences appliquées à Alexandrie*, ed. G. Argoud and J.-Y. Guillaumin (Saint-Etienne: Presses de l'Université, 1998), 189–206; Alain Touwaide, "Therapeutic Strategies: Drugs," in *Western Medical Thought from Antiquity to the Middle Ages*, ed. Mirko D. Grmek (Cambridge, MA: Harvard University Press, 1998), 259–272; Frederick Gibbs, *Poison, Medicine, and Disease in Late Medieval and Early Modern Europe* (London: Routledge, 2018), 15–16; Vivian Nutton, *Ancient Medicine*, 2nd ed. (London: Routledge, 2013), 121–128.

22. The latter was not absent from Aristotle's usage, but this alteration in the context of pharmacology nonetheless represents a significant change; see van der Eijk, *Medicine and Philosophy*, 295–296.

23. Compare Albertus Magnus on plants (and their *vis formativa*) and metals. See Valerie Allen, "Mineral Virtue," in *Animal, Vegetable, Mineral: Ethics and Objects*, ed. Jeffrey Jerome Cohen (Washington, DC: Oliphaunt Books, 2012), 123–152; and Albertus Magnus, *Book of Minerals*, trans. Dorothy Wyckoff (Oxford: Clarendon Press, 1967).

24. On herbals, see Agnes Arber, *Herbals: Their Origin and Evolution* (Cambridge: Cambridge University Press, 1953); and more recently, on uses and meanings of English herbals, Leah Knight, *Of Books and Botany in Early Modern England: Sixteenth-Century Plants and Print Culture* (Farnham: Ashgate, 2009). On the complexities of their use, especially as inflected by gender, see Rebecca Laroche, *Medical Authority and Englishwomen's Herbal Texts, 1550–1650* (Farnham: Ashgate, 2009). In relation to natural historical practices of compilation, see Brian W. Ogilvie, "Encyclopaedism in Renaissance Botany: From *Historia* to *Pinax*," in *Pre-modern Encyclopaedic Texts: Proceedings of the Second COMERS Congress*, ed. Peter Binkley (Leiden: Brill, 1997), 89–99; and Brian W. Ogilvie, "The Many Books of Nature: Renaissance Naturalists and Information Overload," *Journal of the History of Ideas* 64.1 (2003): 29–40.

25. William Turner, *A new Herball, wherein are conteyned the names of Herbes* (London: Steven Mierdman, 1551).

26. Thomas Hill, *The profitable Arte of Gardening, now the thirde time set forth* (London: Henry Bynneman, 1574), 71, 81, and passim; for marginalia, see, e.g., Folger STC 13493, copy 1.

27. Thomas Knell Jr., epistle, in John Northbrooke, *Spiritus est Vicarius Christi in terra. The poore mans Garden, wherein are flowers of the Scriptures* (London: John Kingston for William Williamson, 1571), sig. A4^r.

28. Nicolás Monardes, *Joyfull newes out of the newfound world, wherein are declared the rare and singular vertues of divers and sundrie Herbs, Trees, Oyles, Plants, & Stones*, trans. John Frampton, rev. ed. (London: William Norton, 1580; first ed., 1577), fol. 1^v.

29. On the traffic in plant materials and Monardes's role in it, see Daniela Bleichmar, "Books, Bodies, and Fields: Sixteenth-Century Transatlantic Encounters with New World *Materia Medica*," in *Colonial Botany*, ed. Londa Schiebinger and Claudia Swan (Philadelphia: University of Pennsylvania Press, 2005), 83–99; and Antonio Barrera-Osorio, *Experiencing Nature: The Spanish American Empire and the Early Scientific Revolution* (Austin: University of Texas Press, 2006), 122–128. On the traffic in medicine more broadly, see Harold J. Cook and Timothy D. Walker, "Circulation of Medicine in the Early Modern Atlantic World," *Social History of Medicine* 26.3 (2013): 337–351; and Patrick Wallis, "Exotic Drugs and English Medicine: England's Drug Trade, c.1550–c.1800," *Social History of Medicine* 25 (2012): 20–46.

30. Monardes, *Joyfull newes*, fol. 25^v.

31. Warde, *Alexis*, sig. +.ii^v. Compare also Walter Raleigh's explanation of the presence of these "infused properties" in nature, and his defense of the operation of God therein (*History*, 13).

32. Thomas Hariot, *A briefe and true report of the new found land of Virginia* (Frankfurt: Johann Wechel, 1590), 27.

33. James Kearney, "The Book and the Fetish: The Materiality of Prospero's Text." *Journal of Medieval and Early Modern Studies* 32.3 (2002): 433–468, esp. 438–440.

34. Parkinson, *Paradisi in sole*, sig. **4^r.

35. George Herbert, *The Temple: Sacred poems and private ejaculations* (Cambridge: Printed by Thomas Buck, and Roger Daniel, 1633), sig. D4^v.

36. This picture accords with Terence Cave's account of the generative principle of rhetorical copiousness in *The Cornucopian Text* (Oxford: Clarendon Press, 1979), 11–30.

37. Thomas Hill, *The schoole of skil: Containing two Bookes* (London: Thomes Judson for William Jaggard, 1599), 105.

38. *The History of King Lear*, 4.4.15–19. In the longer quote, I have followed the Norton Shakespeare's edition of the First Quarto (1608). For the original punctuation and spelling of "unpublisht vertues," see William Shakespeare, *M. William Shak-speare: His True Chronicle Historie of the life and death of King Lear and his three Daughters* (London: [by Nicholas Okes] for Nathaniel Butter, 1608), sig. I1^r.

39. W. R. Elton links this passage to Friar Laurence, reading it as evidence of Cordelia's "undiminished faith" in providence. W. R. Elton, *King Lear and the Gods*, 2nd ed. (Lexington: University Press of Kentucky, 1988), 81.

40. *The Riverside Chaucer*, gen. ed. Larry D. Benson, 3rd ed. (Oxford: Oxford University Press, 1988), 23.

41. Edmund Spenser, *The Shepheardes Calender: Conteyning twelve Aeglogues proportionable to the twelve monethes* (London: Hugh Singleton, 1579), sig. M1^v.

42. Thomas Middleton, *The Wisdome of Solomon Paraphrased* (London: Valentine Simmes, 1597), sig. B2^r. A modernized edition appears as Thomas Middleton, *The Wisdom of Solomon Paraphrased*, ed. G. B. Shand, in *Thomas Middleton: The Collected Works*, gen. eds. Gary Taylor and John Lavagnino (Oxford: Oxford University Press, 2007), 1920. Compare also George Chapman, *Ovids Banquet of sence. A Coronet for his Mistresse Philosophie* (London: James Roberts for Richard Smith, 1595), sig. C2^r:

> Sweete sounds and Odors, are the heavens, on earth
> Where vertues live, of vertuous men deceast,
> Which in such like, receive theyr second birth
> By smell and hearing endlesly encreast.

43. Raleigh, *History*, 13. Raleigh's allusion to the Orphic Hymns echoes Marsilio Ficino's *Platonic Theology*, book 2, chap. 9, which calls upon the same lines in the context of an argument that God "sees universal and individual things." Marsilio Ficino, *Platonic Theology*, vol. 1, Eng. trans. Michael J. B. Allen with John Warden, Lat. text ed. James Hankins with William Bowen, I Tatti Renaissance Library (Cambridge, MA: Harvard University Press, 2001), 155.

44. Helen Wilcox, a recent editor of Herbert's poems, describes the first three stanzas as being "packed with potential energy." Helen Wilcox, "Vertue," *FifteenEightyFour* (blog), 17 May 2016, http://www.cambridgeblog.org/2016/05/a-poem-a-day-by-george-herbert-vertue. Helen Vendler finds a "stiffening function" in the pun of the title and in the final stanza; this chapter's approach to "vertue" suggests we attend to the wordplay brought by the *e*, instead of only that suggested by *vis* and *vir*. Helen Vendler, "George Herbert's 'Vertue,'" *Ariel* 1.2 (1970):

54–70, at 62; reprinted in Helen Vendler, *The Poetry of George Herbert* (Cambridge, MA: Harvard University Press, 1975), 9–24. See also Arnold Stein, *George Herbert's Lyrics* (Baltimore: Johns Hopkins University Press, 1968), 178–182. Jonathan Goldberg's deconstruction of the work of writing in the poem might be helpfully considered alongside what I am suggesting is the supplementary logic of virtue. Jonathan Goldberg, "Reading (Herbert's 'Vertue') Otherwise," *Mississippi Review* 11.3 (1983): 51–64.

45. Herbert, *The Temple*, sig. D4^v.

46. As Vendler notes, it is a strange box that can enclose both days and roses ("George Herbert's 'Vertue,'" 61). We might even imagine this "box" as a boxwood, a common varietal in ornamental gardens, especially for hedging out spaces—a suggestion that would layer the proverbial sweetness of an enclosed garden compartment (one we might easily imagine full of days and roses) into Herbert's image.

47. Thomas Elyot, *The image of governance* (London: Thomas Berthelet, 1541), fol. 15^v.

48. Miriam Jacobson, "'Sweets Compacted': Posies and the Poetry of George Herbert," in *George Herbert's Travels: International Print and Cultural Legacies*, ed. Christopher Hodgkins (Newark: University of Delaware Press, 2011).

49. Edmund Tilney, *A brief and pleasant discourse of duties in Mariage, called the Flower of friendshippe* (London: Henry Denham, 1568), sig. A3^r.

50. Thomas Pritchard, *The schoole of honest and vertuous lyfe: Profitable and necessary for all estates and degrees* (London: [William How for] Richard Jones, 1579), sig. A.iii^v.

51. This is a moment where a catalog of virtues becomes explicitly an act of merchandizing. William Shakespeare, *Troilus and Cressida*, 1.2.236.

52. Rich is ultimately skeptical about the possibility of satisfying such a preference. Barnabe Rich, *The Irish hubbub: or, The English hue and crie* (London: John Marriot, 1618), 15.

53. Aristotle attempted to resolve this dilemma by suggesting that virtues bear a reciprocal relation between themselves. See On the history of the concept, see John M. Cooper, "The Unity of Virtue," *Social Philosophy and Policy* 15.1 (1998): 233–274.

54. Contemporary virtue ethicists call this "the enumeration problem." Daniel C. Russell, *Practical Intelligence and the Virtues* (Oxford: Oxford University Press, 2009), 145–176.

55. Plutarch, "On Morall Vertue," in *The philosophie, commonlie called, the morals: written by the learned Philosopher Plutarch of Chaeronea*, trans. Philemon Holland (London: Arnold Hatfield, 1603), 65.

56. Castiglione compares this to the work of a painter: to "meddle divers coulours together, so that throughe that diversitie bothe the one and the other are more sightly to behoulde." Thomas Hoby, trans., *The courtyer of Count Baldessar Castilio divided into foure bookes* (London: William Seres, 1561), sig. L.iiii^v.

57. Compare also the "cement" with the power to sweetly compact virtues in both Donne and Herbert: Donne sees the world decomposing without the cement of Elizabeth Drury ("The Cyment which did faithfully compact / And glue all vertues, now resolv'd, and slack'd"); and Herbert sees the virtuous tiles of the church floor held by the "sweet cement" of love and charity. John Donne, *An Anatomy of the World* (London: Samuel Macham, 1611), sig. A6^r; Herbert, *The Temple*, sig. C5^v.

58. On the organization of mirrors and regiments of princes around the virtues (especially around the cardinal virtues), see Sherman H. Hawkins, "Virtue and Kingship in Shakespeare's *Henry IV*," *English Literary Renaissance* 5.3 (1975): 313–343, at 317–320.

59. In its sixteenth-century articulations, this version of poetic language accords with what Thomas Greene calls a "conjunctive semiotics" in *Poetry, Signs, and Magic* (Newark: University of Delaware Press, 2005), 18–28, 29–42.

60. On the essay and its influence, see John Kerrigan, "The Editor as Reader: Constructing Renaissance Texts" in *The Practice and Representation of Reading in England*, ed. James Raven, Helen Small, and Naomi Tadmor (Cambridge: Cambridge University Press, 1996), 102–124; Tonya Pollard, *Drugs and Theatre in Early Modern England* (Oxford: Oxford University Press, 2005), 9–10; Katherine Craik, *Reading Sensations in Early Modern England* (Basingstoke: Palgrave Macmillan, 2007), 1–6.

61. Holland, trans., *Morals*, 17–50. Further citations are given parenthetically. In most of these cases (and in all pharmacological contexts) the Greek is *dunamis*; Plutarch, *Moralia*, vol. 1, trans. Frank Cole Babbitt, Loeb Classical Library 197 (Cambridge, MA: Harvard University Press, 1927), 71–198. See also Kerrigan's reading of Plutarch in "The Editor as Reader," 114–116.

62. "But like as Physicions are of opinion, that notwithstanding the greene Flies *Cantharides* be of themselves venemous and a deadly poison; yet their wings and feete are helpefull and holsome: yea and of vertue to frustrate and kill the malice of the said flies." Holland, trans., *Morals*, 28.

63. Ibid. On the anatomical style of reading poetry, see Katherine Craik, "'The Material Point of Poesy': Reading, Writing, and Sensation in Puttenham's *The Arte of English Poesie*," in *Environment and Embodiment in Early Modern England*, ed. Mary Floyd-Wilson and Garrett A. Sullivan Jr. (Basingstoke: Palgrave Macmillan, 2007), 153–170, at 159–160; and, more broadly, David Hillman and Carla Mazzio, "Introduction," in *The Body in Parts*, ed. Hillman and Mazzio (New York: Routledge, 1997), xi–xxvvi.

64. Compare Sidney on mingling kings and clowns in the *Defence of Poesie*, and the foundational account of poetic decorum and the joining of diverse materials in Horace's *Ars Poetica* (Thomas Drant, trans., *Horace his arte of Poetrie, pistles, and Satyrs* [London: Thomas Marsh, 1567], sigs. A1ᵛ–A2ᵛ).

65. Intermingling is also a key strategy in the previous essay, on the education of children, where Plutarch and Holland use another medical analogy, to "Physitians mingling and tempering otherwhiles some sweetejuice or liquid with bitter drugs and medicines" (16).

66. Humanist classrooms trained students in this kind of pruning and weeding. See Mary Thomas Crane, *Framing Authority* (Princeton, NJ: Princeton University Press, 1993), 68–71.

67. Arthur Golding, trans., *The .xv. Bookes of P. Ovidius Naso, entytuled Metamorphosis* (London: William Seres, 1567), sig. A3ʳ. He later issues a second warning, that those with stomachs too weak to "brooke, / The lively setting forth of things described in this booke," should abstain until they have grown more strong (sig. A4ʳ). On poison and translation, see Amina Alyal, "Italian Weeds and English Bodies: Translating 'The Adventures of Master F.J.,'" in *Travels and Translations in the Sixteenth Century*, ed. Mike Pincombe (Aldershot: Ashgate, 2004), 104–119. Compare also the bees in Golding's prefatory poem to Baret's *Alvearie* (1573).

68. Whether or not the bee transformed its material or merely conveyed it was a subject of disagreement. See Crane, *Framing Authority*, 68–71; Thomas M. Greene, *The Light in Troy: Imitation and Discovery in Renaissance Poetry* (New Haven, CT: Yale University Press, 1982), 73–74, 98–99 (especially on the "metamorphic implication" of Petrarch's deployment of the bee), 148, 199. See also Francis Bacon's distinction, that "empirics, in the manner of the ant, only store up and use things; the rationalists, in the manner of spiders, spin webs from their own entrails; but the bee takes the middle path: it collects its material from the flowers of field

and garden, but its special gift is to convert and digest it." Francis Bacon, *Novum organum* 1.95, in *The Oxford Francis Bacon*, vol. 11, ed. Graham Rees and Maria Wakely (Oxford: Oxford University Press, 2004), 153.

69. On the circumstances that may have led to this revision, see George Gascoigne, *A Hundreth Sundrie Flowres*, ed. G. W. Pigman III (Oxford: Clarendon Press, 2000), liii; Gillian Austen, *George Gascoigne* (Cambridge: D. S. Brewer, 2008), 84–88; Cyndia Susan Clegg, *Press Censorship in Elizabethan England* (Cambridge: Cambridge University Press, 1997), 103–122; Kirk Melnikoff, *Elizabethan Publishing and the Making of Literary Culture* (Toronto: University of Toronto Press, 2018), 107. On the consequences and framing of these changes, see Meredith Anne Skura, "Erasing an Author's Life: George Gascoigne's Revision of *One Hundreth Sundrie Flowres* (1573) in His *Posies* (1575)," in *Tudor Autobiography: Listening for Inwardness* (Chicago: University of Chicago Press, 2008), 168–196; and Megan Heffernan, who notes the greater number of glosses in the *Posies* and the author's strategies for receding from the revised text. Megan Heffernan, "Gathered by Invention: Additive Forms and Inference in Gascoigne's Poesy," *Modern Language Quarterly* 76.4 (December 2015): 413–445, at 439.

70. Gascoigne, *Posies* (1575), sig. ¶¶.iv ʳ.

71. Gascoigne's narrative redemption—in which he has reformed the aesthetic and sexual libertinism of the 1573 edition—gives him a central place among the young men Richard Helgerson has identified as "Elizabethan prodigals." Helgerson, *The Elizabethan Prodigals* (Berkeley: University of California Press, 1976), 2–6.

72. Gascoigne emphasizes the reader's skill again in a poem responding to the volume's extensive collection of commendatory verse, which he concludes with the couplet: "Smell every poesie right, and you therein shall finde, / Fresh flowres, good hearbes, & holsome weedes, to please a skilfull minde." Gascoigne, *Posies*, sig. ¶¶¶¶¶.iᵛ.

73. Ibid., ¶¶¶.iʳ⁻ᵛ. On the work of authorial inoculation in Gascoigne, see Alyal, "Italian Weeds." As Walter Pagel explains, Paracelsus's interest in the *specific virtues* of matter participated in his critique of humoral medicine and its conception of qualities; Pagel writes of Paracelsus's thought that his interest is in "not the salt as a chemical substance, but its condition which renders it harmful or harmless. It is thus the relationship between 'virtue' and man with which he is concerned; in other words a function and 'power' in matter rather than matter itself is the object of his research" (*Paracelsus* [1982], 133).

74. Paracelsus writes: "What every *Simplex* is in itself, is by art made into many beings, into all shapes and forms like food which stands on the table. If man eats it, it becomes human flesh, through a dog dog's flesh, through a cat cat's flesh. Thus it is with medicine: it becomes what you make of it. If it is possible to make evil out of good, it is also possible to make good out of evil. . . . Though a thing is poison, it may well be turned into non-poison." "Seven Defensiones, the Reply to Certain Calumniations of His Enemies," trans. C. Lilian Temkin, in *Four Treatises of Theophrastus Bombastus von Hohenheim Called Paracelsus*, ed. Henry E. Sigerist (Baltimore: Johns Hopkins University Press, 1941), 23. Jonathan Gil Harris untangles Paracelsian conceptions of poison in the context of early modern political thought in "'Ev'ry Poison Good for Some Use': The Poisonous Political Pharmacy and Its Discontents," in *Foreign Bodies and the Body Politic: Discourses of Social Pathology in Early Modern England* (Cambridge: Cambridge University Press, 1998), 48–78. Andrew Weeks relates Paracelsian arcana to the Lutheran conception of evil in *Paracelsus: Speculative Theory and the Crisis of the Early Reformation* (Albany: State University of New York Press, 1997), 154. For systematic treatments of Paracelsian influence, see Pagel, *Paracelsus* (1958); Charles Webster, *From Paracelsus to*

Newton: Magic and the Making of Modern Science (Cambridge: Cambridge University Press, 1982); and Allen Debus, *The English Paracelsians* (London: Oldbourne, 1965).

75. Gascoigne, *Posies*, sig. ¶¶.ii^v.

76. Ibid., ¶¶.iii^v. Gascoigne repeats this analogy from the previous epistle to the reverend divines, where he attributed it to something "alledged of late by a right reverende father."

77. Whigham and Rebhorn describe book 3 as "Puttenham's masterwork" ("Introduction," *The Art of English Poesy*, 47), both because of its intricate treatment of trope and figure, and because of its more discursive treatment of style and decorum in poetry and at court. It is also the most widely cited by contemporary critics, perhaps because of its catalog-like organization of tropes and figures. As Jenny Mann has noted, Puttenham invents more than a hundred new titles for figures of speech. On the politics of these vernacular names, see Mann, *Outlaw Rhetoric* (Ithaca, NY: Cornell University Press, 2012), 45–46.

78. Puttenham's articulation of this distinction is idiosyncratic. As Linda Galyon has shown, even drawing the distinction was unusual among treatments of rhetoric. More remarkable, perhaps, is the *sonic* luster he derives by displacing the *argos* of *enargia* from light to sound. See Linda Galyon, "Puttenham's *Enargeia* and *Energeia*: New Twists for Old Terms," *Philological Quarterly* 60 (1981): 29–40.

79. Craik, *Reading Sensations*, 35–51; Rebecca Wiseman, "A Poetics of the Natural: Sensation, Decorum, and Bodily Appeal in Puttenham's *Art of English Poesy*," *Renaissance Studies* 28.1 (2013): 33–49, esp. 41–42. On the physiology of reading, see Michael Schoenfeldt, "Reading Bodies," in *Reading, Society and Politics in Early Modern England*, ed. Steven Zwicker and Kevin Sharpe (Cambridge: Cambridge University Press, 2003), 215–243; and Adrian Johns, *The Nature of the Book: Print and Knowledge in the Making* (Chicago: University of Chicago Press, 1998), 380–443.

80. See Crocker, *The Matter of Virtue*, 80–107, on the externality or show of virtue (especially in *Troilus and Cressida*).

81. This is the final full chapter before a true final chapter dedicated to the queen, and so serves as argumentative and thematic conclusion.

82. See Rebecca Bushnell's discussion of art, nature, labor, and pleasure in *Green Desire* (Ithaca, NY: Cornell University Press, 2003), esp. 84–107, as well as her discussion of botanical analogy in *A Culture of Teaching: Early Modern Humanism in Theory and Practice* (Ithaca, NY: Cornell University Press, 1996), 73–116.

83. Sidney, *Defence*, sig.B4^r. Compare Henry Turner's persuasive argument that Sidney approaches *poiesis* as a practical art in *The English Renaissance Stage* (Oxford: Oxford University Press, 2006), 82–113.

84. I agree with Rayna Kalas that Puttenham does not accede to Sidney's ideality and "emphasizes instead the materiality of mental processes"; I am suggesting a shift not from material to immaterial but from iterable to unteachable. Rayna Kalas, *Frame, Glass, Verse: The Technology of Poetic Invention in the English Renaissance* (Ithaca, NY: Cornell University Press, 2007), 141.

85. On the possibilities and limits of the work of instruction in practical manuals, see especially Pamela Smith's recent work, including "Why Write a Book? From Lived Experience to the Written Word in Early Modern Europe," *Bulletin of the German Historical Institute* 47 (Fall 2010): 25–50; and "Craft Secrets and the Ineffable in Early Modern Europe," in Leong and Rankin, *Secrets and Knowledge*, 47–66. For a case study exploring these limits, and asking what other uses such books might serve, see Jennifer Mylander, "Early Modern 'How-To'" Books:

Impractical Manuals and the Construction of Englishness in the Atlantic World," *Journal for Early Modern Cultural Studies* 9.1 (2009): 123–146.

86. Following Daniel Javitch's influential reading of the *Arte* as "one of the most significant arts of conduct of the Elizabethan age," scholars have taken its ambition to be as much social as poetic, a project in training young men for the court more than a practical guide to the writing of poetry. Daniel Javitch, *Poetry and Courtliness in Renaissance England* (Princeton, NJ: Princeton University Press, 1978), 69. See also Frank Whigham, *Ambition and Privilege: The Social Tropes of Elizabethan Courtesy Theory* (Berkeley: University of California Press, 1984); Louis Adrian Montrose, "Of Gentlemen and Shepherds: The Politics of Elizabethan Pastoral Form," *ELH* 50.3 (1983): 433–452; Heinrich F. Plett, "Aesthetic Constituents in the Courtly Culture of Renaissance England," *New Literary History* 14.3 (Spring 1983): 597–621, esp. 610–611; Jonathan V. Crewe, "The Hegemonic Theater of George Puttenham," *English Literary Renaissance* 16 (1986): 71–85; Rosemary Kegl, *The Rhetoric of Concealment: Figuring Gender and Class in Renaissance Literature* (Ithaca, NY: Cornell University Press, 1984), 11–42.

87. In their readings of Puttenham, Derek Attridge and Jonathan Goldberg each take a deconstructive approach to the problem of utility; though their arguments are distinct, each finds a fundamental undecidability at the core of the *Arte*. See Derek Attridge, *Peculiar Language: Literature as Difference from the Renaissance to James Joyce* (Ithaca, NY: Cornell University Press, 1988), 17–45; Jonathan Goldberg, *Sodometries: Renaissance Texts, Modern Sexualities* (New York: Fordham University Press, 2010), 35. In both cases, the rules for poetry and for decorum are constitutively unstable and indeterminate.

Branch: The Traffic in Small Things

1. This dynamic adds small vegetable forms to the mixed economy that Wendy Wall has called the "exchange of love" and the "exchange of texts" in Renaissance poetry and narrative (*Imprint of Gender* [Ithaca, NY: Cornell University Press, 1993], 41, 34). In Jonathan Goldberg's powerful reading of the play, the language of plants participates in *Romeo and Juliet*'s unstable landscape of semiotic and erotic substitutability. Jonathan Goldberg, "*Romeo and Juliet*'s Open Rs," in *Queering the Renaissance*, ed. Jonathan Goldberg (Durham, NC: Duke University Press, 1994), 218–235.

2. On *Romeo and Juliet* and sonnets, see A. J. Earl, "*Romeo and Juliet* and the Elizabethan Sonnets," *English* 27 (1978): 99–119; Gayle Whittier, "The Sonnet's Body and the Body Sonnetized in *Romeo and Juliet*," *Shakespeare Quarterly* 40.1 (1989): 27–41; Rosalie Colie, *Shakespeare's Living Art* (Princeton, NJ: Princeton University Press, 1974), 135–76. I am grateful to Carla Mazzio for several generative suggestions about Juliet's age.

3. *Romeo and Juliet*, 3.5.130, 5.2.18. Unless otherwise stated, all quotations from *Romeo and Juliet* are taken from William Shakespeare, *Romeo and Juliet*, ed. René Weis, Arden Shakespeare, 3rd ser. (London: Bloomsbury, 2012). However, I will consistently bring in readings from the the First Quarto and Second Quarto where appropriate (or where necessary to supplement or clarify Weis's edition.) The Friar's phrase is quoted from William Shakespeare, *An excellent conceited Tragedie of Romeo and Juliet* (London: John Danter, 1597), sig. D4^r. All references to the First Quarto (Q1) are to this edition. All references to the Second Quarto (Q2) refer to William Shakespeare, *The most excellent and lamentable Tragedie, of Romeo and Juliet. Newly corrected, augmented, and amended* (London: by Thomas Creede for Cuthbert Burby, 1599).

4. Gervinus called this an artifice (*Kunstgriff*) or "a trick of nature" (*Naturgriff*), which Shakespeare used "in order to give these passages the deepest and most comprehensive background." G. G. Gervinus, *Shakespeare Commentaries*, vol. 1, trans. F. E. Bunnett (London: Smith, Elder, 1863), 286, 289.

5. Walter Pater, *Appreciations: With an Essay on Style* (New York: Macmillan, 1900), 210–211.

6. See Patricia Fumerton on sonnets as small material forms in "'Secret' Arts: Elizabethan Miniatures and Sonnets," in *Representing the English Renaissance*, ed. Stephen Greenblatt (Berkeley: University of California Press, 1988), 93–133. Heather James shows how rhetorics of diminution shape the fate of erotic poetry in "The Poets' Toys: Christopher Marlowe and the Liberties of Erotic Elegy," *Modern Language Quarterly* 67.1 (2006): 103–127. In the context of modern lyric, see Daniel Tiffany, *Toy Medium: Materialism and Modern Lyric* (Berkeley: University of California Press, 2000).

7. Thomas Elyot, *The boke named the Governour* (London: Thomas Berthelet, 1537), fol. 45^r.

8. John Fisher, *The sermon of John the bysshop of Rochester made agayn the pernicious doctryn of Martin luther* (London: Wynkyn de Worde, [1521?]), sig. B4^v.

9. "As is the bud bit with an envious worm" (1.1.154); "among fresh fennel buds"(1.2.29); "This bud of love" (2.2.128). I will return to the first two examples, spoken by fathers Montague and Capulet, below.

10. See Frederick Gibbs, *Poison, Medicine, and Disease in Late Medieval and Early Modern Europe* (London: Routledge, 2018), on how classical and medieval medicine developed concepts of specific form in conversation with attempts to account for the sometimes incongruous force of venom. The out-of-scale activity of venom informs Diocles's use of *dunamis*, discussed in Chapter 2. See Vivian Nutton, *Ancient Medicine*, 2nd ed. (London: Routledge, 2013), 13.

11. Ruth Nevo, "Tragic Form in *Romeo and Juliet*," *Studies in English Literature, 1500–1900* 9.2 (1969): 241–258, at 242. Naomi Conn Liebler writes that "Barely hidden in the rhapsodic language is a sense that the play magnified for close scrutiny everything that a contemporary sensibility needed in order to understand the complexity of non-tragic life." Naomi Conn Liebler, "The Critical Backstory," in *Romeo and Juliet: A Critical Reader*, ed. Julia Reinhard Lupton (London: Bloomsbury Arden Shakespeare, 2016), 19–52, at 31.

12. I have reproduced the Q1 reading of "small flower," but the differences between that and F1's "weak flower" are subtle but far-reaching. Weakness implies that virtuous inner force is rebelling against a feeble vessel, which is closer to the perspective of Capulet, who seems confused (in his alarm at the force of Juliet's emotions) and resists the possibility that the floods of passion within her might also be *part* of her. The "weak" flower, like Capulet's vision of Juliet, cannot contain the forces for which it serves as a container and is undone by them. The "small" flower of Q1, on the other hand, virtuosically compacts a universe of force into a tiny form.

13. The diversity of distributed virtues demands judgment, prompting the danger of misapplication and the possibility that virtue might turn to vice, as the Friar notes a few lines later. Henry Turner shows how early modern accounts of practical wisdom understand the role of judgment in such situations as part of the exercise of prudence (*The English Renaissance Stage* [Oxford: Oxford University Press, 2006], 53).

14. "Earth hath swallowed all my hopes but she, / Shees the hopefull Lady of my earth." *Romeo and Juliet* (1599), sig. B2^v. The first line does not appear in Q1; Weis chooses to exclude

it from his Arden edition with the argument that the line following represents Shakespeare's revision.

15. See Tanya Pollard's discussion of poison's double virtue in *Romeo and Juliet*, which parallels the play's blending of tragedy and comedy (*Drugs and Theatre in Early Modern England* [Oxford: Oxford University Press, 2005], 55–70).

16. Brooke devotes several lines to a limited defense of occult art, distinguishing between of "skilfulnes" and "lewd abuse." Arthur Brooke, *The tragicall historye of Romeus and Juliet, written first in Italian by Bandell* (London: Richard Tottel, 1562), sig. B.viii[v]. William Painter's prose version of the narrative expands this portrait only slightly, by introducing the Friar as "very skilful in Philosophy, and a great searcher of nature secrets, & exceeding famous in Magike knowledge, and other hidden and secret sciences, which nothing diminished his reputation, bicause he did not abuse the same" (fol. 225[r–v]). In both cases, Romeo's relationship to the Friar is also described in terms of secrets: from a young age, in Painter's account, he did "bare a certein particle amitie to frier Laurence, & departed to him his secrets." William Painter, *The second Tome of the Palace of Pleasure* (London: Henry Bynneman for Nicholas England, 1567), fol. 225[r–v].

17. As quoted in John Henry, "The Fragmentation of Renaissance Occultism and the Decline of Magic," *History of Science* 46.1 (2008): 1–48, at 8; *Natural magick by John Baptista Porta, a Neapolitane: in twenty books* (London: Thomas Young and Samuel Speed, 1658), 2.

18. Weis here follows Q1 in having Juliet "too soon married"; I am persuaded by the happier meter of "made," which appears in Q2–4 and the Folio.

19. Thomas Tusser includes among his points for July's husbandry: "where chamber is swept, & the wormwood is strowne / no flea for his life, dare abyde to be knowne." Thomas Tusser, *Five hundreth points of good husbandry* (London: Richard Tottel, 1573), fol. 53[r]. Gerard notes that wormwood voids worms and keeps away moths and gnats. John Gerard, *The herball, or Generall Historie of Plantes* (London: Adam Islip, Joyce Norton, and Richard Whitaker, 1633), 1097.

20. Sianne Ngai associates the cute with the aesthetic negotiations of lyric poetry with its own scale. "The Cuteness of the Avant Garde," in *Our Aesthetic Categories* (Cambridge, MA: Harvard University Press, 2012). I am grateful to Emma Stapely for a series of conversations about Juliet and the dug from which this paragraph emerged.

21. John Maplet, *The diall of Destiny* (London: Thomas Marsh, 1581), fol. 48[v].

22. See Ioan Couliano's discussion of phantasm, especially in the section, "How a Woman, Who Is So Big, Penetrates the Eyes, Which Are So Small," in *Eros and Magic in the Renaissance* (Chicago: University of Chicago Press, 1987), 21–23.

23. This aspect of my argument offers a quotidian perspective on the debated philosophical role of contingency and fate in the play. For a distinct but important take on this question, see Paul Kottman, "Defying the Stars: Tragic Love as the Struggle for Freedom in *Romeo and Juliet*," *Shakespeare Quarterly* 63.1 (2012): 1–37.

24. Julia Reinhard Lupton shows how the social life of the tragedy turns on a series of spatial transgressions that go by the name of hospitality (especially Capulet's hospitality). Julia Reinhard Lupton, "Making Room, Affording Hospitality: Environments of Entertainment in *Romeo and Juliet*," *Journal of Medieval and Early Modern Studies* 43.1 (2013): 145–172.

25. Thomas Becon, [*The flour of godly praiers*] (London: John Day, 1550), epistle.

26. Isabella Whitney, [*A sweet nosgay, or pleasant posye*] (London: Richard Jones, 1573), sig. A6[v].

27. A still-growing body of scholarship has shown how plague infects the play's pharmacology, epidemiology, and topology: Barbara H. Traister, "'A Plague on Both Your Houses': Sites of Comfort and Terror in Early Modern Drama," in *Representing the Plague in Early Modern England*, ed. Rebecca Totaro and Ernest B. Gilman (New York: Routledge, 2011), 169–182; Paula S. Berggren, "Shakespeare's Dual Lexicons of Plague: Infections in Speech and Space," in Totaro and Gilman, *Representing the Plague*, 150–168; on *Romeo and Juliet* and pharmaceuticals, Pollard, *Drugs and Theatre*, 57–65. Powerful recent arguments about Verona's contagious environments are found in Mary Floyd-Wilson, "'Angry Mab with Blisters Plague': The Pre-Modern Science of Contagion in Romeo and Juliet," in *The Palgrave Handbook of Early Modern Literature and Science*, ed. Howard Marchitello (New York: Palgrave, 2017), 401–22; and Rebecca Totaro, "Embedded in Shakespeare's 'Fair Verona'," in *Contagion and the Shakespearean Stage*, ed. Darryl Chalk and Mary Floyd-Wilson (Cham: Springer, 2019), 255–76.

28. Rebecca Laroche and Jennifer Munroe, *Shakespeare and Ecofeminist Theory* (London: Bloomsbury, 2017), 53–54. The term "transcorporeality" is Stacy Alaimo's, from *Bodily Natures* (Bloomington: Indiana University Press, 2010).

29. Capulet refers to "good Angelica" at 4.4.5; there is some ambiguity as to whether this refers to the Nurse, his wife, or some unspecified culinary procedure, but an address to the Nurse is most likely. On angelica, see Rebecca Laroche, "Lady Brilliana Harley's Angelica Root," in *Early Modern Women* 16.1 (2021): 82–90. See also the discussion of Angelica, a character in Geoffrey Fenton's *Tragicall Discourses*, in Lorna Hutson, *The Usurer's Daughter* (London: Routledge, 1994), 129–134. In the story, translated from Bandello, Fenton describes Angelica in terms of the "operacion and force of true vertue," and her role is to pacify two competing families.

30. As Katharine Wilson suggests, Whetstone's main sources are Ariosto and "Romeo and Juliet," but its central project is revisiting Gascoigne's *Adventures of Master F.J.*; see her *Fictions of Authorship in Late Elizabethan Narratives* (Oxford: Oxford University Press, 2006), 32–36.

31. George Whetstone, *The Rocke of Regard divided into foure parts* (London: [Henry Middleton] for Robert Waley, 1576), 41.

32. Ibid., 42. On floral gifts as an object of suspicion, compare the anecdote concerning the imprisoned Elizabeth Tudor and a young boy who delivered her flowers, described in Lena Cowen Orlin, in *Locating Privacy in Tudor London* (Oxford: Oxford University Press, 2008), 232.

33. See A. Bartlett Giamatti, *The Earthly Paradise and the Renaissance Epic* (Princeton, NJ: Princeton University Press, 1966); Peter Stallybrass, "Patriarchal Territories: The Body Enclosed," in *Rewriting the Renaissance: The Discourses of Sexual Difference in Early Modern Europe*, ed. Margaret W. Ferguson, Maureen Quilligan, and Nancy J. Vickers (Chicago: University of Chicago Press, 1986), 123–142; Amy Tigner, *Literature and the Renaissance Garden from Elizabeth I to Charles II* (Farnham: Ashgate, 2012), 113–125; and Cristina Malcolmson, "The Garden Enclosed/The Woman Enclosed: Marvell and the Cavalier Poets," in *Enclosure Acts: Sexuality, Property, and Culture in Early Modern England*, ed. Richard Burt and John Michael Archer (Ithaca, NY: Cornell University Press, 1994), 251–269.

34. See Juliet's warning when she hears Romeo from below, that "The orchard walls are high and hard to climb, / And the place death" (2.2.63–64).

35. These lines do not appear in Q1.

36. *Romeo and Juliet* (1597, Q1), sig. B2ᵛ; *Romeo and Juliet* (1599, Q2), sig. B2ᵛ. Compare "buds" in the *Sonnets*, where they rarely blossom on schedule or at all; there, failed budding represents an interruption of circulation—especially in Sonnet 1. Cankers and buds are also joined in Sonnets 35 and 70.

37. Quoted from the Second Quarto (*Romeo and Juliet* [1599], sig. B2ᵛ.) On "heiress," see George Steevens, quoted in H. H. Furness, ed., *A New Variorum Edition of Shakespeare*, vol. 1, *Romeo and Juliet* (Philadelphia: J. B. Lippincott, 1871), 32. As noted above, some editions exclude the first of these these lines, which is present in the Second Quarto and the Folio.

38. Weis (Arden, 3rd ser.) glosses this line to note that Shakespeare might here be rewriting a description applied to Romeo in Brooke's poem that deploys a common Petrarchan image: "Thy stearles ship (O Romeus) . . . wracke thy sea beaten barke" (Brooke, *Romeus and Juliet*, fol. 23ʳ).

39. He threatens to drive her beyond the walls, into the streets where Romeo has been all along, making her an animal of the fields:

> Graze where you will, you shall not house with me.
> Look to't, think on't; I do not use to jest.
> Thursday is near. Lay hand on heart, advise.
> An you be mine, I'll give you to my friend;
> An you be not, hang, beg, starve, die in the streets,
> For, by my soul, I'll ne'er acknowledge thee,
> Nor what is mine shall never do thee good.
>   (3.5.189–195)

Capulet here makes explicit that fatherly acknowledgment is contingent on Juliet's enclosure.

40. *Romeo and Juliet* (1597, Q1), sig. B2ᵛ.

41. This phrasing is from Q2 (sig. M2ʳ). Q1 reads, "There shall no statue of such price be set, / As that of *Romeos* loved *Juliet*" (sig. K4ʳ).

42. The status of the traffic in women in the play is complex. The comic pattern that *Romeo and Juliet* seems initially to follow affirms and enacts that kinship dynamic: breaking a young woman out from the authority of her father and delivering her to heterosexual marriage. But, like the other kinds of traffic in the play, its traffic in Juliet is interrupted. As Dympna Callaghan shows, both feuding families initially seem marked by incest, with their refusals to turn outwards; it is the Prince's declaration of an end to the feud that authorizes exogamy under the central aegis of the state. Romeo and Juliet's initial self-trafficking is subsumed into this centralized form. In this light, we should hesitate before claiming utopian potential in the decentered "free play" of the tragedy's traffic. The unchecked course of virtues across the stage and across Verona, with its transgression of paternal enclosure and exercise of a liberty indifferent to authority, looks awfully like the ideology of romantic love that feminist and queer theorists have seen restored in the play's conclusion and canonized by its legacy. See Dympna Callaghan, in "The Ideology of Romantic Love: The Case of Romeo and Juliet," in Dympna Callaghan, Lorraine Helms, and Jyotsna Singh, *The Weyward Sisters: Shakespeare and Feminist Politics* (Oxford: Blackwell, 1994), 59–101; and, on the unstable paths of small things and of vectors of desire, Goldberg, "*Romeo and Juliet*'s Open Rs." In its interest in porousness, Kathryn Schwarz's recent account of "the seductive potential of contagion" in the play, and the way in which dynamics associated with the plague "render subjects pervious to

one another," offers a provocative counterpoint to my own here ("*Held in Common*: Romeo and Juliet and the Promiscuous Seductions of Plague," in *Queer Shakespeare: Desire and Sexuality*, ed. Goran Stanivukovic [London: Bloomsbury, 2017], 245–261.)

43. The contours of this virtuous cosmology are more fully described in Chapter 2; see Laurie Shannon, *The Accommodated Animal: Cosmopolity in Shakespearean Locales* (Chicago: University of Chicago Press, 2013), at 44; and Julia Reinhard Lupton, "Creature Caliban," *Shakespeare Quarterly* 51.1 (2000): 1–23

44. Gayle Rubin, "The Traffic in Women: Notes on the 'Political Economy' of Sex," in *Toward an Anthropology of Women*, ed. Rayna R. Reiter (New York: Monthly Review Press, 1975), 157–210; and Eve Kosofsky Sedgwick, *Between Men: English Literature and Male Homosocial Desire* (New York: Columbia University Press, 1985), 21–27. Perhaps ironically, in the traffic of *Romeo and Juliet*, these nonhuman agencies do some of the same work that Maureen Quilligan attributes to incest, as a strategy that effects a "halt in the orderly traffic in women." Maureen Quilligan, *Incest and Agency in Elizabeth's England* (Philadelphia: University of Pennsylvania Press, 2008), 32. On the connection to poetry, see Meredith L. McGill, introduction to *The Traffic in Poems*, ed. Meredith L. McGill (New Brunswick, NJ: Rutgers University Press, 2008), 3.

Chapter 3

1. Plat's collection inspired Isabella Whitney's complex response in *A Sweet Nosgay* (1573), the subject of Chapter 4.

2. Most of these identifications are advertised on the works themselves and can be confirmed in the records of the Inns. Additional biographical information is available in the *ODNB*: A. H. Bullen, "Gifford, Humphrey (*fl.* 1580)," rev. Elizabeth Goldring; Emma Smith, "Whetstone, George (*bap.* 1550, *d.* 1587)"; Matthew Steggle, "Grange, John (*b.* 1556/7)."

3. Jessica Winston, *Lawyers at Play: Literature, Laws, and Politics at the Early Modern Inns of Court, 1558–1581* (Oxford: Oxford University Press, 2016), 46–75. Mary Thomas Crane argues that this generation of poets in the 1570s rewrote the humanist conventions of gathering they had learned in school according to the collision between those models and the values of courtly culture (*Framing Authority* [Princeton, NJ: Princeton University Press, 1993], 162–196).

4. Richard Helgerson, *The Elizabethan Prodigals* (Berkeley: University of California Press, 1976), 1–15. See also Georgia Brown, *Redefining Elizabethan Literature* (Cambridge: Cambridge University Press, 2004), 18–26.

5. These rhetorical renderings of the limits of enclosure might be considered alongside Michelle O'Callaghan's recent work challenging perceptions of the Inns as cloistered homosocial enclosures, showing the involvement of women (as wives, daughters, poets) in those networks. Paper presented at "The Early Modern Inns of Court and the Circulation of Text" conference, 14 June 2019. See also her *The English Wits: Literature and Sociability in Early Modern England* (Cambridge: Cambridge University Press, 2010).

6. Winston, *Lawyers at Play*, 77–98; and Jessica Winston, "Lyric Poetry at the Early Elizabethan Inns of Court: Forming a Professional Community," in *The Intellectual and Cultural World of the Early Modern Inns of Court*, ed. Jayne Elisabeth Archer, Elizabeth Goldring, and Sarah Knight (Manchester: Manchester University Press, 2011), 223–244.

7. See Arthur Marotti, *Manuscript, Print, and the English Renaissance Lyric* (Ithaca, NY: Cornell University Press, 1995), esp. 35–37. On manuscript circulation and cultures of semi-

publicity in the Inns, see Harold Love, *Scribal Publication in Seventeenth-Century England* (Oxford: Clarendon Press, 1993), 224–229; and Arthur Marotti, *John Donne, Coterie Poet* (Madison: University of Wisconsin Press, 1986), chap. 1.

8. On this doubled address, see Lorna Hutson, *Usurer's Daughter* (London: Routledge, 1994), 122–125; Crane, *Framing Authority*, 166–169, 174.

9. J. W. Saunders, "The Stigma of Print: A Note on the Social Bases of Tudor Poetry," *Essays in Criticism* 1.2 (1951): 139–164. Scholars have revised Saunders's thesis from a number of angles since its publication. See, for example, Steven May's argument that it is poetry, not print, that brings discredit in "Tudor Aristocrats and the Mythical 'Stigma of Print,'" *Renaissance Papers* 10 (1980): 11–18; Wendy Wall, *The Imprint of Gender* (Ithaca, NY: Cornell University Press, 1993); Nita Krevans, "Print and the Tudor Poets," in *Reconsidering the Renaissance*, ed. Mario A. di Cesare (Binghamton, NY: Medieval and Renaissance Texts and Studies, 1992), 301–314. For Gascoigne, Whetstone, and others, poetic production served an aspirational practice of preferment, though each seems to have had more success with later, more moralizing writing (see Crane, especially on the ambivalent role of Lord Burghley, in *Framing Authority*, 165–180.)

10. Fitzherbert's *Husbandrie* (first published ca. 1523) prescribes the enclosure of pastureland by both hedge and ditch. The process of enclosure was gradual and uneven, and in practice could denote a range of changes in land use; see Joan Thirsk, "The Common Fields," *Past and Present* 29 (1964): 3–25; Thirsk, "Changing Attitudes to Enclosure in the Seventeenth Century," in *The Festschrift for Professor Ju-Hwan Oh on the Occasion of His Sixtieth Birthday*, ed. Jan Cygan (Taegu [Korea], 1991), 518–543; and Thirsk, "Enclosing and Engrossing," in *The Agrarian History of England and Wales*, vol. 4, *1500–1640*, ed. Joan Thirsk (Cambridge: Cambridge University Press, 1967), 200–255; J. R. Wordie, "The Chronology of English Enclosure," *The Economic History Review* 36.4 (1983): 483–505; Andrew McRae, *God Speed the Plough* (Cambridge: Cambridge University Press, 2002), chaps. 1, 2, 5, and 6. On enclosure as a literary dynamic, see Richard Burt and John Michael Archer, eds., *Enclosure Acts* (Ithaca, NY: Cornell University Press, 1994); and Jennifer Munroe, *Gender and the Garden in Early Modern English Literature* (Aldershot: Ashgate, 2008), 18–20.

11. Hugh Plat, *Floures of Philosophie* (London: Francis Coldock and Henry Bynneman, 1581), sig.M6^{v-r}. The leaves are damaged in the only copy of the 1572 edition. On their ostensibly Senecan origin, see the introduction to Richard J. Panofsky, ed., *The Floures of Philosophie (1572) by Hugh Plat and A Sweet Nosgay (1573) and The Copy of a Letter (1567) by Isabella Whitney* (Delmar, NY: Scholars' Facsimiles and Reprints, 1982), vi–viii.

12. Plat, *Floures* (1581), sig. M6^r.

13. On the rhetorical use of hedges as an icon of enclosure, including their thorniness, see Frances E. Dolan, *Digging the Past* (Philadelphia: University of Pennsylvania Press, 2020), 134.

14. The population of London approximately quadrupled over the course of the sixteenth century. See Roger Finlay, *Population and Metropolis: The Demography of London, 1580–1660* (Cambridge: Cambridge University Press, 1981); Vanessa Harding, "The Population of London, 1550–1700: A Review of the Published Evidence," *London Journal* 15 (1990): 111–128; Paul Griffiths and Mark S. R. Jenner, eds., *Londinopolis: Essays in the Social and Cultural History of Early Modern London* (Manchester: Manchester University Press, 2000), 2–3. On how Londoners struggled to live with density in this period, see Lena Cowen Orlin, "Temporary Lives in London Lodgings," *Huntington Library Quaterly* 71.1 (2008): 219–242.

15. "Although gardens were to be places of recreation and pleasure," Henderson writes, "this was increasingly available to only a select few." During the sixteenth century, gardeners' positions at the Inns switched from tenancy relationships to waged positions. Paula Henderson, "The Evolution of the Early Gardens of the Inns of Court," in Archer, Goldring, and Knight, *Intellectual and Cultural Worlds*, 179–198, at 182–184. Henderson notes that much of the planting also served the purposes of enclosure and division: of recorded plant purchases, many served for hedging, as borders and divisions and for mazes (192).

16. Locks appear with greater frequency in the Inns' records for this period (ibid., 179–184); Henderson cites a Lincoln's Inn record from 1613, charging the porter with "lookinge to such nusances as shall happen in the House by the sluttishness of laundresses and others," "in case hee finde any such nusance in the Garden or backside, to admonishe the Panierman and Gardiner respectivelie thereof." See also David Jacques, "'The Chief Ornament' of Gray's Inn: The Walks from Bacon to Brown," *Garden History* 17.1 (1989): 41–67; Tia Sedley, "Inner Temple Garden: 'A New Faire Garden, Envoironed with Stronge Brick Walls,'" *London Gardener* 7 (2001–2002): 46–51. Other examples may be found in Inns' surviving record books, largely through payments for supplies or to gardeners for enforcing increased security. See F. A. Inderwick, ed., *A Calendar of the Inner Temple Records*, vol. 1 (London: Published by the Order of the Masters of the Bench and sold by Henry Sotheran; Stevens and Haynes; Stevens and Sons, 1896), 77, 106, 151, 303, 380, 382; and *The Black Books of Lincoln's Inn*, vol. 1 (London: Lincoln's Inn, 1897), 89–90.

17. Wenceslaus Hollar, "A sheet from a bird's-eye plan of London: from St Giles on the left to Chancery Lane on the right, Holborn at top, the Thames from Savoy Stairs to Essex Stairs at the bottom," (1660/6), etching. British Museum Q,6.136. On the history of Lincoln's Inn Fields, which were not established until later in the seventeenth century, see Walter Thornbury, *Old and New London*, vol. 3 (London: Cassell, Petter & Galpin, 1878), 44–50.

18. Paul Raffield, *Images and Cultures of Law in Early Modern England: Justice and Political Power, 1558–1660* (Cambridge: Cambridge University Press, 2004), 3, 6.

19. "Textual networks of address and exchange," she writes, "operated as an experimental, quasi-corporate form of alternative polity—what we might even venture to call a 'republic-in-waiting.'" Laurie Shannon, "Minerva's Men: Horizontal Nationhood and the Literary Production of Googe, Turberville, and Gascoigne," in *The Oxford Handbook of Tudor Literature, 1485–1603*, ed. Mike Pincombe and Cathy Shrank (Oxford: Oxford University Press, 2009), 437–454, at 440.

20. Dolan, *Digging the Past*, 124–128. On bordered title pages, see the series of articles by Juliet Fleming discussed at greater length in Chapter 1.

21. Walter Ong suggests that space-making metaphors like gardens were key to the ways that humanist print culture structured newly spatial ways of thinking, especially the practices of rhetorical invention associated with commonplacing. Walter J. Ong, *Ramus, Method, and the Decay of Dialogue* (Cambridge: Harvard University Press, 1983), 112–118. On Ong's spatial logic and its significance for the more wayward forms of Renaissance rhetoric and poetics, see Jenny C. Mann, *Outlaw Rhetoric: Figuring Vernacular Eloquence in Shakespeare's England* (Ithaca, NY: Cornell University Press, 2012), 3–8, 22, 31.

22. Roger Chartier, *The Order of Books* (Stanford, CA: Stanford University Press, 1992), vii, 1–24.

23. John Grange, *The Golden Aphroditis a pleasant discourse, penned by John Grange Gentleman, student in the common lawe of England* (London: Henry Bynneman, 1577), sig. N.iii^v, sig. A.iii^r.

24. Plat, *Floures* (1581), sig. M6^v.

25. Both in George Whetstone, *The Rocke of Regard divided into foure parts* (London: [Henry Middleton] for Robert Waley, 1576), sig. ¶¶.i^{r-v}.

26. See Kathy Eden, *Friends Hold All Things in Common: Tradition, Intellectual Property, and the Adages of Erasmus* (New Haven, CT: Yale University Press, 2001); and Laurie Shannon, *Sovereign Amity: Figures of Friendship in Shakespearean Contexts* (Chicago: University of Chicago Press, 2002), 50–55.

27. On the meanings of "license," another term that appears in this setting, in the context of Elizabethan printing, see Cyndia Susan Clegg, *Press Censorship in Elizabethan England* (Cambridge: Cambridge University Press, 1997), 12–15.

28. Heather James, "Ovid and the Question of Politics in Early Modern England," *ELH* 70.2 (2003): 343–373. This argument is more expansively made in Heather James, *Ovid and the Liberty of Speech in Shakespeare's England* (Oxford: Oxford University Press, 2021). See also Patrick Cheney, *Marlowe's Counterfeit Profession: Ovid, Spenser, Counter-Nationhood* (Toronto: University of Toronto Press, 1997), who writes: "for Marlowe, as to some extent for Lucan and Ovid, *libertas* means, above all, freedom of expression: in thought, word, action and (for some Elizabethans) print" (21).

29. On *parrhesia*, see David Colclough, "*Parrhesia*: The Rhetoric of Free Speech in Early Modern England," *Rhetorica: A Journal of the History of Rhetoric* 17.2 (1999): 177–212; Michel Foucault, *Fearless Speech* (Los Angeles: Semiotext(e), 2001); and John Kerrigan, "The Editor as Reader: Constructing Renaissance Texts" in *The Practice and Representation of Reading in England*, ed. James Raven, Helen Small, and Naomi Tadmor (Cambridge: Cambridge University Press, 1996), 102–124. Giving the reins to the reader specifically immunizes poet and publisher against accusations of lascivious verse—a commonplace of anti-poetic sentiment. See also Chapter 2 above.

30. The nature of this scandal is never made fully explicit, and Gascoigne's revisions (however much he advertised them) were minimal when it came to potentially offensive content. See Gillian Austen, *George Gascoigne* (Cambridge: D. S. Brewer, 2008), 84–87. Cyndia Clegg draws a distinction between censorship and censure (*Press Censorship*, 103–122).

31. Susan Staub, "Dissembling His Art: 'Gascoigne's Gardnings,'" *Renaissance Studies* 25.1 (2011): 95–110. Staub's argument is shaped by Rebecca Bushnell's illumination of the role of these poetic and rhetorical categories in the making of Renaissance gardens, in *Green Desire* (Ithaca, NY: Cornell University Press, 2003).

32. George Gascoigne, *A Hundreth Sundrie Flowres*, ed. G. W. Pigman III (Oxford: Clarendon Press, 2000), 2 (hereafter cited as Pigman, ed., *Flowres*). The quotation is taken from the table of contents; the "devises" begin on p. 217.

33. Kirk Melnikoff argues for Richard Smith's authorship of this epistle in *Elizabethan Publishing and the Makings of Literary Culture* (Toronto: University of Toronto Press, 2018), 99–136, esp. 108–117.

34. Pigman, ed., *Flowres*, 4.

35. On Gascoigne's strategies of miscellaneity, see Megan Heffernan, *Making the Miscellany: Poetry, Print, and the History of the Book in Early Modern England* (Philadelphia:

University of Pennsylvania Press, 2021), 89–123; Matthew Zarnowiecki, *Fair Copies: Reproducing the English Lyric from Tottel to Shakespeare* (Toronto: University of Toronto Press, 2014), 47–70.

36. Pigman, ed., *Flowres*, 3.

37. *Songes and Sonettes* (London: Richard Tottel, 1557), epistle.

38. One confusing aspect of how the volume is printed is that the epistles by H.W. and G.T. appear not with that from the printer to the reader, but before the beginning of *The Adventures of Master F.J.*, following *Supposes* and *Jocasta*. Adrian Weiss has described the somewhat unusual circumstances of the volume's printing in "Shared Printing, Printer's Copy, and the Text(s) of Gascoigne's *A Hundreth Sundrie Flowres*," *Studies in Bibliography* 45 (1992): 71–104. Kirk Melnikoff challenges Weiss's understanding of Richard Smith's role in this process (*Elizabethan Publishing*, 106–117).

39. On other examples of poets with friends like these, most prominently Barnabe Googe, see Saunders, "Stigma," 145–147.

40. Pigman, ed., *Flowres*, 142.

41. In the 1575 *Posies*, Gascoigne compares his poems to Theodore Beza's "Poëmata castrata," offering them "gelded from all filthie phrases, corrected in all erronious places, and beautified with addition of many moral examples." "To the reverend Divines," in Pigman, ed., *Flowres*, 361. See Alan Stewart, "Gelding Gascoigne," in *Prose Fiction and Early Modern Sexualities in England, 1570–1640*, ed. Constance C. Relihan and Goran V. Stanivukovic (Basingstoke: Palgrave, 2003), 147–169.

42. Susan C. Staub, "The Lady Frances Did Watch: Gascoigne's Voyeuristic Narrative," in *Framing Elizabethan Fictions: Contemporary Approaches to Early Modern Narrative Prose*, ed. Constance C. Relihan (Kent, OH: Kent State University Press, 1996), 41–54, esp. 44–46.

43. Kerrigan writes, "Gascoigne was peculiarly alert to the mixed nature of his audience, and to the danger of encountering spiders. But an awareness of reader diversity was widespread among his contemporaries, almost a condition of authorship in the expanding market for print" ("The Editor as Reader," 112; "reader's share" appears at 111, 116).

44. Pigman, ed., *Flowres*, 141–142.

45. Ibid., 245, 293, 263.

46. Michael Hetherington observes along similar lines that Gascoigne's "hundreth" participates in the title's vagueness of quantity, suggesting a round and unified figure without committing to a precise quantity, "taunting its readers with the vexed question of its unity of multiplicity." Michael Hetherington, "Gascoigne's Accidents: Contingency, Skill, and the Logic of Writing," *English Literary Renaissance* 46.1 (2016): 29–59. Compare Tusser's "hundreth" (and later five hundred) points, discussed in Chapter 5.

47. See Jessica Wolfe's discussion of the adage in relation to Erasmus's treatment of religious strife and toleration, *Homer and the Problem of Strife* (Toronto: University of Toronto Press, 2015), 94–95.

48. Whetstone, *Rocke*, epistle. See also Humphrey Gifford, *A posie of Gilloflowers eche differing from other in colour and odour, yet all sweete* (London: [Thomas Dawson] for John Perrin, 1580), sig. II^r ("Though al the flowers herein contayned, carie one name, yet eche of them differs from other, both in colour and savour, the better to satisfie the diversitie of eyes that shall view them, and variety of noses that shall smell them"); and George Pettie, "Letter of G.P. to R.B. concerning this woorke," in *A petite Pallace of Pettie his pleasure* (London: Richard Watkins, 1576) ("Tragicall trifles, whiche you have heard mee in sundrie companies at

sundrye times report, and so neare as I could I have written them word for word as I then told them"(sig. A.iii^r).

49. Pigman, ed., *Flowres*, 274.

50. Laurie Shannon, "Poetic Companies: Musters of Agency in George Gascoigne's 'Friendly Verse,'" *GLQ: A Journal of Lesbian and Gay Studies* 10.3 (2004): 453–483, esp. 463–464. See also Henry S. Turner, *The Corporate Commonwealth: Pluralism and Political Fictions in England, 1516–1651* (Chicago: University of Chicago Press, 2016); Drew Daniel, *The Melancholy Assemblage: Affect and Epistemology in the English Renaissance* (New York: Fordham University Press, 2013). On the homosociality of collective authorship, see Jeffrey Masten, *Textual Intercourse: Collaboration, Authorship, and Sexualities in Renaissance Drama* (Cambridge: Cambridge University Press, 1997).

51. The poems appear in George Gascoigne, *A Hundreth sundrie Flowres bounde up in one small Poesie* (London: [Henry Bynneman and Henry Middleton] for Richard Smith, 1573), sig. Cc4^{v-r}. On the "close walk" and the importance of walks to Inns' gardens, see Henderson, "Evolution of the Early Gardens," 193. Bacon will famously add walks to the Grey's Inn gardens in the 1590s. On the importance of both walks and groves to learned discourse, also see Jacques, "'Chief Ornament,'" 41–67.

52. On the "network of associations between gardens, galleries, walking, and intimacy," see Lena Cowen Orlin, *Locating Privacy in Tudor London* (Oxford: Oxford University Press, 2008), 237. We might also compare this "close walke" to the fateful gallery from *The Adventures of Master F. J.*, which Orlin places in the context of Tudor domestic and landscape architecture (*Locating Privacy*, 242–243).

53. On the etymological and conceptual links between falling, occasion, and accident, see Hetherington, "Gascoigne's Accidents," 43–44.

54. Gascoigne, *Hundreth sundrie Flowres* (1573), sig. Cc4^v.

55. Stewart, "Gelding Gascoigne," 164.

56. Pigman, ed., *Flowres*, 360. See also Saunders, "Stigma," 149–150.

57. Crane, *Framing Authority*, 68–73.

58. William Webbe, *A Discourse of English Poetrie* (London: John Charlewood for Robert Walley, 1586), sig. D.iii^v–D.iv^r.

59. Gascoigne, *Posies* (1575), ¶¶.iii^v.

60. Timothy Kendall, *Flowers of epigrammes, out of sundrie the moste singular authours selected* (London: John Kingston and John Shepherd, 1577), sig. A5^{r-v}. Martial was seen as especially in need of expurgation—see, for example, the editions of Hadrianus Junius (1568), who wrote that wise readers should run from the obscene epigrams like a dog runs from the crocodiles in the Nile (after getting a drink). On Martial in the Renaissance, see J. P. Sullivan, *Martial: The Unexpected Classic* (Cambridge: Cambridge University Press, 2001), 253–294.

61. Gifford, *Gilloflowers*, sig. I1^v.

62. Thomas Lodge, *The workes of Lucius Annaeus Seneca Newly Inlarged and Corrected* (London: William Stansby, 1620), sig. B1^{r-v}.

63. Thomas Hill, *The Gardeners Labyrinth: Containing a discourse of the Gardeners life* (London: Henry Bynneman, 1577), sig. F4^{r-v}.

64. Ibid., 47.

65. Pigman also notes Grange's "pastiche" of the prefatory letter from Gascoigne's *Flowres* in specific phrases; see his note in *Flowres*, 169 (note 144.10).

66. Grange, *Golden Aphroditis*, sig. N.iii^v.

67. On Zoilus, see Heidi Brayman *Reading Material in Early Modern England: Print, Gender, and Literacy* (Cambridge: Cambridge University Press, 2005), 123; David Carlson, *English Humanist Books: Writers and Patrons, Manuscripts and Prints, 1475–1525* (Toronto: University of Toronto Press, 1993), 227 n. 18, who ties it to the Grammarians' War; on Zoilus and patronage, see H. S. Bennett, *English Books and Readers, 1558–1603* (Cambridge: Cambridge University Press, 1965), 6–10.

68. Grange, *Golden Aphroditis*, sig. N.iii^v.

69. *Collected Works of Erasmus*, vol. 35, *Adages III iv 1 to IV 2 100*, trans. and annotated Denis Drysdall, ed. John N. Grant (Toronto: University of Toronto Press, 2005), 222.

70. Ibid. The proverb also appears in Elizabeth's *Sententiae*, where she quotes directly from Suetonius's *Lives of the Caesars*. Janel Mueller and Joshua Schodel, eds., *Elizabeth I: Translations, 1544–1589* (Chicago: University of Chicago Press, 2009), 366.

71. Jonson continues: "He is an ill prince that so pulls his subjects' feathers as he would not have them grow again; that makes his exchequer a receipt for the spoils of those he governs. No, let him keep his own, not affect his subjects'; strive rather to be called just than powerful." Ben Jonson, *Timber, or Discoveries Made upon Man and Matter*, ed. Felix E. Schelling (Boston: Ginn, 1892), 41.

72. The *OED* suggests that the sense that is now most common (s.v. "carp," 5a: "To talk querulously, censoriously, or captiously; to find fault, cavil") appears rarely before the sixteenth century. Though the primary Latin sense of *carpere* was in reference to plants, *Lewis & Short* notes that it had also come to mean to enjoy or make use of, or, in a negative sense, to gnaw or tear at someone's character, or, on the other hand, to consume completely or destroy; it could also mean to break down into parts or cut into pieces. Charlton T. Lewis and Charles Short, *A Latin Dictionary. Founded on Andrews' edition of Freund's Latin Dictionary. Revised, Enlarged, and in Great Part Rewritten* (Oxford: Clarendon Press, 1879). Each of these senses might be reconsidered in light of the analysis of *carpe diem* poetry in Wendy Beth Hyman, *Impossible Desire and the Limits of Knowledge in Renaissance Poetry* (Oxford: Oxford University Press, 2019).

73. Julia Reinhard Lupton, *Thinking with Shakespeare* (Chicago: University of Chicago Press, 2011), 37. Like Thomas Howell's appeal for patrons to water his soil (Chapter 1), this moment in Grange can be understood in light of the contrast that Garrett Sullivan draws between the "landscape of stewardship" and landscapes of custom and of absolute property in Garrett A. Sullivan Jr., *The Drama of Landscape: Land, Property, and Social Relations on the Early Modern Stage* (Stanford, CA: Stanford University Press, 1998).

74. Grange, *Golden Aphroditis*, sig. N.iii^v.

75. On sensory resonances of violets, see Rebecca Laroche, "Ophelia's Plants and the Death of Violets," in *Ecocritical Shakespeare*, ed. Lynne Bruckner and Dan Brayton (Farnham: Ashgate, 2011), 211–222; and Steven Turner and Rebecca Laroche, "Robert Boyle, Hannah Woolley, and Syrup of Violets," *Notes and Queries* 58.3 (2011): 390–391; and on their earliness, the Duchess of York's question in *Richard II*: "Who are the violets now / That strew the green lap of the newcome spring?"(5.2.46–47).

76. Patricia Akhimie, *Shakespeare and the Cultivation of Difference* (New York: Routledge, 2018), 5–32.

77. Keith Thomas shows the increasing deferral of adult responsibility in sixteenth-century England. Members of the Inns were forced to wait an especially long time to take on the

authority granted to their elders. Keith Thomas, "Age and Authority in Early Modern England," *Proceedings of the British Academy* 62 (1976): 205–248, esp. 208, 219.

78. Roger Ascham, *The Scholemaster* (London: John Day, 1570), sig. H.ii^v.

79. Ascham refers to the ages seventeen to twenty-seven; cited by Thomas in "Age and Authority," 220. On the framing of verse by Elizabethan poets prior to Spenser, through the lens of Spenser's self-fashioning against their models, see Richard Helgerson, "The New Poet Presents Himself: Spenser and the Idea of a Literary Career," *PMLA* 93.5 (1978): 893–911.

80. Rebecca Bushnell, *A Culture of Teaching*, 73–116; Helgerson, *Elizabethan Prodigals*; Helgerson, "The New Poet."

81. Katharine Wilson, *Fictions of Authorship in Late Elizabethan Narratives* (Oxford: Oxford University Press, 2006), 32–36.

82. Whetstone, *Rocke*, sig. ¶.ii^v.

83. This connection will be further explored in the second branch, following Chapter 4.

84. Readers are ultimately responsible for their own (deferred) pleasure: "but if the blastes be loathed, the blossoms shall not bee liked: for though the one be in youre hands, yet the other are in my hold: and if you like not the coulour of the Fethers, you shall never tast the carving of the Fowle." Austen Saker, *Narbonus: The Laberynth of libertie* (London: Richard Jones, 1580), 126. George Pettie frames his work as fruits of earlier times, pairing it with work of the present moment and asking his readers to use their judgment accordingly: "Thus have I sent you in that booke some fruites of my former folly, and in this letter the profession of my present fayth, desiring you to use the one to your honest pleasure, and to follow the other to your godly profite" (Pettie, *A petite Pallace*, sig. A.iii^v).

85. John Florio, *Florio His firste Fruites which yeelde familiar speech, merie Proverbes, wittie Sentences, and golden sayings* (London: Thomas Dawson for Thomas Woodcock, 1578), sigs. *4^v, **2^r.

86. Breton signs his early publications from "his Chamber in Holborne," which also implies geographical proximity to the Inns.

87. Nicholas Breton, *The workes of a young wyt* (London: Thomas Dawson, 1577), sig. A.iii^r.

88. Hyder Rollins suggests that *Workes* was composed slightly prior to *Fancie*, though both reached the press at about the same time. Hyder E. Rollins, "Nicholas Breton's *The Works of a Young Wit* (1577)," *Studies in Philology* 33.2 (1936): 119–133.

89. See the discussions in William Turner, *A new Herball, wherein are conteyned the names of Herbes* (London: Steven Mierdman, 1551), sig. Evi^r ("Ther are ii. kyndes of otes: the one is called in English comonly, otes: and the other . . . wild otes"); and Rembert Dodoens, *A niewe herball, or historie of plantes*, trans. Henry Lyte (Antwerp: Printed by Henry Loë for Gerard Dewes, 1578), 467.

90. Levinus Lemnius, *An Herbal for the Bible*, trans. Thomas Newton (London: Edmund Bollifant, 1587), sigs. Q1^v–Q2^r.

91. This aspect of the Primordium echoes Gascoigne's epistle to the Reverend Divines, where he defends including chokeweeds among the more wholesome grains of the *Posies*: "I coulde aswell sowe good graine, as graynes or draffe. And I thought not meete (beeing intermingled as they were) to cast away a whole bushell of good seede, for two or three graynes of Darnell or Cockle" (Pigman, ed., *Flowres*, 361). As in the similar phrase quoted above (on trading a bushel of good will for a pint of peevish choler), Gascoigne's logic is quantitative, a mathematical rationalization of what is an acceptable loss.

92. Breton's references to the lightness of his oats also suggests the "*tenui . . . avena*" of Eclogue 1's opening verses.

93. Thomas Heywood, *A pleasant conceited Comedie, Wherein is shewed, how a man may chuse a good Wife from a bad* (London: Matthew Law, 1602), sig. C1^r; Thomas Dekker and John Webster, *West-ward hoe* (London: John Hodget, 1607), sig. F1^v; and *The London Prodigall* (London: Thomas Creede for Nathaniel Butter, 1605), sig. B4^r.

94. Thomas Becon, *A pleasaunt newe Nosegaye, full of many godly and swete floures* (London: John Mayler for John Gough, 1543), sig. E.iii^r. This is also the earliest usage cited in the *OED*.

95. Choke seeds like cockle and darnel carried further moral and proverbial currency. The choking effect of wild oats on barley is offered as an analogy for the pestilence of a feigned friend in Francis Meres's *Palladis Tamia*: "As Choak-weede is an enemy to Ciches and Orobos, as Cockle is hurtfull unto Wheate, as wild Otes is noysom unto Barley, as Henbane is mortall unto Lentilles, and all these do kill by embracing: so the friendship of some is more pestilent, then their enmitie." Francis Meres, *Palladis tamia, Wits treasury* (London: Peter Short for Cuthbert Burby, 1598), fol. 126^r (citing Pliny's *Natural History*, bk. 18, chap. 45).

96. To the contrary, "neyther age nor nature bring vertues upon their backe," he says. "For vertues are habits, which are gotten by many actions of our owne." Christopher Fetherston, *A Dialogue agaynst light, lewde, and lascivious dauncing* (London: Thomas Dawson, 1582), sigs. B8^v–C1^r. Fetherston was also a translator of Calvin and François Hotman.

97. Fetherston's dedication to William Lewin, a judge and member of Elizabeth's high commission for ecclesiastical matters, frames necessary moral correction in the language of uprooting: "To whom shall the servant, who hath espied weedes in the fieldes complayne, if not to the maister whose the fielde is? And whom shold I rather certify of this thing then you, who hath authoritie to plucke up suche weeds by the rootes." Ibid., sig. ¶5^r.

98. Amy Tigner, *Literature and the Renaissance Garden from Elizabeth I to Charles II* (Farnham: Ashgate, 2012), 102.

99. On soil amendment, see Dolan, *Digging the Past*, 14–44; Hillary Eklund, "Introduction," in *Ground-Work: English Renaissance Literature and Soil Science*, ed. Hillary Eklund (Pittsburgh: Duquesne University Press, 2017). Joan Thirsk notes that oats were often sown as the first crop on ley ground newly ploughed. See Joan Thirsk, "Farming Techniques," in *The Agrarian History of England and Wales*, vol. 4, *1500–1640*, ed. Joan Thirsk (Cambridge: Cambridge University Press, 1967), 161–199, at 166.

100. See Catherine Bates, *Masculinity, Gender, and Identity in the English Renaissance Lyric* (Cambridge: Cambridge University Press, 2007), 28–88; and Stephen Guy-Bray, *Against Reproduction: Where Renaissance Texts Come From* (Toronto: University of Toronto Press, 2009), 144–175, on the "poetics of abjection," especially in Milton. We might also draw a connection to the accounts of subjectivity in relation to self-shattering and to vulnerability as articulated, respectively, by Rebecca Lemon, *Addiction and Devotion in Early Modern England* (Philadelphia: University of Pennsylvania Press, 2018); and by James Kuzner in *Open Subjects* (Edinburgh: University of Edinburgh Press, 2012).

Chapter 4

1. Isabella Whitney, [*A sweet nosgay, or pleasant posye*] (London: Richard Jones, 1573), sig. A.vi^r. The only known copy of the octavo survives without a title page; the title by which the collection is generally known is taken from the first heading following the preliminaries (sig.

B.ii[r], where Whitney's versified "Phylosophicall Flowers" begin). All parenthetical citations refer to this edition. The last several decades have seen lively scholarly interest in Whitney's poetry, spurred by Betty Travitsky's foundational critical and editorial work. See Betty S. Travitsky, "'The wyll and testament' of Isabella Whitney', *English Literary Renaissance*, 10 (1980): 76–95; "'The lady doth protest": Protest in the popular writings of Renaissance Englishwomen," *English Literary Renaissance* 14 (1984): 255–83; and "Isabella Whitney," in *The Early Modern Englishwoman: A Facsimile Library of Essential Works*, ser. I, pt. 2, vol. 10, ed. Susanne Woods, Betty S. Travistky, and Patrick Cullen (London: Routledge, 2001), ix–xi. The body of scholarship on Whitney since (cited in their particulars in this chapter's notes) has focused on labor and authorship, on the spatial and legal politics of Whitney's rhetorical and imaginative strategies, and on the importance to her poetry of craft practices in printing house and household.

2. "Hugh Platt" of London is recorded as admitted May 4 (1571/2), *The Records of the Honorable Society of Lincoln's Inn*, vol. 1 (London: Lincoln's Inn, 1896), 79. The open space now known as Lincoln's Inn Fields was not laid out until the seventeenth century; the fields that existed in that space adjacent to Lincoln's Inn were in the hands of the Crown. "Lincoln's Inn Fields: Introduction," in *Survey of London*, vol. 3, *St. Giles-in-The-Fields*, pt. 1, *Lincoln's Inn Fields*, ed. W. Edward Riley and Laurence Gomme (London: London County Council, 1912), 3–22. Whitney devotes a passage in the "Wyll" included in the *Nosgay* to the Inns, specifically leaving them gentlemen ("a youthfull roote, / full of Activytie"), books, and means of recreation (sig. E.vi[r]). On Geoffrey Whitney (better known as the author of *A Choice of Emblemes and Other Devises* [Leiden, 1586]) and his likely association with Thavies Inn or Furnival's Inn, see Andrew King, "Whitney, Geoffrey (1548?–1600/01)," *ODNB*. George Mainwairing, Isabella Whitney's dedicatee, was also linked to the Inns. Carolyn Sale reads Whitney's engagement with the law of property as a retort to this community from which she was excluded. Carolyn Sale, "The Literary Thing: The Imaginary Holding of Isabella Whitney's 'Wyll' to London (1573)," in *The Oxford Handbook of English Law and Literature, 1500–1700*, ed. Lorna Hutson (Oxford: Oxford University Press, 2017), 431–447, at 435. For an analysis of the social and literary significance of Whitney's encounter with Plat, see the introduction to Richard J. Panofsky, ed., *The Floures of Philosophie (1572) by Hugh Plat and A Sweet Nosgay (1573) and The Copy of a Letter (1567) by Isabella Whitney* (Delmar, NY: Scholars' Facsimiles and Reprints, 1982).

3. In this way, Whitney also invokes the paradoxical principle of "Virescit vulnere virtus" (Virtue flourishes with a wound), discussed in Chapter 2; and in Juliet Fleming, "The Renaissance Collage: Signcutting and Signsewing," *Journal of Medieval and Early Modern Studies* 45.3 (2015): 443–456; and in Whitney Trettien's essay in the same volume, discussed below.

4. On the significance of the common in sixteenth-century England, see Neil Rhodes, *Common: The Development of Literary Culture in Sixteenth-Century England* (Oxford: Oxford University Press, 2018). On its importance for Whitney, see Crystal Bartolovich, "'Optimism of the Will': Isabella Whitney and Utopia," *Journal of Medieval and Early Modern Studies* 39.2 (2009): 407–432; Stephanie Elsky, *Custom, Common Law, and the Constitution of English Literature* (Oxford: Oxford University Press, 2020), 133–158; Sale, "The Literary Thing," 431–447.

5. Trettien shows how this kind of mixing and patching was often women's work, for example, as mending, culling, or distilling. Whitney Trettien, "Isabella Whitney's Slips: Textile Labor, Gendered Authorship, and the Early Modern Miscellany," *Journal of Medieval and Early Modern Studies* 45.3 (2015): 505–521. On slips and embroidery, compare the work of Bess of Hardwick and Mary Queen of Scots, in Santina M. Levey, *Elizabethan Treasures: The Hardwick*

Hall Textiles (New York: National Trust, distributed by Harry N. Abrams, 1998); and Nicole LaBouff, "Embroidery and Information Management: The Needlework of Mary Queen of Scots and Bess of Hardwick Reconsidered," *Huntington Library Quarterly* 81.3 (2018): 315–358. On Jones, see Michelle O'Callaghan, "'My Printer Must, Haue Somwhat to His Share': Isabella Whitney, Richard Jones, and Crafting Books," *Women's Writing* 26.1 (2019): 15–34; Kirk Melnikoff, "Jones's Pen and Marlowe's Socks: Richard Jones, Print Culture, and the Beginnings of English Dramatic Literature," *Studies in Philology* 102 (2005): 184–209; and Megan Heffernan in *Making the Miscellany: Poetry, Print, and the History of the Book in Early Modern England* (Philadelphia: University of Pennsylvania Press, 2021), 54–88.

6. On Whitney's strategies of authorization, see Wendy Wall, *The Imprint of Gender: Authorship and Publication in the English Renaissance* (Ithaca, NY: Cornell University Press, 1993), 279–340; and, in a different form, Wendy Wall, "Isabella Whitney and the Female Legacy," *ELH* 58.1 (1991): 35–62; as well as Laurie Ellinghausen, "Literary Property and the Single Woman in Isabella Whitney's *A Sweet Nosgay*," *Studies in English Literature, 1500–1900* 45.1 (2005): 1–22.

7. On this tradition, see A. Bartlett Giamatti, *The Earthly Paradise and the Renaissance Epic* (Princeton, NJ: Princeton University Press, 1966). On the connections of the *hortus conclusus* to the bodies of women, see Amy Tigner, *Literature and the Renaissance Garden from Elizabeth I to Charles II* (Farnham: Ashgate, 2012), 113–158; Frances E. Dolan, *Digging the Past* (Philadelphia: University of Pennsylvania Press, 2020), 146; Richard Burt and John Michael Archer, eds., *Enclosure Acts* (Ithaca, NY: Cornell University Press, 1994). On the enclosure of women's bodies, see Peter Stallybrass, "Patriarchal Territories: The Body Enclosed," in *Rewriting the Renaissance: The Discourses of Sexual Difference in Early Modern Europe*, ed. Margaret W. Ferguson, Maureen Quilligan, and Nancy J. Vickers (Chicago: University of Chicago Press, 1986), 123–142. For a richly historicist account of women's relationship to land and property, see Pamela S. Hammons, "The Gendered Imagination of Real Property in Renaissance England," in *Gender, Sexuality, and Material Objects in Renaissance Verse* (Burlington, VT: Ashgate, 2010), 115–136.

8. In this way, Whitney's waywardness echoes Juliet's abortive unhousing, discussed above in Branch 1.

9. Wall, *Imprint of Gender*, 300–307.

10. Hugh Plat, *Floures of Philosophie* (London: Francis Coldock and Henry Bynneman, 1581), sig. A.5^r. The phrase is printed in the same location in the edition of 1572 (see Panofsky, ed., *The Floures of Philosophie*.) The saying also appears in Anthony Munday's conclusion to the second part of *Zelauto* (London: John Charlewood, 1580), 104; and as a proverbial translation of "De petit petit" in Randle Cotgrave's *Dictionarie of the French and English Tongues* (London: Adam Islip, 1611), s.v. "petit."

11. Plat, *Floures* (1581), sig. M6^r.

12. Compare Wendy Wall's discussion of John Chamberlain's use of "license" to attack Mary Wroth, who (he writes) "takes great libertie or rather licence to traduce whom she please." Wendy Wall, "Isabella Whitney," 37.

13. Bartolovich, "Optimism of the Will," 415. Bartolovich argues that it represents a temporal utopia in which the goods of London are redistributed in a "collective inheritance for all its citizens." Sarah Hogan further develops the spatial dimensions of this utopian reading in *Other Englands: Utopia, Capital, and Empire in an Age of Transition* (Stanford, CA: Stanford University Press, 2018), 122–138. Carolyn Sale places Plat's conception of literary and

territorial property in the context of legal understandings of use and possession ("The Literary Thing," 445–447).

14. As Frances Dolan shows, hedges never only enclose territory; they also generate new spaces and spur new forms of relation. See Dolan, *Digging the Past*, 122–161.

15. Plat, *Floures* (1572), sig. A4ᵛ.

16. This connection was well established: labyrinths featured in romance narratives, and some Renaissance garden mazes featured a statue of Venus at the center. Cf. *Hypnerotomachia Poliphili* (Venice, 1499); and Cosimo de' Medici's Villa Castello in Florence. Claudia Lazzaro, *The Italian Renaissance Garden* (New Haven, CT: Yale University Press, 1990), 174–176.

17. *Jus abutendi*, a prerogative associated in later legal traditions with outright ownership or dominion. Carolyn Sale argues that Whitney's engagement with Plat's garden does not amount to *fructus*, but I find her mode of consumption to be transformative enough to qualify. Recent work by Elsky (*Custom*) and Sale ("The Literary Thing") gives important legal context to Whitney's and Plat's tactics around property. My reading of Whitney's claims to common property is indebted to Bartolovich, who, challenging a liberal feminist tradition that reads Whitney's literary tactics as a claim of authorial property, argues we would better understand the *Nosgay* in light of a Marxist-feminist assertion of collective goods.

18. Leah Price observes the frequency with which this point is made in an assessment of the state of the field in "Reading: The State of the Discipline," *Book History* 7 (2004): 303–320.

19. Roger Chartier, *The Order of Books* (Stanford, CA: Stanford University Press, 1992), viii.

20. Michel de Certeau, *The Practice of Everyday Life* (Berkeley: University of California Press, 1984), 174.

21. Consider also the significance of "spoliation" as a literary tactic; on Renaissance *spolia* and poetic reuse, see Andrew Hui, *The Poetics of Ruin in Renaissance Literature* (New York: Fordham University Press, 2017). We should also acknowledge the violent turn in de Certeau's language, and the fine line in his account between the poaching of the dispossessed and the vagabond and the appropriation of the colonizer.

22. As she writes,

> If any other thing be lackt
>   in thee, I wysh them looke
> For there it is: I little brought
>   but no thing from thee tooke.
>   (sig. E.vʳ)

23. *De Doctrina Christiana*, trans. R. P. H. Green (Oxford: Oxford University Press, 1996), 125–126.

24. See Kathy Eden, *Friends Hold All Things in Common: Tradition, Intellectual Property, and the Adages of Erasmus* (New Haven, CT: Yale University Press, 2001), 22–24.

25. While Northbrooke's framework reflects other precedents (notably William Alley's *The Poore Mans Librarie* [London: John Day, 1565]), he also signals an affiliation with other mid-Elizabethan flower books. His dedication echoes the prefatory materials from poetic and miscellaneous works published in the same years (like Gascoigne's) through its use of humility topoi and in the more specific reference to "certayne of my freendes" whose "earnest request" to publish he "wel . . . could not denye." John Northbrooke, *Spiritus est vicarius Christi in terra.*

The poore mans garden, wherein are flowers of the scriptures (London: John Kingston for William Williamson, 1571), sig. A3ʳ; this passage is marked with a manicule beside it in Cambridge University Library Syn.8.57.71. Northbrooke also closely echoes the language ubiquitous in the period for describing (and potentially dissuading) detractors, asking for his patron's defense against "momishe affections of bityng zoilous persons" and other bad readers (ibid.).

26. In a 1571 pamphlet, Knell linked recent devastating floods to God's punishment of enclosers and engrossers—"against them that joygne house to house and lande to lande (till there be no more place left for the poore)." Thomas Knell Jr., *A declaration of such tempestious, and outragious Fluddes, as hath been in divers places of England* (London: William How for John Allde and William Pickering, 1571), sig. A.iiiʳ.

27. Thomas Knell Jr., epistle, in Northbrooke, *Garden*, sig. A4ʳ.

28. Ibid., sig. A4ᵛ.

29. John Northbrooke, *Spiritus est vicarious Christi in terra. A treatise wherein Dicing, Dauncing, Vaine playes or Enterluds with other idle pastimes . . . are reproved* (London: Henry Bynneman for George Bishop, 1577), sig. A.iiiʳ. On Northbrooke's *Treatise*, see Patrick Collinson, *The Birthpangs of Protestant England: Religious and Cultural Change in the Sixteenth and Seventeenth Centuries* (London: Macmillan, 1988), 112–113.

30. Philip Stubbes, *Anatomie of Abuses* (London: Richard Jones, 1595), 57. See also the discussion in Paula Henderson, *Tudor House and Garden* (New Haven, CT: Yale University Press, 2006), 144.

31. Knell's critique of "private commodity" (sig. B1ʳ) echoes other complaints about enclosure, where the phrase marks violations of the values of the common or the commonwealth. For example, residents of Hingham in 1539–1540 complained that their landlord, in infringing on common pastureland, only regarded his "private lucre and peculyere commodyte . . . to the decay and utter dystruccone of the Comon welthe of the seid Towne." Cited in Anthony Fletcher and Diarmaid MacCulloch, *Tudor Rebellions*, 5th ed. (London: Routledge, 2008), 84. Similar phrasing appears in Holinshed's account of Henry VIII's attempts to counter these dynamics—in particular, nobles and gentlemen intent on turning arable ground to pasture, engrossing and enclosing land, and selling at prices "as might stand most with their owne private commoditie." Raphael Holinshed, *Chronicles of England, Scotlande, and Irelande*, vol. 6 (London: Henry Denham, 1587), 862.

32. Knell, in Northbrooke, *Garden*, sig. B1ʳ.

33. Rebecca Laroche, *Medical Authority and Englishwomen's Herbal Texts, 1550–1650* (Farnham: Ashgate, 2009), 151–166.

34. "Epistle" in Lyte, trans., *A Niewe Herball* (1578), sig.*3ʳ. Cited in Laroche, *Medical Authority*, 147.

35. On the social and cultural meanings of neighborliness, see Naomi Tadmor, "Friends and Neighbours in Early Modern England: Biblical Translations and Social Norms," in *Love, Friendship and Faith in Europe, 1300–1800,* ed. Laura Gowing, Michael Hunter, and Miri Rubin (London: Palgrave Macmillan, 2005), 150–176; Keith Wrightson, "The 'Decline of Neighbourliness' Revisited," in *Local Identities in Late Medieval and Early Modern England*, ed. Norman L. Jones and Daniel Woolf (London: Palgrave Macmillan, 2007), 19–49. As Dolan observes, hedges, in addition to enclosing, could also provide the poor with a common medicinal resource, through access to the plants growing within and beneath them (*Digging the Past*, 153).

36. Historians of medicine have shown how printed medical books saw rapidly widening audiences in early modern England. See Paul Slack, "Mirrors of Health and Treasures of Poor Men: The Uses of the Vernacular Medical Literature of Tudor England," in *Health, Medicine, and Mortality in the Sixteenth-Century*, ed. Charles Webster (Cambridge: Cambridge University Press, 1979), 237–274; Mary Fissell, "The Marketplace of Print," in *Medicine and the Market in England and Its Colonies*, ed. Mark S. R. Jenner and Patrick Wallis (Basingstoke: Palgrave Macmillan, 2007), 108–132; Deborah Harkness, *The Jewel House: Elizabethan London and the Scientific Revolution* (New Haven, CT: Yale University Press, 2007), chap. 3, on medical books; Andrew Wear, "The Popularization of Medicine in Early Modern England," in *The Popularization of Medicine, 1650-1850*, ed. Roy Porter (London: Routledge, 1992), 17–41. The project of popularization met special urgency at times of plague, and books with titles like *The Treasure of Poore Men* (1560) and *The Poor Mans Jewel* (1578) advertised access to techniques of preservation. On access to practitioners and the regulation of medical practice, see especially Margaret Pelling, *Medical Conflicts in Early Modern London: Patronage, Physicians, and Irregular Practitioners, 1550-1640*, with Frances White (Oxford: Clarendon Press, 2003); Margaret Pelling and Charles Webster, "Medical Practitioners," in Webster, *Health*, 165–236.

37. William Bullein, *A dialogue bothe pleasaunte and pietifull wherein is a goodly regimente against the fever pestilence* (London: John Kingston, 1564), sig. A2ᵛ. Laroche suggests that Whitney's Medicus may draw specifically from the Medicus who appears in Bullein's dialogue (*Medical Authority*, 162–163).

38. Herbal "publication," in this polemic sense, echoes Tottel's rhetorical framing of *Songes and Sonettes* (1557) as making public the poems "which the ungentle horders up of such treasure have heretofore envied thee." *Songes and Sonettes* ([London]: Richard Tottel, 1557), "To the reder."

39. Ellinghausen, "Single Woman," 5. As a woman out of service, Whitney is both "at liberty and at risk" (O'Callaghan, "'My Printer,'" 29). On publication and feminine itinerary, see also Patricia Phillippy, "The Maid's Lawful Liberty: Service, the Household, and 'Mother B' in Isabella Whitney's *A Sweet Nosegay*," *Modern Philology* 95.4 (1998): 439–462.

40. Scholars who have made arguments about patterns across the *Nosgay* as a whole include Laurie Ellinghausen ("Single Woman," 3) and Meredith Anne Skura, who reads the first two parts of the *Nosgay* against one another, focusing on how the contrast frames the text's autobiographical dimensions (*Tudor Autobiography* [Chicago: University of Chicago Press, 2008], 159).

41. To the other, she worries that

> none can tell, if you be well,
>   nor where you doo so turne:
> Which makes me feare, that I shall heare
>   your health appaired is:
> And oft I dread, that you are dead,
>   or somthyng goeth amys.
>   (sig. C.viiʳ)

42. Hogan observes that Whitney's "Wyll" follows a "distributive logic" that effects a horizontal dispersal of goods across London rather than following a patrilineal line of descent

(*Other Englands*, 130). On the strange temporality of willing, see Wall, *Imprint of Gender*, 298–302.

43. The word "store" recurs thirteen times in the "Wyll," where it powers an image of the bustling city in line with the resource-logic of humanist *copia*: stores of goods to fuel future use, like a garden full fraught with virtuous flowers. When "store" appears in Whitney's earlier *Copy of a Letter* (London: Richard Jones, 1567), it names the latent utility of texts: there, she requests "when you shall this letter have / let it be kept in store" (sig. A.v^r); or, of the wisdom of the lesson:

> Trust not a man at the fyrst sight,
>   but trye him well before:
> I wish al Maids within their brests
>   to kepe this thing in store.
>   (sig. A.vii^v)

In her "Admonition" to young gentlewomen, "store" names an art of false tears that suitors learn from Ovid, who "within his Arte of love, / doth teach them this same knacke," and she asks, "Why have ye such deceit in store? / have you such crafty wile?" (sig. A.vi^r).

44. On ideas about health and the environment, see Andrew Wear, "Making Sense of Health and the Environment in Early Modern England," in *Medicine in Society*, ed. Andrew Wear (Cambridge: Cambridge University Press, 2010), 119–148. On plague in London's environment in particular, see Margaret Pelling, "Skirting the City? Disease, Social Change and Divided Households in the Seventeenth Century," in *Londinopolis: Essays in the Cultural and Social History of Early Modern London*, ed. Paul Griffiths and Mark S. R. Jenner (Manchester: Manchester University Press, 2000), 154–175.

45. Most other examples of the idiom prior to 1570 appear in translations by Arthur Golding, curiously: in one case, from his *Metamorphoses*, describing the evasive maneuvers of a hunted beast; in another example, from a sermon by Calvin, describing the actions of an untrustworthy friend. We might imagine the evasive maneuvers of Whitney and other single women as the "windlasse" path of Golding's hunted quarry, who, giving the slip, turns "as swift about as spinning wheele he whips." Arthur Golding, trans., *The .xv. Bookes of P. Ovidius Naso, entytuled Metamorphosis* (London: William Seres, 1567), fol. 94. The *OED*'s first example of the usage of "slip" in this phrase is also from 1567: s.v. "slip," n.5, III.8.a.

46. Edward Hake, *Newes out of Powles Churchyarde* (London: John Charlewood and Richard Jones, 1579), sig. G.ii^r. First published by Henry Denham in 1567. See also the anonymous rebuttal, *A Letter sent by the Maydens of London, to the virtuous Matrones and Mistresses of the same, in the defense of their lawfull Libertie* (London: Henry Bynneman for Thomas Hacket, 1567). Patricia Phillippy shows the importance of Hake's urban satire and the rebuttal to Whitney's text in "Lawful Liberty" (441). Charlewood and Jones acquired from Denham the right to print Hake's satire later in the 1570s before publishing the 1579 edition.

47. As Wall notes, the word encompassed the circulation that equally characterized "publication, travel, and harlotry," implanting in the *Nosgay* a concern with the dangers of circulation in public ("Isabella Whitney," 48). Phillippy links both the word and Whitney's travel beyond domestic space to her other "tropes of contagion" ("Lawful Liberty," 168).

48. John Gerard, *The herball, or generall Historie of Plants* (London: Adam Islip, Joyce Norton, and Richard Whitaker, 1633), 260.

49. The violence of scattering "abroad" further aligns publication and dispersal with the form of the blazon, a form of praise that, as Nancy Vickers shows, links the publication of women's bodies to the violence of scattering. Nancy Vickers, "Diana Described: Scattered Woman and Scattered Rhyme," *Critical Inquiry* 8.2 (1981): 265–279.

50. Questions about the portability and longevity of plant virtues were of great significance to those involved in the global traffic in plant materials. Nicolás Monardes, for example, offers advice on how to preserve the virtue of China root from the East Indies, by keeping it warm "for that therwith it doeth preserve the vertue the better, and dureth longer tyme, before it be corrupted" (*Joyfull Newes out of the newfound world*, trans. John Frampton, rev. ed. [London: William Norton, 1580], fol. 14ʳ); or, on the freshness of Mechoacan (see fol. 26ᵛ). For related debates on the power of mineral spring water when packaged and removed from the source, see Lorraine Daston and Katharine Park, *Wonders and the Order of Nature, 1150–1750* (New York: Zone Books, 2001), 138 n. 13.

51. Thomas Becon, [*The flour of godly praiers*] (London: John Day, 1550), epistle. Remarkably prolific, Becon was also the author of a *Nosegay*, discussed below.

52. Elsky, *Custom*, 141–150.

53. Compare the version of "taking" in Whitney's receipt to the prescription that Arthur Golding gives for the administering of his translation of the *Metamorphoses*, discussed in Chapter 2.

54. Thomas Elyot, *The Dictionary of syr Thomas Eliot knyght* (London: Thomas Berthelet, 1538), s.v. "fasciculus."

55. N.B., *A smale handfull of fragrant flowers* (London: Richard Jones, 1575).

56. Plat, *Floures*, sig. A.iiᵛ.

57. Carla Mazzio shows how Shakespeare riffs on Bellot's catalogs alongside print culture and poetry in *Love's Labour's Lost* in "The Melancholy of Print: *Love's Labour's Lost*," in *Historicism, Psychoanalysis, and Early Modern Culture*, ed. Carla Mazzio and Douglas Trevor (London: Routledge, 2000), 186–227. See also Anne Lake Prescott, "Elizabeth's Garden of Virtue: Jacques Bellot's Sonnet Sequence for the Queen," *ANQ* 5.2–3 (1992): 122–124.

58. Jacques Bellot, *The Englishe Scholemaister* (London: Henry Dizle, 1580), sig. F4ʳ. The repetition of "posy" in Bellot's English title renders the French "bouquet" and "devise" respectively. This nosegay is followed by a "Salatte of love, conteyning the posies of things that are commonly put in a Salatte" (sig. G5ʳ).

59. Isaiah 40:6. As given on the title page of *An epitaph, or funerall inscription, upon the godlie life and death of the right worshipfull Maister William Lambe Esquire* (London: Henry Denham for Thomas Turner, [1580]).

60. Thomas Becon, *A pleasant newe Nosegaye, full of many godly and swete floures, lately gathered by Theodore Basille* (London: John Mayler for John Gough, 1543), sig. A1ᵛ.

61. "The Ballet of Ballettes of Solomon, called in Latin, *Canticum Canticorum*," 1:10. *The holie Bible* (London: Richard Jugge, 1568).

62. For example, in Henry Finch's 1615 gloss: "Christs dwelling in her heart by faith, which maketh her both gracious, and sweete as a nosegay of mirrh in a weomans bosome." Henry Finch, *An exposition of the Song of Solomon* (London: John Beale, 1615), sig. C3ʳ.

63. Gaspar Loarte, *The godly garden of Gethsemani furnished with wholesome fruits* (London: [William. Carter], 1576). Within, the book is introduced as both the fateful garden of its title and as the Solomonic nosegay, "a posie of the bitter paynes and sorowes that Christe suffered for hir and hir faythfull children" (sig. *4ʳ).

64. St. Bernard of Clairvaux, *Sermones in Cantica Canticorum*, 43.3. Cited in Erich Auerbach, *Literary Language and Its Public in Late Latin Antiquity and the Middle Ages*, trans. Ralph Manheim (Princeton, NJ: Princeton University Press, 1993), 74. For another English Catholic example, see Matthew Kellison, *A myrrhine posie of the bitter dolours of Christ his passion* (Douai: By Laurence Kellam, 1639), sig. C2ʳ.

65. Jones assembled a number of poetic collections beginning in the 1560s and frequently couched these gatherings in the language of plants. On Whitney and Jones's collaboration, see Melnikoff, "Jones's Pen and Marlowe's Socks" and "Richard Jones"; O'Callaghan, "'My Printer,'" 20; Lynette McGrath, *Subjectivity and Women's Poetry in Early Modern England* (Aldershot: Ashgate, 2002), 123–133; Robert J. Fehrenbach, "Isabella Whitney and the Popular Miscellanies of Richard Jones," *Cahiers Élisabéthains* 19 (1981): 85–87.

66. On possible earlier editions, including an extant fragment, see Hyder E. Rollins ed., *A Handful of Pleasant Delights (1584) by Clement Robinson and Divers Others* (Cambridge, MA: Harvard University Press, 1924), x–xv.

67. Michelle O'Callaghan suggests that Jones's publication of N.B.'s *Smale Handfull of Fragrant Flowers* in 1575 might have been inspired by Whitney's *Nosgay* ("'My Printer,'" 26.) On authorship, see Hyder E. Rollins, "*A Small Handful of Fragrant Flowers* (1575)," *Huntington Library Bulletin* 9 (1936): 27–35, who dismisses the attribution to Nicholas Breton that survives in the STC. In defense of Breton's authorship, see Jean Robertson, "Nicholas Breton and 'A Smale Handfull of Fragrant Flowers,'" *Modern Language Review* 37.3 (1942): 359–363.

68. N.B., *Handfull* (1575), sig. A.iiiʳ.

69. Ibid., sig. A.iiᵛ.

70. Clement Robinson, *A handefull of pleasant delites, containing sundrie new sonets and delectable histories* (London: Richard Jones, 1584), sig. A2ʳ.

71. Not quite everything is given a named tune, though the title page reads "Newly devised to the newest tunes that are now in use, to be sung: everie Sonet orderly pointed to his proper Tune."

72. Robinson, *Handefull*, sig. A2ʳ.

73. On fantasies of and recipes for winter blooms, see Rebecca Laroche, "Roses in Winter: Recipe Ecologies and Shakespeare's Sonnets," in *Ecological Approaches to Early Modern Texts: A Field Guide to Reading and Teaching*, ed. Jennifer Munroe, Edward J. Geisweidt, and Lynne Bruckner (London: Routledge, 2016), 51–60.

74. Robinson, *Handefull*, sig. A3ᵛ.

75. George Gascoigne, *A Hundreth sundrie Flowres bounde up in one small Poesie* (London: [Henry Bynneman and Henry Middleton] for Richard Smith, 1573), sig. C.ivᵛ.

76. Lorna Hutson, *The Usurer's Daughter* (London: Routledge, 1994), 116–129. On the rich resonance of scent in the period, see Holly Dugan, *The Ephemeral History of Perfume: Scent and Sense in Early Modern England* (Baltimore: Johns Hopkins University Press, 2011).

77. On the multiplicity of Whitney's audience, see Boyd M. Berry, "'We Are Not All Alyke or of Complexion One': Truism and Isabella Whitney's Multiple Readers," in *Renaissance Papers 2000*, ed. T. H. Howard-Hill and Philip Rollinson (Rochester, NY: Camden House, 2000), 13–23, at 17; and Ann Rosalind Jones, who observes that Whitney is "attempting to win multiple literary admirers," of both sexes (*The Currency of Eros: Women's Love Lyric in Europe, 1540–1620* [Bloomington: Indiana University Press, 1990], 47–48).

78. O'Callaghan, "'My Printer,'" 23.

79. Nicholas Breton, *The workes of a young wyt* (London: Thomas Dawson, 1577), sig. A.ii^{r-v}.

80. C. Thimelthorpe, *A Short Inventory of certayne Idle Inventions: The Fruites of a close and secret Garden of great ease, and litle pleasure* (London: Thomas Marsh, 1581), sigs. A.iii^r-A.iv^r.

81. On English ideas of complexion, see Mary Floyd-Wilson, *English Ethnicity and Race in Early Modern Drama* (Cambridge: Cambridge University Press, 2003), esp. 23–47; Gail Kern Paster, *The Body Embarrassed: Drama and the Disciplines of Shame in Early Modern England* (Ithaca, NY: Cornell University Press, 1993); and Steven Shapin, "Why Was 'Custom a Second Nature' in Early Modern Medicine?," *Bulletin of the History of Medicine* 93.1 (2019): 1–26. On the fate of Galen in early modern Europe, see Mary Lindemann, *Medicine and Society in Early Modern Europe* (Cambridge: Cambridge University Press, 1999), 17–25, 84–90; Vivian Nutton, "The Fortunes of Galen," in *The Cambridge Companion to Galen*, ed. R. J. Hankinson (Cambridge: Cambridge University Press, 2008), 355–390.

82. Levinus Lemnius, *The Touchstone of Complexions*, trans. Thomas Newton (London: Thomas Marsh, 1576), sig. N4^v.

83. Ibid., sig. N5^r.

84. Michael Marder, *Plant-Thinking: A Philosophy of Vegetal Life* (New York: Columbia University Press, 2013) 107–111.

85. Michael Warner, *Publics and Counterpublics* (Princeton, NJ: Princeton University Press, 2002). Whitney's formulation is also not quite what Benedict Anderson will call print capitalism, though it registers some of the simultaneity Anderson attributes to that social formation. On these points, see the wide range of scholarship that emerged from the Making Publics project, including the special issue "Printing Publics," ed. Patricia Fumerton, *Early Modern Culture* 8 (2010); Bronwen Wilson and Paul Yachnin, eds., *Making Publics in Early Modern Europe: People, Things, Forms of Knowledge* (London: Routledge, 2011); and Marlene Eberhart and Paul Yachnin, eds., *Forms of Association* (Amherst: University of Massachusetts Press, 2015). The rational liberty that Habermas ascribes to the Enlightenment public sphere sits uneasily with the tangle of transactions and obligations that links Whitney's imagined readership. For a nuanced analysis of the relation of early modern English textual culture to Habermas's conception of the public sphere, see Mark Rose, "The Public Sphere and the Emergence of Copyright: The Stationers' Company, *Areopagitica*, and the Statute of Anne," in *Privilege and Property: Essays on the History of Copyright*, ed. Ronan Deazley, Martin Kretschmer, and Lionel Bently (Cambridge: Open Book Publishers, 2010), 67–88.

Branch: How to Read Like a Pig

1. The pig is frequently collectivized, as it is here, as a stand-in for the commons or populace as such. In this sense, this moment in Erasmus stands as a kind of prelude to Edmund Burke's famous invocation of the "swinish multitude" in his 1790 *Reflections on the Revolution in France*, under whose hooves "learning will be cast into the mire." On the many satirical responses to Burke, see Darren Howard, "Necessary Fictions: The 'Swinish Multitude' and the Rights of Man," *Studies in Romanticism* 47.2 (2008): 161–178. Compare also Martin Marplelate's denunciation of the bishops as a "swinish rable" (John Petheram, ed., *An Epistle to the Terrible Priests of the Convocation House* [London, 1843], 32).

2. Edward Topsell, *The historie of foure-footed beastes: Describing the true and lively figure of every Beast* (London: William Jaggard, 1607), 675.

3. On this woodcut, see Adam G. Hooks, "Sidney's Porcupine," *Anchora* (blog), 9 November 2021, http://www.adamghooks.net/2011/04/sidneys-porcupine.html; and R. L. Eagle, "The *Arcadia* (1593) Title-Page Border," *The Library*, 5th ser., 4 (1949): 68–71. On the frontispiece, see also the discussions in Stephen Orgel, "Textual Icons: Reading Early Modern Illustrations," in *The Renaissance Computer: Knowledge Technology in the First Age of Print*, ed. Neil Rhodes and Jonathan Sawday (London: Routledge, 2000), 57–67, esp. 62–63; and Margery Corbett and R. W. Lightbown, *The Comely Frontispiece: The Emblematic Title-page in England, 1550–1660* (London: Routledge and Kegan Paul, 1979), 58–65.

4. Erasmus glosses the aphorism as "meaning that to stupid people the very best things are stinking and unpleasant." *The Collected Works of Erasmus, Adages I i 1 to I v 100*, trans. Margaret Mann Phillips (Toronto: University of Toronto Press, 1982), 347. The earliest versions of the proverb cite the perfume amaracine instead of marjoram, which, according to Lucretius, "drive[s] away the pig, which fears all perfume." See Shane Butler, "Making Scents of Poetry," in *Smell and the Ancient Senses*, ed. Mark Bradley (London: Routledge, 2014), 74–89, at 78. For a Renaissance example of the proverb, see John Conybeare's commonplaced lessons, which include: "Nihil cum fidibus graculo: Nihil cum amaracino sui: The dawe hath naught to doe with a lute, nor the sowe with oyle of majoram." *Letters and Exercises of the Elizabethan Schoolmaster John Conybeare*, ed. Frederick Cornwallis Conybeare (London: Henry Frowde, 1905), 46.

5. *The Holy Bible conteyning the Old Testament, and the New* (London: Robert Barker, 1611).

6. Augustine, *The Lord's Sermon on the Mount*, trans. John J. Jepson (New York: Paulist Press, 1948), 2.20.68.

7. Charles G. Osgood, trans., *Boccaccio on Poetry* (New York: Liberal Arts Press, 1956), 62.

8. Augustine tries to offer a solution to this problem, and to avoid the implication that it is possible to harm that which is holy; "even though it cannot be torn to pieces and impaired and remains whole and inviolate, yet we must consider what their intentions are who stand opposed to it like bitter enemies" (*The Lord's Sermon on the Mount*, 2.20.68).

9. On the material realities of textual destruction, and the argument that it was much more common that we may believe, see Adam Smyth, *Material Texts in Early Modern England* (Cambridge: Cambridge University Press, 2018), 55–74.

10. Charles I, *Effata regalia: Aphorismes divine, moral, politick*, ed. Richard Watson (London: Robert Horn, 1661), 8.

11. George Whetstone, *The honorable reputation of a Souldier* (London: Richard Jones, 1585), sig. E.ii^v. Envy is the passion most associated with destructive readers; see Lynn Sermin Meskill, *Ben Jonson and Envy* (Cambridge: Cambridge University Press, 2009). On destructive swine in gardens: "How can it by any reason go-well upon the Earth? For the Sheepe are committed and put-in-trust unto the Wolfe, for to be kept / the little Fishes, to the Cat / and the sweet Hearb-garden, to the Swine." Hendrik Niclaes, *Proverbia HN: The proverbes of HN* (Cologne: N. Bohmburg, 1575), fol. 30.

12. An indispensible The classic discussion of the pig as a figure of transgression is found in Peter Stallybrass and Allon White, *Politics and Poetics of Transgression* (Ithaca, NY: Cornell University Press, 1986).

13. Bartholomew Chappell, *Garden of Prudence: Wherein is contained, A patheticall discourse, and godly meditation* (London: Richard Jones, 1595), sig. A2^v.

14. Isabella Whitney, [*A sweet nosgay, or pleasant posye*] (London: Richard Jones, 1573), sig. A.viii^r.

15. The swine and the dog are frequently threats. See, for example, the proverb of the dog in the manger, who neither eats the grain there nor allows others to eat, e.g., in Humphrey Gifford, *A posie of Gilloflowers* (London: [Thomas Dawson] for John Perrin,1580), sig. *3ᵛ.

16. See especially the nominal definitions: *OED*, s.v. "ravin," n.1, 1a–c, 2–d, and 3. The bird has a separate, Germanic etymology. The root is the same word that Ausonius, in his famous *carpe diem* lyric, gives to the ruin wrought by the seasonal passage of time: "Mirabar celerem fugitiva aetate rapinam." Like the greedy guts who pluck *rashly* and the bad readers who *rush* into Plat's garden, the ruin described by Ausonius operates by acceleration.

17. Arthur Golding, trans., *The .xv. Bookes of P. Ovidius Naso, entytuled Metamorphosis* (London: William Seres, 1567), fol. 188.

18. Topsell, *Historie*, 667.

19. R. P. Knight, *Symbolical Language of Ancient Art and Mythology* (London: Black and Armstrong, 1836), 36–37.

20. *Maimonides' Mishneh Torah*, ed. Philip Birnbaum (New York: Hebrew Publishing, 1967), Damages to Property, 5.9.

21. Francis Thynne, *Emblemes and Epigrammes*, ed. F. J. Furnivall (London: Early English Text Society, 1876), 22. See Stephen Greenblatt, *Renaissance Self-Fashioning: From More to Shakespeare* (Chicago: University of Chicago Press, 1980), 157–192.

22. The fatality of the swine haunts Richard and his governance in Shakespeare's *Richard III*, where he is, as Margaret says, an "abortive, rooting hog" (1.3.224). In the play's last act, Richmond extends Richard's deadly, hoggish effect to a field that stands for all of England:

The wretched, bloody, and usurping boar,
That spoiled your summer fields and fruitful vines,
Swills your warm blood like wash, and makes his trough
In your embowelèd bosoms—this foul swine
Lies now even in the center of this isle.

(5.2.7–11)

23. William Shakespeare, *Venus and Adonis*, lines 1115–1116, in *The Complete Sonnets and Poems*, ed. Colin Burrow, Oxford Shakespeare (Oxford: Oxford University Press, 2002), 232. The action of "nuzzling" is echoed by another pig against the future, from Breton's *The uncasing of Machavils instructions to his sonne* (London: Edward Griffin for Richard Higgenbotham, 1615), where it forms a metaphor for treachery: "Swine eates the flowers, then nusles up the roote, / And none but beastly mindes will surely doo't" (sig. G1ᵛ).

24. The ambidexterity of the boar's gender in this moment—from penetrating tusk to a maternally nuzzling groin—replays the role reversal that characterizes Venus's seduction of Adonis throughout Shakespeare's poem. See *OED*, s.v. "groin"; "groin" (n.1, 2a) meaning "snout" derives from the sound made by hogs; "groin" meaning the fold formed by the thighs (n.2, 1a), our more common contemporary sense, may derive from the Old English "grynde" for valley or abyss. The transformation from "grind" to "groin" occurred in the sixteenth century. In Golding's translation, Adonis is wounded "in his codds" (*Metamorphosis*, fol. 134ᵛ).

25. Edmund Spenser, *The Faerie Queene*, ed. A. C. Hamilton, Longman Annotated English Poets (New York: Pearson, 2001), 2.12.87. All subsequent references are to this edition, though I have modernized the lettering.

26. Stanzas 8 and 9. Robert Matz argues that the language of looseness in book 2 participates in its recoding of aristocratic virtues of hospitality as vices; thus when the porch's grapes offer themselves for gathering, their echo of lyric hospitality is not gracious but treacherous ("an embracing vine, / Whose bounches hanging downe, seemd to entice / All passers by, to taste their lushious wine, / And did them selves into their hands incline, / As freely offering to be gathered" [2.12.54]). Robert Matz, *Defending Literature in Early Modern England* (Cambridge: Cambridge University Press, 2004), 120.

27. At the moment we encounter him, the young knight has hung up his arms, "the ydle instruments / Of sleeping praise, were hong upon a tree," and has turned instead to prodigality and vanity ("But in lewd loves, and wastfull luxuree, / His dayes, his goods, his bodie he did spend") (2.12.80). Verdant seems to possess a distinctly vegetal energy, one whose passivity and effeminacy Robert Matz has linked to Elizabethan attacks on poetry (*Defending Literature*, 94).

28. Until brought back to life and present action by the "vertue" of the Palmer's staff. Spenser asks us to pity seeing "Him his nobility so fowle deface," while also admiring the new tenderness of his young manhood: as he sleeps, "on his tender lips the downy heare / Did now but freshly spring, and silken blossoms beare" (2.12.79). On the vegetality of Verdant, specifically in connection with sleep and the vegetable soul, see Garrett A. Sullivan Jr., *Sleep, Romance, and Human Embodiment: Vitality from Spenser to Milton* (Cambridge: Cambridge University Press, 2012), 29–46. Loewenstein draws a connection to the representation of vegetative growth in the May eclogue of Spenser's *Shepheardes Calender* (Joseph Loewenstein, "Gryll's Hoggish Mind," *Spenser Studies* 22 (2007), 243–256, at 245).

29. Edmund Spenser, *Fowre Hymnes* (London: [Richard Field] for William Ponsonby, 1596), sig. A.ii^r.

30. Timothy Kendall, *Flowers of epigrammes* (London: John Sheppard, 1577), sig. A.iiii^r. On the identification of Gascoigne with his Greene Knight, see Richard Helgerson, *The Elizabethan Prodigals* (Berkeley: University of California Press, 1976), 44–47; Meredith Anne Skura, *Tudor Autobiography: Listening for Inwardness* (Chicago: University of Chicago Press, 2008), 195–199.

31. "To the gentle Gentlewomen Readers," in George Pettie, *A petite Pallace of Pettie his Pleasure* (London: Richard Watkins, 1576).

32. As G.W. writes in a commendatory poem to Spenser's *Amoretti and Epithalamion* (1595), "Because no malice of succeeding daies, / can rase those records of thy lasting praise." *Amoretti and Epithalamion* (London: William Ponsonby, 1595), sig. A1^r. On the materiality of razing, see Joshua Calhoun, *The Nature of the Page* (Philadelphia: University of Pennsylvania Press, 2020), 73–98. For the argument that these verbs "owe their historical and moral force to the Reformation," see Jennifer Summit, *Memory's Library: Medieval Books in Early Modern England* (Chicago: University of Chicago Press, 2008), 133. Greenblatt links the stanza's "inventory of violence" to the "principle of regenerative violence" that links the destruction of the Bower to Spenser's colonial projects, in which "the act of tearing down is the act of fashioning" (*Renaissance Self-Fashioning*, 188).

33. For an account of how the Bower's landscape elements engage with Renaissance garden design, see Michael Leslie, "Spenser, Sidney, and the Renaissance Garden," *English Literary Renaissance* 22.1 (1992): 3–36. Jennifer Summit links these dynamics in book 2 (specifically in the Bower and in Eumnestes' library) to John Bale's description of winnowing the wheat from the chaff in the relics of the monasteries (*Memory's Library*, 110–112). On images of culling

and uprooting in humanist reading practices, see Chapter 3 above; and Mary Thomas Crane, *Framing Authority* (Princeton, NJ: Princeton University Press, 1993), 58–70. Thomas Elyot's good reader, when faced with heathen poetry, becomes the swine of Matthew 7:6 who "treadeth the nettils under his feete, whiles he gadreth good herbes" (*The boke named the Governour* [London: Thomas Berthelet, 1537], fo. 49ʳ).

34. See especially Patricia Parker's reading of Verdant's suspended instruments ("Suspended Instruments: Lyric and Power in the Bower of Bliss," in *Literary Fat Ladies* [New York: Routledge, 1987], 54–66); and Wendy Beth Hyman's reading of the Bower's *carpe florem* poem (in *Impossible Desire and the Limits of Knowledge in Renaissance Poetry* [Oxford: Oxford University Press, 2019], 143–155), both of which persuasively make this link. Stephen Greenblatt associates the episode with the conflict between art and nature (*Renaissance Self-Fashioning*, 157–192). On the relation of Spenser to this slightly earlier generation of poets, see Richard Helgerson, "The New Poet Presents Himself: Spenser and the Idea of a Literary Career," *PMLA* 93.5 (1978): 893–911.

35. Hyman, *Impossible Desire*, 143–155.

36. As Chris Barrett argues, there is an anti-allegorical force in the (occasionally expressed) natural historical tendency in Spenser. Chris Barrett, "Cetaceous Sin and Dragon Death: *The Faerie Queene*, Natural Philosophy, and the Limits of Allegory," *Spenser Studies* 28 (2013): 145–164, at 147.

37. The language of kind also appears in the line from Pliny that might be a source: "in luto volutatio *generi* grata" (*Natural History* 8.77, my italics; rolling in the mud is pleasing to that kind/species). Pliny, *Natural History*, vol. 3, Books 8–11, trans. H. Rackham, Loeb Classical Library (Cambridge, MA: Harvard University Press, 1940).

38. "Sylva iuvat capras: unda lutúmque sues." Also appropriate is 2 Peter 2:22, "It is come unto them, according to the true proverbe . . . the sowe that was washed [is returned] to the wallowing in the myer," as Hamilton cites in his notes (2.12.87, note).

39. This suggests a happy affinity between what James calls "flower power" and what we might call "pig power." See Heather James, *Ovid and the Liberty of Speech in Shakespeare's England* (Oxford: Oxford University Press, 2021), 20–54.

40. This aspect of the Bower extends Richard Helgerson's argument, that Spenser, as the "new poet" of the *Shepheardes Calender*, breaks from the model of containment in which the production of poetry was an established way station on a young man's progress through prodigality (Helgerson, "The New Poet," 893–902).

41. The connection between Guyon and *carpe diem* is richly argued in Hyman, *Impossible Desire*, 43–55. Kasey Evans gives an elegant reading of Gryll as a figure of mourning (and Guyon as its refusal) (Kasey Evans, *Colonial Virtue: The Mobility of Temperance in Renaissance England* [Toronto: University of Toronto Press, 2012], 86–94.)

Chapter 5

1. Thomas Tusser, *A hundreth good pointes of husbandrie* (London: Richard Tottel, 1557), sig. A.iiᵛ. My translation; on the Latin proverb, see n. 35 below.

2. John Crowe Ransom, "Shakespeare at Sonnets," *Southern Review* 3 (1938): 531–353, at 531.

3. Yvor Winters, "Poetic Styles, Old and New," in *Four Poets on Poetry*, ed. Don Cameron Allen (Baltimore: Johns Hopkins University Press, 1959), 49. This trend in Shakespearean criticism was first identified by Rosalie Colie, whose discussion of the force of the epigrammatic

tradition on the sonnet form I discuss below. Rosalie Littell Colie, "*Mel* and *Sal*: Some Problems in Sonnet-Theory," in *Shakespeare's Living Art* (Princeton, NJ: Princeton University Press, 1974), 68–134. Ransom was not the first to take exception with Shakespeare's sonnets (consider Steevens's explanation that they were not included in his 1793 edition "because the strongest act of Parliament that could be framed, would fail to compel readers into their service"), but a resurgence of such criticism did follow upon Ransom's salvo through the 1940s and 1950s. Winters, following Ransom's lead, opens his discussion of the sonnets by noting that "in the past ten years or so I have found them more and more disappointing." Among others, we might add the feelings of disappointment expressed by C. L. Barber, Edward Hubler, G. Wilson Knight, and, somewhat more recently, Thomas Greene, whose argument I will return to below. Barbara Herrnstein Smith discusses some of these perceived "closural failings" in *Poetic Closure: A Study of How Poems End* (Chicago: University of Chicago Press, 1968), 214–220. Helen Vendler's emphasis on "couplet ties" in her commentary on the *Sonnets* offers a counterweight to these complaints of inorganicism—that is, the closer we look, the better attached the poems seem. Helen Vendler, *The Art of Shakespeare's Sonnets* (Cambridge, MA: Belknap, 1997).

4. Ransom, "Shakespeare at Sonnets," 533.

5. Winters, "Poetic Styles," 48.

6. Paul Fussell, *Poetic Meter and Poetic Form* (New York: McGraw Hill, 1979), 122. M. M. Mahood makes an analogous point in *Shakespeare's Wordplay* (London: Methuen, 1957), 103.

7. See, for example, Edward Hubler, *The Sense of Shakespeare's Sonnets* (Princeton, NJ: Princeton University Press, 1952), 24.

8. Colie, "*Mel* and *Sal*," 70.

9. Coleman Hutchison, "Breaking the Book Known as Q," *PMLA* 121.1 (2006): 33–66.

10. All references to the *Sonnets* are to William Shakespeare, *Shake-speares Sonnets. Never before Imprinted* (London: by George Eld for Thomas Thorpe, 1609); sonnets are cited by number. As Hutchison likewise acknowledges, it is unlikely (and impossible to determine with certainty) that Shakespeare had any hand in these patterns, or in the layout and editing of the volume in general. For a very useful discussion of what is unusual or regular in the 1609 quarto (including other aspects of the layout of the page and rhetorics of authorization), see Marcy L. North, "The Sonnets and Book History," in *A Companion to Shakespeare's Sonnets*, ed. Michael Schoenfeldt (Oxford: Blackwell, 2010), 204–222; and Arthur Marotti, "Shakespeare's Sonnets as Literary Property," in *Soliciting Interpretation: Literary Theory and Seventeenth-Century English Poetry*, ed. Elizabeth D. Harvey and Katharine Eisaman Maus (Chicago: University of Chicago Press, 1990), 143–173.

11. Philip Sidney, *The Defence of Poesie* (London: for William Ponsonby, 1595), sig. F4^r.

12. Wendy Wall, *The Imprint of Gender* (Ithaca, NY: Cornell University Press, 1993), esp. 70–73 on "the fixity of form."

13. Dubrow argues that Drayton, Gascoigne, and Puttenham all emphasize the restrictive and cohesive force of stanzaic form; they "insistently redefine malleability as modularity, thus rendering it a source of, not a threat to, the unity of the text." Heather Dubrow, *The Challenges of Orpheus: Lyric Poetry and Early Modern England* (Baltimore: Johns Hopkins University Press, 2008), 166, 169.

14. Dubrow sees the indented couplet as a shaky visual foundation to the architecture of the poem: "in instances where one or both lines of the couplet are indented, especially if the second line is not capitalized, the base may seem far less reliable, and the visual effect can be that of a column whose base is apparent but insecure. The column may even appear to be threat-

ening to topple over, its *rime* potentially *sparse*, its customary function as an icon for restraint hence toppled as well" (ibid., 173).

15. George Puttenham, *The arte of English poesie: Contrived into three Bookes* (London: Richard Field, 1589), 73. Puttenham shares with George Gascoigne the image of "shutting up" with rhyme. Gascoigne, in his "Certayne Notes of Instruction" (first published in his 1575 *Posies*) describes the structure of the rhyme royal stanza in these terms: "the first and thirde lines do aunswer (acrosse) in like terminations and rime, the second, fourth, and fifth, do likewise answere eche other in terminations, and the two last do combine and shut up the Sentence" (*The posies of George Gascoigne Esquire* [London: Henry Bynneman for Richard Smith, 1575], sig. Uiᵛ). In Puttenham's discussion of rhyme, this "good enough" sound of the distich stands for "the most vulgar proportion of distance of situation," in which all such verses are less strongly bound to the poem as a whole. For Puttenham, these distinctions of taste are explicitly distinctions of class. Skelton, with Chaucer and Gower, was faulted for "being in deede but a rude rayling rimer & all his doings ridiculous, he used both short distaunces and short measures pleasing onely the popular eare" (*Arte*, 69).

16. Thomas Greene, "Pitiful Thrivers: Failed Husbandry in the Sonnets," in *Shakespeare and the Question of Theory*, ed. Patricia Parker and Geoffrey Hartman (New York: Methuen, 1985), 230–244.

17. For a definitive treatment of these genres, see Andrew McRae, *God Speed the Plough* (Cambridge: Cambridge University Press, 2002), esp. part 2, pp. 133–228; on Tusser in particular, see 146–151.

18. Sidney, *Defence*, sig. F4ʳ.

19. It is impossible to rule out entirely that they exist, or that they once did but no longer survive, but I have found no earlier examples in an extensive survey.

20. Thomas Tusser, *A hundreth good pointes of husbandrie* (1557), sig. D.iʳ⁻ᵛ. For a reading that emphasizes the sophistication of Tusser's strategies to distance his verse from Elizabethan courtly contexts, see Scott Oldenburg, "Thomas Tusser and the Poetics of the Plow," *English Literary Renaissance* 49.3 (2019): 273–303. On the account Tusser gives of his own life, see Meredith Anne Skura, *Tudor Autobiography: Listening for Inwardness* (Chicago: University of Chicago Press, 2008), 126–148.

21. In the decades following the publication of the Tottel's miscellany, "sonnet" was used to describes a variety of kinds of poems to which we would not apply the word—all symptoms, Sidney Lee complained, of a "reluctance of the Elizabethans to accept the sonnet's distinctive principles." Sidney Lee, "The Elizabethan Sonnet," in *The Cambridge History of English Literature*, vol. 3, ed. A. R. Waller and A. W. Ward (Cambridge: Cambridge University Press, 1908), 249. This may only make it more noteworthy, then, that all of the "sonets" that appear in editions of Tusser's *Pointes* adhere reasonably closely to a more precise formal definition. By following the "sonnet" as it operated as a maker's term through the 1560s and 1570s, Cathy Shrank finds that these poems are often not fourteen lines, often not in pentameter, and— significantly for our purposes here—not necessarily about love. As Shrank notes, collections immediately in the wake of Tottel's were more likely to use the sonnet form for "sober reflection or even blatant didacticism." Cathy Shrank, "'Matters of Love as of Discourse': The English Sonnet, 1560–1580," *Studies in Philology* 105.1 (2007): 35. Gascoigne prefaced his formal definition by complaining that "some thinke that all Poemes (being short) may be called Sonets, as in deede it is a diminutive worde derived of *Sonare*," before correcting them: "but yet I can beste allowe to call those Sonnets whiche are of fourtene lynes, every line conteyning tenne

syllables. The firste twelve do ryme in staues of foure lines by crosse meetre, and the last twoo ryming together do conclude the whole" (Gascoigne, *Posies* [1575], sig. U.i^v). As Gascoigne complains here, "sonnet" often meant nothing more precise than a brief lyric, frequently invoked to echo Tottel's title and to capitalize on the success of that *other* collection of 1557 (the title of which thus may have suggested something more like "short poems and also shorter poems").

22. In this sense, it carries what Susan Stewart calls the basic ideological form of miniaturized language, which, as she argues, always plays with abstraction and closure. Susan Stewart, *On Longing: Narratives of the Miniature, the Gigantic, the Souvenir, the Collection* (Durham, NC: Duke University Press, 1984), 53.

23. On stationers as readers, see Zachary Lesser, *Renaissance Drama and the Politics of Publication* (Cambridge: Cambridge University Press, 2004).

24. None of the sonnets of Googe (1563), Turberville (1567), or Gascoigne (1573) has indented couplets. Nonetheless, the indentation of couplets seems to have been commonly practiced by 1591, when the concluding couplets in Sidney's *Astrophel and Stella* and the sonnets in Spenser's *Ruines of Rome* and *Visions of the worlds vanitie* were indented. Even with the couplet's confirmed visual distinction, compositors did not regularly follow the mold now familiar from Shakespeare's 1609 quarto. In 1592, the sonnets in Samuel Daniel's *Delia* were indented, as were the first lines of each quatrain. The printer of Constable's *Diana*, also printed in 1592, followed the Petrarchan model, with the first lines of each quatrain at the left margin and the next lines indented, but with an alteration marking the exception of the couplet: these last two lines are indented even farther than those quatrain lines. (This seems to render concrete a native tweak to an Italianately inclined collection, in which each poem is titled in Italian, as *Sonnetto Primo, Secondo*, and so on.) George Turberville's *Epitaphes, Epigrams, Songs and Sonets* (London: Henry Denham, 1567) does, however, include some pointed couplet conclusions to longer poems in which the couplets are set off from the preceding verse in italic or roman type (cf. fols. 19^r, 29^r, 105^v, 129^r), and, in one case, in brackets (fol. 62^r).

25. Thomas Tusser, *Five hundreth points of good husbandry united to as many of huswiferie* (London: Richard Tottel, 1573), sig. A1^v.

26. Thomas Tusser, *A hundreth good pointes of Husbandry, lately maried unto a Hundreth good poyntes of Huswifery: newly corrected and amplified* (London: Richard Tottel, 1570), preface.

27. *Shake-speares Sonnets* (1609), E1^v.

28. First formally called "Tottel's Miscellany" by Thomas Warton in the late eighteenth century, again in John Payne Collier's limited reprint of 1867, and widely referred to as such since Edward Arber's edition published with that title in 1870. For this attribution, see Matthew Zarnowiecki's analysis in *Fair Copies: Reproducing the English Lyric from Tottel to Shakespeare* (Toronto: University of Toronto Press, 2014). For a thorough account of its initial publication and circulation, see J. Christopher Warner, *The Making and Marketing of Tottel's Miscellany, 1557: "Songs and Sonnets" in the Summer of the Martyrs' Fires* (Farnham, England: Ashgate, 2013); and on later editions, Paul Marquis, ed., *Richard Tottel's "Songes and Sonettes": The Elizabethan Version* (Tempe: Arizona Center for Medieval and Renaissance Studies, 2007). On the organization and influence of *Songes and Sonettes*, see Megan Heffernan, *Making the Miscellany* (Philadelphia: University of Pennsylvania Press, 2021), 19–53; and the essays collected in Stephen Hamrick, ed., *Tottel's "Songes and Sonettes" in Context* (Farnham, Surrey: Ashgate, 2013). On the miscellanies that followed its publication, see Steven May, "Popu-

larizing Courtly Poetry: *Tottel's Miscellany* and Its Progeny," in *The Oxford Handbook of Tudor Literature, 1485–1603*, ed. Mike Pincombe and Cathy Shrank (Oxford: Oxford University Press, 2009), 418–433. I have also relied on Hyder Rollins's essential edition (Hyder E. Rollins, ed., *Tottel's Miscellany (1557–1587)*, 2 vol. [Cambridge, MA: Harvard University Press, 1928.])

29. Tusser's *Pointes* beats out the eleven editions of Tottel's Miscellany with sixteen of its own. (There would be nearly twenty-five in total by the end of the seventeenth century.) There are indications that both works were popular soon after publication, including fines levied by the Stationers' Company against the printer of an unauthorized edition and three separate editions in the span of two months in the summer of 1557. See W. W. Greg, "Tottel's Miscellany," *The Library*, 2nd ser., 18 (1904): 118–123.

30. Lewis nonetheless finds some reason to return: "The truth is that, after Wyatt, Tusser is the most readable of all the Drab versifiers. The pleasure, no doubt, results partly from our nostalgia for the land and for an age which, if not much softer than our own, was hard in different places." C. S. Lewis, *English Literature in the Sixteenth Century, Excluding Drama* (Oxford: Oxford University Press, 1944), 262. Sir Walter Scott, in other respects a fan of the *Pointes*, was perhaps more harsh, writing that "the poetry of Tusser is obviously the least recommendation of his work." Walter Scott, ed., *A Collection of Scarce and Valuable Tracts on the Most Entertaining Subjects*, 2nd ed., vol. 3 (London: T. Cadell et al., 1810), 406.

31. John Thompson, *The Founding of English Metre* (London: Routledge, 1961), 1–2.

32. In his thoughtful consideration of oral cultures in early modern England, Adam Fox confirms this stance, painting Tusser as a kind of wandering rural stenographer, in whose "couplets we hear the language of the countryside, abounding with old saws which were probably ancient when he chanced to weave them into the fabric of his text, so providing some of their earliest recordings." Adam Fox, *Oral and Literate Culture in England* (Oxford: Clarendon, 2000), 152. Wendy Wall argues that this way of viewing Tusser was already attached to *Pointes* in the seventeenth century, when part of their appeal was a sense of his regional and antique quaintness. Wendy Wall, *Staging Domesticity* (Cambridge: Cambridge University Press), 36–37.

33. Michael Spiller notes the singular exception of Nicolo di Rossi in the early fourteenth century, whose terminal couplets do not seem to have spawned any imitators. Michael Spiller, *The Development of the Sonnet* (London: Routledge, 1992), 199 n. 4. No scholarly consensus exists as to why such a mutation should have occurred. Some (including Patricia Thomson) have noted the proximity of the Italian *strambotto*, or the likely influence of the rhyme royal stanzas so popular in English poetry of the fifteenth and sixteenth centuries, while Jiří Levý has attributed the innovation to the innate "distichic tendency" of the Germanic languages. Patricia Thomson, *Sir Thomas Wyatt and His Background* (Stanford, CA: Stanford University Press, 1964), 227–234; Jiří Levý, "On the Relations of Language and Stanza Pattern in the English Sonnet," in *Worte und Werte: Bruno Markwardt zum 60. Geburstag*, ed. Gustav Erdmann and Alfons Eichstaedt (Berlin: de Gruyter, 1961), 214–231, at 220.

34. Tusser, *A hundreth good pointes* (1557), sig. A.ii^v. Roughly translated, "In harmony, small things grow. In discord, the biggest things are destroyed."

35. Quentin Skinner describes this as "one of the most widely quoted *dicta* on politics throughout the Renaissance," attributing the source of its authority partially to Sallust. Quentin Skinner, *Visions of Politics* (Cambridge: Cambridge University Press, 2002), 23; Gisela Bock and Quentin Skinner, *Machiavelli and Republicanism* (Cambridge: Cambridge University Press, 1993), 129.

36. This implication is intensified if we consider the sense of "concord" we find in Puttenham—namely, the aural concord between words, or rhyme.

37. Tusser, *A hundreth good pointes* (1557), sig. A.ii^v.

38. Tusser, *A hundreth good pointes* (1570), sig. A.ii^r.

39. Robert Recorde, *The pathway to knowledg, containing the first principles of geometrie, as they may moste aptly be applied unto practise* (London: Reynold Wolfe, 1551), sig. A1^r.

40. Tusser addresses both men and women, but not with the same points. Beginning in the edition of 1570, Tusser uses pilcrows to mark that particular points within the calendrical progression are directed to housewives, thus discriminating rationing and redirecting his readers' attention according their gender. In these editions, however, these points are thus not among those that are numbered—they literally don't count. Formally identical but finally inconsequential, they therefore have a liminal place within the economy of the point that governs the volume.

41. See especially William Sherman, *Used Books: Marking Readers in Renaissance England* (Philadelphia: University of Pennsylvania Press, 2008), 25–52.

42. G. K. Hunter, "The Marking of *Sententiae* in Elizabethan Printed Plays, Poems, and Romances," *The Library*, 5th ser., 6.3–4 (1951): 171–188; Zachary Lesser and Peter Stallybrass, "The First Literary *Hamlet* and the Commonplacing of Professional Plays," *Shakespeare Quarterly* 59.4 (2008): 371–420; Claire Bourne, *Typographies of Performance in Early Modern England* (Oxford: Oxford University Press, 2020), 32–76.

43. On the pointing of verse, and the interplay of visual, grammatical, and rhetorical pointing, see Malcolm Parkes, *Pause and Effect: An Introduction to the History of Punctuation in the West* (Berkeley: University of California Press, 1992), 97–114. Though it does not directly address poetry, the insights of Parkes's essay on *ordinatio* and the hierarchy of the page are also relevant. See his "The Influence of the Concepts of Ordinatio and Compilatio on the Development of the Book," in *Medieval Learning and Literature: Essays Presented to Richard William Hunt*, ed. J. J. G. Alexander and M. T. Gibson (Oxford: Clarendon Press, 1976), 115–141.

44. Parkes, *Pause and Effect*, 101.

45. This is in contrast to other examples of didactic small verse forms, such as William Lily's "epigramma" (or "Carmen ad discipulos de moribus"), an imitation of the *Distichs of Cato*, which was printed in 1521 with breaks between metrical lines, as the *Distichs* normally were, but with no empty space left between epigrams and with pilcrows at the left margin given the duty of marking the beginning of a new saying. William Lily, *Epigrammata Guil. Lilii. Angli* (London: Richard Pynson, 1521). In this context, the line breaks between points in Tusser are a typographic luxury. Compare also the proverbs of Christine de Pizan, which appear as distichs with white space between them in Harley MS 4431, but which are printed without space between couplets in Caxton's edition of 1478. Christine de Pizan, *The Morale Proverbes of Cristyne* (Westminster: William Caxton, 1478).

46. Megan Heffernan unfolds the poetics of the parcel in *Making the Miscellany*, 31–38. As Wendy Wall notes, the term also potentially designates the poems' circulation: the first uses of "parcel" to mean something sent and delivered date to the mid-sixteenth century. Wall, *Imprint of Gender*, 25. Seth Lerer considers parcels as units of land in "Cultivation and Inhumation: Some Thoughts on the Cultural Impact of Tottel's *Songes and Sonettes*," in *Tottel's "Songes and Sonettes" in Context*, ed. Stephen Hamrick (London: Routledge, 2013), 147–161.

47. The *Treatise* had first been published by Edward Whitchurch in 1547 and had already gone through four editions by the time Tottel tried his hand at an unauthorized and "aug-

mented" edition in 1555. The competition between the two stationers warmed up to a minor publishing war through the 1550s and 1560s. On the significance of this back-and-forth, see the discussion in Joshua Phillips, *Fictions of English Communal Identity, 1485–1603* (Farnham: Ashgate, 2010), 106–107, 110–113.

48. Louis B. Wright places the *Treatise* among the large set of texts he classes as Tudor "handbooks to improvement." Louis B. Wright, *Middle-Class Culture in Elizabethan England* (Chapel Hill: University of North Carolina Press, 1935), 148. John King describes the *Treatise* as a whole as "a Renaissance reformulation of this encyclopedia of prudential wisdom" and argues that the "pyththie meters" are directly modeled on the *Distichs*. John King, *English Reformation Literature: The Tudor Origins of the Protestant Tradition* (Princeton, NJ: Princeton University Press, 1982), 363. See also Mary Thomas Crane, *Framing Authority* (Princeton, NJ: Princeton University Press, 1993), 169. Baldwin wrote in verse in a range of practical, instructional, and interpretive contexts. His edition of the Song of Songs, published in 1549 out of Whitchurch's shop, combines a similar layering of substance, commentary, and summation, offering biblical text in translation, the argument, and the metrical "paraphrase," and prescribing an "order of reading" for all of these elements. The edition amounts to a collection of small verse forms (including quatrains, couplets, ballads, *strambotti*, and sonnets) more than a continuous translation. On the range of verse, see Sister Francis Camilla Cavanaugh, ed., *A Critical Edition of "The Canticles, or Balades of Salomon Phraselyke Declared in English Metres" by William Baldwin* (St. Louis, MO: St. Louis University Press, 1964), 49–70. Baldwin writes that he renders the canticles in meter because they are, to begin with, canticles, or ballads, and in the dedication to Edward VI notes that he was inspired in part by the success of the metrical psalms. He instructs the reader, however, to take the verse itself as a secondary quality: "in reading note the sentence more than the rime, with the argumentes whiche go before and after the songes. And reade them orderly, so shall the proces of the matter helpe the muche." William Baldwin, *The Canticles, or Balades of Salomon* (London: Edward Whitchurch, 1549), sig. A1ᵛ. Noam Flinker describes Baldwin's *Canticles* as "the first collection of English poetry" in *The Song of Songs in English Renaissance Literature: Kisses of Their Mouths* (Cambridge: D. S. Brewer, 2000), 31–65.

49. Chloe Rachel Wheatley, "Epitomes of Early Modern History" (PhD diss., Columbia University, 2001); and her *Epic, Epitome, and the Early Modern Historical Imagination* (London: Routledge, 2016).

50. A similar process of abstraction appears in early editions of the metrical psalms. Though no copy is currently known of the edition published by Tottel in 1554 (it has not been seen since a Sotheby's auction in the 1920s), an edition published a year earlier with the same title (from which Tottel may well be drawing his edition) presents each of Sternholde's psalms with a brief verse argument beforehand. Like Baldwin's and Tusser's abstracts, these are printed in roman type, while the matter from which they draw is printed in black letter. Thomas Sternholde, *All Suche Psalmes of David as Thomas Sterneholde, late Grome of the kynges Majesties Robes, did in his lyfe tyme drawe into Englishe metre* (London: John Kingston and Henry Sutton, 1553).

51. William Baldwin, *A treatyce of Morall philosophy containing the sayinges of the wise* (London: Richard Tottel, 1557), sig. I.viʳ.

52. *Songes and Sonettes* (1557), sig. A.iiᵛ.

53. Tusser, *A hundreth good pointes* (1557), sig. D.iʳ⁻ᵛ.

54. Dympna Callaghan, "Confounded by Winter: Speeding Time in Shakespeare's Sonnets," in Schoenfeldt, ed., *A Companion to Shakespeare's Sonnets*, 104–117, at 110–111.

55. Tusser, *A hundredth good pointes* (1570), sig. F.ii^r.

56. Ibid., sig. F.i^v.

57. Tusser, *Five hundreth points* (1573), sig. A.i^v.

58. Compare also the "description of woman's age" that appears in Tusser's section on huswifery, where an analogous juxtaposition of chronology and prudence receives similar typographical differentiation. The poem gives one line for every fourteen years of her life (numbered at the left margin by the age it epitomizes), making a series of rhyming couplets, with "A lesson" printed beneath with its content condensed in four brief lines of blackletter. Tusser, *Five hundreth points* (1573), sig. X.iii^v.

59. Tusser, *Hundreth good pointes* (1570), sig. K.ii^v; and Tusser, *Five hundreth points* (1573), sig. Y.i^r.

60. A third poem is entitled a "sonet" in the table of contents of the 1573 edition, though the word does not appear in the title of the poem as it appears in the text ("A sonet how to set a candle afore the Devill"). In three octets and a couplet, its layout resembles the 1573 composition of the "Sonet to Lady Paget" (Tusser, *Five hundreth points* [1573], sig. Q.iii^r).

61. The sonnet is also a play on the convention of the lover's experience of the passage of time, here with "love" markedly replaced by "author." Compare, for example, the first poem, by Surrey, in Tottel's Miscellany ("The sunne hath twise brought furth his tender grene, / Twise clad the earth in lively lustinesse" [*Songes* (1557), sig. B.ii^r]) and Shakespeare's Sonnet 104.

62. On the poetics and semiotics of this problem of closure, see Barbara Herrnstein Smith, *Poetic Closure*; and Roland Barthes, *S/Z*, trans. Richard Miller (New York: Hill and Wang, 1974), esp. 113–114 and 216–217, on enumeration, description, and the "*et cetera* of plenitudes"; as well as Giorgio Agamben, *The End of the Poem: Studies in Poetics*, trans. Daniel Heller-Roazen (Stanford, CA: Stanford University Press, 1999), 109–115.

63. Giorgio Melchiori, *Shakespeare's Dramatic Meditations* (Oxford: Clarendon Press, 1976), 15; David Parker, "Verbal Moods in Shakespeare's Sonnets," *Modern Language Quarterly* 30.3 (1969): 331–359.

64. Thomas Wilson, *The Arte of Rhetorique, for the use of all suche as are studious of Eloquence* (London: Richard Grafton, 1553), sigs. F.iv–I.ii^v.

65. On pedagogical scripts and the sonnets' debt to Wilson and Erasmus, see Katharine Wilson, *Shakespeare's Sugared Sonnets* (London: George Allen & Unwin, 1974), 146–167; on the stylistic implications of these connections, see Lynne Magnusson, "A Pragmatics for Interpreting Shakespeare's Sonnets 1 to 20: Dialogue Scripts and Erasmian Intertexts," in *Methods in Historical Pragmatics*, ed. Susan M. Fitzmaurice and Irma Taavitsainen (Berlin: Mouton de Gruyter, 2007), 167–184. As Margreta de Grazia has suggested, the opening poems in the sequence would thus likely have "evoked the pedagogical context which prepared fair young men to assume the social position to which high birth entitled them." Margreta de Grazia, "The Scandal of Shakespeare's Sonnets," *Shakespeare Survey* 46 (1994): 35–49, at 45.

66. All of these methods belong to what David Glimp has called "the reproductive imperative" in *Increase and Multiply* (Minneapolis: University of Minnesota Press, 2003). Vin Nardizzi has written insightfully on the consequences of the instructional discourses in the *Sonnets*, using early modern how-to books to argue against their forms of increase as versions of parthenogenesis. His reading of grafting is especially relevant to the discussion of Sonnet

15 below. Vin Nardizzi, "Shakespeare's Penknife: Grafting and Seedless Generation in the Procreation Sonnets," *Renaissance and Reformation* 32.1 (2009): 83–106.

67. It will not be possible here to extend this reading into Sonnets 127–154, but several scholars have noted that these themes are significantly transformed in the sonnets addressed to the Dark Lady, those following Sonnet 126. See for example Greene, "Pitiful Thrivers," 242; Lars Engle sees the economy of the *Sonnets* shifting from a generative to a depressed paradigm at this moment in the sequence. Lars Engle, *Shakespearean Pragmatism* (Chicago: University of Chicago Press, 1993), 49.

68. These two qualities are differentially distributed across Sonnets 5 and 6, which play out between them what is more often the logic of partition within a single sonnet, as 5 extends a conceit (Those hours . . . will play, For never-resting time leads, Then were not summer's distillation left . . .) that 6 converts to imperative or hortatory advice (Then let not, Make sweet, Be not). Sonnet 5 is the first in the sequence without any first- or second-person pronouns, and the couplet does not so much turn outward in address, or forward or backward in time, as it distills the poem's logic of distillation into a general law, leaving the young man's personal prescription to be inferred from this floral truism about show and substance, and leaving readerly expectation dangling between the two poems.

69. On the recuperative capacities of the sonnets, see Martha R. Lifson, "The Rhetoric of Consolation: Shakespeare's Couplets," *Assays: Critical Approaches to Medieval & Renaissance Texts* 2 (1982): 95–114.

70. Greene, "Pitiful Thrivers," 234. Greene specifically mentions Sonnets 15, 18, 19, 54, 60, 63, and 65.

71. With his use of this term, Greene condenses *energeia* and *enargia*, language's efficacity and its vivacity, into a name for the force of figurative language in general. We should also keep in mind Margreta de Grazia's observation that "the poet generally reserves figurative language to describe less what he would preserve than the mutations that threaten to destroy it." Margreta de Grazia, "Revolution in *Shake-speares Sonnets*," in Schoenfeldt, *A Companion to Shakespeare's Sonnets*, 57–69, at 65.

72. Greene, "Pitiful Thrivers," 234.

73. Stephen Booth, *An Essay on Shakespeare's Sonnets* (New Haven, CT: Yale University Press, 1969). Booth writes: "Most of the sonnets become decreasingly complex as they proceed. The effect of the couplet usually is to sum up the poem or draw a moral. Essentially, it offers the reader a sound, simple reason why the poem was written and an oversimplified suggestion of what it was about. The couplet is often gnomic; it is almost always so in tone. It sounds simple and is usually easily grasped. The couplet ordinarily presents a coincidence of formal, syntactical, and logical structure, and it ordinarily gives the impression that the experience of the preceding twelve lines has been a good deal simpler than in fact it has been" (130).

74. Hubler, *The Sense of Shakespeare's Sonnets*, 25 (ellipsis in original). Hubler has here suppressed the maternal environment for mental conception suggested by Holofernes's phrase, "nourished in the womb of *pia mater*."

75. Ibid.

76. *Shake-speares Sonnets* (1609), 11.14. Citations from the *Sonnets* are given in the text with poem numbers and line numbers, where appropriate, and follow the Folger Shakespeare Library copy (shelfmark STC 22353).

77. Aaron Kunin, "Shakespeare's Preservation Fantasy," *PMLA* 124.1 (2009): 92–106, at 96.

78. De Grazia, "Revolution in *Shake-speares Sonnets*," 65.

79. For sixteenth-century debates on the morality of husbandry and household accumulation within the context of a closed or infinite economy (the latter supported by good husbandry and the abundance of nature), see Lorna Hutson, *The Usurer's Daughter* (London: Routledge, 1994), 17–51.

80. As Fineman argues, these aren't quite Petrarchan oxymorons, because "relatively consistently and univocally, their equivocations—"still telling what is told"—illustrate the way a second time calls up its difference from the first, the way a copy is unlike the original it remembers." Joel Fineman, *Shakespeare's Perjured Eye: The Invention of Poetic Subjectivity in the Sonnets* (Berkeley: University of California Press, 1986), 270.

81. No authoritative explanation of the brackets that appear at the end of Sonnet 126 has ever been offered, though they most likely seem a printing-house intervention or gloss. Benson left the poem out of his 1640 edition entirely, and many editors have omitted the curved brackets, treating them as nonauthorial accidentals. See Colin Burrow's defense of their inclusion in his Oxford edition. Colin Burrow, ed., *The Complete Sonnets and Poems* (Oxford: Oxford University Press, 2002), 632. For another view, see John Lennard, *But I Digress: The Exploitation of Parentheses in English Printed Verse* (Oxford: Oxford University Press, 1991), 41–43. Joseph Pequigney sees the parentheses as part of the narrative design of the sequence. Joseph Pequigney, *Such Is My Love: A Study of Shakespeare's Sonnets* (Chicago: University of Chicago Press, 1985), 206. I am indebted to Rayna Kalas's reading of this sonnet and the history of its editorial treatment in "Fickle Glass," in Schoenfeldt, *A Companion to Shakespeare's Sonnets*, 261–276.

82. Nothrop Frye, "How True a Twain," in *The Riddle of Shakespeare's Sonnets* (New York: Basic Books, 1962), 23–54, esp. 39.

83. Its closural force is strong enough that it has been described as explicitly apocalyptic and even as a "metacouplet" "parodying the sonnet form" that takes the 125 preceding sonnets as quatrains. See Katherine Duncan-Jones, "Playing Fields or Killing Fields: Shakespeare's Poems and *Sonnets*," *Shakespeare Quarterly* 54.2 (2003): 127–141; Michael J. B. Allen, "Shakespeare's Man Descending a Staircase: Sonnets 126 to 154," *Shakespeare Survey* 31 (1978): 127–138, at 134.

84. Greene himself finds Sonnet 126 "slighter" than the poem that precedes it and prefers the "mutual render" of Sonnet 125 as a satisfying closure to the economic tensions of the sequence addressed to the young man ("Pitiful Thrivers," 230).

85. Cited in Ian Robinson, *The Establishment of Modern English Prose in the Reformation and the Enlightenment* (Cambridge: Cambridge University Press, 1998), 189.

86. Puttenham, *Arte*, 140.

87. Kalas, "Fickle Glass," 274–275.

Epilogue

1. Hugh Plat, *Floraes paradise: Beautified and adorned with sundry sorts of delicate fruites and flowers* (London: Humphrey Lownes for William Leake, 1608), sigs. A3ʳ–A4ʳ.

2. The most comprehensive published treatment of Plat's notebooks appears in Angus Vine, *Miscellaneous Order* (Oxford: Oxford University Press, 2020), 158–190; Vine shows that Plat's production of knowledge relied "on a complex system of first-, second-, and third-order notes." For a reading that places Plat's notebooks richly in the context of social networks of

knowledge that linked Elizabethan Londoners, see Deborah Harkness, *The Jewel House* (New Haven, CT: Yale University Press, 2007), 211–252.

3. William Rawley, "To The Reader," in Francis Bacon, *Sylva sylvarum: or A naturall historie. In ten centuries* (London: John Haviland and Augustine Mathewes for William Lee, [1626]), sig. A1^r. Rawley echoes the "rude and undigested heap" (*rudis indigestaque moles*) evoked at the outset of Ovid's *Metamorphoses*. Poliziano, reviving the classical generic designation most associated with Statius, used similar language: "sylva indigesta materia a philosophis apellatur, ea quam Graeci hylen vocant" ("*silva* is called by the philosophers raw material, which the Greeks call wood." Cited in and translated by Dustin Mengelkoch, *Papinian Mutability: Statius and Early Modernity* [PhD diss., University of North Carolina Chapel Hill, 2010], 18.). On this same passage in the context of Renaissance commonplacing, see Eric MacPhail, *Dancing around the Well: The Circulation of Commonplaces in Renaissance Humanism* (Leiden: Brill, 2014), 10. Corrine Saunders unpacks the important connections drawn by medieval thinkers between *silva* and primal chaos (by way of the Greek *hulē*), including the association in Bernardus Silvestris's *Cosmographia* between *silva* and chaos: "Congeries informis adhuc, cum Silva teneret / Sub veteri confusa globo priordia rerum" ("when Silva, still a formless chaotic mass, held the first beginnings of things in their ancient state of confusion"). Corrine J. Saunders, *The Forest of Medieval Romance: Avernus, Broceliande, Arden* (Cambridge: D.S. Brewer, 1993), 17–27, at 23. A wide-reaching account of the forest's uncivilized rawness is given in Robert Pogue Harrison, *Forests: The Shadow of Civilization* (Chicago: University of Chicago Press, 1992), 1–60.

4. Deborah Harkness argues that Bacon defines himself by suppressing the influence of Plat and the interconnected world of London science (*The Jewel House*, 211–252.) See also Malcolm Thick, *Sir Hugh Plat: The Search for Useful Knowledge in Early Modern London* (Totnes, Devon: Prospect Books, 2010); Ayesha Mukherjee, *Penury into Plenty: Dearth and the Making of Knowledge in Early Modern England* (London: Routledge, 2015); and Mukherjee, "The Secrets of Sir Hugh Platt," in *Secrets and Knowledge in Medicine and Science, 1500–1800*, ed. Elaine Leong and Alisha Rankin (London: Routledge, 2016), 69–86. See also the chapters on Plat and Bacon, respectively, in Vine, *Miscellaneous Order*, 158–190 and 191–223.

5. See Harkness, *The Jewel House*; and Vine, *Miscellaneous Order*.

6. Vine's analysis of Plat and Bacon's note-taking extends to the sixteenth and early seventeenth centuries a renewed interest among scholars of early modern science in the textual practices by which knowledge was generated, stored, and shared in early modern Europe. See especially Elizabeth Yale, *Sociable Knowledge: Natural History and the Nation in Early Modern Britain* (Philadelphia: University of Pennsylvania Press, 2016); Yale, "With Slips and Scraps: How Early Modern Naturalists Invented the Archive," *Book History* 12.1 (2009): 1–36; and Richard Yeo, *Notebooks, English Virtuosi, and Early Modern Science* (Chicago: University of Chicago Press, 2014). On practices of note-taking, see Lorraine Daston, "Taking Note(s)," *Isis* 95.3 (2004): 443–448; Ann Blair, "The Rise of Note-Taking in Early Modern Europe," *Intellectual History Review* 20.3 (2010): 303–16; and Blair, "Note Taking as an Art of Transmission," *Critical Inquiry* 31.4 (2004): 85–107.

7. H.C., *The Forrest of Fancy* (London: Thomas Purfoote, 1579), sigs. A.ii^r–A.iii^r.

8. George Gascoigne, *A Hundreth Sundrie Flowres*, ed. G. W. Pigman III (Oxford: Clarendon Press, 2000), 4.

9. "Filum Labyrinthi," in *The Works of Francis Bacon*, ed. James Spedding, Robert Leslie Ellis, and Douglas Denon Heath, vol. 3 (London: Longman 1858), 498; and Francis Bacon, *The Advancement of Learning*, ed. Michael Kiernan, The Oxford Francis Bacon iv (Oxford University Press, 2000), 124. On this point, see Stephen Clucas, "A Knowledge Broken': Francis Bacon's Aphoristic Style and the Crisis of Scholastic-Humanist Knowledge Systems," in *English Renaissance Prose: History, Language, and Politics*, ed. Neil Rhodes (Tempe, AZ: Medieval and Renaissance Texts and Studies, 1997), 147–72; James Stephens, *Francis Bacon and the Style of Science* (Chicago: Chicago University Press, 1975), 98–120; Brian Vickers, *Francis Bacon and Renaissance Prose* (Cambridge: Cambridge University Press, 1968), 60–95. A persuasive account of the preliminary nature of the *Sylva*'s matter is found in Daniel Garber, "Merchants of Light and Mystery Men: Bacon's Last Projects in Natural History," *Journal of Early Modern Studies* 3.1 (2014): 91–106.

10. *The Works of Francis Bacon*, ed. James Spedding, Robert Leslie Ellis, and Douglas Denon Heath, vol. 7 (London: Longman 1859), 312.

11. On the loose form of the *Commentarius solutus*, see Vine, *Miscellaneous Order*, 23; Vine shows how the *solutus* in Bacon's title repurposes the rhetorical use of the term to mean a discontinuous style. The question of Bacon's looseness is illuminated by the discussion of *disinvoltura* and Bacon's styles of "unwinding" in David Carroll Simon, *Light Without Heat: The Observational Mood from Bacon to Milton* (Ithaca, NY: Cornell University Press, 2018), chap. 1.

12. Alan Stewart, "Introduction," *Promus of Formularies and Elegancies (1594–1595)*, in *The Oxford Francis Bacon*, vol. 1, *The Early Writings (1584–1596)*, Oxford Scholarly Editions Online (Oxford: Oxford University Press, 2013). Later, in *The Advancement of Learning*, he would refer again to this pair of terms, drawing the distinction (and his own valuation) along these lines: "the one to preserve or continue themselves, & the other to dilate or Multiply themselves; whereof the latter seemeth to be the worthyer" (*Advancement*, 139). The forces of dilation and multiplication—spending, in other words—are worthier than mere conservation. On these points, see Vine, *Miscellaneous Order*, 18–26.

13. Rawley concludes the epistle by quoting Bacon that, "this work of his *Naturall History*, is the *World*, as God made it and not as men have made it; For that it hath nothing of Imagination." Rawley, "To the Reader" in Bacon, *Sylva sylvarum*, sig. A3^r.

14. Bacon, *Advancement of Learning*, 22. Bacon's position will be memorably echoed by Thomas Sprat, in his *History of the Royal-Society of London, For the Improving of Natural Knowledge* (London, 1667), which calls for a return to that "primitive purity, and shortness, when men deliver'd so many *things*, almost in an equal number of *words*" (113). On the traditional rhetorical balance between *res* and *verba*, to which Bacon alludes here, see A. C. Howell, "*Res* and *Verba*: Words and Things," *ELH* (1946): 131–142; in the context of the Royal Society, Peter Dear, "*Totius in Verba*: Rhetoric and Authority in the Early Royal Society," *Isis* 76.2 (1985): 145–161; and Brian Vickers, "The Royal Society and English Prose Style: A Reassessment," in *Rhetoric and the Pursuit of Truth* (Los Angeles, CA: William Andrews Clark Memorial Library, 1985), 3–76. Margreta de Grazia reframes this distinction in "Words as Things," *Shakespeare Studies* 28 (2000): 231–235.

15. On possession in Plat's *Floures*, see Crystal Bartolovich, "'Optimism of the Will': Isabella Whitney and Utopia," *Journal of Medieval and Early Modern Studies* 39.2 (2009): 407–432; Stephanie Elsky, *Custom, Common Law, and the Constitution of English Literature* (Oxford: Oxford University Press, 2020), 133–158; and Carolyn Sale, "The Literary Thing: The

Imaginary Holding of Isabella Whitney's 'Wyll' to London (1573)," in *The Oxford Handbook of English Law and Literature, 1500–1700*, ed. Lorna Hutson (Oxford: Oxford University Press, 2017), 431–447. On the variety of possessive authorship at stake in John Harington's digs at Plat in his *Metamorphosis of Ajax*, see Joseph Loewenstein, *The Author's Due: Printing and the Prehistory of Copyright* (Chicago: University of Chicago Press, 2002), 135–138.

16. Plat, *Floraes paradise*, sig. P3ᵛ.

17. Plat, *Floraes paradise*, sig. B8ᵛ. On these senses of "profit," see Ayesha Mukherjee, "*Floraes Paradise*: Hugh Platt and the Economy of Early Modern Gardening," *The Seventeenth Century* 25.1 (2010): 1–26; and Andrew McRae, *God Speed the Plough* (Cambridge: Cambridge University Press, 1996), 135–156. On the rise of market gardening in the late sixteenth and early seventeenth centuries, see Joan Thirsk, "Farming Techniques," in *The Agrarian History of England and Wales, 1500–1640*, vol. 4, ed. Joan Thirsk (Cambridge: Cambridge University Press, 1967), 195–196; and Malcolm Thick, *The Neat House Gardens: Early Market Gardening Around London* (Devon: Prospect Books, 1998). Thick's monograph on Plat places him richly in this context (Thick, *Sir Hugh Plat*.)

18. The most memorable version of this argument is the account of Bacon as a founding figure of instrumental rationality in Theodor Adorno and Max Horkheimer, *Dialectic of Enlightenment*, trans. John Cumming (New York: Verso, 1997), 3–8; on Bacon and industrial science, see Benjamin Farrington, *The Philosophy of Francis Bacon* (Chicago: University of Chicago Press, 1966). Related questions about man's dominion over nature shape the debate inspired by Carolyn Merchant, *The Death of Nature: Women, Ecology, and the Scientific Revolution* (San Francisco: Harper & Row, 1980); for criticism of her view of Bacon, see Peter Pesic, "Wrestling with Proteus: Francis Bacon and the 'Torture' of Nature," *Isis* 90.1 (1999): 81–94; as well as Merchant's response in "The Scientific Revolution and *The Death of Nature*," *Isis* 97.3 (2006): 513–533. These issues are productively reframed in Katharine Park, "Women, Gender, and Utopia: *The Death of Nature* and the Historiography of Early Modern Science," *Isis* 97.3 (2006): 487–495. On the complexity of concepts of dominion, see Peter Harrison, "Having Dominion: Genesis and the Mastery of Nature," in *Environmental Stewardship: Critical Perspectives, Past and Present*, ed. R. J. Berry (London: T & T Clark, 2006), 17–31; and Stephen Gaukroger, *Francis Bacon and the Transformation of Early Modern Philosophy* (Cambridge: Cambridge University Press, 2001), 166–220.

19. Martin Heidegger, *The Question Concerning Technology and Other Essays*, trans. William Lovitt (New York: Garland, 1977), 17–18.

20. They were often associated with *supellex*, or supply, which in the context of rhetoric referred to the furniture of the mind. Bacon referred in *The Advancement of Learning* to "mindes emptie and unfraught with matter, & which have not gathered that which *Cicero* calleth *sylva* and *supellex*" (*Advancement*, 59). Compare Pedro Mexía's influential *Foreste*, in Thomas Fortescue's 1571 translation, which advertised that "this present Foreste, whiche for good cause me thought, I so might name, or title, for that beyng a collection of divers, and sundrie matters, is as a Foreste, well furnished with many trees, birdes, and beastes, of different, and contrary natures" (*The Forest, or Collection of Histories* [London: John Kingston for William Jones, 1571], sig. a.ivᵛ-b.iʳ). On textual furniture, see Jeffrey Todd Knight, "'Furnished' for Action: Renaissance Books as Furniture," *Book History* 12.1 (2009): 37–73, at 54. On *supellex* and humanism, see Kathy Eden, "Intellectual Property and the *Adages* of Erasmus: *Coenobium* vs. *Ercto non cito*," in *Rhetoric and Law in Early Modern Europe*, ed. Victoria Kahn and Lorna Hutson (New Haven, CT: Yale University Press, 2001), 269–284. On this dimension of

silvae, see Alastair Fowler, "The Silva Tradition in Jonson's *The Forrest,*" in *Poetic Traditions of the English Renaissance,* ed. Maynard Mack and George deForest Lord (New Haven, CT: Yale University Press, 1982), 163–180.

21. Isabella Whitney, [*A sweet nosgay, or pleasant posye*] (London: Richard Jones, 1573), sig. A.viii[r].

22. On *silvae* and occasional poetry, including Statius's *Silva* and Ben Jonson's *Forrest,* see Fowler, "The Silva Tradition," 174. On Statius and the heat of occasional poetry, see the especially rich work of Dustin Mengelkoch in "The Mutability of Poetics: Poliziano, Statius, and the *Silvae,*" *Modern Language Notes* 125.1 (2010): 84–116; and *Papinian Mutability,* esp. chap. 1.

23. Mukherjee, "Floraes Paradise," 14. See also Vine, *Miscellaneous Order,* 178–179.

24. As Steven Shapin has shown, the solution to this epistemic dilemma was neither mechanical nor metaphysical but social: experiments needed to be hosted, carried out, and witnessed by trustworthy (usually, genteel) persons. Steven Shapin, "The House of Experiment in Seventeenth-Century England," *Isis* 79.3 (1988): 373–404.

25. John Milton, *Areopagitica,* in *Complete Prose Works of John Milton,* vol. 2, ed. Ernest Sirluck (New Haven, CT: Yale University Press, 1959), 492.

26. Though standard in Plat's publications, the suggestion in *Floraes Paradise* that readers look forward is ironic—as he confessed in the epistle, he knew that his days were "drawing to their periode" (sig. A3[v].) While he would provide no new supply of fresh inventions during his lifetime, the work's 1652 reissue as *The Garden of Eden* would be followed by a second volume drawn from Plat's notes (*The second part of the Garden of Eden, or, An accurate Description of all Flowers and Fruits growing in England* [London: William Leake, 1659.])

27. "It is not an idle curiosity," the philosopher of plants Michael Marder observes, "that 'enjoyment' shares its grammatical root with 'fruit.'" Marder turns to these same concepts of *uti* and *frui* when, against modernity's instrumentalizing and destructive styles of thought, he suggests an environmental ethic attentive to earlier distinctions between modalities of use. Michael Marder, *The Philosopher's Plant* (New York: Columbia University Press, 2014), 64.

28. Plat, *Floraes paradise,* sigs. M1[r], E4[r].

29. Mukherjee, *Penury into Plenty,* 63–92.

30. Bacon, *Sylva,* 131.

31. Bacon sought light-bearing experiments before fruit-bearing, cautioning that "as the army of particulars is so vast and so scattered and dispersed that it dissipates and confounds the intellect, we should have no good hopes for the latter's cursory sorties and ineffectual flights" (*Instauratio Magna,* ed. Graham Rees, The Oxford Francis Bacon xi [Oxford: Oxford University Press, 2004], 159–160.) Nonetheless, as Rhodri Lewis argues, it was these fruit-bearing experiments that had the greatest legacy in the later seventeenth century, both in the midcentury reformist circles around Samuel Hartlib and later with the formation of the Royal Society (Rhodri Lewis, "Francis Bacon and Ingenuity," *Renaissance Quarterly* 67.1 [2014]: 113–163, at 145–147). The role of craft and technical knowledge is a central point of debate in scholarship on Bacon and on seventeenth-century science; see Antonio Pérez-Ramos, *Francis Bacon's Idea of Science and the Maker's Knowledge Tradition* (Oxford: Clarendon, 1988); Sophie Weeks, *Francis Bacon's Science of Magic* (Cambridge: Cambridge University Press, 2015); Charles Webster, *The Great Instauration: Science, Medicine, and Reform, 1626–1660* (London: Duckworth, 1975); Cesare Pastorino, "The Philosopher and the Craftsman:

Francis Bacon's Notion of Experiment and its Debt to Early Stuart Inventors," *Isis* 108.4 (2017): 149–768.

32. Le Doeuff writes: "Bacon says that nature is conquered by local movement, man being able to do no more than put together or separate. But the efficiency of such motions can only be understood if one imagines a gardener pruning, grafting, transplanting, exposing plants to varying degrees of sunshine, in short, demonstrating that supreme craft which consists in denaturing things with nature's assistance." See Michèle Le Doeuff, "Man and Nature in the Gardens of Science," in *Francis Bacon's Legacy of Texts*, ed. William A. Sessions (New York: AMS Press, 1990), 119–138, at 126. As Vera Keller shows, a practice of philosophical gardening would develop over the course of the seventeenth century in parallel with but distinct from philosophical husbandry. See Vera Keller, "A 'Wild Swing to Phantsy': The Philosophical Gardener and Emergent Experimental Philosophy in the Seventeenth-Century Atlantic World," *Isis* 112.3 (2021): 507–530.

33. Bacon, *Sylva*, 113.

34. On this experiment and Bacon's use of della Porta, see Doina-Cristina Rusu, "Rethinking *Sylva Sylvarum:* Francis Bacon's Use of Giambattista della Porta's *Magia Naturalis*," *Perspectives on Science* 25.1 (2017): 1–35, 10. On Bacon's citational patterns in the *Sylva,* see Graham Rees, "An Unpublished Manuscript by Francis Bacon: *Sylva Sylvarum* Working Drafts and Other Notes," *Annals of Science* 38 (1981): 377–412.

35. Plat, *Floraes Paradise,* sig. B2^{r-v}.

36. The author of the *The Fruiterers Secrets* writes that fruiterer Richard Harris made the king an orchard from a collection of foreign grafts; since then, "by reason of the great increase that now is growing in divers parts of this Land, of such fine & serviceable fruit, there is no need of any foraigne fruite, but we are able to serve other places." N. F., *The Fruiterers Secrets* (London: by Richard Braddock, to be sold by Roger Jackson, 1604), sig. A.ii^{r-v}.

37. James Delbourgo, "What's in the Box? The Time Machines of Sir Hans Sloane," *Cabinet Magazine* 41 (2011). See his *Collecting the World: Hans Sloane and the Origins of the British Museum* (Cambridge, MA: Harvard University Press, 2019). See also Martha Fleming, "Afterword: What Goes Around, Comes Around: Mobility's Modernity," in *Mobile Museums: Collections in Circulation,* ed. Felix Driver, Mark Nesbitt, and Caroline Cornish (London: UCL Press, 2021), 328–342; and Victoria Pickering, "Putting Nature in a Box: Hans Sloanes's 'Vegetable Substances' Collection," PhD diss., (Queen Mary University of London, 2017).

38. Luke Keogh, *The Wardian Case: How a Simple Box Moved Plants and Changed the World* (Chicago: University of Chicago Press, 2020), 33. See John Woodward, *Brief Instructions for Making Observations in All Parts of the World; as also for Collecting, Preserving and Sending over Natural Things* (London: Richard Wilkin, 1696); Robert Boyle, *General Heads for the Natural History of a Country, Great or Small: Drawn Out for the Uses of Travellers and Navigators* (London: John Taylor, 1692).

39. James Petiver, *Brief directions for the easie making, and preserving collections of all natural curiosities* [London: s.n., 1709?].

40. "Sir Hans Sloane, Bart. Pr. R. S. His Answer to the Marquis de Caumont's Letter, Concerning This Stone," *Philosophical Transactions* 40 (1737–1738): 376.

41. John Evelyn, *Acetaria: A discourse of sallets* (London: B. Tooke, 1699), sig. O8^r.

42. Mangoes were not an important commodity or cultivar in early modern Europe, though the first accounts of them in European languages appeared in the early sixteenth century, written by Spanish and Portuguese travelers. The path of mangoes from India to the

Caribbean is unclear, but it may have been through the eastern coast of Kenya, where they had first been carried on Arabian trade routes. R. J. Knight and R. J. Schnell, "Mango Introduction in Florida and the 'Haden' Cultivar's Significance to the Modern Industry," *Economic Botany* 48.2 (1994): 139–145. On Fairchild, see Amanda Harris, *Fruits of Eden: David Fairchild and America's Plant Hunters* (Gainesville: University Press of Florida, 2015).

INDEX

Note: Italicized page numbers refer to figures.

ACKNOWLEDGMENTS

This book had its origin half a lifetime ago, in an economic botany course with John Gruber spent wandering fields and woodlands of suburban Philadelphia and catching leaves from the air. I realized soon after, listening to a lecture by Peter Stallybrass, that those leaves might have something to do with Shakespeare. They have been scattered and regathered many times since, but I owe a great deal to the friends and teachers who have enabled the final gathered form of this book. Peter has since been a source of support and a model for the joyful deflation of abstract ideas for two decades now. Any sharpness in the form those pieces eventually took is due to Margreta de Grazia, who has unfailingly seen through the thickets of material to the questions that mattered (including the unanswerable ones); her hospitality in Fairmount and in London provided some of the sunniest moments in this long process. Lynn Festa was a mentor to my earliest attempts to think about grafting; these current efforts still bear the sign of her advice and friendship. I would not have asked those initial questions about old leaves and old books without the encouragement of Laurie Schmitt, Terry Guerin, Jim Green, and Katharine Park. Zachary Lesser, with Margreta de Grazia and Peter Stallybrass, advised the dissertation that grew into this book and helped me think through issues ranging from print popularity to the couplet; he continues to give some of the best advice out there.

My research and writing were supported by a Provost's Postdoctoral Fellowship at the University of Southern California; a Barbara Thom Postdoctoral Fellowship at the Huntington Library; and the ongoing support of the University of Miami, which has enabled this book in multiple ways, including a research leave, the Provost's Research Award, the Creative and Scholarly Activities Award, and the Fellowship in the Arts and Humanities. Key chapters were written while a 2016–17 fellow at the Center for the Humanities, and I am grateful to Mihoko Suzuki for her support of the project and for the intellectual community she formed there. That year's group of fellows read and responded to chapters with helpful suggestions, as did the Center's Medieval and Early Modern Studies research group and its Animal Studies and Environmental Humanities research group. I am especially grateful for suggestions from Anthony Barthelemy, Karl Gunther, Mary Lindemann, Frank Palmeri, Guido Ruggiero, Maria Galli Stampino, Mihoko Suzuki, Hugh Thomas, Robyn Walsh, and Ashli White. I have been lucky in my time in Miami to have had three exemplary chairs in the English Department; Pamela Hammons, Timothy Watson, and Tom Goodmann each protected my time for writing and research while somehow finding time of their own to actually talk about ideas. Melissa Reittie and Lydia Starling provided exemplary material and logistical support throughout.

Rare book libraries made the research possible, including the Kislak Center for Special Collections at the University of Pennsylvania, the Library Company of Philadelphia, the Folger Shakespeare Library, Houghton Library at Harvard University, the Newberry Library, the Huntington Library, and the University of Miami's Richter Library and Kislak Center for Special Collections. For their particular help, I would like to thank: at Penn, John Pollock, Lynne Farrington, and Mitch Fraas; at the Folger, Caroline Duroselle-Mellish, Owen Williams, and Heather Wolfe; at Houghton, Karen Nipps; at the Huntington, Vanessa Wilkie, Karla Nielsen, and Joel Klein; and at Miami, Cristina Favretto and Jay Sylvestre. Preparing a manuscript during a pandemic means asking a lot of favors, and I am grateful to the imaging departments at Emory's Rose Library, the Rare Book and Manuscript Library at the University of Illinois, Princeton University Library, the British Library, the Bodleian, and the Huntington. Manuel Flores at the Huntington was exceptionally helpful with more image requests than I can count. Virginia Schilling of the ESTC project at the University of California, Riverside, supplied invaluable assistance in sharing multiple rounds of data and seemed somehow undeterred by the five spellings of "ortyard." Paige Morgan helped me process, interpret, and think critically about what to do with that data. Ruth Shannon Trego spent hours helping clean and interpret piles of spreadsheets and somehow remained cheerful and exacting through it all.

This book was written in Philadelphia, Southern California, and Miami and was nurtured by intellectual communities in each location. At the University of Pennsylvania, my research and thinking developed with the support of the Material Texts and Medieval-Renaissance seminars and the Program in Comparative Literature and Literary Theory, including Rita Copeland, Joan DeJean, JoAnne Dubil, Ania Loomba, Ann Moyer, Melissa

Sanchez, Barbara Traister, Daniel Traister, and Liliane Weissberg. I was lucky there to have a group of allies whose influence persisted, including Kate Aid, Claire Bourne, Kara Gaston, Dianne Mitchell, Marissa Nicosia, Alan Niles, Simran Thadani, and Thomas Ward. Matt Goldmark, Emma Stapely, and Emily Weissbourd all helped hash out ideas in various Philadelphia dive bars, and my sense of what matters in the project is still fueled by those conversations. At USC, Rebecca Lemon first welcomed me to California, and her friendship and insight have been sustaining since. I am grateful to Bruce Smith for wide-ranging conversation on Shakespeare, flowers, and cuts; to Peter Mancall for inviting me into and for fortifying the region's community of early modernists; and to Natania Meeker and Antónia Szabari for speculative conversations about plants and politics. At the Huntington, more than a few ideas were generated on long walks in the garden with Heidi Brayman, Dympna Callaghan, Heather James, and Carla Mazzio, each of whom read chapters at an early stage and offered invaluable feedback, as did J. K. Barret, Urvashi Chakravarty, Will Fisher, and Marjorie Rubright. The 2018–19 cohort of Huntington Library long-term fellows supported work on this book in tangible and intangible ways, including especially helpful feedback from Katherine Cox, Marjoleine Kars, Alexander Statman, and Danielle Terrazas Williams. Lori Anne Ferrell and Naomi Tadmor generously leant their expertise on all matters of early modern social and cultural history. Multiple chapters are sharper and more searching because of the intensity with which Kate Adams and Andrea Denny-Brown engaged with drafts and knocked around ideas. My work throughout that year was inspired by Daniela Bleichmar's sharp readings and creative capacities for reaching outside genres and disciplines. I am grateful to Steve Hindle for welcoming me to the group and to Juan Gomez and Natalie Serrano for making it all happen; Catherine Wehrey-Miller's wry generosity helped make it feel like home.

My arguments have benefited from the engagement of audiences at UC Davis, SUNY Stony Brook, Scripps College, and the University of Southern California, as well as half a dozen seminars at the Shakespeare Association of America, where various limbs of this book had their start. The organizers, conveners, and audiences at each of these events challenged and improved the book immensely. Rebecca Bushnell, Frances Dolan, Rebecca Laroche, Jennifer Munroe, and Vin Nardizzi have all offered vital support and improved my thinking about horticulture and husbandry. Julia Reinhard Lupton's ongoing collaboration and advice have shaped my understanding of early modern virtues and given life to more than one of these chapters. My thinking in this time has been sustained, and the book improved, by conversations with Joshua Calhoun, Lara Langer Cohen, Andy Crow, Adhaar Desai, Mary Fissell, Juliet Fleming, Musa Gurnis, Lauren Kassell, Heather Love, Lucía Martínez Valdivia, Jeffrey Masten, Roy Ritchie, Colleen Rosenfeld, Barbara Savage, Debapriya Sarkar, Steven Shapin, Karen Raber, Anna Rosensweig, Kyla Wazana Tompkins, and Tiffany Werth. Laurie Shannon read portions of the manuscript and talked ideas with an uncanny eye for the embers that had the most spark in them. Audra Wolfe and Anna Glass, at different points, offered wise advice on form and structure. Grace Lavery read several chapters and talked me off of a complex of ledges. Laura Kolb read every page and somehow persuaded me it looked like a book. Molly Yarn went through the full manuscript with care and immensely improved its final form.

Finishing a book with any sense of community during COVID is difficult, but I have been lucky in both text threads and talk threads. I must especially thank: Tassie Gwilliam, Pamela Hammons, Gema Pérez-Sánchez, Marina Magloire, Brenna Munroe, and Allison Schifani for their company and conversation in backyards and on Zoom; Chris Hunter and Jennifer Jahner, for their friendship and Cali hospitality; Kat Lecky and Stephanie Shirilan, for the most supportive writing pod; Megan Heffernan and Laura Kolb (and Penny and Imogen), for their insight and good humor on matters bibliographic, veterinary, and otherwise; and Yumi Lee and Golnar Nikpour, for getting me through it, fighting. The friendship and intellectual community of Jan Radway and Laurie Shannon provided both heat and light through a long COVID winter and made it possible to see something beyond the stipulated present.

This project arrived at Penn under the wings of Jerry Singerman, whose patience, wisdom, and insight made the manuscript both possible and immeasurably better, as those qualities have for so many other books in the field. Jenny Tan took on the project at a crucial moment without a false step and offered sage advice on both argument and framing. Jennifer Shenk copy edited the manuscript with care and precision, and Kristen Bettcher brought it ably through production. The final text has been significantly improved by the suggestions of Jennifer Munroe and an anonymous reader; I am grateful to them for their attentive readings and thoughtful engagement with the project. All errors of course remain my own.

A portion of Chapter 2 was published in earlier form as "Poetic Language, Practical Handbooks and the 'Vertues' of Plants," in *Ecological Approaches to Early Modern English Texts: A Field Guide to Reading and Teaching*, edited by Lynne Bruckner, Edward J. Geisweidt, and Jennifer Munroe (Farnham, Surrey: Ashgate, 2015), 61–69. An earlier version of Chapter 5 appeared as "The Point of the Couplet: Shakespeare's *Sonnets* and Thomas Tusser's *A hundreth good pointes of husbandrie*," in *English Literary History* 83.1 (Spring 2016): 1–41. I am grateful to Ashgate and to Johns Hopkins University Press, holders of the original copyright, for the permission to include them here.

I must single out a few people for their exceptional endurance. My parents first modeled the value of taking ideas seriously and never questioned too loudly when that lesson sometimes took me down seriously arcane paths, but they and Alice also reminded me of the value of leaving rabbit holes to spend time with balls, fields, and ponds. Leah Rosenberg has been a tireless source of solidarity on all things prose-and Florida-related, and I am further indebted to her and Apollo Amoko for their exemplary hospitality in face of both hurricanes and revisions. Muffet McGraw disapproved of the project from Day One, but her companionship, ferocity, and insistence on routine made finishing it possible. Finally, Lindsay Thomas has been the steady beating heart of this book for the last five years, with her wisdom, good humor, and uncanny capacity for both solving seemingly impossible intellectual problems and knowing when it is time to just take a walk. I am sure she is very glad to see it over, but I hope she sees her impression on its pages.

CPSIA information can be obtained
at www.ICGtesting.com
Printed in the USA
JSHW010921230922
30745JS00001B/4